# FAITH
## *in motion*

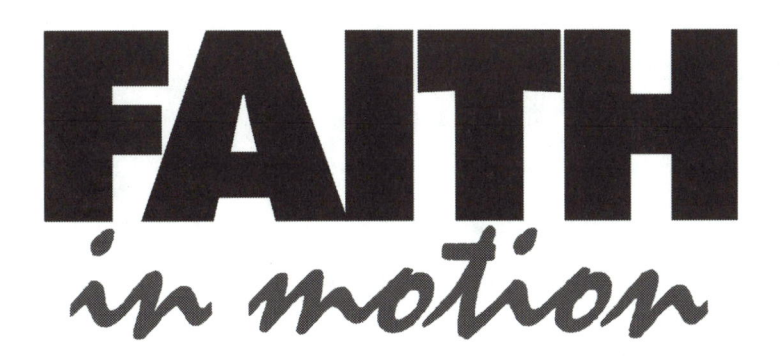

# E. LARRY BEAUMONT

**WinePress Publishing**
MUKILTEO, WA 98275

Faith in Motion
Copyright © 1998 by E. Larry Beaumont

Published by:
WinePress Publishing
PO Box 1406
Mukilteo, WA 98275

All rights reserved. No part of this publication may be reproduced, stored in a retrieval system or transmitted in any way by any means, electronic, mechanical, photocopy, recording or otherwise, without the prior permission of the publisher, except as provided by USA copyright law.

Scripture is quoted from the New International Version of the Bible.

Printed in the United States of America

ISBN 1-57921-069-4
Library of Congress Catalog Card Number: 97-61897

# DEDICATION

Surely I will forget to acknowledge someone who played a role in bringing this book to reality. If I have, please forgive me. But I cannot forget all of these dear souls:

Jeff Hale, Jim Knutson, Gary Ehman, Bing Peng, Dave Sherman, Rick Stookey of my Monday morning Bible study; Steve and Mary Meyer, John and Mary Hasler, Sandy Ceas, John Benz, Jeff Winters, Jeff Hetschel, Jeff Beste, Greg Peterson, Jamie and Rod Shanks, all past and present Board members of Oasis Hospitality International. Drs. Craig Blomberg and William Klein at Denver Seminary, who taught me to appreciate good scholarship, even if I have not yet achieved it. The FOOLS (Fellowship of Older Students) at Denver Seminary, who have prayed for me throughout this work; and friends from Foothills Bible Church, too numerous to mention, who provided encouragement along the way.

But I can't stop there. Special mention must go to my incredible family, without whom I have no identity: to Mom, who taught me never to give up; to my sister Ruth Beaumont Cook, a *real* writer, who far surpasses my talent and makes me so proud; to Michelle and Mitch, my wonderful children who survived, despite all of my travels; but most of all to "Saint" Sue, my wife, lover, prayer warrior and best friend of almost thirty years, to whom I dedicate this book. I love you all beyond words.

# Foreword

As I open the last few revisions to the pages of *Faith In Motion*, I am both exhilarated and saddened. Joyful, because this work is going off to press almost four years after the founding of Oasis Hospitality International. Sad, because I will no longer have it to anchor my being after hundreds of 5:00 a.m. writing sessions. Happy, because individual devotions contained in this book have touched traveling members of the Christian Travelers Network where they needed them most—in hotel rooms around the world. And a *little* melancholy, just because it has been a labor of love and a means of total immersion in God's word. But now, instead of hiding behind a computer screen to the exclusion of the real world, I must use this book to minister in the secular world!

If you are a frequent business traveler, you already know the need for this book. But if you are not a traveler in the geographic sense, you might be surprised to learn that this book is for you, too. Every human being is on a spiritual journey, and every thought shared in this book applies to that journey, as much as to a Saturday night stay-over. That's because a book based on the Bible is a book based on universal truth, applicable to all. What speaks to a jet-setting business executive speaks also to a spouse at home, taking care of the kids. And it is written with women in mind, just as much as men.

I hope and pray that you do not think it is inappropriate to share so many stories about my own personal experiences in travel and in life. One thoughtful reader suggested that I have accomplished nothing more than self-promotion. But for that one honest opinion, there have been hundreds of others who have thanked

# FOREWORD

me for being vulnerable, for sharing the shaky, human part of my nature, for encouraging them to let God raise them above their own limitations. And that indeed has been my intent. I am no saint, and this book will confirm that. (I have changed the names of people where negative implications are included, to protect confidentiality.) But if God can use my weaknesses for His glory, then amen, so let it be. So I have taken the risk of transparency for the sole purpose of encouraging you.

I hope you will draw from these devotions how God is everywhere and can be found in everything. He goes before us, He goes with us, and He protects our back sides, too! My experiences are only a small smattering of what He is accomplishing and wants to accomplish through each person who reads this book. My prayer is that your own memories of God's presence in your travels will be triggered, and that you will share those memories with me. If enough of you will do so prayerfully, we can look forward to a sequel—written by you!

Although this book emerged from a study of travel-related stories in the Bible, I was surprised to find another theme rising inexorably from its core. One cannot travel through the Old Testament without beginning to thirst for the Messiah, the Son of God. One cannot drink-in Jesus of Nazareth, the greatest frequent traveler of all time, without tasting how easily He interacted with those He encountered. One cannot digest His flood of encounters with strangers without drawing nourishment from how much we all have in common. One cannot be energized by how much we have in common without sharing this sweetest of drinks throughout the Christian church. And one cannot involve the Christian church without choking on our lack of unity.

I did not set out to write a book about unity. But Bible authors did. Unity is central to everything Jesus taught, amplified repeatedly by Paul, Peter and John. I have come to believe that without unity, we spend more time canceling out each others' efforts than in actually spreading the gospel. I feel just as strongly about this as Martin Luther felt about salvation by faith. I have even wondered if a radical call to unity is the stuff of the Second Reformation. I don't know all the answers, but I do know where to start—at the grass roots level. It is a matter of personal conviction. And it starts with you and me.

Our role as travelers, then, is to be ambassadors for Christ, celebrating what we have in common, not jamming obscure theological dogma down the throat of someone who cannot escape the window seat. In the end, I hope this book will challenge you to love sacrificially all those you encounter, attracting them toward the kingdom of God, not repelling them. Perhaps true hospitality is the *oasis* created by true Christian unity—welcoming strangers in from the sandstorms of life.

May God be glorified!

E. LARRY BEAUMONT
Morrison, Colorado
September 2, 1997

## *January 1*
## PRESENCE AND POWER

> ". . . hovering over the waters . . ."
> (Genesis 1:2)

Traveler: *Spirit of God*
**Read: Genesis 1:1–26**

A hummingbird hovers like a graceful ballerina, siphoning sweet nectar from a fragile blossom, hanging motionless in the air. Or so it seems from a distance. Up close, the hummingbird is a powerful presence, wings scooping air too fast to see, hovering close.

For frequent travelers caught up in the frantic pace of modern business, God may seem distant, too, watchful but uninvolved. Coming close to God while on the go is tricky, like refueling a fighter jet in mid-air. But when that connection is made, God suddenly becomes closer than breathing, a transformation more startling than the hovering of a hummingbird.

"In the beginning God created the heavens and the earth. Now the earth was formless and empty, darkness was over the surface of the deep, and the Spirit of God was hovering over the waters" (Genesis 1:1–2). From the instant of creation, God was intensely active, tangible, hovering close to His creation, refining its features with light and sky and dry ground and vegetation and animals. And you. God's intimacy has never wavered, sustaining those who decide to move toward Him for a closer look.

That's what this book is about—God's hovering presence and power—and your faith in motion. You'll start by journeying through the Bible with me and studying the actions of God's faith-travelers. As you seek intimacy with God during your travels, you'll feel refreshed, energized and encouraged. Then, you'll begin to turn outward, to sense a more urgent purpose for your itinerary: "I, the Lord, have called you . . . to open eyes that are blind, to free captives from prison and to release from the dungeon those who sit in darkness" (Isaiah 42:6,7).

As we move along together each day, through God's word, I pray each Bible hero and heroine will help you see God, His angels, the Holy Spirit and Jesus Christ as fellow frequent travelers, hovering close to the sweetness that is your life, nurturing everything you do and redirecting your steps: ". . . seek first his kingdom . . ." (Matthew 6:33).

## January 2
## PERFECT PLAN

"... fill the earth and subdue it."
(Genesis 1:28)

Travelers: *God's People*
**Read: Genesis 1:27–2:3**

Memories of warm, fizzy South Pacific surf were quenched like an icy dive into the North Atlantic, even before I arrived home from paradise. Between planes in San Francisco, I called the office, since I had intentionally avoided business on my twenty-fifth wedding anniversary trip to Hawaii. Dozens of urgent messages reported a major company "down-sizing" and the shocking termination of my entire senior staff. The peace of strolling on beaches, holding hands and watching fiery red sunsets evaporated instantly.

In the next few weeks, like so many others, I lost my job too. Fifteen years of intense dedication, building a new consulting business from the ground up had suddenly capsized. I had always thought God's plan for me was to retire from that company, because of the great success I achieved there. Now I was starting over.

Does God's plan for you seem hard to figure out, too?

What was God's plan for us from the beginning? His very first words came in the form of a plan: "God blessed them and said to them, 'Be fruitful and increase in number; fill the earth and subdue it'" (Genesis 1:28). So God's first instructions were for travel. How else would people "fill the earth?"

God intended it to be easy, full of blessings and richness. Imagine what it would be like today if His original plan had not been spoiled. No flight delays. No turbulence. No pickpockets. Only the ease of implementing God's perfection. But when Adam and Eve chose to learn about good and evil (Genesis 3:5), humanity lost its chance to have it easy.

In losing my job, I could have felt as hopelessly banished as Adam and Eve, the victim of my own sins. But I knew Jesus Christ had paid for all sins, including mine. Instead of eternal condemnation, I was being set free to pursue God's true plan for me, not my plan: "If you hold to my teaching, you are really my disciples. Then you will know the truth, and the truth will set you free" (John 8:32).

Whose plan are you following today? Yours or God's?

## January 3
### BEETLE BATTLES

"... to work it and take care of it."
(Genesis 2:15)

Traveler: *Adam*
Read: Genesis 2:4–15

Dad's house was easy to find among the monotonous similarity of post-World War II tract housing. His flower garden could be seen from two blocks away. Many loads of damp, musty peat moss had transformed brick-like Ohio clay into plush fertility, from spring's delicate yellow daffodils to fall's burnt orange zinnias.

When I was twelve, Dad gave me a job. It was very hot and dry that year, and hundreds of rose blossoms, each as dear to him as a member of the family, were under attack by Japanese beetles. He was working overtime at his office job and beetle battles could not wait until he came home each night. So he filled an old coffee can half full of used motor oil and showed me how to pluck beetles off each blossom and into the can. I felt pretty important and did my job with great vigor.

Looking back, I realize what an easy job it was. I didn't have to mow grass, pull weeds or pick vegetables. Dad did all that, probably after I went to bed. He gave me a job I could handle. I was just a boy, secure in my Dad's garden, doing my little job with no other responsibilities.

I think God took Adam on his first trip to the Garden of Eden with the same thing in mind: "The Lord God took the man and put him in the Garden of Eden to work it and take care of it" (Genesis 2:15). It was a picture of harmony and peace.

Wouldn't you like to be given simple jobs like that today, instead of the intensity of modern business? Wouldn't you like to rely on someone else to handle all the details?

You can. The answer lies in how you view your daily tasks. It's your choice: to play God and try to be responsible for everything yourself, or to obey as a child of God, doing the job He gives you, letting Him manage the garden. If you choose, each day can be as easy as flicking beetles from a rose.

## January 4
### WET PAINT: DO NOT TOUCH

> "... you will surely die."
> (Genesis 2:17)

Traveler: *Adam*
**Read: Genesis 2:16–17**

Opening day. There are no two sweeter words to baseball fans and no two greater baseball lovers than my son and me. Traditionally, opening day for a major league team is on a weekday afternoon. Even the strictest parents have been known to let kids miss school for the big day.

But one April, I had to say no. My son's grades had dropped. Given that a teenager's behavior cannot be changed by overt threats of physical doom, only one approach would get his attention—missing opening day.

My son took his punishment quietly. But when his grades came out again in June, I was shocked to see almost straight A's. This had never happened before. As we celebrated his great comeback, he confided, "Dad, there's no way I'm going to miss opening day next year, with the grand opening of Coors Field!"

I had never threatened him with that. He realized on his own that what I hadn't said was more alarming than the punishment already received.

If only Adam and Eve had been as perceptive. As He put Adam to work in the Garden of Eden, God made the potential risks very clear: "You are free to eat from any tree in the garden; but you must not eat from the tree of the knowledge of good and evil, for when you eat of it you will surely die" (Genesis 2:16–17). That was like calling attention to a "Wet Paint" sign, which tempts everyone to see if the paint is really wet. Adam and Eve couldn't resist. Note, God didn't say what would happen if they ate fruit from the other trees in the garden. They should have listened not only to what God said, but also to what He didn't say.

Only after the forbidden fruit had been eaten and Adam and Eve were banished from the Garden of Eden, God revealed that the tree of life, not the tree of knowledge of good and evil, offered eternal life (Genesis 3:22–24).

What's this have to do with frequent travelers? Everything. There are many "Wet Paint" signs along the road.

## *January 5*
## LONELINESS LOSES

"It is not good for the man to be alone."
(Genesis 2:18)

Traveler: *Adam*
**Read: Genesis 2:18–25**

It was Sunday afternoon, the end of an agonizing third straight weekend at a construction site two thousand miles from home. The phone rang. I heard my wife crying hysterically. My teenage daughter had fainted, hit her head on the corner of the TV and opened a nasty gash over her eye. In panic, my wife had called me instead of someone closer. I quickly told her to call our family doctor to deal with the emergency. There was nothing else I could do.

Then began the longest two hours of my life, waiting for word on my daughter's condition. Totally alone, I broke down. I just wasn't designed for long periods of loneliness. My daughter recovered nicely, but I was scarred with feelings of guilt for being gone at the wrong time.

If you travel frequently, chances are loneliness is your biggest problem too. Some quiet time is nice, but not weeks or years of it.

God knew this from the beginning: "It is not good for the man to be alone. I will make a helper suitable for him" (Genesis 2:18). This was right after He warned Adam about the tree of knowledge of good and evil (verse 17). God realized, even in such a perfect setting as the Garden of Eden, loneliness is bad.

Today, it's rare when a traveler can take along God's designated helper/spouse. Eve went with Adam, but modern business travel almost always means loneliness. I've been there and felt it, for many years.

But you have an advantage which Adam and Eve didn't have: "If you love me, you will obey what I command. And I will ask the Father, and he will give you another Counselor to be with you forever—the Spirit of truth. The world cannot accept him, because it neither sees him nor knows him. But you know him, for he lives with you and will be in you. I will not leave you as orphans; I will come to you" (John 14:15–18).

The Holy Spirit, packed safely inside of you by your faith in Jesus Christ, is even better than traveling with your spouse. Take Him along.

## *January 6*
## COMMANDER OF THE CAMP

"... the sound of the Lord God as he was walking..."
(Genesis 3:8)

Traveler: *God*
**Read: Genesis 3:1–13**

Mayor Hinsley knew everyone in town. Looking very official, he marched up to the registration counter at about 7:00 p.m. and asked for my room number. Even though giving out such information is against hotel policy, the clerk never hesitated.

After a long day of baking in the hot North Carolina sun, sniffing the bouquet of raw garbage at the town's landfill and enduring a concert of flies, I had returned to my room about 6:30 p.m. and showered. Still dripping from the intense July humidity and dressed only in my undershorts, I began working diligently on the mayor's project. Papers and books were spread everywhere across the room when the knock came.

Assuming it was a only a housekeeper checking that my room was properly made-up, I opened the door just a crack, and the mayor burst in. That's when I learned this small town mayor resented big city consulting fees; he expected me to be available to him twenty-four hours per day. If only I had heard him coming. I was not ready for a visitor. Neither were Adam and Eve: "Then the man and his wife heard the sound of the Lord God as he was walking in the garden in the cool of the day, and they hid from the Lord God among the trees of the garden" (Genesis 3:8). They couldn't hide from God any more than I could hide from the mayor.

You may think anything you do in the privacy of your hotel room is your business alone. Not true for God's people: "For the Lord your God moves about in your camp to protect you and to deliver your enemies to you. Your camp must be holy, so he will not see among you anything indecent and turn away from you" (Deuteronomy 23:14).

Your hotel room is your camp. God always has the keys. If He sees it as unholy, it could be your business will go very badly. I learned my lesson: my room is always ready for a white glove inspection from my Commander In Chief.

## January 7
### GARDEN OF GOD

"Cursed is the ground because of you . . ."
(Genesis 3:17)

Travelers: *Adam and Eve*
**Read: Genesis 3:14–24**

My home in Colorado sits in the foothills of the Rocky Mountains, surrounded by majestic green pine trees, blue sky and red sandstone. But very little grows in our red rocks soil except the hardiest weeds known to humanity. The key: don't plant vegetables for redeeming social value. Those not strangled by the weeds will provide dietary fiber for the plentiful wildlife. If I try to live on the fruits of that soil, I will starve. "Cursed is the ground because of you . . ." (Genesis 3:17). My land is a direct descendant of that curse. So am I.

Instead of working the ground like Adam, my life's painful toil came in the form of frequent business travel, and many times I felt cursed indeed. Despite being a Christian, I often allowed myself to forget God's promises and focused only on the Old Testament drudgery of it all.

It doesn't need to be that way for you.

In this first "week" of Bible travel, you have seen God's original plan, before the fall of Adam and Eve, was for you to travel, to subdue the earth with God's power, to perform work that is easy and enjoyable, to share your life with others and to eat from the tree of eternal life. As you read the Old Testament, it's easy to realize how far you have fallen from God's desire for you, but it's hard to remember God's promises, which are still available.

Even though "all have sinned and fall short of the glory of God" (Romans 3:23), there is actually a purpose for enduring the modern business lifestyle. You are working toward a goal shared with the Apostle Paul: "I consider that our present sufferings are not worth comparing with the glory that will be revealed in us. . . . Creation itself will be liberated from its bondage to decay and brought into the glorious freedom of the children of God. . . . Who shall separate us from the love of Christ?" (Romans 8:18,21,35).

One day it will all pay off. You will be free. And the fruit of God's garden will be sweeter than anything you have ever tasted. That's a promise, not a curse!

## January 8
### THE KEY TO PROTECTION

> "'... sin is crouching at your door....'"
> (Genesis 4:7)

Traveler: *Cain*
**Read: Genesis 4:1–16**

Loaded with luggage, Fred nudged open the door to Room 262 with the edge of his briefcase and flicked on the light switch with his elbow. Shrugging off his shoulder bag, he bounced the rest of his bags on the bed. Red digits on a bedside clock amplified his fatigue. Tonight had become tomorrow.

Suddenly the telephone clanged, as only hotel phones can. Fred's first thought was, "Man, my boss will stop at nothing to track me down!" He answered reluctantly. A polite voice said, "Mr. Smith, this is the front desk. I'm afraid you left the lights on in your rental car and locked the door. I hate to disturb you, but you'll have no battery in the morning." Fred thanked the man, reached for his keys and began to open his door.

Without warning, the door smashed into his face. A knife was at his throat and his mouth was taped shut. His money, computer and clothes were gone in seconds. Fortunately, Fred was not seriously harmed.

Looking back, Fred told me he regretted not having paid more attention as he checked into the hotel. Someone had been watching. There were so many things he could have done differently to protect himself.

How diligent have you been in protecting yourself when you're alone? God told Cain, "... if you do not do what is right, sin is crouching at your door; it desires to have you, but you must master it" (Genesis 4:7). Sin is crouching at your door, too. But you have something Cain did not have: freedom from sin through Jesus Christ: "But thanks be to God that, though you used to be slaves to sin, you wholeheartedly obeyed the form of teaching to which you were entrusted. You have been set free from sin and have become slaves to righteousness" (Romans 6:17–18).

You have protection. It's obedience to what you've been taught by Jesus Christ. Not just nominal obedience, but wholehearted, total, joyful obedience. Sin is very close at hand when you travel. Are you protected?

## *January 9*
### REMEMBERING STEVE

"... God took him away."
(Genesis 5:24)

Traveler: *Enoch*
**Read: Genesis 5:1–24**

"Six . . . gee . . . eighteen . . . sense . . . h . . . vee . . ." At first, the incoherent string of numbers, letters and words sounded like a bingo game from across the hall. My door was open and so was Steve's. We were both studying in our dorm rooms on a quiet Friday morning when everyone else was in class. But then I heard a *thump* and a chair hitting the floor.

Although I had known him only two weeks since the fall quarter began, Steve was not the kind of guy to fool around or make noise. He was a born-again Christian, a member of the Navigators, and he was always telling someone about Jesus Christ, though not obnoxiously. In fact, Steve was the happiest, most peaceful guy I had ever met. He just couldn't keep the Good News of his life bottled up inside! If only I had known him a little longer. It took me 24 more years to find what he had.

Getting up from my desk to see what was happening, I found Steve sprawled on the floor, in a trance. Moments ago he had been studying. Forty-five minutes later, he was dead. Brain hemorrhage. I believe he never felt a thing. Steve walked with God on earth. God simply took him away.

"Enoch walked with God; then he was no more, because God took him away" (Genesis 5:24). Enoch's departure was more miraculous than Steve's, because Enoch just disappeared. But Steve's trip was almost as quick. And I believe Steve experienced something quite beautiful—the sudden presence of Jesus Christ. Steve's brief appearance in my life reminds me of the priest Levi: "True instruction was in his mouth and nothing false was found on his lips. He walked with me in peace and uprightness, and turned many from sin" (Malachi 2:6).

How is your walk with God? If you were to die suddenly, what would people say about you? Is there still work to do before people will remember you as favorably as I remember Steve? "And what does the Lord require of you? To act justly and to love mercy and to walk humbly with your God" (Micah 6:8).

It's a good way of remembering Steve.

## *January 10*
## THE BOTTOM LINE

">... an accounting for the life of his fellow man."
(Genesis 9:5)

**Traveler:** *Noah*
**Read: Genesis 9:1–17**

Aging boss. Power struggle. Competition. Choosing sides. Winners. Losers.

Bob hired, mentored and promoted me. So when he challenged Sam for leadership of the office, he expected me to support him. But over the years, he had become an alcoholic and a tyrant. Sam understood my discomfort with Bob's deteriorating condition and smoothly recruited my support, promoting me even faster than Bob had. Even though Bob had serious personal problems, I just let him crash and burn. It didn't take long to help Sam complete the coup.

Sam and I were in. We made a great team. That is, until ten years later, when Sam decided I had become a threat to his power. Now it was my turn to go. Sam used my young top gun to run me out of the company. Why hadn't I seen it from the beginning? Because ambition is one of Satan's very best tools: "be sure your sin will find you out" (Numbers 32:23). Today, Bob is a bitter and lonely man. Shouldn't I have found a way to help him?

This episode is not easy to confess. But incredibly, God has forgiven me through the blood of Jesus Christ.

Just after the great flood, Noah and his sons were given a chance to start over after the overwhelming wickedness that preceded the flood. The principle that God set down was simple: "And from each man, too, I will demand an accounting for the life of his fellow man" (Genesis 9:5). There is no great difference between Abel's blood crying out from the ground (Genesis 4:10) and what I did to Bob.

Have you done similar things in your career? Are your footprints implanted on the backsides of people you scrambled over? Don't deceive yourself by saying, "Well, at least I'm not a murderer like Cain." God's accounting makes no distinction—sinning against a fellow man is shedding his blood, whether figuratively or literally.

Is your bottom line being accountable for the lives of your associates?

## *January 11*
### YOUR TICKET, PLEASE

> "... so that we may make a name for ourselves and not be scattered..." (Genesis 11:4)

**Travelers:** *The People*
**Read: Genesis 11:1–9**

In 1973, long before he became hero of the Persian Gulf War, H. Norman Schwartzkopf accepted an assignment at the Pentagon in Washington, D.C. In his autobiography he wrote, "For the first time in my Army career, I'd opted for an assignment not because I wanted it, not because I felt it was where I could make the greatest contribution to the Army or my country, but because I thought it would help me get ahead. I'd decided to ticket punch."[1]

In the military, "ticket punching" means taking jobs which enhance your potential for promotion, even if you must subordinate your ideals and beliefs.

But Schwartzkopf said, "To accomplish anything in Washington meant having to compromise, manipulate and put in the fix behind the scenes... I worked hard and gained a reputation as a team player who knew how to get things done in the bureaucracy—something of which I wasn't entirely proud. I knew I had to make a change."

He quickly took an assignment no one else would accept. Leaving Washington, he said, "I was free. But while my friends offered congratulations, they couldn't understand why I would give up a plum career assignment in order to command troops in the Arctic, in the dead of winter, working for a notoriously fierce boss. The ticket punchers thought I was crazy."

As a frequent traveler, you may feel quite isolated at times and far from the source of power in the home office, which can be like the tower of Babel, full of people making names for themselves, so they don't get sent into the field, where people like you make great sacrifices: "Come, let us build ourselves a city, with a tower that reaches to the heavens, so that we may make a name for ourselves and not be scattered over the face of the whole earth" (Genesis 11:4).

You are the most important part of the organization—what customers see. Your work has meaning that few in the home office can understand. But God does. He wants you out there, totally dependent on Him.

God doesn't punch tickets.

## January 12
### WHEN GOD SAYS GO

"... go to the land I will show you."
(Genesis 12:1)

Traveler: *Abram*
**Read: Genesis 12:1–5**

In May, 1985, I was disillusioned with all the travel I had done for many years and my engineering job was not going well. I felt called to serve Jesus Christ and believed God had brought job dissatisfaction into my life as a signal. So I responded to a vision God had given me for a new ministry for frequent travelers.

But right in the midst of setting up a non-profit corporation and applying for charitable tax status for my new ministry, God suddenly said, "No." Or at least, "Not yet." In a dizzying sequence of events, I was sent to a major construction project on the East coast and was handed challenges far beyond anything I could handle on my own. I learned how small I am and what total dependence on God is all about.

God told Abram to pull up his roots, too: "Leave your country, your people and your father's household and go to the land I will show you" (Genesis 12:1). He promised to bless Abram greatly, but only after much suffering (Acts 7:6). Looking back, I can see God was telling me something very similar. He was saying I was not ready to serve Him until I had been completely humbled. And, I must serve Him for the right reasons, not just to run from some other situation.

Why do you travel? Is it because you hate sitting behind a desk? Or it gets you away from the kids for some peace and quiet? Is it for your purpose or God's?

If it's for your purposes, you'll probably end up miserable, as I did. But if you travel for God, then His plan for you has very important implications. Even if He doesn't speak directly to you as He did to Abram, you can still look back and see how His plan has unfolded in your life. Celebrate that. Your everyday travel troubles will seem much smaller.

Go when God says.

## January 13
### CHECKING IN WITH GOD

"... so he built an altar there ..."
(Genesis 12:7)

**Traveler:** *Abram*
**Read: Genesis 12:6–9**

My first day as Owner's Representative at the power plant site where God sent me in 1985 included an immediate test. Construction was well underway when I arrived, and the contractor chose that day to slap my client with a major claim for more money. My job was to be firm enough with the contractor to send a message of toughness, while not being so harsh as to poison our relationship for the next three years. Balancing on the edge of a sharp knife would have been easier. If I could not handle this initial meeting well, I'd be out of a job before the end of the first week.

Feeling much like David facing Goliath for the first time, I claimed the words of Jesus: "... do not worry beforehand about what to say. Just say whatever is given you at the time, for it is not you speaking, but the Holy Spirit" (Mark 13:11). The words I was given were calm, confident and competent. They set the stage for a tough but fair relationship with the contractor.

When that first meeting was over, my stiff-upper-lip East coast client took me aside and called me the "Country Bumpkin" because of my easy-going style of conducting the meeting. He said, "Your biggest asset is that you are easy to underestimate." There was ironic humor in the statement and in the nickname, but also great respect. You only get a nickname if they are going to keep you on the job.

I found a quiet place and gave thanks to God.

Abram must have felt the same way when he saw the Promised Land, filled with people who must be driven out. But God appeared to Abram and reassured him: "To your offspring I will give this land" (Genesis 12:7). In response, Abram built an altar to the Lord.

As you travel, do you face problems alone, or do you claim God's word against the enemy? Do you listen for His reassurance by praying before a big meeting? And do you take time when it's over to thank Him for being at your side?

Check in with God regularly.

## January 14
### GOD'S GRACE

> ". . . Abram went down to Egypt . . ."
> (Genesis 12:10)

**Traveler:** *Abram*
**Read: Genesis 12:10–20**

I confess. One of the biggest challenges I face as a Christian is my behavior when I'm driving a car. My wife must wonder how such a pillar in the community can turn into a snarling fool at the slightest provocation. My demeanor can switch on a dime, although I've matured recently. Now I don't shake my fist at perpetrators of injustice, for fear of being shot!

Here's how I sound: "Oh honey, look at the deer over there in the . . . *Did you see that guy cut right in front of me? I don't believe he did that!* . . . Now what was I saying?" I've also been known to observe: "She can't possibly go that slow down hill!" Worst of all, when I speed up to keep someone from passing me on the right, I rationalize that the other guy's actions are unsafe.

By the grace of God, I am not permanently condemned for my weakness. I know this because I usually arrive at my destination safely, and the car rarely breaks down on the freeway. But I certainly deserve any penalty.

Abram did some very compulsive things too, when the heat was on. He lied to Pharaoh about his wife: "'Say you are my sister, so that . . . my life will be spared'" (Genesis 12:13). But instead of penalizing Abram for lying, God inflicted serious diseases on the unsuspecting ruler and his household. In fact, Abram gained considerable wealth as a payoff, which probably helped him survive the famine after he was kicked out of Egypt (verse 19).

I thought dishonesty didn't pay. How did Abram get off the hook? Because he belonged to God. I don't think God condoned Abram's behavior any more than He likes my driving, but God had a covenant with Abram. God's love simply overpowered his human weaknesses. That's called grace. And it makes us not want to fail Him any more.

Do you belong to God? Isn't your life lots better than you deserve? Isn't His grace hard to comprehend? Stop right now and do what Abram did: call on the name of the Lord (Genesis 13:4) and give thanks.

## January 15
### LOT'S LOSS

"... Lot chose for himself..."
(Genesis 13:11)

**Traveler:** *Lot*
**Read: Genesis 13:5–18**

I wanted to be elected "Partner" in my company so badly. That's capital "P." But when my election finally came, after 10 years of striving, something changed. I began to realize that in a secular partnership, I was expected to put the company first in my life. In fact, the Uniform Commercial Code says that I could be sued by my partners if they could prove that I had not committed myself to their financial well-being. Yet some of my partners took bad risks that endangered all of us. I felt like someone who discovers he has married the wrong woman.

After six years of "marriage" I found the problem: "Do not be yoked together with unbelievers... what fellowship can light have with darkness?" (2 Corinthians 6:14). My relationship with Jesus Christ had been growing strongly during that time, and I realized I could not live with non-Christian values as the top priorities in my life.

Abram's nephew Lot started out with wrong priorities, too. He chose for himself the most fruitful land around—land so beautiful it was, "... like the garden of the Lord..." (Genesis 13:10). But the people who lived there were, "... wicked and sinning greatly against the Lord" (verse 13). The land was attacked and conquered, and Lot was taken captive (Chapter 14). Later, God himself found the place so vile He destroyed it with burning sulfur (Chapter 19). Lot escaped only by divine intervention, but his wife did not survive.

I escaped the partnership, but not without emotional damage.

Do you have the "perfect plan" for success? Are your goals very clear? Do you know exactly where you want to go with your life? Are you reading all the popular "How-To" books and building your own plan for personal wealth?

Don't be like me, or like Lot. It's not too late to reevaluate your priorities and to let God write your master plan. He already has: "But seek first his kingdom and his righteousness, and all these things will be given you as well" (Matthew 6:33).

God must come first. All other priorities will bring you emptiness and dissatisfaction, even if you win the "Lot-tery."

## *January 16*
## NOT EVEN A THREAD

"... accept nothing ..."
(Genesis 14:23)

Traveler: *Abram*
**Read: Genesis 14:1–24**

The first day of sixth grade was when I was supposed to claim the turf I'd earned, after five years of working my way to the top. But despite the surging mob of cavorting kids, I was alone. I didn't know a soul. I had just moved into town.

The bell clanged. Instantly I was jostled and shoved in an unruly thrust toward the school door. Just before I squirted through the bottleneck, five brand new yellow pencils with perfect erasers were thrust in front of my face. "Here," a boy said. "I'm Jack, and you can have these for free. Will you be my friend?" I was thrilled.

But at lunch time, I found out there was a catch. Everyone in the school hated Jack, because he played nasty tricks on them. Even before I opened my lunch sack, Jack was in a fight. To my horror, he immediately yelled for me to come to his aid. "You said you'd be my friend. Now prove it!"

Not a good start.

As you travel through life, beware of gifts from strangers. Any business acquaintance, at home and on the road, might involve people like Jack. And gifts from adults are more subtle than new pencils with perfect erasers. But they always have a price—recruiting your influence for the future.

Abram showed us the right way to deal with this problem. He had saved the King of Sodom from defeat and the King wanted Abram to take all the spoils of victory. Abram knew that if he accepted, it would come back to haunt him later. So Abram told the King: "I have raised my hand to the Lord, God Most High, Creator of heaven and earth, and have taken an oath that I will accept nothing belonging to you, not even a thread or the thong of a sandal, so that you will never be able to say, 'I made Abram rich'" (Genesis 14:22–23). Abram relied on two things: looking first to God as his authority and avoiding obligations to anyone.

God's people must show that the wisdom and the material goods they acquire come from God, not from men. Are you relying on God or on your "network" today?

## January 17
## GOD HEARS!

> "... so she fled from her."
> (Genesis 16:6)

**Traveler:** *Hagar*
**Read: Genesis 16:1–16**

Our three-year assignment in Connecticut was nearly over and the renters of our home in Denver were leaving. My wife and I did not want to commit to another long lease, only to find that we would be returning home before the lease ended. So I reluctantly stayed behind, thinking it would only be a month or two, and my family moved back to Colorado. But suddenly my project in Connecticut turned into a nightmare of problems and it was another full year before I could leave.

I missed my family so badly, especially on weekends. I wanted to run. Forget the job; forget my responsibilities! More than once I started to pack my bags and flee. But I stuck it out, and God blessed me with the pinnacle of my professional career, guiding me as I helped straighten out the mess.

Have you ever run away from an assignment? If not, there's a good chance you have felt like it.

Hagar, the servant of Abram's wife Sarai, was mistreated by Sarai (Genesis 16:6). Hagar was anything but innocent, having openly despised Sarai for being barren. "... So she fled from her" (verse 6).

Instead of feeling sorry for Hagar and letting her off the hook, an angel of the Lord sent Hagar back, in submission to her mistress (verse 9). The angel told Hagar that her descendants would be too numerous to count if she would obey. The angel also said, "You are now with child and you will have a son. You shall name him Ishmael, for the Lord has heard of your misery" (verse 11). Hagar was humbled by the presence of God and went back and gave birth to Ishmael (verse 15), which means "God hears."

If you feel like running away, don't take matters into your own hands without trusting God. Stick it out, prayerfully. Your business career is filled with times when you are taken advantage of. But God's way is to hang in there, to submit to His authority. He will bless you beyond comprehension.

God hears!

## *January 18*
### LAUGHING AT THE LORD

> "Yes, you did laugh."
> (Genesis 18:15)

**Traveler:** *Sarah*
**Read: Genesis 18:1–15**

At the age of sixteen I was incredibly naive. Apparently everyone in our high school knew that Greg was going to ask Kim to the prom, except me. Even though Greg was one of my best friends, we talked about basketball, not girls. I thought Kim was pretty and that was that.

I asked, she accepted (because in those days it was politically correct to accept the first offer), and the scandal began. To make matters worse, Kim was elected prom queen, and she had to endure the entire pomp and circumstance with me, instead of with Greg. She wasn't very nice about it, and the whole process was agony for both of us.

At the picnic the day after the prom, the guys drifted off to one side of the picnic area to share horror stories from the night before, while the gals held their own pow-wow. Instead of swallowing my fate graciously, I asked aloud, "Why didn't she just turn me down, if she didn't want to go with me?" Little did I know that my voice carried easily to where the girls could hear. I had swallowed my foot, up to the kneecap, and I didn't hear the end of it until I moved away, after high school.

God overheard Sarah, too, as she eaves-dropped from inside the tent, at the prospect of having a child in her old age: "After I am worn out and my master is old, will I now have this pleasure?" (Genesis 18:12). But God heard her and confronted her. She lied about it and was caught. We can almost see her face burning with shame today.

Do you laugh at God when He asks you to do something?

God has promised many wonderful things in His word. Do you believe Him? Or does God see your many acts of unfaithfulness as laughing at Him? In business, in travel, do you often act as if you are alone, and He is not in control? Does God overhear your doubt and shake His head sadly?

Remember how humiliated Sarah must have been to be confronted with a lie.

I certainly have no problem remembering how I was overheard at the prom picnic.

## January 19
## ALCOHOL AND LONELINESS

> "Let's get our father to drink wine . . ."
> (Genesis 19:32)

**Travelers:** *Lot's Daughters*
**Read: Genesis 19:30–38**

"It is not good for . . . man to be alone" (Genesis 2:18). Yet that is exactly what happens in business travel. And it's not just a problem for men. The number of women traveling alone is increasing dramatically. Since your God-given helper often cannot be with you on a business trip, alcohol can become a substitute. Like a poisonous snake, slithering unseen in tall grass, a little alcohol becomes more alcohol on the next trip; it can coil and strike suddenly, devastating mind, spirit and body.

This is not a pretty subject. But our passage through Genesis demands that it not be skipped. Here I must confess that in the past I resorted to numbness rather than face the pain of separation from my family. I knew alcohol was not good for me, and I certainly never got raging drunk. But I rationalized that a couple beers before bed were better than all sorts of other trouble I could get into. Two became three. Three became six. Only my imperfect faith in Jesus Christ at that time, and the undeserved grace of God, kept me from becoming an alcoholic.

Alcohol and loneliness simply don't mix.

Lot's daughters were lonely and isolated, living with their father in a cave after the destruction of Sodom and Gomorrah. They had no hope of meeting eligible young men and getting married. So they said, "Let's get our father to drink wine and then lie with him and preserve our family line through our father" (Genesis 19:32). Loneliness and alcohol were used as justification for immorality.

It is hard to suggest that a little wine in fellowship with family and friends is wrong, when Christ himself changed water into wine at a wedding (John 2:1–10). But when you are alone, alcohol is a welcome-mat at the front door of your mind, making you feel comfortable with evil in your presence.

How about you? Do you need a drink when you're alone "to forget your troubles?" Let God and God alone meet your "medicinal" needs!

## January 20
### FEAR AND FAITH

"... when God had me wander..."
(Genesis 20:13)

Traveler: *Abraham*
Read: **Genesis 20:1–18**

My internal survival alarms flashed red—danger, danger! My client's lawyer had suddenly become friendly, after months of open hostility. As he sidled up to me at a reception, his eyes never stopped darting around the room. Superficially friendly words belied hawk-like intensity. That must be how a rabbit feels, knowing it's too late, just before the talons sink in.

In casual conversation across the room, he had just overheard that I had once memorized the Gospel of Mark and performed it on stage as a one-man dramatic recital. I often share that experience with professional friends, whenever social conversation turns to religion. Now, while faking amazement at my "remarkable" talent, my predator was asking to borrow the videotape of my performance. In a sudden, heart-stopping premonition, I saw the trap. He was Jewish. He would claim that my portrayal of the Scribes and the Pharisees was anti-Semitic. At long last, he would be able to discredit me in public. I did not have the faith to give him the tape.

Abraham did the same thing when he lied and told Abimelech that Sarah was his sister. She was his half sister, but she was also his wife. Poor Abimelech believed Abraham's deception, and he was almost ruined by God because of it (Genesis 20:7). In explaining why he lied to Abimelech, Abraham twisted his powerful calling from God (Genesis 12), whimpering that God had caused him to "wander from my father's household" (Genesis 20:13). His fear of Abimelech kept him from boldly proclaiming his mission.

I, too, lost a valuable opportunity to share my faith with a Jewish man, who could certainly have gained from meeting Jesus. This man later tried to ruin me, so what did I gain from failing to meet the challenge? What if I had shown the courage to share my true faith?

Does business travel put you in dangerous situations which test your faith? Do you recoil and hide behind God's apron strings? Or do you seize the opportunity? You never know how your testimony might affect someone in the future.

## January 21
## GOD'S GRAND SLAM

"God heard the boy crying..."
(Genesis 21:17)

Travelers: *Hagar and Ishmael*
Read: **Genesis 21:8–21**

Commuting to a job site 2,000 miles away and coming home every third weekend was tough. Arriving late Friday night and leaving again on Sunday afternoon, for another three weeks, left me only thirty-six jet-lagged hours with my family at a time. By April 1988 this had been our plight for four months. No end was in sight.

Then, I had to give up a precious Saturday with my family because I had just been elected partner in the company and had to sign all the papers. To make it even worse, on this day, when my career had reached its pinnacle, I reached a new family low-point—I would be absent from my son's first competitive baseball game. I dragged myself off to work, fulfilling the responsibility society had given me, but neglecting the one God had given me. My job meant that I could not be part of my own community. I was outside, looking in.

Abraham's wife's servant Hagar also knew what it was like to be on the outside. After Isaac was born to Abraham and Sarah, Hagar's son Ishmael was no longer welcome. Mother and son were sent off to the desert. As they ran out of food and water, both Hagar and Ishmael cried out in misery. But an angel came and told Hagar, "God has heard the boy crying as he lies there. Lift the boy up and take him by the hand, for I will make him into a great nation" (Genesis 21:17–18). God not only saved them, but blessed them.

God heard my boy crying, too. While I was at work that Saturday, the baseball game was rained out and rescheduled for Sunday *morning*, not afternoon. So I was able to attend before leaving again for the airport. In an affirmation only God could arrange, my son hit his first home run while I was coaching third base!

If you find yourself in a desperate situation, let your heart cry out. God hears your crying, too.

## January 22
### THE LORD WILL PROVIDE

"On the mountain of the Lord..."
(Genesis 22:14)

Travelers: *Abraham and Isaac*
**Read: Genesis 22:1–19**

Putting our Colorado home up for sale—because we couldn't afford it anymore—was very emotional. We were moving to Connecticut for three years and there was no way to keep our home and have a second one back East. We loved our home in the Colorado foothills and considered each mule deer to be a member of the family. Even though it hurt, Sue and I knew this was the Lord's direction for us.

Just as we bought our Connecticut house, the Colorado housing market crashed, and we could not sell our old house at any price. Over the next three years, we endured three renters, bridge loans and considerable discomfort, but we managed to stay afloat.

Even potential bankruptcy was not as terrifying as what Abraham endured when God told him to kill his only son Isaac: "Then he reached out his hand and took the knife to slay his son. But the angel of the Lord called out to him from heaven, 'Abraham! Abraham!' 'Here I am,' he replied. 'Do not lay a hand on the boy . . . Now I know that you fear God . . .'" (Genesis 22:10–12). Abraham was willing to sacrifice his son, but God gave him a ram to kill instead (verse 13).

Ironically, the house we bought in Connecticut appreciated over 60% in just two years. When God sent us back to Colorado, we made enough money on the second house to fix up the first. God provided for us first by not letting us sell the Colorado house and then by allowing us a profit in Connecticut to resolve our financial difficulties.

We were willing to sacrifice our house and God gave it back to us.

God Himself made a sacrifice far beyond anything you can comprehend. Unlike Abraham, He did sacrifice His Son: "God so loved the world that he gave his one and only Son, that whoever believes in him shall not perish but have eternal life" (John 3:16).

He made that sacrifice for *you*. Have you thanked Him today?

## January 23
### GOD'S TRAFFIC SIGNALS

> "O Lord . . . give me success today . . ."
> (Genesis 24:12)

**Traveler:** *Abraham's Chief Servant*
**Read: Genesis 24:1–51**

Today is November 26, 1994. I write this devotion as an act of faith. I do not know how it will turn out.

Next Monday, I will make an offer to buy a bankrupt dinner theater. I believe that God has led me to turn the theater into a Christian hospitality center, a place for the body of Christ to gather for fellowship and encouragement. I believe that He will show me the path to follow, even though I have no idea how I will raise the money. According to conventional business practice, the proposition seems absurd, yet God spurs me on.

I take much good-natured kidding from my prayer partners about my "Field of Dreams." If I buy it, will they come?

Abraham's chief servant had to rely on faith, too. He had to travel to a distant land, find Abraham's relatives and seek a wife for Isaac. When he reached the town of Nahor, he prayed for the Lord's guidance, asking that he be greeted a certain way, as a sign of the Lord's favor: "'O Lord, God of my master Abraham, give me success today. . . . May it be that when I say to a girl, 'Please let down your jar that I may have a drink,' and she says, 'Drink and I'll water your camels, too'—let her be the one you have chosen for your servant Isaac'" (Genesis 24:12, 14). Rebekah was the one.

My offer letter to the theater owner is the same thing. It is a prayer for guidance. But just as Abraham's servant left the decision up to Laban and Bethuel, whether Rebekah would be allowed to go to Isaac (verse 49), I am prepared to go on to another project if this one does not work out. I have left the result to God.

How do you make tough decisions? Are you willing to proceed until God says "Stop?"

*Postscript:* The theater owner allowed only three months to raise the money—impossible. That was God's stop sign. In 1996, another Christian group followed my vision, bought the theater, and it is now functioning as I had dreamed.

## January 24
### PEACE WITHOUT A PRICE

"Let us make a treaty with you."
(Genesis 26:28)

Traveler: *Isaac*
Read: Genesis 26:1–31

I took my chiropractor friend to a basketball game, hoping that the medical doctor who has season tickets right beside me wouldn't show up. Both are people I think highly of, yet their professions often conflict over the subject of medical care.

But the medical doctor did come to the game that night. It was inevitable that during a time out, I would have to introduce the two.

When my guest proudly announced that he was a chiropractor, I braced for fireworks. But the doctor said to the chiropractor, "It's good to meet you. I really respect what you're doing, and I wish more of my colleagues did. The medical profession doesn't want to admit it, but you are healing folks we can't. And sometimes we heal folks you can't. Isn't that what it's supposed to be all about—healing?" The doctor was able to put the health and well-being of people ahead of a professional rivalry. She recognized the fires of caring and competence burning in the eyes of my friend.

Abimelech, powerful King of the Philistines, had a rivalry with the people of Israel. But when he saw that the Lord was with Isaac, he sought a treaty of peace: "We saw clearly that the Lord was with you; so we said, 'There ought to be a sworn agreement between us . . .'" (Genesis 26:28). Abimelech, like my doctor friend, saw the bigger picture. He understood the need to take care of his people and humbled himself to make peace.

Have your enemies ever wanted to make peace with you? If so, they probably see you as a servant of God, like Isaac. They recognize they can't beat God. But if your enemies are always attacking, think about how you appear to them. Are you exhibiting true faith? Do you reflect the qualities of integrity which scare a dishonest opponent? Are you confident that God is with you in all battles? Or do you need to fix some things in your life, in order to gain that kind of invincible presence?

## January 25
### STONE PILLOW

"I ..will watch over you . . ."
(Genesis 28:15)

**Traveler:** *Jacob*
**Read: Genesis 28:10–22**

Somewhere down the hall a door slammed. I leaped out of bed, pulse pounding, totally disoriented. It was 3:00 a.m. in the dark, and I had no idea where I was. Milwaukee on Thursday, for a 7:00 a.m. breakfast appointment? Or Newark on Friday, before an early wake-up call to fly home? It had been one of those hectic weeks, with one or two airplane flights each day to a different city and a new hotel every night. This was one of the scariest moments of my life.

If you travel frequently, particularly to different places each day, you may feel jumbled, too. It's easy to fall into a state of suspended animation, where you just go through the paces, enduring it until you arrive home. Are you missing something that would make the whole process more tolerable?

While traveling toward Haran, Jacob stopped and slept along the way, placing a rock—not unlike some of the hotel pillows I've had—under his head. In the depths of sleep, God came to him: "I am with you and will watch over you wherever you go, and I will bring you back to this land. I will not leave you until I have done what I have promised you" (Genesis 28:15). No heart-stopping disturbances. No disorientation in the night. Just a stunning sense of God's presence: "How awesome is this place! This is none other than the house of God; this is the gate of heaven" (verse 17).

Has any hotel room ever seemed like that to you?

Wouldn't it be nice if God talked directly to you as He did to Jacob? Wouldn't it be easier to carry on if God told you that your trip was important to His plan and that He would bless you and bring you home safely?

God *is* that close to you. His promise to Jacob is His promise to you. You simply need to focus on God's purpose for your travel. That's what may be missing. Ask Him today to clarify your calling and to enter your conscious thought—and your dreams. You'll never again wonder where you are in the middle of the night.

## January 26
### ANGELS OF ACTION

> ". . . and the angels of God met him."
> (Genesis 32:1)

Travelers: *The Angels of God*
**Read: Genesis 32:1–2**

In the comic strip "Rose Is Rose," little Pasquale has a guardian angel who literally clears all threats from his path. Yet the angel often gets no respect for his efforts, because he can't be seen.

I haven't given my guardian angel much respect either. Looking back over my years of business travel, I've been too quick to remember the trials and tribulations but too slow to recall all the times when things went right, even miraculously right. Nor have I always contemplated how much worse things could have been.

I remember easily the exasperation of a weather-delayed flight, but the fact that it arrived safely is quickly forgotten. The sudden cancellation of a meeting, planned months in advance, is easy to recall, but not the subsequent sale when my customer remembered he had inconvenienced me. Or the sudden breakthrough in contract negotiations, when it looked as if another weekend would be lost.

Do you think angels protect you as you go, or do you focus on all the bad things that happen? Are God's angels frequent travelers? The Bible is a travel book, full of angels protecting travelers. Whether it's Hagar (Genesis 16) or Elisha (2 Kings 6), angels tread where your enemies can't see them: "The angel of the Lord encamps around those who fear him, and he delivers them" (Psalm 34:7). Angels literally "lift you up in their hands . . ." (Psalm 91:12), to protect you.

The author of Hebrews, though, gives us the best mission statement for angels: "Are not all angels ministering spirits sent to serve those who will inherit salvation?" (Hebrews 1:14). So angels are sent. They travel. But not to everyone. Only to those who know God.

The source of all power and protection is Jesus Christ. If you don't feel that kind of protection, it's an indication of a poor relationship with Him. There is no better time than right now to invite Him into your heart for the first time, or to renew your faith in the angels He sends to you. Then, nothing can come between you and His love.

## *January 27*
## HOW MANY FOREIGN GODS?

"... no one pursued them."
(Genesis 35:5)

**Traveler:** *Jacob*
**Read: Genesis 35:1–15**

Lawyers, with all due respect, make my brain feel like a pretzel. They love all the convoluted details of complex contracts, because they are trained to consider each provision from every possible angle and to pose hypothetical questions which bear little resemblance to reality. As a professional engineer, I am often involved in contract negotiations with lawyers who possess intellectual capacities far greater than mine. But I can choose a weapon which gives me the advantage, no matter how smart the lawyer.

Before entering any negotiation meeting, I ask God to sit right next to me. I ask Him to give me the words to say and the actions to take. If God is on my side, I have nothing to fear. But how do I know God is there? Have I chosen the right weapon?

Jacob's people had acquired many bad habits during their sojourn in the city of Shechem. But when they offended Hamor and his sons, after the sons had defiled Jacob's daughter Dinah, they were under serious threat of attack. They needed to leave quickly and they needed protection (Genesis 34). Jacob told his people to get rid of all their foreign gods, as a sign that they belonged to the one true God. When they had done so, they set out on their journey, "... and the terror of God fell upon the towns all around them so that no one pursued them ..." (Genesis 35:5).

Have you developed some bad habits when you travel, or in any facet of your life? Do you stretch the rules a little when there is no threat to your safety, but then call on God when things get tough? What foreign gods have you picked up along the way? Wouldn't it be better to get rid them? There is no guarantee God will save you from trouble, if you offend Him enough. The only way for the weapon to be effective is when your righteousness causes your enemies to sense God's presence.

I learned in my negotiating experience that when I was not right with God, He was noticeably absent from the chair beside me. And opposing lawyers made that absence very painful indeed.

What weapon will you choose?

## *January 28*
### BLESSINGS IN CAPTIVITY

"... the Lord gave him success in everything..."
(Genesis 39:3)

**Traveler:** *Joseph*
**Read: Genesis 39:1–23**

I had been left for dead—professionally. When I was transferred to Connecticut in 1985, no one expected me to return to the home office. I would be out of sight and out of mind. I would bring in lots of money to the company, but I would not be in the way. I was essentially a refugee in my client's office.

The lesson of Joseph showed me how to survive. Joseph was sold by his jealous brothers, into slavery in Egypt (Genesis 37). But God was with Joseph: "When his master saw that the Lord was with him and that the Lord gave him success in everything he did, Joseph found favor in his eyes ... the Lord blessed the household of the Egyptian because of Joseph" (Genesis 39:3–5).

There were two keys to Joseph's survival. First, the master knew that Joseph's success came from the Lord. The text does not tell us how he knew, but we can assume that Joseph did not take credit for himself. Whenever something good happened, Joseph probably gave thanks to God in visible ways. He was not shy about expressing his source of strength, in a foreign land.

Second, even the household of his master was blessed. The better it got for Joseph's master, the more Joseph was put in charge. Not a bad way to live out your captivity.

My client in Connecticut liked my work so much that I was asked to join their staff as an executive on loan, to help clean up some internal problems. They respected me far more than my own company did. I let them know that my success came from the Lord. God was good to me and to my client.

When you are put in a difficult place, make the best of it. Make sure your "captor" knows of your dependence on God and that his blessings may come from God blessing you. Serve with excellence, even if the situation is not of your design.

It is God's design.

## *January 29*
## GREAT DELIVERANCE

"God sent me ahead . . ."
(Genesis 45:5)

**Travelers:** *Joseph's Brothers*
**Read: Genesis 44:14–45:11**

This was a sudden drop-everything-and-go vacation. In the preceding month, Sue had suffered her second miscarriage, and we were not sure, after four years of trying, whether we would ever have children. And my power plant in Michigan had been sabotaged in a labor dispute and was badly damaged. We both needed a rest and impulsively hopped a plane to Colorado.

You probably have had months like that, where everything seems to go wrong at once. If so, consider what happened to Joseph. His brothers sold him into slavery and reported that he was dead. Imagine how hard that must have been for Joseph. How could God put him through such an ordeal? How can God put you through some of the things you must face?

Joseph answered that question for all generations when he revealed his identity to his starving brothers, many years later, after Joseph had become master of all Egypt. Instead of blaming his brothers, he said, "God sent me ahead of you to preserve for you a remnant on earth and to save your lives by a great deliverance. So then, it was not you who sent me here, but God" (Genesis 45:7–8).

Sometimes we suffer because God has a higher purpose in mind. If Joseph had not suffered at the hands of his brothers, God's people would not have survived the famine. And if my wife and I had not suffered during that month in Michigan, we probably would never have come to Colorado nor found the personal relationships with Jesus Christ which we now enjoy. We knew the moment we got off that airplane in Denver, in 1973, that God had sent us ahead to Colorado for a reason. Almost a quarter century later, God is still revealing to us the nature of that mission.

God puts his own special signature on His "great deliverances," too. Pharaoh gave Joseph the very best of Egypt, so that he could enjoy the fat of the land (verse 18).

And our daughter Michelle was born exactly nine months after our arrival in Colorado! What special package does He have in mind for you?

## January 30
ON BEING USED

> "... but God intended it for good ..."
> (Genesis 50:20)

**Travelers:** *God's People in Egypt*
**Read: Genesis 50:15–26**

The ink on my diploma was barely dry. It was only my second day on my very first job, and I was training in the control room of a large power plant. A huge boiler was being started up, so I began writing down water pressures and temperatures, just to familiarize myself with the maze of gauges and instruments.

Incredibly, I noticed that the boiler water was too hot. At that temperature it could "flash" to steam and explode, like water thrown onto a sizzling grill. But I was sure that I must be wrong. Here were men who had been going through the same procedure for 25 years, men recognized as among the best in the business. How could a green engineer like myself see a problem that easily?

Hesitantly, I asked the boiler operator about the data. His icy response was, "Obviously, your readings are wrong. I've done this a thousand times. You're in the way, kid."

I decided to go out in the plant where the temperature measuring device was located, to see if the instrument was malfunctioning. Just as I arrived, there was a rumble and then an explosion. Suddenly I was enveloped by roaring steam and I ran for my life.

Later, I learned that a pipe ruptured directly under the I-beam I had been standing on. The beam deflected the steam, preventing it from hitting me directly. If I had been standing inches to either side of the beam, I would have been scalded to death.

In the subsequent investigation, management confiscated my notes and used them against the operator, who was disciplined but kept his job. I immediately became the enemy of every operator in that plant, for "squealing" on one of their own. I felt like Joseph among his brothers: "but God intended it for good to accomplish what is now being done, the saving of many lives" (Genesis 50:20).

Trust in God in all places and situations, no matter how difficult. He has a purpose. He has selected you specially. That is the lesson of Joseph.

## January 31
## WHO AM I?

*"So now, go. I am sending you . . ."*
(Exodus 3:10)

Traveler: *Moses*
Read: Exodus 3:1–15

Among the three of us, the other two men's speech impediments complemented my hearing loss. Each of us had important career accomplishments to communicate to our potential client. We knew we were the most qualified for the job. But physical handicaps can become deterrents in formal sales presentations in the competitive business world. Every word counts. Guessing whether you heard a question correctly could be fatal. In the consulting business, you can do a great presentation and still lose the job.

Conventional wisdom would have kept us from pursuing that project. Any real marketing expert would have said that we did not have enough flash to impress the client. But I was not a real marketing expert. Rather I was a manager who believed in the potential of all people.

After some careful thought, we crafted a way to help each other. I spoke at key points where the others might have stuttered, and they fielded questions when I might have had trouble hearing. In the process, the client saw what a good team we were. And we won the job, not because someone felt sorry for us, but because we were the best. We refused to let our handicaps stop us.

Do you have physical or mental traits that hold you back? Moses did, too. But God called him to lead His people out of Egypt. Moses was so lacking in confidence because of his slowness of speech that God became very angry at him.

When Moses could not understand how he would impress the great Pharaoh, God told him how He uses people with handicaps: "See, I have made you like God to Pharaoh, and your brother Aaron will be your prophet" (Exodus 7:1). So it's not your physical drawbacks that impress people, when God is involved. God literally alters how you appear. You appear as God to an adversary! That's a powerful transition.

And when God has successfully used you to accomplish His mighty work, be sure to acknowledge God in the same way God instructed Moses (Exodus 3:12): worship Him formally, for He is the source of power. Without Him, every person is severely handicapped.

## February 1
### BETTER LATE THAN NEVER

"... the Lord kept vigil that night ..."
(Exodus 12:42)

Travelers: *The Israelites*
**Read: Exodus 12:1–42**

Working the "graveyard" shift, Patrice Secora often left the hospital after 1:00 a.m. Driving home at that late hour one night, she decided to return a video tape to the rental store. The store was completely dark—not even a security light was on. Looking around, to make sure no one was lurking near, she jumped out of the car quickly and hurried to the "mail slot" used for after-hours returns.

Just as she dropped the tape into the slot, she heard a sickening jangle as her car keys slipped off the end of her finger, accompanied the tape down the slot and bounced on the floor inside the locked shop. Patrice froze in horror. Not a soul around. No pay phone in sight. No all-night coffee shop. No car keys. A solitary woman, defenseless in the darkness. "Oh Lord," she cried aloud, "help me!" She wasn't just whistling in the dark; she knows Jesus Christ as her best friend.

Just then, out of the darkness inside the store, a young woman emerged, silently picked up the keys, slipped them back through the slot to Patrice's shaking fingers, and disappeared back into the shadows, without a word.

The Israelites were delivered out of Egypt in a similar way. Despite impossible odds, God chose Moses to lead the way after 430 long years: "During the night Pharaoh summoned Moses and Aaron and said, 'Up! Leave my people' . . . Because the Lord kept vigil that night to bring them out of Egypt, on this night all the Israelites are to keep vigil to honor the Lord for the generations to come" (Exodus 12:31, 33, 42). Passover is the remembrance of God's vigilance that enabled the Israelites to leave quickly.

Patrice has no idea who the woman in the video store was, or why she was there in total darkness, but she knows her prayer was answered—instantly. She witnessed her own "Passover." She has a personal relationship with God, and He was there in her time of need. Evil was banished at her cry for help.

How is your relationship with God? Can you call on Him in a crisis? Do you really believe He can deliver you from an impossible situation?

## February 2
### IN HOT PURSUIT

"... wandering around the land in confusion ..."
(Exodus 14:3)

Travelers: *The Israelites*
Read: Exodus 14:1–12

My client was convinced that we would lose. I was being called to testify in a trial which seemed hopeless. I told the truth, but as the opposing lawyers rose to cross examine me, they actually mocked me, so confident were they of their victory. Their questions were brutal. They attacked not only my testimony, but my credibility. After two long days of testimony, I felt like I had been led to the slaughter.

That's how the Israelites felt when they left Egypt. God specifically ordered them to backtrack on their route, so Pharaoh would pursue them: "Pharaoh will think, '"The Israelites are wandering around the land in confusion..'" (Exodus 14:3). The Israelites did not realize that this was part of God's plan, and they complained bitterly about their hardships: "It would have been better for us to serve the Egyptians than to die in the desert!" (verse 12). But God was in control throughout. What followed was the spectacular parting of the Red Sea and the Israelites' miraculous escape.

God had a plan for my testimony at trial, too. The opposition called its witnesses, whose job it was to contradict everything I had said. But when their lawyers tried to put words in their mouths, they resolutely refused to lie. Even though they were on the other side, and they had opposed me many times over the years, they were men of integrity. They had a perfect chance for revenge on me, but they told the truth. The lawyers looked like Egyptians as the case collapsed around them in minutes.

Has God placed you in situations which seemed absolutely hopeless? If so, remember His goal is to bring glory to Himself through you. Sometimes it takes years before His victory is complete. You may not be able to see His plan until you look back over time and see what He was doing in your life. But if things seem confusing, and if the enemy is chasing you and gaining ground quickly, don't lose faith. Trust Him. He is luring the enemy toward destruction. All you have to do is watch with anticipation.

## *February 3*
### UNFAILING PROTECTION

> ". . . the angel of God . . . went behind them."
> (Exodus 14:19)

Travelers: *The Israelites*
**Read: Exodus 14:13–20**

Before my friend died of brain cancer at a very young age, he asked me to conduct his memorial service. The procession to the cemetery was the longest I have ever seen. A string of at least a hundred cars streamed through the city toward the cemetery. I was a little frightened as we sped through red lights and busy intersections.

Only two motorcycle policemen escorted our caravan. Their teamwork and timing were impeccable. As the procession approached an intersection, one policeman blocked crossing traffic and remained in that position until the last car in line passed through. By this time, the other officer was already guarding the next intersection. The first then leap-frogged his partner, racing with break-neck speed and screaming siren to the next intersection, arriving only moments before our limousine which led the procession. Watching them work was terrifying, as they risked their own safety for ours.

The angel of God went in front of the Israelites when they left Egypt. But when they reached the Red Sea with Pharaoh in hot pursuit, the angel changed positions: "Then the angel of God, who had been traveling in front of Israel's army, withdrew and went behind them. The pillar of cloud also moved from in front and stood behind them. . . . Throughout the night the cloud brought darkness to one side and light to the other side; so neither went near the other all night long" (Exodus 14:19–20).

Sometimes our only mental picture of God's angels is as an invisible shield in front of us to deflect the bad guys. Actually, they cover us from all angles, just like the policemen escorting our convoy. When God's plan is being implemented, and when we submit ourselves to Him, His angels rush from point to point, covering all vulnerable areas, front and rear.

Do you feel a sense of total protection? If not, think about whether you have totally submitted your well-being to God. If you have been trying to provide your own protection, give it up. You can't beat the Egyptians by yourself. Join the convoy of God's people who are secure in their escort of angels.

## February 4
### GOD'S INFINITE PATIENCE?

> "... the people ... put their trust in him ..."
> (Exodus 14:31)

Travelers: *The Israelites*
Read: Exodus 14:21–31

Not since the Viet Nam war had our country faced such a grave military challenge. We had been drawn into numerous small conflicts in the intervening years. But the invasion of Kuwait by Saddam Hussein launched an armada of American troops in response. The risks were immense, and no one could predict what would happen. Everyone feared a great loss of life and another enervating commitment in a hostile environment.

But something remarkable happened. After decades of moral decay, our nation suddenly begged for God's support. Not the politicians and certainly not the media, but millions of individual families—grass roots America was on its knees, all faiths unified in prayer.

The results were stunning—one of the most thorough military victories in history. The opposition nearly melted away in the face of our advance. Tens of thousands of lives were saved by the brilliance of our military leadership and the bravery of our troops. Those who died will never be forgotten. But I believe that the results of the Persian Gulf War would have been very different if our people had not responded in prayer as they did. No such unity was found during Viet Nam, and the results were disastrous.

The Israelites also saw the awesome beauty of God's deliverance: "And when the Israelites saw the great power the Lord displayed against the Egyptians, the people feared the Lord and put their trust in him and in Moses his servant" (Exodus 14:31). For awhile, they realized what it meant to be God's chosen people. Later, the memory faded and they rebelled time and again (Exodus 15:24).

America, too, has returned quickly to its sinful ways. God finally lost His patience with the Israelites and scattered them across the earth (Jeremiah 30:11). Will we pay the penalty of God's wrath one day? Is God's patience infinite?

How about you personally? Do you call on God in times of trouble, only to forget Him as soon as the good times roll again? How long before He loses His patience with you?

## February 5
### JUST DESERTS

">. . . I will not bring on you any . . . diseases"
(Exodus 15:26)

Travelers: *The Israelites*
Read: Exodus 15:22–27

Looking back to that day over twenty years ago, I don't even remember what it was I accomplished. I was a brash, self-confident young engineer and I had just successfully completed a very tough assignment. I thirsted for recognition. So I strutted into my boss's office, tossed out a little casual conversation and eventually asked if he knew that I had completed the job. Yes, he knew. I lingered, hoping for some sort of reward.

My boss was much wiser than I realized. He knew exactly what I was doing. He picked up the phone and asked a couple of other senior managers to stop in. While we were waiting for them to arrive, he wrote something on an old napkin. When the others arrived, he presented it to me with great flair, congratulating me on a job well done.

Then he asked me to read aloud what he had written on the napkin. It said, "YGTKYJ." Everyone else was smiling; they knew what the acronym meant. Finally, I looked quizzically at my boss for an interpretation. He whispered, "You Get To Keep Your Job."

He wasn't kidding. That was my reward.

God was not kidding, either, when He told the Israelites to stop grumbling against Moses as if he had caused the harsh desert conditions they encountered. He didn't say they would be given riches or comfort. No milk and honey talks on that day: "He said, 'If you listen carefully to the voice of the Lord your God and do what is right in his eyes, if you pay attention to his commands and keep all his decrees, I will not bring on you any of the diseases I brought on the Egyptians, for I am the Lord, who heals you'" (Exodus 15:26). In other words, they got to keep their jobs. But if they didn't toe the line fairly soon, God would treat them just like the Egyptians.

Would other people say you complain about lots of things? God hears your grumbling as well as your prayers. Let God heal your bad attitude. Job or no job? Disease or no disease? Desert or dessert?

## *February 6*
HURRICANE!

"... some of them paid no attention ..."
(Exodus 16:20)

Travelers: *The Israelites*
Read: Exodus 16:1–35

Which is worse, a tornado or a hurricane? Tornadoes are unpredictable and sudden. As an Ohio native, I saw many. There is no real way to prepare, so there is very little worry expended. The chances of actually getting hit are not that great. So people go through the motions when a warning comes. It's over in half an hour and life goes on.

Hurricanes are usually not quite as deadly as tornadoes, but their paths of destruction are much wider. The chances of being hit are much greater. Thanks to modern satellite technology, we get several days' notice before a hurricane strikes. This time allows people to prepare—and to worry.

As Hurricane Gloria approached New England in 1985, we went to the store for bottled water and candles. They were gone. There were none left in the city. All the food was gone, too. Store shelves were stripped bare by panicky buyers.

Everyone worries about survival in the face of disaster. It's human nature. It was true of the Israelites, who worried that the amount of manna God gave them each day would not be enough. They tried to store up extra provisions, despite Moses' warnings: "However, some of them paid no attention to Moses; they kept part of it until morning, but it was full of maggots and began to smell" (Exodus 16:20). God was extremely displeased with their lack of faith in His provision: "How long will you refuse to keep my commands and my instructions?" (verse 28).

God also gave commandments through His Son Jesus Christ. "And do not set your heart on what you will eat or drink; do not worry about it. For the pagan world runs after all such things, and your Father knows that you need them. But seek his kingdom, and these things will be given to you as well" (Luke 12: 29–31).

Are you paying attention to God and His priorities in your life. If so, you will never lack for the essentials in life, as long as you seek His Kingdom first, whether it's in the face of a tornado, a hurricane or the daily grind of life.

## *February 7*
## OUR GREATEST NEEDS

"'Is the Lord among us or not?'"
(Exodus 17:7)

Travelers: *The Israelites*
Read: Exodus 17:1–7

Frequent business travelers encounter no greater feeling of desperation than trying to get home on the eve of a holiday. One Wednesday evening before Thanksgiving, I rushed to Chicago's airport just in time for the announcement that my flight home had been canceled—bad weather in Denver. I had been away a great deal recently and had consoled my family by anticipating a four day holiday weekend together. I needed desperately to find a way home.

The Israelites were desperate, too—for water. And they grumbled once again against God: "Is the Lord among us or not?" (Exodus 17:7). But God said to Moses, "I will stand there before you by the rock at Horeb. Strike the rock, and water will come out of it for the people to drink" (verse 6). God did not just perform a mighty work. He stood among them!

God stood with me that Thanksgiving eve. As I walked dejectedly through the terminal ticketing area, I looked up and saw the ticket counter of a competing airline. I walked up and said to the agent, "Look, I know there's a blizzard in Denver and this is a dumb question, but do you have any flights going to Denver?" The agent said, "Why yes, there's one pulling away from the gate right now, but you'll never catch it."

Without a moment's hesitation, I hoisted bag and briefcase, racing through the airport. Of course, the gate was the farthest one, at the end. In Chicago, that's more like a marathon than a sprint. As I approached the gate, the agent was watching for me. He grabbed me by the sleeve, physically pushed me onto the plane and slammed the door in my face. A waiting flight attendant gripped my shoulders and pushed me backwards into an open seat. "But I don't have a first class tick . . ."

"Shush! No time for that now. We've gotta' go—NOW!"

We were the last plane allowed to land in Denver during that Thanksgiving blizzard of 1982. And flying first class was the dressing on the turkey. God knew my desperate need to get home. He knows your deepest longings, too.

## February 8
### CALLING FOR HELP

> ". . . you cannot handle it alone."
> (Exodus 18:18)

**Traveler:** *Jethro*
**Read: Exodus 18:1–27**

I was retained as an engineering consultant to study the operating efficiency of a power plant. My client had too much cost for the kilowatt. He had decided that several of his staff were not performing well, and he asked me to consider a re-organization, including some layoffs. Not a fun assignment.

Jethro, Moses' father-in-law, may have been the very first traveling consultant. Traveling from Midian out to the desert, Jethro observed Moses buckling under his crushing load of work: "What you are doing is not good. You and these people who come to you will only wear yourselves out. The work is too heavy for you; you cannot handle it alone. Listen now to me and I will give you some advice, and may God be with you" (Exodus 18:17–19). Jethro then gave Moses some very practical advice which delegated authority and probably raised morale.

As I interviewed each of my client's employees, in grisly anticipation of pinpointing the ones who would have to go, an interesting pattern began to emerge. Finally, I completed my research, went home to write the report and traveled back the next week, to meet with my client. Not knowing how my opinions would be received, I described what I had found, realizing I would probably be fired on the spot.

"Sam," I started, "I'm afraid I have some bad news. The problem is not with any of the plant's staff. It's with your own management team. The staff get such mixed messages from you and the other partners that they don't understand what you want them to do." Long silence and stare. Sam scowled and cleared his throat; I waited for my dismissal. Finally he growled, "You're right, of course. What should I do?"

Sam accepted my advice. His new policies were so successful that he was able to finance a new plant. And the employees that didn't get fired say I saved their jobs.

An outside view is always valuable, whether in business or with a personal problem. Are you, like Moses, wearing yourself out, and everyone around you? Get help from someone you can trust. And may God be with you, too.

## *February 9*
### AN ENEMY TO YOUR ENEMIES

"... to guard you along the way ..."
(Exodus 23:20)

Travelers: *The Israelites*
**Read: Exodus 23:20–22**

"So how was New York?" I asked my new employee, who was just returning from his first business trip. Rick was fresh out of engineering school and I had no idea that he'd never been beyond Indiana in his life.

"Well, my flight was six hours late, so I got to LaGuardia at 3:00 in the morning. I didn't take enough cash for a cab, so I took the subway ... Why are you looking at me like that?"

"You took the subway at three in the morning? How were you dressed?" I asked incredulously.

Rick answered, "I had on my white summer three piece suit."

"You took the subway at three in the morning, dressed in a white business suit and carrying suitcases? How did you know where to get off the subway?"

"I just asked for help." I stood there dumbfounded, looking at a walking miracle. Surely a guardian angel had gone with this naive young man that night.

The Israelites faced an extremely difficult trip as they set out for the Promised Land. But God sent an angel ahead of them as a guard "... to bring you to the place I have prepared" (Exodus 23:20). Don't you wish angels would protect you like that today?

Guess what! They do and they have! Look back on your life right now with perfect hindsight and recall all the times when things could have turned out very badly for you. Perhaps you even deserved worse? God sent an angel before you. It should make you feel special. You are.

But there's more to the story: "Pay attention to him and listen to what he says. Do not rebel against him ... since my Name is in him. If you listen carefully to what he says and do all that I say, I will be an enemy to your enemies ..." (verses 21–22).

Do you just go out on your own, expecting God to protect you, or do you listen for guidance from God's angel? If you don't listen and do all he says, your protection may not be so great next time. Make sure your enemies are His enemies.

## February 10
## OUTLASTING THE COMPETITION

"Little by little I will drive them out . . ."
(Exodus 23:30)

Travelers: *The Israelites*
**Read: Exodus 23:27–33**

Our competition had moved more quickly and had earned a significant lead in a new consulting market. I was given the job of penetrating their position of strength. But at professional conferences, they had all the significant speaking slots and all the prestige. I couldn't even get on the program. For two years it seemed we would never win that "flagship" project that would show the market what we could do.

As the Israelites approached the Promised Land, they must have felt the same way. The opposition looked overwhelming. But God was in control all the way. At first it sounded like God would deliver the Promised Land in a single, cataclysmic punch: "I will send my terror ahead of you and throw into confusion every nation you encounter. I will make all of your enemies turn their backs and run. I will send the hornet ahead of you to drive the Hivites, Canaanites and Hittites out of your way" (Exodus 23:27–28).

But then God said something which serves as a great reminder that the difficulties we experience have purpose: "But I will not drive them out in a single year, because the land would become desolate and the wild animals too numerous for you" (verse 29). The claiming of the Promised Land would be a process, not a single victory. God was telling us for all generations that too much success, too quickly, spells trouble.

And so it was with our new market. Eventually we got that first break, and then another, and another. Slowly we climbed toward respectability and ultimately became a leader.

What I never considered in those early days was that, if we had been successful immediately, we would have built our business on a foundation of sand. We would not have had the skills nor the experience to do bigger jobs with excellence, and soon our customers' confidence would have eroded. The long fight was far better for us than a quick killing.

This is the perfect model for a Christian business perspective. Follow God's plan. He'll make it plenty tough on the competition, but are you able to trust Him and persevere long enough for the process to run its course?

## *February 11*
FIRST-NAME BASIS

". . . I will give you rest."
(Exodus 33:14)

Traveler: *Moses*
**Read: Exodus 33:12–23**

For the vast majority of frequent fliers, travel is not fun. Late arrivals, strange hotel beds, early breakfast appointments and warped time zones drain you.

How do you combat fatigue? Start before you leave home!

Before setting out, Moses reaffirmed his relationship with God: "'If you are pleased with me, teach me your ways so I may know you and continue to find favor with you . . .' The Lord replied, 'My Presence will go with you, and I will give you rest.' Then Moses said to him, 'If your Presence does not go with us, do not send us up from here. How will anyone know that you are pleased with me and with your people unless you go with us? What else will distinguish me and your people from all the other people on the face of the earth?'" (Exodus 33:13–16).

In other words, make sure that God is going with you. And how do you know that God will accompany you? To Moses, God said, "I will do the very thing you have asked, because I am pleased with you and I know you by name" (verse 17). And to us, Jesus says, "I am the good Shepherd; I know my sheep and my sheep know me—just as the Father knows me and I know the Father—and I lay down my life for the sheep" (John 10:14–15). So the critical question is: Does God know you by name? He certainly would not go with a stranger! Do you go to Him so often that you're on a first-name basis? Without that, you're outside looking in. And it's when you're just a wolf stalking the sheep pen that you get tired and lonely.

Seek God before you leave and learn His ways while you're going. Feel His Presence, guiding and strengthening you, calling you by name. Fatigue doesn't stand a chance, and neither does Satan.

## *February 12*
### FRAME OF REFERENCE

"... the cloud lifted..."
(Numbers 10:11)

Travelers: *The Israelites*
**Read: Numbers 10:11–13**

Everyone has seasons in life when the winds of discontent whistle through the cracks in their materialistic facades. Life seems to move in a cycle, with periods of relative happiness and contentment followed by the need for change. Each person has a different cycle. Throughout my adult life, I have gone through such a cycle about every four years.

Times of internal turbulence can be as upsetting as seasickness, if you have no fixed frame of reference, no guiding light, no solid rock. You feel adrift. The older you are, the scarier it feels. Everyone starts whispering behind your back about mid-life crisis. The world views your searching as weakness.

As the Israelites wandered in the desert, it was easy for them to feel lost. Though they recognized that the ultimate goal was to claim the Promised Land, they did not know where they were going from day to day. Would they ever get out of the desert?

But they did have a frame of reference. They had a cloud which settled over their meeting place: "In all the travels of the Israelites, whenever the cloud lifted from above the tabernacle, they would set out; but if the cloud did not lift, they did not set out—until the day it lifted" (Exodus 40:36–37).

Once, they stayed in Sinai until the "... twentieth day of the second month of the second year..." (Numbers 10:11), almost fourteen months! This was a time when God spoke to them at length about their future. "Then the Israelites set out from the Desert of Sinai and traveled from place to place until the cloud came to rest..." (verse 12).

Could your times of uncertainty be viewed as a cloud settling over you? Could it be God's cloud? Perhaps He wants to teach you something during that time. Instead of letting the experience be negative and depressing, let the cloud become your frame of reference. And when the cloud lifts, it will be God's signal to move on—maybe continuing the same journey, maybe something new. Just watch and follow.

## *February 13*
OVERLOAD

". . . the burden is too heavy for me."
(Numbers 11:14)

**Traveler:** *Moses*
**Read: Numbers 11:4–34**

I had been a hostage for six months when I finally broke down.

My family had already moved back to Colorado from Connecticut. But I could not leave until my construction job was complete, and it was mired in trouble. I was allowed thirty-six hours every third weekend to commute home, but that short of a visit only intensified the pain.

One Sunday afternoon, just as I was leaving for yet another three weeks, my kids began to fight with each other. I felt like a stranger in my own home. It was as if I didn't recognize my family and they didn't recognize me. Instead of assuming my normal role of taking the time to counsel my family and resolve the dispute in a Godly way, I had to get up and leave.

Suddenly, I burst into tears. Each member of my family froze for a moment, then realized how their fight was robbing me of precious moments with them. In a rush, they mobbed me and we cried together. They realized for the first time that big, strong Dad was not so strong, and I needed their help.

Moses needed help, too. The burdens of leading the Israelites were too great for one man. He cried out to God, who told him to find people to help him: "I will come down and speak with you there, and I will take of the Spirit that is on you and put the Spirit on them. They will help you carry the burden of the people so that you will not have to carry it alone" (Numbers 11:17).

It was another six months before my commuting ended. But from the moment I unintentionally sought my family's help, I knew we would survive. God put His Spirit on them and they helped carry my burden.

Are your burdens too heavy? Are you ready to break? Cry out to God and call on family and friends for help. God will actually give them some of His Spirit to help you. And if they're like my family, they're just waiting for you to ask.

## February 14
### THE TRUE PROMISED LAND

"Send some men to explore the land . . ."
(Numbers 13:2)

Travelers: *Israelite Explorers*
Read: Numbers 13:1–33

Mike had been my client for twelve years. I had made dozens of trips to Ohio over the years and had helped solve many problems at his power plant. But I never got to know him personally. There was always an invisible barrier.

Recently, while we were touring a plant in another state together, Mike said he was very fearful of flying on airplanes. I mentioned almost casually that I had overcome that battle by reading my Bible while I fly.

The next day, as the plant tour continued, Mike suddenly asked me to climb a one-hundred-foot high ladder to inspect a certain piece of equipment. Gasping for air, we reached the top, and Mike said, "Good. Now we're alone. I've been waiting all day for this chance. Yesterday, you said you read your Bible when you are afraid. Are you a Christian?"

I confirmed that I am a Christian and that I had founded a Christian ministry for travelers. Mike said, "Well, we're traveling today, and that gives us the opportunity to share together. I was saved about three months ago. I've known all these years there was something different about you; now I know what it is." And there, one hundred feet above the ground on a catwalk in a power plant, Mike and I bear-hugged and prayed together briefly.

God instructed Moses: "Send some men to explore the Land of Canaan, which I am giving to the Israelites" (Number 13:2). He sends you to do the same. But what is the Promised Land for you?

For many years, I thought exploring the Promised Land meant pursuing my career and being successful in the eyes of the world. Mike taught me that there is a completely different and infinitely more exciting way of exploring—by sharing my faith with those I encounter. Jesus described it way: "The harvest is plentiful but the workers are few. Ask the Lord of the harvest, therefore, to send out workers into his harvest field" (Matthew 9:37–38).

Where is your true Promised Land?

## *February 15*
COVERING THE BASICS

"Their protection is gone . . ."
(Numbers 14:9)

**Travelers:** *The Israelites*
**Read: Numbers 14:1–9**

Call it a hunch. Or call it divine inspiration. I prefer the latter.

We were competing for a huge consulting contract which could supply us with work for months to come. Realistically, there were only two companies who could do the job—ourselves and the "Darth Vader" of consulting companies, our bitter competitor.

Knowing the competition is a big part of any business, and we knew exactly what "Darth" would do. Funded by a major international conglomerate, they would spare no expense in preparing the latest in multimedia, Madison Avenue sales presentations, designed to awe the client into hiring them. They had done it before, successfully. Quality of work after they won the job did not matter. Only market-savvy flash and pizzazz.

We had no such funding. But we did have a commitment to, and a reputation for, quality. Our marketing department decided that, if we were going to win the job, we would have to out-glitz the competition, to spend big money on the boldest presentation we had ever done. Ultimately, I said no, because I believed that integrity would sell better than sparkle. Over the very vocal protests of my staff, I proceeded to plan a "Prairie Home Companion"-like presentation.

When the day of the presentation arrived, our competition was interviewed first, so we were there to watch them go in. They had the nicest looking visual aids I had ever seen. Later we learned that they had produced a video especially for this client! My staff panicked, very much like the Israelites: "Why is the Lord bringing us to this land only to let us fall by the sword?" (Numbers 14:3). Everyone thought I was as crazy as Moses, for intentionally failing to copy the competition.

But I'm guessing that our competition forgot the basics: prayer. As a result: "Their protection is gone, but the Lord is with us" (verse 9). Our presentation went very well, and the contrast I had hoped for was glaring. After all the zing of the previous presentation, ours looked very professional, yet human. The client liked real people more than entertainment. We won. Are you covering the basics each day?

## February 16
### A DIFFERENT SPIRIT

">. . . not one of them will ever see the land I promised . . ."
(Numbers 14:23)

Travelers: *The Israelites*
**Read: Numbers 14:20–38**

Like an un-poked potato in a microwave, the man in line in front of me exploded. His first class upgrade certificate had just been rejected because the flight was already too full. Instead, he had been assigned a middle seat near the back of the plane. To any frequent flier, that's like being served rancid hamburger instead of succulent filet mignon. The man berated the agent mercilessly, using some of the foulest language I had ever heard.

I was next in line. The agent was near tears. Handing me *my* middle seat assignment, she cringed, waiting for another verbal barrage. I smiled and said, "Looks like you've had a long day. I'll pray for your strength." That's all I said. It was offered in a different spirit than the angry man who preceded me.

The Israelites rebelled against Moses, because they expected to be killed by the residents of the Promised Land. God eventually forgave them, but swore that ". . . not one of them will ever see the land I promised . . . No one who has treated me with contempt will ever see it. But because my servant Caleb has a different spirit and follows me wholeheartedly, I will bring him into the land . . ." (Numbers 14:23–24).

Caleb received a great gift because his spirit contrasted with his peers.

So did I. After I boarded the plane, I was paged on the loudspeaker and asked to bring my bags to the front of the plane. I groaned, thinking I was being "bumped" from the flight because it had been over-sold. But a smiling flight attendant stopped me at the doorway and sat me down in first class. I said, "There must be some mistake. I don't have an upgrade certificate." The attendant just winked.

Then I realized that my earlier compassion for the ticket agent was being rewarded. To this day, I'm not sure how she pulled it off.

Do you rebel against situations in life and in the process show contempt for God? Or are you like Caleb, communicating God's promises with a different spirit?

## *February 17*
## TO GO OR NOT TO GO

"... go ... but do only what I tell you."
(Numbers 22:20)

**Traveler:** *Balaam*
**Read: Numbers 22:1–38**

Green has always been my favorite color. But not in thunderstorms. Green thunderclouds often contain hail and don't mix well with flying airplanes.

I was in Mississippi for a business meeting. In the time it took to drive from downtown to the airport, the weather changed from sunny and steamy to mostly ominous. Just as my friend and I were getting on the plane, I looked out the window and saw a towering thundercloud, trimmed green in a way any Ohio native recognizes as trouble.

Suddenly a voice inside me said, "Get off the plane." Embarrassed, I picked up my baggage and left the plane. My friend did not ridicule me. He knew the risk but decided to stay with it because of an important appointment the next morning.

Balaam was on a trip, too: "But God was very angry when he went, and the angel of the Lord stood in the road to oppose him" (Numbers 22:22). Once Balaam realized that it was God's angel, he submitted himself, offering to cancel his trip. But God wanted to use Balaam against Balak, an enemy of Israel: "Go ... but speak only what I tell you" (verse 35).

Just as the plane I had rejected took off, a tremendous lightning bolt hit the airport and knocked out all the power. Hail dimpled everything in sight. On the phone the next day my friend said, "You made the right choice. It was the scariest flight I've ever taken. I think the pilot definitely was wrong in deciding to fly through that storm."

Thankfully, my friend was spared. But God knew I would have been terrified on that flight and told me personally to avoid it. Fortunately, I listened and did what He said, just as Balaam did. But, like Balaam, I too often rage against physical restraints rather than acknowledge God's presence.

Do you listen for God's instructions? Or are you too busy or too embarrassed to change your course of action? Listen and obey; each act of faith brings you closer to Him on a daily basis. He is where you are.

## February 18
### WHY SO LONG?

> "... he made them wander ... forty years ..."
> (Numbers 32:13)

Travelers: *The Israelites*
Read: Numbers 32:1–15

Only fifteen more years and I would have been wandering as long as the Israelites did. I had worked twenty-five years in a career I really hated before I realized I was lost. How could God let me wander so long?

Moses tells us: "The Lord's anger burned against Israel and he made them wander in the desert forty years..." (Numbers 32:13). Could it be that God was angry with me? He clearly called me to ministry in the spring of 1969. But I ignored Him when my first "real" job offer in the engineering field arrived. Did I make God angry, rationalizing that my business career was really my ministry? Did I allow God's expectations to be overshadowed by the world's? Did his anger burn against me, and did He allow me to wander for twenty-five years? Probably.

I thought I had known Jesus Christ all my life. But as A. W. Tozier has pointed out: "A man can die of starvation knowing all about bread, and a man can remain spiritually dead while knowing all the historic facts of Christianity."[2] All my life I had known of Him and even loved Him, but I had never promised to obey Him. I knew the rules and did the best I could. But I never came to grips with the totality of my sinful nature until 1992, when I was baptized and born again. Only then did I see how my life could have angered Him. Only then did I see that I had been starving to know Him personally. Now, since my baptism, He has allowed me to stop wandering.

Are you struggling in a situation that seems to have gone on forever? Is it possible that God's anger has been burning against you and He has allowed you to wander until you make a commitment? You can end that spiritual sojourn right now. Stop, wherever you are, and acknowledge that you have spent more time knowing about Jesus than just knowing Jesus.

## February 19
### FIGHTING FIRE WITH FIRE

"... the Lord your God himself will fight for you."
(Deuteronomy 3:22)

**Traveler:** *Joshua*
**Read: Deuteronomy 3:21–28**

Only a skeleton crew remained. It was New Year's Eve and all but a few supervisors had left early, anticipating a long holiday weekend. I was left in charge of our brand new processing plant. It was full of thousands of tons of solid waste—trash, garbage—fuel. It was bitterly cold that last day of 1987, the worst possible time for a fire.

Within moments of the first shouts, we were choking and coughing in dense smoke and sloshing through ankle-deep water gushing from ruptured fire protection pipes. The TV helicopter arrived before the fire trucks; for the first time I appreciated how disaster victims feel as they are exploited by media hype. We had worked so hard on this plant. And now there was no doubt it would burn to the ground on live television.

No doubt, that is, except for a supervisor named Lloyd. He said that most of the smoke came from a pile of fuel at one end of the plant. If the unburned part of the pile could be cut away from the fire, it would burn out and the building would be saved. He asked permission to attack the pile with our big bulldozer. I said no; I was not willing to risk a man's life.

Against my orders, Lloyd disappeared into the smoke. I thought I would never see him again. But fifteen minutes later, he emerged, covered with soot, his white toothy grin all the more visible. He had moved the fuel away from the fire, and it was out. Lloyd himself fought the fire for me, fearlessly.

Joshua also had no doubt how to fight fires: "Do not be afraid ... the Lord your God himself will fight for you" (Deuteronomy 3:22). How about you? Do you wait until your whole life is involved in a fire before figuring out how to fight it? Or do you plan ahead, knowing exactly who will be fighting for you?

## February 20
### THE MOST UNUSUAL PEOPLE

"So they . . . entered the house of a prostitute . . ."
(Joshua 2:1)

Travelers: *Joshua's Two Spies*
Read: Joshua 2:1–24

In the here-today, gone-tomorrow world of modern business, learning about the competition's plans is critical. But I considered it unethical to ask my clients to betray my competition's strategy, even though the competition did it to me regularly. God led me to a better way—listening to the competition's employees.

Most businesses have periodic national conferences attended by clients, vendors, government representatives and competing consultants. The conferences are full of displays and technical meetings, where scholarly papers are presented on current issues in the field. There is also plenty of socializing. So I always trained my staff to be very careful what they said at these gatherings, especially concerning our strategic plans for the future.

What I did not realize, until I started attending these conferences myself, was that we had achieved a reputation for the best working conditions in the industry. As the leader of that image, I was an easy target at a conference for any up-and-coming youngster who would gladly jump ship from a competitor for a better offer (exactly the kind of person I was not interested in). In their zeal to impress me with their knowledge of the industry, they would often tell me what their employers were planning without my asking. All I had to do was show up.

I felt that God was delivering the enemy to me, and I always gave Him the credit for our success. I'd feel a little guilty about this windfall were it not for the story of Joshua's spies, who hid from the enemy in Jericho by staying with a prostitute named Rahab. She protected them in return for her family's safety: ". . . please swear to me by the Lord that you will show kindness to my family because I have shown kindness to you" (Joshua 2:12). I never got that creative in my research!

God uses the most unlikely heroes to help His people. If we act with integrity and faith, He always provides an answer. It's just that some answers are more surprising than others. Are you trusting God's creativity in your battles?

## February 21
### BETTER THAN A HUNCH

"... since you have never been this way before."
(Joshua 3:4)

**Travelers:** *The Israelites*
**Read: Joshua 3:1–17**

After the 1990–91 season, the Denver Nuggets were a sorry bunch. A great tradition from years past had crumbled, but when they drafted 7'-2" Dikembe Mutombo at the end of that dismal season, I saw an opportunity. I believed that there would never be a better chance to get season tickets located close to the court.

But my hunch was full of risk. What if the team suddenly picked-up and left town? Or what if Mutombo was a bust and the team never obtained a good supporting cast? They could flounder for years. But as management consolidated, I took the plunge. My seats were just four rows back from the court, and the action was "fan-tastic."

They became the hottest seats in town. The arena was sold out almost every night—the best business decision I ever made. But it sure would have been easier if I had been guaranteed the kind of success the Nuggets ultimately enjoyed only a few years after I bought the tickets.

I always felt like the Israelites had it made. God's signs in those days seemed like guarantees. When it was time to cross the Jordan, they did not have to play hunches: "When you see the ark of the covenant of the Lord your God . . . you are to move out from your positions and follow it. Then you will know which way to go, since you have never been this way before" (Joshua 3:3–4). How simple!

Do you feel that God doesn't give you clear signals on your journey? Oh, rest assured, He can. But He seeks something far more valuable—your faith. Jesus said, "Therefore I tell you, whatever you ask for in prayer, believe that you have received it, and it will be yours" (Mark 11:24).

Pray and believe. That's no hunch.

*Postscript:* That was 1994. Two years later, the Nuggets were once again in disarray, one of the most stunning collapses in memory. So ultimately my worldly hunch wasn't so good. But where to put my faith has not changed!

## February 22
### TRUTH ALWAYS WINS

"Are you for us or for our enemies?"
(Joshua 5:13)

Traveler: *Commander of the Army of the Lord*
**Read: Joshua 5:13–6:20**

Tom and I worked on opposite sides of a major construction project. We developed mutual respect for each other as professionals who wanted a "win-win" project for our respective companies. When I discovered that Tom was a serious Christian, we began to play tennis together, and we became close friends.

Eventually, our project got into trouble and there were frequent battles between my client and Tom's boss. Behind the scenes, Tom and I often discussed options for resolving each dispute. It was amazing how both "camps" exaggerated and warped the real issues, drumming personality conflicts into open hatred. We prayed together for the truth to win and for the project to recover.

> Now when Joshua was near Jericho, he looked up and saw a man standing in front of him with a drawn sword in his hand. Joshua went up to him and asked, "Are you for us or for our enemies?" "Neither," he replied, "but as commander of the army of the Lord I have now come." (Joshua 5:13–14)

God's angel told Joshua that he had no favorites; that as commander of God's army, his only interest was in executing God's plan to deliver Jericho into the hands of the Israelites. The angel was doing his job for truth, not as an advocate for the Israelites.

Tom was like God's angel to me. He didn't play favorites, even at the risk of his job. He wanted the truth only. When he discovered that his boss was a liar, he quit his job rather than be required to cover for his boss against me, a Christian brother. Now that's integrity.

I faced many long months of conflict after Tom left. But I always knew I had truth on my side. Tom gave me the courage to carry on through some very dark days.

Remember that there are often Christians on both sides of any dispute in life. If you can't pray with them, pray for them. The truth always wins.

## February 23
### ONE NATION UNDER GOD

"... do not be discouraged."
(Joshua 8:1)

**Travelers:** *Joshua and His Army*
**Read: Joshua 8:1–22**

My friend Dr. Ken Knoll lived in Malaysia and is steeped in Asian culture. He tells me that Asians respect America as a Christian nation. Even though the vast majority of Asians are not Christians, they believe in many of the same values, including family, honesty and hard work. They respect our Christian heritage and feel honored to work with God-fearing people like Ken.

Asians cannot understand what they see happening in America today. They cannot understand how a Christian nation can have such severe problems with crime, racial hatred and greed. How perceptive. What they don't understand is that we have fallen. We are no longer a Christian nation.

The Israelites fell, too: "So the Lord was with Joshua, and his fame spread throughout the land. But the Israelites acted unfaithfully ... So the Lord's anger burned against Israel" (Joshua 6:27–7:1). When Joshua attacked the town of Ai, God withdrew His protection, and the Israelites were defeated. God explained, "Israel has sinned; they have violated my covenant, which I commanded them to keep" (Joshua 7:11).

Later, after Joshua had purged the evil from his people, God said, "Do not be afraid; do not be discouraged. Take the whole army with you, and go up and attack Ai. For I have delivered into your hands the king of Ai, his people, his city and his land" (Joshua 8:1). When the Israelites obeyed, God forgave them. But not forever. Eventually, Israel sinned so many times against God that He finally gave up and allowed them to be scattered into captivity.

What about America? Have we forgotten His judgment in Viet Nam since our victory in the Persian Gulf? How much more will God bear before He gives up on us as a nation? When will it be too late to return to Him as "one nation under God?"

What about you? Have you forgotten past defeats because of recent success? Did God bless you only to watch you sin again? How long will He tolerate that kind of disloyalty?

*Faith in Motion*

## *February 24*
## ACADEMY AWARD

"The men of Israel . . . did not inquire of the Lord."
(Joshua 9:14)

**Travelers:** *The Gibeonites*
**Read: Joshua 9:1–27**

I should have seen it coming. All the clues were right in front of me. But he seemed to be the perfect solution to my problem, so I ignored the warning signs.

I needed to hire an experienced draftsman to handle an extremely demanding project. He would be required not only to work long hours on the drafting board, but also to supervise other draftsmen involved in the project. When I first met Bill, I thought he had it all—he was mature, extroverted, experienced, aggressive.

Yet there was something mysterious about him. So, with what I thought was great wisdom, I hired Bill on a 90 day trial period; if he didn't fit in, I could let him go after that time.

Bill fit in quite well for 90 days—exactly 90 days. On day 91 he underwent the most radical personality change I have ever seen. Of course, it was not a personality change at all. He had successfully acted out the role he thought I wanted to see, until I signed him on as a full-time employee. He fooled everyone and then instantly became a tyrant, using his title as "supervisor" to take over the office. He literally thought the term meant unconditional authority over everyone and everything, including me. Three days later I had to fire him.

If only I had listened to that inner prompting.

If only the Israelites had done the same with the Gibeonites: "The men of Israel . . . did not inquire of the Lord" (Joshua 9:14). The Gibeonites deceived them into signing a treaty by acting as if they came from far away. Actually, they were from the nearby town of Gibeon. But the Israelites fell for the trick because they did not inquire of the Lord for guidance. This violated God's command to conquer all the peoples living in the Promised Land and severely complicated their relationships long into the future.

Do you inquire of God before you make important decisions? Or do you move ahead quickly, only to be deceived by the evils of the world? Inquire of God constantly. He will help you see through Academy Award performances.

## February 25
## GOLD WATCH

> "Then Joshua blessed Caleb . . . and gave him . . . his inheritance." (Joshua 14:13)

**Traveler:** *Caleb*
**Read:** Joshua 14:6–15

The first half of the 1990s will be remembered as a time when businesses showed their true colors. An entire new language was created, including "downsizing," "re-engineering" and "career programming." These new terms attempted to mask the true agenda: "You are now on your own. No one can count on continuous employment. Loyalty of the company to the employee is passé. There will be no gold watch."

Some of the changes have been good. They have reminded us that we must be competitive in a global marketplace and that every person must pull his or her weight for a business to survive. But many American businesses have gone too far. They have alienated even their most loyal, productive employees. Even those surviving the cuts look over their shoulders, wondering when they will be next.

Why can't it be like it was for Caleb, who served Joshua for 45 years, loyally and capably? When the time came to retire, Caleb asked: "Now give me this hill country that the Lord promised me . . ." (Joshua 14:12). Joshua gave him all of Hebron. I certainly expected a great retirement from my company when I was elected partner at the age of 40. But six years later I was gone. Of course I was not alone. Millions of good people lost their jobs. Too bad things have changed.

Or is it so bad? Christians *do* have a secure retirement. We will receive an entire city of gold: "The wall was made of jasper, and the city of pure gold, as pure as glass" (Revelation 21:18). The retirement that waits for us will make us glad that we underwent the losses of the current day, because we can learn now where true security lies! Forget the gold watch!

"The city does not need the sun or the moon to shine on it, for the glory of God gives it light, and the Lamb is its lamp" (Revelation 21:23). Put your hope in the Lamb, the Lord, the salvation of Jesus Christ. That's what to "watch" for!

## February 26
## RETURNING HOME

"... serve him with all your heart and all your soul."
(Joshua 22:5)

**Travelers:** *The Eastern Tribes*
**Read: Joshua 22:1–5**

I call it the "rubber leg syndrome." That's the feeling on Saturdays, after traveling all week and arriving home late Friday night. Jet lag, fatigue and business stress leave me feeling weak. It's like staggering across the finish line at a marathon and then collapsing. And sleeping late on Saturday doesn't help when it's 5:30 a.m. Mountain time and I spent the week on Eastern time; I wake up two hours early, whether I want to or not.

At times like that, my legs do feel like rubber. It's very easy to feel sorry for myself and to dodge other weekend responsibilities. Just prop me up in front of the tube and let me catch a couple of ball games. I'll be back to normal on Sunday. Why do I feel so tired? I must be missing something.

Joshua provides the answer to the rubber leg syndrome. When he allowed the Reubenites, Gadites and Manasseh to return home after conquering the Promised Land, he commended them for a job well done (Joshua 22:3). But he also cautioned them that their jobs didn't end there. He reminded them that they must obey the commandments of God when they went home: "... to love the Lord your God, to walk in all his ways, to obey his commands, to hold fast to him and to serve him with all your heart and all your soul" (verse 5).

God protected them in their travels, but Joshua wanted to make sure they didn't crash when they returned home.

That's what I was missing. And it's true for you, too. If you want God's protection when you travel, you must be diligent in serving Him when you're home, even if that's the last thing you want. Rely on God's strength, not your own.

When rubber legs threaten to stop you, try turning the day over to God. Pray, read your Bible and then serve Him with all your heart. That may mean working around the house or giving your wife a break from the kids or helping the homeless. Let God provide the strength.

You can't do it by yourself.

## *February 27*
## THE ARRANGEMENT

"... they will become snares and traps for you ..."
(Joshua 23:13)

**Travelers:** *The Israelites*
**Read: Joshua 23:1–16**

It seemed natural to be invited to dinner with fellow travelers. They were engineers like myself, helping to start-up a new power plant. I was the new guy on site; they had been there for several months.

After dinner, they suggested the three of us stop in the hotel bar to hear a little country music and relax. Not long after we arrived, three women came in. My new friends knew them, so they were asked to join us. About 10:00 p.m., my friends got up to leave, and each took one of the women with him. The third woman asked me if I would like to go home with her. Suddenly I realized that the whole evening had been a setup. I was out of there like a flash.

The next day I learned that the entire construction site had an "arrangement." Field engineers are often paid a "per diem," a daily payment for hotel and meals. By pairing up with single women, they were sharing their money—and their beds—by living together. Everyone was expected to do it. If anyone "squealed" it would ruin many careers and marriages; that's why my "friends" were so anxious to draw me into the plot.

Joshua recognized human nature as he bade farewell to the Israelites. He had led them to the Promised Land and was about to die. So he gave them a warning which rings down through the centuries: "... the Lord your God fights for you, just as he promised. So be very careful to love the Lord your God. But if you turn away and ally yourselves with ... these nations ... and if you intermarry with them and associate with them ... they will become snares and traps for you ... until you perish ..." (Joshua 23:10–13).

By refusing to go along with the arrangement, I lost my two friends and word raced quickly around the job. I was ostracized throughout the assignment and even threatened a few times. But the Lord defended me and continues to fight for me wherever I go. Judging by what happened to my "friends" in the years after that, even though I kept their secret, I'd say they forfeited God's protection.

One went bankrupt. The other died very young.

## *February 28*
## PICKING SIDES

> "... they will be thorns in your sides ..."
> (Judges 2:3)

Traveler: *Angel of the Lord*
**Judges 2:1–4**

With big businesses gobbling up small businesses at every turn, strategic alliances among not-so-big companies are common. If the right kind of teammate with just the right combination of skills, experience and shared values can be found, a new team can compete successfully against large companies.

In our haste to team up with a certain company several years ago, we checked only surface qualities and did not take the time to get to know each other, to learn what made their company tick. What a mistake!

As the Israelites took possession of the Promised Land, they broke God's command to drive out the Canaanites and other inhabitants. Instead they tried to coexist and they made God angry. At Bokim, the angel of God appeared and said, "Yet you have disobeyed me. Why have you done this? Now therefore I tell you that I will not drive them out before you; they will become thorns in your sides and their gods will be a snare to you" (Judges 2:2–3).

The subsequent history of the Israelites was filled with opposition from the people that God had been willing to completely destroy, a conflict among Jews, Arabs and Palestinians that continues to this day.

Our covenant with another engineering company had the same result. They wanted only to dash off a report to a client at minimum cost; we had high standards of quality. They plagiarized our own proprietary material and used it against us in competition. When a client became unhappy, they blamed us. They became thorns in our sides and their god of profit-without-quality became a snare to us. It was two long years before we could withdraw from that relationship.

Do you compromise your values in choosing your business associates? Be very careful. Talk with their customers and their employees. Visit their offices and spend some time comparing core values. If you sense warning signals, don't be afraid to go it alone, because you are not alone at all. Wouldn't you rather have the power of God on your side?

## *February 29*
## THE WATERING PLACES

> ". . . consider the voice of the singers . . . They recite the righteous acts of the Lord." (Judges 5:10–11)

Traveler: *Deborah*
**Read: Judges 4:1–5:12**

In the early days of my traveling, before I realized the evil lurking at my feet, I spent many hours in hotel bars, almost exclusively where there was live music, just to drown out the evening. That seemed better than the isolation of my room or driving around getting lost and running the risk of robbery. In other words, I was seeking fellowship. Something was missing.

Our sojourn through the Bible, one travel story at a time, is beginning to highlight, one insight at a time, what's wrong with modern business travel. An obvious theme up to this point has been loneliness; and a corollary of loneliness is the lack of consistent Christian fellowship. There is no place to go to find it in every city a person visits. And today's traveling business women are even more isolated than men. Local churches certainly do not reach out in this way.

The song of Deborah (Judges 5:1–31) provides the answer. I love this story because it introduces us to the first female business traveler. Deborah was the leader of Israel who teamed with Barak, son of Abinoam, to defeat the Canaanite king Jabin after twenty years of oppression (Judges 4). Deborah's song celebrates God's deliverance of the Israelites from Jabin.

Deborah tells travelers to ". . . consider the voice of the singers at the watering places. They recite the righteous acts of the Lord . . ." (Judges 5:10–11). I've seen many singers at the "watering places" along the road, but never ones who praise God. In Israelite culture there were places to go for fellowship with people who worshipped God and kept their compass set straight. In our culture, no such fellowship exists.

A new kind of watering place is needed—one which attracts the kind of people who know God and Jesus Christ. One where the singers recall the miracles of the kingdom of God instead of the Pop 40. One where men and women can gather in perfect safety and in fellowship to share stories of the road and to meet local folks with a heart for hospitality. Will you pray right now that God will move to nurture our brothers and sisters in this way?

## *March 1*
### GIVE ME A SIGN

"Go in the strength you have . . . I will be with you . . ."
(Judges 6:14,16)

Travelers: *God with Gideon*
**Read: Judges 6:1–40**

The principal at our son's school had been tutoring a dozen eighth-graders in math, even though he was overloaded with managing a growing school. In an act of blind submission to God, I agreed to dedicate a full semester, two hours per day, to helping these kids make it to ninth-grade.

I traveled light-years from the cocoon of my home office to the cacophony of junior high. With no formal teaching experience, taking them from failing to passing in a school with extremely tough standards seemed impossible.

Gideon had the same experience when the angel of the Lord appeared and told him to defeat Midian: " 'But Lord,' Gideon asked, 'how can I save Israel? My clan is the weakest in Manasseh, and I am the least in my family'. The Lord answered, 'I will be with you, and you will strike down all the Midianites together'" (Judges 6:15–16). Still unconvinced, Gideon asked for a sign (verse 17) and God provided one (verse 21). In fact, Gideon asked for more signs (verses 36–40) before he truly believed.

Don't you wish God would give you signs as clear as the ones He granted Gideon? Especially in travel, the physical effects and the isolation from your loved ones can make you wonder if you've really listened to God.

Tell me: what could be a stronger sign than the blood of Jesus Christ, who died on a cross? If He could lay down His life, we can certainly endure the hardships He assigns to us in this life. That's the sign I was given. No sacrifice, neither teaching nor traveling, can compare with the agony He suffered first for us.

Gideon wasn't more fortunate than you because God gave him signs. You are more blessed than Gideon because Jesus gave you an even bigger sign.

*Postscript:* Praise God, eleven of my twelve charges passed eighth grade math!

# March 2
## TENNIS TENACITY

"In order that Israel may not boast . . ."
(Judges 7:2)

Traveler: *Gideon*
**Read: Judges 7:1–21**

In the early 1960s, I was among a group of guys who could play tennis very well, and we begged our high school administration to let us have a tennis team. But there was no money for facilities or coaches. Boldly, we made a proposal: If we could beat the league champions on their own courts, would the school let us be a team? The answer was a bureaucratic, "We'll see."

They had gleaming white tennis uniforms; we had cut-off jeans. They played in a stadium; we practiced with wire nets that sagged. They played tennis by the book; we had never seen the book. They seemed embarrassed to be on the courts with us; we felt out of place.

Gideon knew about being overmatched: "The Lord said to Gideon, 'You have too many men . . . In order that Israel may not boast against me that her own strength has saved her . . .'" (Judges 7:2), God told Gideon to choose only three hundred men to fight tens of thousands. So Gideon chose only those who lapped water like dogs (verse 6). I imagine these men were like our Marines today. But they were far outnumbered and stood no chance at all except for the power of God.

Our mob of misfits sneaked-up on that championship tennis team much like Gideon did to the Midianites: "While each man held his position . . . all the Midianites ran, crying out as they fled" (verse 21). We beat them six to three.

If we had played them again, they probably would have overwhelmed us. But on that one day, God allowed us to see how His kingdom works: "Blessed are you when people insult you, persecute you and falsely say all kinds of evil against you because of me. Rejoice and be glad, because great is your reward in heaven, for in the same way they persecuted the prophets who were before you" (Matthew 5:11–12).

Are you outnumbered? You can win a championship far greater than any tennis match by "serving" your Lord Jesus Christ.

## March 3
### CREWING FOR CASH

"All Israel prostituted themselves by worshipping it . . ."
(Judges 8:27)

**Traveler:** *Gideon*
**Read: Judges 8:22–27**

Times were good when I was hired by a growing engineering company in 1978. My new boss had just used his bonus check to pay cash for a new sail boat. And this was no small row boat. He promised if I worked hard, I'd make the same kind of money in just a few years. His words sounded good—hard work and financial rewards. I was ready to follow this man to the promised land, the wrong promised land.

After Gideon defeated the Midianites, he was asked to rule over Israel. His words sounded good, too: "I will not rule over you, nor will my son rule over you. The Lord will rule over you" (Judges 8:23). But Gideon proceeded to make a gold idol from the people's jewelry and everyone worshipped the idol. This sin plagued Gideon's family in future generations.

My boss was like Gideon. He worshipped an idol, too—his boat. If he liked an employee, he would invite him to "crew" on his boat on weekends. When an employee was not chosen to crew on his boat, word got around the office that this employee "doesn't have what it takes." Of course, that prompted intense competition to get selected. Just like the Israelites, we all prostituted ourselves by worshipping the boat, or at least the coveted invitation to sail on the boat.

By the grace of God, I realized after my first crewing invitation that my boss was using his boat to recruit favor in his drive to become manager of the entire office. I never accepted another invitation. For years I fell behind my peers in promotions and influence. But when my boss began to self-destruct from his materialistic foundation of sand (Matthew 7:26–27), so did all of his "boys."

Everyone needs a mentor. But think back. Have there been times when you were a prostitute instead of a student? Now is a good time to reset your compass. Will you continue worshipping false idols like the Israelites, or will you seek true integrity through the true mentor, Jesus Christ?

## March 4
### A TRAVELING COMPANION TO AVOID

"God sent an evil spirit . . ."
(Judges 9:23)

Traveler: *Evil Spirit*
**Read: Judges 9:22–57**

Have you ever felt the presence of evil? I certainly have, especially while traveling. But I never thought God could be the one to send me an evil spirit. Isn't that Satan's realm? It's chilling to think that God might actually cause trouble in order to get my attention.

Now I have never done anything as bad as Abimelech: "God sent an evil spirit . . . in order that the . . . shedding of . . . blood might be avenged on . . . Abimelech" (Judges 9:23–24). But I'm not perfect, either. There is no doubt that I have done many things which angered God.

God could deal with me just as He did with Abimelech, who murdered all seventy of his brothers in order to gain power (Judges 9:5). God sent an evil spirit to avenge the murder of his brothers by causing the people of Shechem to oppose him. At first, Abimelech had the upper hand, winning battles against the people of Shechem and even slaughtering a thousand people inside a burning tower (verse 49). But as he stormed the tower, a woman dropped a millstone on his head, all but killing him. To be dropped by a woman, in that culture, was the ultimate disgrace. "Thus God repaid the wickedness that Abimelech had done to his father by murdering his seventy brothers" (verse 56).

Notice that the evil spirit sent by God didn't just strike down Abimelech with a bolt of lightning. It was more subtle than that. Abimelech was allowed some success in destroying the people of Shechem. Then without warning, God took him down.

If things are going well for you right now, is it possible that God is setting you up for disgrace? God is not evil. But He can use evil to bring you into submission to Him, even if you think you're getting away with something right now.

All it takes is a prayer. Get down on your knees right now and acknowledge those actions in your life which have angered God. Ask Him to forgive you in the name of Jesus Christ who died for you.

An evil spirit sent by God is a traveling companion to avoid.

# *March 5*
## SURPRISING POWER

"... he tore the lion apart with his bare hands ..."
(Judges 14:6)

Travelers: *Samson and the Spirit of the Lord*
**Read: Judges 14:1–20**

At the time I had no idea where I got the strength. Looking back, it's even harder to understand. From a purely human perspective, there is no way I could have found the time to memorize the Gospel of Mark while traveling frequently and building a consulting business. But from a heavenly perspective, it is clear that the Spirit of the Lord came on me with power, just as He did to Samson.

Samson was set aside by God before his birth to Manoah's wife, who had been sterile and childless (Judges 13:1–3). Samson first sensed the Spirit of the Lord as a young man. And he found that the Spirit of the Lord can give extraordinary physical strength: "The Spirit of the Lord came upon him in power so that he tore the lion apart with his bare hands as he might have torn a young goat" (Judges 14:6).

I was given a different kind of physical strength when I was set aside and the Spirit came on me. Instead of raw power, I was given endurance. For sixteen months, I memorized scripture every waking moment, rarely tiring of the challenge.

Have you ever thought that God may have set you aside for something special? Even if you are older and you have never felt the Spirit come upon you, it is not too late. God's timing in your life may not make sense from a human perspective. He may have been waiting for the right time to use you, just as Manoah's wife was left barren for a long time before conceiving.

It could be that God is simply waiting—for you to acknowledge His sovereignty in your life. An exciting challenge could be waiting for you, designed especially by God. You may be the only person in the world who can do what He needs done.

God set you aside just as surely as He did Samson. He needs to hear that you are ready. Tell Him now.

## March 6
### SURPRISING WEAKNESS

> "... he did not know that the Lord had left him."
> (Judges 16:20)

Traveler: *Samson*
Read: Judges 16:1–22

I had become a member of senior management in 1991. For three years, I managed a major division of the company, with over one hundred employees. I was on top of the world and even began to envision myself as head of the whole company. But at some point during those years, the senior partners who had promoted me decided they had made a mistake. My Christian values often conflicted with their purely materialistic ones, and I was not afraid to speak my mind on tough issues. They preferred a "yes" man who would be quiet and do what they wanted; that's the type of person they expected when they promoted me.

My romance with senior management was similar to Samson's with Delilah. I did not understand the implications of being "unequally yoked" (2 Corinthians 6:14) any more than Samson understood the danger of consorting with a seductive enemy of Israel. And just as the Philistines took a long time to work out their plot against Samson (Judges 16:5–21), management's decision to get rid of me took awhile to unfold.

Samson finally told Delilah the secret of his strength (verse 17): "If my head were shaved, my strength would leave me, and I would be as weak as any other man" (Judges 16:17). When the Philistines came to capture him, "... he did not know that the Lord had left him. Then the Philistines seized him, gouged out his eyes and took him ..." (verses 20–21). When I confronted the ethics of my partners, I assumed God was right there with me; but my lust for power had shaved my head and God had left me. He allowed me to become surprisingly weak and he allowed my career to be gouged out. It was the worst thing, and the best thing, that ever happened to me.

Do you allow the temptations of the world to seduce you away from doing God's work? If so, your potential for receiving God's surprising power may suddenly be overshadowed by your own surprising weakness.

## *March 7*
### PRACTICE HOSPITALITY

"You are welcome at my house . . . don't spend the night in the square." (Judges 19:20)

**Traveler:** *A Levite*
**Read: Judges 19:16–21**

It happens every day, all around the business world. Perhaps its a member of a Baptist church in Denver who travels to Orlando for two weeks of training at corporate headquarters. She stays in a modern hotel downtown, isolated from everything but the people she trains with all day—all strangers. She meets no one who invites her home in the name of good hospitality. Nor would she consider such an offer; how could she know she'd be safe?

The story of a Levite traveling to the town of Gibeah (Judges 19) offers an example of what's missing in modern hospitality. The Levite had no place to stay when he arrived in the town square of Gibeah. Clearly he was not safe. When an old Benjamite returned to Gibeah from working in the fields and saw the Levite sitting in the square, he invited him to his house immediately. He also offered whatever the Israelite needed to continue on his journey: "You are welcome at my house . . . Let me supply whatever you need. Only don't spend the night in the square" (Judges 19:20). Then the Benjamite provided food and drink for his guest and his donkeys, and he even protected his guest from evil just outside the door (verse 22).

In other words, the host had no higher priority than the welfare of an unannounced guest.

Why can't we do that today? We need places sponsored by local Christians which are dedicated to the welfare of travelers. Isn't this an issue of Christian unity (John 17:23)? Remember that the Levite and the Benjamite were of different tribes but they were both Jews. Why can't Christians gather together in the same way, caring for our own when they are far from the home flock? Many "Bed & Breakfast" establishments have the kind of atmosphere offered by the Benjamite, but they lack the round-the-clock service often needed by business travelers.

Please pray that one day we'll find a way to meet this need.

## March 8
ASK FIRST

"The Israelites went up . . . and inquired of God."
(Judges 20:18)

Travelers: *The Israelites*
**Read: Judges 20:1–48**

I have one deaf ear. So when I get a head cold just before leaving on an airplane, I run the risk of bursting my good ear drum. I could become totally deaf in minutes.

If you travel, you know what it's like. As your plane begins its descent for landing, the pressure inside clogged ears begins to build because there is no release. By the time you touch down, the pain can be excruciating. I have seen grown men cry, myself included, from the pain.

Recently, I had a serious allergy attack before I left on a trip. It was the worst attack I'd had in years. Even decongestant drugs did not unclog my ears. Before I left for the airport, I prayed with my wife for relief, and my family continued to pray after I left. Hours later, as my plane was landing, the familiar pressure built up, but never hurt. At one point during landing, when I was sure my good ear would be damaged, the pressure suddenly relieved enough to get me through. Minutes later, as soon as I got off the plane, my ears clogged up even worse than before, and I had a difficult time hearing during the rest of the trip. But my ear was spared.

The Israelites inquired of God before they fought the Benjamites. And they continued to do so, even when the battle seemed to be going against them. Ultimately, God gave them the victory because they had inquired of Him first: ". . . tomorrow I will give them into your hands" (Judges 20:28).

I believe I was given victory over my clogged ears because I "inquired of the Lord" by praying with my wife first. Do you inquire of the Lord before setting out? How about forming a regular prayer team and seeking the Lord's presence before you leave? Ask the team to keep you in constant prayer while you're gone. And compare notes with them when you return. You'll be amazed how things change for the better as you go. When a difficult situation changes in your favor, you'll learn that someone was praying for you at that exact time.

God bless you and your inquiring team!

## March 9
## POURING OUT

"... I was pouring out my soul to the Lord."
(1 Samuel 1:15)

**Traveler: Hannah**
**Read: 1 Samuel 1:1–20**

"Excuse me, sir," said the elderly man sitting next to me. "Are you a pastor?" "No," I answered, "not really. Why do you ask?"

"Well, ever since we left Boston four hours ago, you've been studying that Bible. I've never seen someone so intense. It was as if you didn't even realize you were on an airplane. I just assumed you were getting ready for a sermon."

I asked the man if he was a Christian. He said he and his wife had never been able to get into it, but then, he'd never met anyone like me before. Our brief discussion piqued his curiosity, if not his heart. He was fascinated that anyone could become so interested in religion. I told him he was missing the adventure of a lifetime.

Elkanah's wife Hannah was on a trip also, a pilgrimage to Shiloh. She had been unable to have children and she pleaded bitterly with God to give her a son. Her prayers were so fervent that she probably forgot where she was: "Hannah was praying in her heart, and her lips were moving but her voice was not heard. Eli thought she was drunk . . . 'Not so, my lord,' Hannah replied, 'I am a woman who is deeply troubled. I have not been drinking wine or beer; I was pouring out my soul to the Lord . . . I have been praying here out of my great anguish and grief '" (1 Samuel 1:13–16).

In Hannah's case, it was Eli the priest who observed her and who blessed her intensity. In my case it was an elderly man and his wife who did not know the Lord.

What about the people you encounter in travel? You can witness to them without saying a word, through the material you read and your reverence toward it while sitting next to them.

Hannah poured out her heart to God and received her long-awaited child. I poured out my devotion to the word on that flight and received many thoughts that went into this book. As you witness to others, even if they simply observe your devotion silently, unimaginable blessings will be poured out on you as you go.

## March 10
### THE WAY TO SHILOH

> "The Lord continued to appear . . . and . . . he revealed himself . . . through his word." (1 Samuel 3:21)

Traveler: *Samuel*
**Read: 1 Samuel 3:1–21**

Maybe it's the spectacular views from above God's creation. Or perhaps it's knowing that I am completely insulated from the telephone and fax machine for awhile. Whatever the reason, I have experienced the presence of God more on airplanes than anywhere else, especially during early morning flights. Although commercial air travel is not as spectacular as a jet fighter pilot's experience—nor would I want it to be—something of what I feel is captured in the poem "High Flight," by John Gillespie Magee, Jr.:

> Oh, I have slipped the surly bonds of earth,
> And danced the skies on laughter silvered wings . . .
> And, while with silent, lifting mind I've trod
> The high untrespassed sanctity of space,
> Put out my hand, and touched the face of God.[3]

God frequently appeared to Samuel as he was growing up in Shiloh: "The Lord continued to appear . . . and . . . he revealed himself . . . through his word" (1 Samuel 3:21). As Samuel learned from God, "he let none of his words fall to the ground" (1 Samuel 3:19). That means Samuel took God's words with him wherever he went.

Has God ever appeared to you? If you don't think so, maybe you need to think about your Shiloh. Has there ever been a special place where you have felt the presence of God? Where might you go frequently to study God's word and to listen to Him, quietly and alone? It might be in your closet at home or in the middle of Central Park or in Seat 16D at 35,000 feet. Or simply in the still of the morning in your most comfortable chair. It doesn't matter.

Find that place where you sense God. Go there often. Take His words with you and don't let them fall to the ground. God will use you in amazing ways, just as He did Samuel.

## March 11
### HOME BASE

> "But he always went back . . . home. . . . And he built an altar there . . ." (1 Samuel 7:17)

**Traveler:** *Samuel*
**Read: 1 Samuel 7:2–17**

A few years ago, our family decided to have prayer time just after breakfast each weekday. We listen to each other's concerns and prayer requests for the day; then each member prays for another around the circle. It's a daily "sending out" ceremony and it really sets the stage for great discussion each evening at the dinner table: "How was your test?" "Was your knee stronger at practice?" "What happened with that problem relationship at school?" "How did your Bible study go?" "Did your client finally pay that money he owes you?" Caring all around is our altar at home.

It's very hard for me to leave on business trips and miss that morning family prayer time. But it's doubly pleasant to return and catch up on family prayer requests. It's also pretty emotional when a small voice whispers, "Thank you for bringing my Daddy home safely," a prayer request already answered.

Samuel was a "circuit" judge in ancient Israel: "From year to year he went on a circuit from Bethel to Gilgal to Mizpah, judging Israel in all those places. But he always went back to Ramah, where his home was, and there he also judged Israel. And he built an altar there to the Lord" (1 Samuel 7:16–17).

Samuel's circuit was very much like our modern day frequent travel. And Samuel teaches us where our anchor ought to be—at home. Samuel didn't just come and go. He built an altar at home as the core of his existence.

What is your home base like? Is it just a place to flop on weekends where everyone needs to stay out of your way so you can rest up for next week? Or do you have an altar there to worship the Lord and gather strength? What kind of regular "ceremony" can you conduct when you are home, which will support you while you're away, appearing as secure and inviting as the deck of an aircraft carrier to a fighter returning from a mission?

## March 12
### PURPOSE OF THE TRIP

"...the Lord will come upon you..."
(1 Samuel 10:6)

Traveler: *Saul*
**Read: 1 Samuel 10:1–8**

To celebrate our twenty-fifth wedding anniversary, Sue and I took a two-week trip to Maui, Hawaii. Since our favorite times together are walking the beaches for miles and reading quietly together, Sue and I packed more books than clothes. Even though it seemed strange, I took my Bible concordance and my laptop computer, not to do regular work, but to do some long-delayed Bible study.

During our first week, Sue was still exhausted from our daughter's wedding the previous week. While she slept late each morning, I would awake just before sunrise (because of the four-hour time difference between Colorado and Hawaii) and sneak out on the verandah overlooking the pounding surf.

Oasis Hospitality International had been founded just a month before, but I had not had time to study the biblical concept of hospitality. Putting down the novel I had brought along, I felt strongly called to study what the Bible says about travel. I began to look-up travel-related words in the concordance and found hundreds of scriptural references. It took four hours a day for two weeks to catalog the 828 Bible stories which became the basis for this book, all while my wife slept. We didn't miss a moment of togetherness.

I intended the trip for one purpose. God intended it for another.

Saul went on a trip with his servant for the purpose of finding some lost sheep. God used the trip to lead Saul to Samuel, who anointed Saul King of Israel: "The Spirit of the Lord will come upon you in power... and you will be changed into a different person" (1 Samuel 10:6). The sheep became secondary to God's purpose, just as the scenery became secondary to God's leading me in the word.

As you set out on a trip that has an obvious business purpose, remember that God may have an entirely different purpose for you. Be alert, be open, sense the excitement of being tabbed by God as His servant. The drudgery of travel will never feel quite the same.

## March 13
### ATTACKING THE HIGHER GROUND

"Perhaps the Lord will act in our behalf."
(1 Samuel 14:6)

Travelers: *Jonathan and His Armor Bearer*
**Read: 1 Samuel 14:1–14**

Recently I traveled to present the results of an engineering study to a new client, a billion dollar company. They brought eight experts—legal, environmental, various engineering disciplines, accountants—to the meeting to critique my presentation.

This happens quite frequently. As a consultant, I have specialized knowledge in a fairly narrow field. But my clients need to understand that expertise from many different angles, so they bring all their big guns. I go into this kind of meeting knowing that my client's wizards are usually much smarter, more educated and more knowledgeable about their specific business than I. That's why Jonathan, son of Saul, is such an inspiration.

The tall cliffs Jonathan encountered when he decided to attack the Philistines with only his armor bearer at his side (1 Samuel 14:4–5) remind me of mahogany board rooms and the smell of leather—an intimidating setting. By the numbers Jonathan did not stand a chance. He was outnumbered and he had to climb toward the Philistine camp from below, one toehold at a time.

But Jonathan had what we all need when we're outnumbered. He had an adventuresome spirit, secure in his faith in almighty God: "Perhaps the Lord will act in our behalf. Nothing can hinder the Lord from saving, whether by many or by few" (verse 6). The Philistines taunted Jonathan and his companion, but as they tried to attack him from above, twenty of them fell off the cliff where they were easily killed. This brazen attack sent the Philistines into a panic and they were later defeated by the Israelites, who had been hiding in the hills with no weapons, facing certain defeat (Chapter 13).

Jonathan's best friend became a pretty good warrior himself. His name was David and he beat a giant named Goliath: "All those gathered here will know that it is not by sword or spear that the Lord saves; for the battle is the Lord's, and he will give all of you into our hands" (1 Samuel 17:47).

Remember that next time you find yourself looking up at the enemy.

## March 14
### THE SOURCE OF AUTHORITY

"So the men rescued Jonathan . . ."
(1 Samuel 14:45)

Travelers: *Saul and Jonathan*
Read: 1 Samuel 14:24–45

The primary reason I left the relative security of a large consulting partnership to form my own company was that the partnership's values had changed from providing top service, no matter the cost, to making a profit, no matter how poor the service. But history has shown that the risks of going it alone are very great, especially when client spending in my area of expertise was in an extended decline. Yet I have been blessed far beyond my expectations by a small group of loyal clients who continue to give me work, even though my new company's financial stature is minuscule compared to my old company. Why?

After Jonathan miraculously delivered the Israelites from the Philistines, he and his men were extremely tired and hungry. But Jonathan's father Saul had decreed that no one could eat food before evening, an apparent ego trip by a king who had abused the power granted by God. But Jonathan did not know about the decree and ate some honey. As a result, Saul declared that Jonathan should die, because he broke the king's rule (1 Samuel 14:24–44).

But the men in the army saw Saul's hypocrisy: Jonathan had just delivered them from certain death, and now Jonathan was to be killed by his father's strange rule? They rallied around Jonathan: "Never! As surely as the Lord lives, not a hair of his head will fall to the ground, for he did this today with God's help" (verse 45). Jonathan's authority came from the people he served, not from those in charge.

In my case, my clients rescued me because I had served them well over the years, and they knew my commitment to service mattered more than the profit motives of my old company. That company still has its profit standards, but I have their clients. My source of authority comes from the people I serve.

What about you? Are you languishing under the canopy of a big company with big profits and poor commitment to service? If you truly believe in God's salvation as Jonathan did, you will be rescued by your co-workers and your customers, not by your boss.

## March 15
### TRUE OBEDIENCE

"Because you have rejected the word of the Lord, he has rejected you . . ." (1 Samuel 15:23)

**Traveler:** *Saul*
**Read: 1 Samuel 15:1–35**

I grew up in a main-line denomination, which taught that we should make decisions in life using "scripture, tradition, experience and reason." The church was saying that the Bible can only be understood by modifying historical scripture with modern, rational thought. Did God say something back then which doesn't make sense today? No problem. If it isn't reasonable, it must not be true. I was forty-two years old before I realized the tragic error in that teaching.

King Saul was the perfect model of a rational thinker in his day. God told him to totally destroy the Amalekites, because they had attacked the Israelites as they left Egypt (Exodus 17:8–14). But Saul spared their king and the best of their animals to take as the spoils of battle. When confronted by Samuel, Saul rationalized that the animals would be used ". . . in order to sacrifice them to the Lord your God at Gilgal" (1 Samuel 15:21).

Samuel's response is one which every traveler should take personally, because we face tantalizing choices every day which can be justified with rationalization. Read this as if Samuel were talking to you personally:

> Does the Lord delight in burnt offerings and sacrifices as much as in obeying the voice of the Lord? To obey is better than sacrifice, and to heed is better than the fat of rams. For rebellion is like the sin of divination, and arrogance like the evil of idolatry. Because you have rejected the word of the Lord, he has rejected you as king. (verses 22–23)

Do you think of yourself as a diviner and an idolater, full of arrogance? Probably not. But how many of us, if confronted by a prophet like Samuel, would not wilt under the scrutiny of having compromised God's clear commands?

"And the Lord was grieved that he had made Saul king over Israel" (verse 35). Is He grieved over what He has done for you?

## March 16
### A BOOK AND ITS COVER

". . . but the Lord looks at the heart."
(1 Samuel 16:7)

**Traveler:** *Samuel*
**Read:** 1 Samuel 16:1–13

When I was in tenth grade, I tried out for the high school baseball team. Although I had grown to almost six-feet-tall, I was extremely thin, weighing only about 110 pounds. I had been a pretty good pitcher throughout Little League, but I never received any formal coaching. We were lucky to have a team in those days; our coaches were World War II vets who had lost their youth in the war. Most were happy to be alive; they knew little about the game.

My high school coach was no different. Teaching had nothing to do with it. Either you were a "natural," with a splendid physical body, or you were rejected quickly, mostly by appearance. I got to pitch just two innings on the junior varsity that season. I gave up one hit, no runs, and struck-out three batters. But I never pitched again, because I looked more like Ichabod Crane than a ballplayer.

Samuel was told to choose Israel's next king from Jesse's sons (1 Samuel 16:1). God told Samuel, "Do not consider his appearance or his height. . . . The Lord does not look at the things man looks at. Man looks at the outward appearance, but the Lord looks at the heart" (verse 7). As a result, David was chosen instead of his brothers.

If only my high school baseball coach had possessed the wisdom of Samuel. He would have seen a kid with a great heart for baseball. He would have known that my body would catch up with the others, and he would have taught me the game. But I have no regrets, because that experience gave me the wisdom I use now, as a high school baseball coach. I delight in finding that young player whose skills are deficient but whose heart burns for baseball. Then the teaching is easy.

What does God see in your heart? If Samuel the prophet came looking past your physical appearance, what would he find? If you have a heart after God, He will come to you in a thousand ways and anoint you, never judging the book by its cover.

## March 17
### TIP FOR A TIRED TRAVELER

> "Then relief would come . . . and the evil spirit would leave . . ."
> (1 Samuel 16:23)

**Traveler:** *David*
**Read: 1 Samuel 16:14–23**

For years, whenever I checked into a hotel room, the first thing I did was turn on the television. I thought it was my friend; it blocked out the silence of loneliness. It was a far better alternative than going out alone, in a strange city.

It was also addictive. Unable to sleep, I watched television for hours, depriving me of sleep. It was a vicious cycle which God could have broken at any time. But for a long time, I wouldn't let Him. I know now that during this time I was much like Saul.

"Now the Spirit of the Lord had departed from Saul, and an evil spirit from the Lord tormented him" (1 Samuel 16:14). His servants recommended harp music as a way to soothe Saul. "Whenever the spirit from God came upon Saul, David would take his harp and play. Then relief would come to Saul; he would feel better, and the evil spirit would leave him" (verse 23). The Lord's spirit had departed from Saul because of his disobedience to God's word. And each time I turned on the television, it was the same as being tormented by an evil spirit. Unlike Saul, I had no David to come and play the harp.

But most hotel rooms do have radios with classical and Christian music stations. Now, I leave the television off, and as soon as I enter a room I turn to great music on the radio. The Holy Spirit fills the void through the vehicle of music, just as He did for Saul. What a change! I get more work done, I rarely have trouble sleeping, and I greet each new day enthusiastically, instead of with fatigue.

Aren't the parallels between modern travel and the Bible amazing? Leave that television off when you check in at the hotel! Find some good music on the radio. You will feel relieved, instantly.

## March 18
### THE DAVID IN YOU

"... who delivered me from the paw of the lion ..."
(1 Samuel 17:37)

Traveler: *David*
**Read: 1 Samuel 17:1–37**

Instead of relating one of my experiences on this page, let's look at you. You may be facing some challenge in your life that looks as impossible as Goliath looked to the Israelite army. If so, there is something of David in you that wants to shout, "What is this problem that it should defy a child of the living God" (compare 1 Samuel 17:26)?

When David asked Saul to allow him to fight Goliath, Saul told him that a boy stood no chance against such an experienced fighting man. David said, in my paraphrase, "Oh, really? You're out here with a whole army, equipped with swords and spears. But as a shepherd, I've had to face lions and bears completely alone, and I have killed them myself. 'The Lord who delivered me from the paw of the lion and the paw of the bear will deliver me from the hand of this Philistine'" (verse 37).

Maybe you have quaked with fear like the Israelite soldiers. But think back over your life. Haven't there been times when you did some surprising things, all by yourself? Wasn't there a problem or two which you solved with amazing resourcefulness? Did you know the source of your strength at those times?

David knew. He knew that it was not just his own strength that allowed him to kill lions and bears when they attacked. No, he knew that he had been delivered, just as he would be from the Philistine giant: "You come against me with sword and spear and javelin, but I come against you in the name of the Lord Almighty, the God of the armies of Israel, whom you have defied" (verse 45).

That same God is the God of your army, and that problem of yours is defying God. Step up to it in faith, declare the source of your strength and make sure your stones are smooth and round (verse 40).

## March 19
### CRUMBLING OPPOSITION

"But the Spirit of God came even upon him . . ."
(1 Samuel 19:23)

**Traveler:** *Saul*
**Read: 1 Samuel 19:1–24**

I was wearing down. In my seventh consecutive day of expert witness testimony in Utah, the opposing lawyer had just informed me that I would probably be on the stand for three more days. Although I couldn't betray my true feelings to him, I knew I couldn't last that long. So during a short break, I called home and talked to my wife. She assured me that everyone she knew was praying for me and told me not to worry about missing my son's baseball games. God gave me strength, through my wife, and I went back to the battle.

David went under God's protection, too, by fleeing to Samuel when Saul tried to kill him. When Saul sent men to capture David, they were overcome by Samuel's power and did not take David. Finally Saul himself came. "But the Spirit of God came even upon him, and he walked along prophesying . . ." (verse 23). God's power overcame Saul's evil intent.

As I continued my seventh day of testimony, the attorney continued pounding me with the same questions he had asked for days, trying to get me to answer one differently than I had before. Suddenly, he looked up from his notes, his eyes glazed over and he stopped. This snarling, rude, unethical attorney just gave up. He closed his briefcase and left the room without another word. It was over.

Recorded in my personal log book on August 28, 1991 are the ironies of his sudden surrender: "First, God knew what I could bear; second, I have been supported by endless prayer; third, I'll get home tonight to see Mitch's ball game, just when that seemed impossible; fourth, I had to experience the adversity to appreciate God's power; fifth, I was out of vitamins which I can only buy at home; and sixth, apparently God even knew I was out of underwear!"

God knows what you can handle. He will come to you, if you will come to Him.

## March 20
### OLD FRIENDS

"... for we have sworn friendship with each other..."
(1 Samuel 20:42)

Travelers: *Jonathan and David*
**Read: 1 Samuel 20:1–42**

It had been fourteen years since we saw Linda and Denny. We had gone to college together in Michigan, gotten married in the same month and lived in the same first shabby apartment building. On Friday nights, they had to bring their own folding chairs to our apartment for a game of "Monopoly"‘ since neither couple owned more than two chairs.

As the years went by, they moved to California to pursue their careers and we headed for Colorado. An outside observer would have thought the friendship was dead, because so many years passed without seeing each other.

But, ah, we cherish those rare occasions when our paths cross! Recently Sue and I stopped in their town on our way to a vacation and invited Linda and Denny to lunch. It was like time had stood still. After three hours of much laughter and a few tears, the restaurant staff had to ask us to leave so they could prepare the dining room for dinner. Our hearts were warmed as they had not been in years. We realized that close friendship is a matter of the heart, not of physical distance.

David and Jonathan were close friends. Jonathan even risked his life to affirm their friendship when David was being pursued by Saul (1 Samuel 20). Jonathan made sure that David knew to flee for his life, rather than allowing him to walk back into Saul's snare.

As we grow older, it's easy to lose track of old friends. Sit back and remember for a few minutes. Who is that close friend in your life "who sticks closer than a brother" (Proverbs 18:24)? What close friends do you have that you haven't seen in awhile? Why not arrange to visit, during one of your next trips? Jesus said, "Greater love has no one than this, that he lay down his life for his friends" (John 15:13).

All you'd have to do is lay down part of a trip for your friend.

## March 21
### HOSPITALITY HINT

> "Now then, what do you have on hand?"
> (1 Samuel 21:3)

**Traveler:** *David*
**Read: 1 Samuel 21:1–9**

Small budget hotels have become very successful out along the interstate highways. The price of a clean room is much less than a major downtown hotel chain, and the budget hotel is easy to find. But there is another reason why they are so popular.

Probably three quarters of my business trips start late on a weekday, so that I arrive at my destination close to midnight, usually hungry and thirsty. There is nothing more frustrating than checking into a big hotel, in a deserted city, at $120 per night, only to find that all food services are closed. Or maybe room service is open, but a glass of milk will cost you $5, plus tip, plus room delivery charge, plus tax. If you want a cup of coffee early in the morning, the restaurant doesn't open until 7:00. Despite all of the fancy decorations and architecture of a big downtown hotel, it feels more like being committed to an institution than being a guest, in need of hospitality.

Small budget hotels have an advantage that has defined good business for a long time: location. They are usually near an all-night pancake house and a 24-hour convenience store. Just before checking in, I can stop at the store, buy some milk and cookies and take them to my room. In the morning, when I want to write devotions at 5:00 a.m., I can always run over and get coffee.

David's definition of hospitality was informal too. The issue was how to feed his hungry men, not whether they were ceremoniously clean enough to eat consecrated bread from the temple: "As for my men . . . what do you have on hand? Give me five loaves of bread, or whatever you can find" (1 Samuel 21:3).

On this devotional walk through the Bible, God continues to offer hints concerning Christian hospitality. This one has to do with midnight snacks. When we're finished with this book, we'll have the blueprint for an entirely different format for providing hospitality. Are you enjoying the search?

FAITH IN MOTION

## *March 22*
WHO IS YOUR PROPHET?

"Do not stay . . . Go . . ."
(1 Samuel 22:5)

Traveler: *David*
**Read: 1 Samuel 22:1–5**

Unless you are independently wealthy and travel for fun, you probably travel frequently to make a living, to survive, to do the work God has assigned you. The company you work for gives you a mission. It might be sales or engineering or management. But the company's focus on that mission is probably unwavering. And that focus is on the company's best interests, not necessarily on your own. You may be expected to stay at a project site for weeks, to fix a problem, regardless of the effect it may have on your personal life. Or you may expand into international sales, because that's where the market is, not realizing that you'll be away from home many weekends at a time.

I've often envied the Old Testament heroes, and here's another case. David was on a mission to flee from Saul, who wanted to kill him (1 Samuel 22). As a man of God, he had a prophet, or "seer" as they were called then, to watch out for him. If he went to a place where he would be in danger, the prophet Gad warned him not to stay but to go somewhere else. It's easy to wish that we had prophets like that today, who could warn us of the dangers of travel.

But we can have such a support system. I meet one morning each week with a group of other men whose sole purpose is to guard each other from bad decisions. As time goes on, I find that I can rely more and more on their judgment as I face critical decisions, and I know they are praying for me when I am gone. This didn't come easily; it took a long time to build that kind of trust. But as a group, they are just as powerful in judgment as the prophet Gad.

Find a group like that outside of your company, but then bring them up to speed on how your company works. They'll be able to see dangers which you are too close to the fire to see.

And when they say, "Do not stay . . . Go!" (1 Samuel 22:5), you'd better listen, because the Spirit of God may be upon them.

## *March 23*
ASKING FOR HELP

"Please give . . . whatever you can find . . ."
(1 Samuel 25:8)

**Traveler:** *David*
**Read: 1 Samuel 25:1–8**

In 1988, when my family moved back to Colorado, I was forced to stay behind in Connecticut, for nearly a full year. In the previous two years, we had become part of a small local church community whose members loved us greatly. But after my family left, I went to church alone. Each week, everyone wanted to know how my family was, and that just intensified my loneliness. It became easier to stop going to church than to confront how much I missed my family. I nose-dived into a state of suspended animation, blocking out the pain, forming a shell which even the love of friends at church could not penetrate. Looking back, I'm not sure why I reacted that way. But it's clear I did not follow David's example.

As he fled from Saul, David must have felt lonely, too. And he was never sure where the King's spies might be. Yet he never hesitated to ask for help from the people he encountered. In the Desert of Maon, he simply went to a wealthy property owner in Carmel: ". . . be favorable toward my young men . . . Please give your servants and your son David whatever you can find for them . . ." (1 Samuel 25:8). Nabal's response is covered in the next devotion. The focus here is that David did not hesitate to ask. I not only failed to ask for help, but I withdrew in a very unhealthy way when help would have been freely offered.

Christian hospitality involves providing help to travelers who need it. But it cannot be provided if it is not requested. As a traveler, are you too proud to accept help from caring local residents? I hope not. I made that mistake.

Where do you go for fellowship when you travel? Have you tried just stopping in at a local church? Ones that hold Wednesday night services would love to have you, and you'd make friends that would be there every time you go back. Be like David, not like me. Seek out local churches and ask to join their fellowship!

# March 24
## IN THE BUNDLE OF THE LIVING

"Praise be to the Lord . . . who has sent you today to meet me."
(1 Samuel 25:32)

Traveler: *David*
**Read: 1 Samuel 25:1–39**

I have always dealt with my loneliness in travel by being alone. I try to live through each trip, in an emotional cocoon. As a result, I get grumpy and less than diplomatic in important business meetings. And when trips begin to pile up, one week after another, people start asking what's wrong with me. The truth, which I can never tell them, is that I feel trapped. If a local Christian were to offer to meet me and provide fellowship, I probably would make an excuse and decline. And many others have told me the same thing: they are too tired or too busy to take time to meet someone.

My question is, "Has this 'poor me' attitude ever negatively affected my performance?" It certainly affected David's!

At least David tried to find help. But when Nabal refused, the stress of David's predicament caused him to over-react. He angrily prepared to kill all the men in Nabal's service (1 Samuel 25:21–22). It was only when Nabal's wife Abigail heard of her husband's affront to David that true hospitality took place. She brought food, kind words and advice to David: ". . . let this gift . . . be given to the men . . . Let no wrongdoing be found in you . . . [your] life . . . will be bound securely in the bundle of the living by the Lord your God . . . [you] will not have on [your] conscience the staggering burden of needless bloodshed . . ." (verses 28–31).

David's near-tragic reaction was changed through his encounter with Abigail.

God can change our hearts too, as we travel. He can provide us valuable counsel after a tough day of business meetings. But not if we hide out in a hotel room for many nights a year. That's what happened to me.

We hope that one day the Christian Travelers' Network will help you locate a friendly, good listener in each city you visit. But until then, find a local church and reach out! Someone you hardly know might, through the work of the Holy Spirit, come up with just the right answer to that knotty problem you've been facing.

## March 25
### LETTING GOD JUDGE

"Who can lay a hand on the Lord's anointed and be guiltless?"
(1 Samuel 26:9)

**Travelers:** *David and Saul*
**Read: 1 Samuel 26:1–25**

In every chapter of my business career, I observed many men (and a few women) jockeying for promotion. I saw it happen inside my own company and outside, from a consultant's perspective. They were so obvious about their ambition! It would have been easy to do them in, to leak word to management about how they took advantage of their co-workers for their own advancement. Yet I always chose to let things go, because I never knew when it was God's plan for such a person to advance.

God has chosen many leaders whom I would not have chosen. And I'll guess you can think of a few questionable ones too. But Jesus taught us to follow them and honor them, even when it's very difficult: "Give to Caesar what is Caesar's . . ." (Matthew 22:21). That's not an easy teaching to practice.

David had a perfect opportunity to sneak up on Saul and to kill him in his sleep, the man who had pursued him with intent to kill. But David recognized that Saul was still the king and therefore God's anointed: "Who can lay a hand on the Lord's anointed and be guiltless?" (1 Samuel 26:9). He recognized that judgment belonged to God, not to himself. He let Saul sleep, even though he could expect Saul to continue pursuing him.

What a great lesson for modern business leaders! The competition is so tough, and we've all heard the phrase "dog eat dog." But that is man's way, not God's.

Have you pursued someone's career with intent to kill? Have you put the word out that so-and-so is no good, with the intent to limit his or her advancement? Consider David's example. You can accomplish much more by treating that person as God's anointed and leaving the judgment to God. He will determine the proper timing: ". . . the Lord will strike him; either his time will come and he will die, or he will go into battle and perish" (1 Samuel 26:10).

That's how to deal with corrupted leaders today.

## March 26
### IN HIS TIME

"Because you did not obey . . . the Lord has done this to you today." (1 Samuel 28:18)

Traveler: *Saul*
**Read: 1 Samuel 28:1–25**

Coal dust. Asbestos fibers. Heavy metals. Solid waste. Even dioxin. Over the years I worked in heavy industry, my body ingested many residues which could, at any time in the future, cause serious health problems. I've asked my wife if I glow in the dark, but she says, "Not yet."

Saul also carried a residue from which he could not escape. He had failed to destroy the Amalekites as God had told him (1 Samuel 15) and had made light of God's reprimand. A considerable amount of time passed, during which Saul remained king, but eventually his kingdom went into decline, and he pursued David, to kill him. Finally he consulted a witch, who told him he would lose his kingdom: "Because you did not obey . . . the Lord has done this to you today" (1 Samuel 28:18). Saul's residue of sin finally caught up with him.

Sometimes I get scared, wondering how my body is dealing with all the stuff I have breathed. But there's another residue which is far more dangerous, one which each person contacts at birth—sin. But unlike all the dust in my lungs, which could come back to haunt me later, there is a cleanser for my sin. It is Jesus Christ, who makes me white as snow (Isaiah 1:18), inside and out.

What residue do you carry around? Take time to think about what God would say, if asked about your life. Hopefully He would reply immediately, "For I will forgive [his] wickedness and will remember [his] sins no more" (Jeremiah 31:34). But if He does not know you as one of his forgiven, your residue of sin will eventually catch up to you. It may take quite a long time, like it did for Saul, but God does not forget.

The answer is so simple. Now is the time to get down on your knees and ask Jesus Christ into your life. Even if you are a believer, has your record been perfect? Purge your residue and change your life. Do it now!

## March 27
### BE SURE OF YOUR CALLING

"... each one was bitter in spirit because of his sons and daughters." (1 Samuel 30:6)

Traveler: *David*
**Read: 1 Samuel 30:1–25**

Frequent business travel can take a tremendous toll on families.

When David returned to Ziklag, where the families of all his men were staying, he found the town destroyed and all the women and children taken captive. "David was greatly distressed, because the men were talking of stoning him . . ." (1 Samuel 30:6). They had been gone too long and had left their families unprotected.

Among my professional friends, I have never heard of a business traveler returning home to find his town destroyed and his family kidnapped. But I have heard stories of empty homes, where wives could no longer stand the loneliness and isolation from a husband too often absent. And I know of homes where teenagers, in the absence of parental leadership, have gotten into serious trouble with "friends" who *would* spend time with them—selling them drugs and encouraging an immoral lifestyle. Those spouses and children definitely may have felt like stoning their absent leader.

To survive, David turned to God to reaffirm his calling. Read in Psalms 27 and 56 how David poured out his pain to God, but then trusted God and His timing: "Wait for the Lord; be strong and take heart and wait for the Lord" (Psalm 27:14). "When I am afraid, I will trust in you . . . What can mortal man do to me?" (Psalm 56:3–4).

I would add something to what David did. I would seek the Lord's guidance frequently with my entire family, confirming God's calling for my travel and affirming my love for my family. When they are part of the inquiring process, they too are strengthened as David was, and they are better able to withstand the stresses of my travel.

Do it together. It is your responsibility to affirm your calling and trust God to protect your family while you are gone. It beats getting pelted with rocks when you return late some Friday night.

## March 28
### GRAVEYARD LEADERSHIP

"But by these slave girls . . . I will be held in honor."
(2 Samuel 6:22)

**Traveler:** *David*
**Read:** 2 Samuel 6:1–23

I spent the summer of 1984 trying to fix a power plant in Ohio. Like a forensic pathologist searching for the cause of death, I was asked to catalog all the problems and count the number of hours the plant could not operate because of each problem.

One of the keys to problem solving is listening to the plant operators. They know the plant far better than most people imagine, but management often ignores their opinions. Many workers do not have the education nor the experience to know why a certain problem exists, but they provide observations which no one else sees.

The "graveyard" shift, from midnight to eight in the morning, is often made up of people who just don't fit the regular world. They are often "loners," people who prefer to avoid normal society. Many are deep thinkers, with a surprising ability to analyze quietly the problems they observe.

By spending a week drinking coffee and eating donuts with the graveyard shift in Ohio, I learned a critical piece of information which I simply could not have learned in any other way. And my willingness to listen to some humble men, who work on the fringe of society, sent a message to the entire operating staff that I was there to help them, not to intimidate or judge them.

David had the same idea. When the ark of God was returned to Jerusalem, David danced and leaped for joy and wore linen instead of his kingly robes. His wife criticized him for "disrobing in the site of the slave girls . . . as any vulgar fellow would" (2 Samuel 6:20). But David knew that a leader derives support from his people: "I will become even more undignified than this . . . but by these slave girls . . . I will be held in honor" (verse 22).

I was criticized too, for spending so much time with the graveyard shift. But I will be remembered as the one who fixed the plant by sitting down and listening to them.

The people you encounter with the least influence may have the most wisdom.

## *March 29*
### DESPISING GOD'S WORD

"... the sword will never depart from your house ..."
(2 Samuel 12:10)

Traveler: *Nathan*
Read: 2 Samuel 12:1-14

My life of crime was short-lived. One Sunday morning at the age of five, I stole some gum from my mother's purse. I'm not sure what tipped her off, but within five minutes I was caught. If she had just spanked me, I would have taken my penalty and gone along. But she sat me down first and made sure I understood why she was going to spank me—not because she wanted the gum, but because it was wrong to steal. Of course, the anticipation of the "whuppin'" made it hurt even worse when it was finally administered. It was a lesson I never forgot.

Had there been chewing gum in his day, David would have had all he wanted. He was king. God anointed him king over Israel, delivered him from Saul, gave him his master's house and wives and gave him the houses of Israel and Judah. Through Nathan the prophet, God told David there was no limit to what God would have done: "And if all this had been too little, I would have given you even more" (2 Samuel 12:8). Yet something in his fallen human nature led David to steal Uriah's wife and to arrange for Uriah's death. God forgave David (verse 13), but He inflicted severe punishment on him, which affected his entire family forever.

Whether it's stealing gum as a little child or a major sin committed as an adult, we all fall short of God's standards. And we take risks that could affect our families for years to come. But we have an intercessor whom David did not have. We have Jesus Christ, who died for our sins, and who sets us free. All we have to do is admit our mistakes to Him. Then, we must do as Jesus told the man he healed by the pool, "Stop sinning or something worse may happen to you" (John 5:14).

It's up to us. Shall we despise God's word or honor it?

## March 30
### IN TRANSIT

"... to refresh those who become exhausted ..."
(2 Samuel 16:2)

Travelers: *David and Ziba*
**Read: 2 Samuel 16:1–4**

When David was on the run from his son Absalom, he hid in the wilderness, high on the Mount of Olives. Just past the summit David was met by Ziba, the servant of Mephibosheth. Earlier (2 Samuel 9), David had shown great kindness to Ziba and Mephibosheth, Jonathan's son, who was severely crippled. Now it was time for Ziba to return the favor.

Ziba met David's fleeing party, high on the mountain: "'The donkeys are for the king's household to ride on, the bread and fruit are for the men to eat, and the wine is to refresh those who become exhausted in the desert'" (2 Samuel 16:2). Ziba anticipated David's need and went out to meet him.

In modern business travel, we are not usually fleeing from something, but we are often in serious need of refreshment. And missing a plane on Friday night, because of a traffic jam on the way to the airport, can leave us near tears, just as David was (2 Samuel 15:30). Don't you think there is a great need for Christian hospitality in airports? (See also 2 Samuel 17:27–29.) Haven't you ever sat at home during a big storm and wondered about all the poor travelers coping with it at the airport? With the current increase in international travel, fatigue and discouragement are never far away.

Airports have airline travel clubs, which are very nice if you have enough money. And there are restaurants and bars to sit in if you get stranded before closing time. But where are the Christian brothers and sisters who are willing to pack up a "care package" and carry it to the airport, along with personal love, to encourage and refresh travelers? Couldn't youth groups and senior groups take time, say once a quarter, to meet travelers at the airport and encourage them?

Jesus said, "Greater love has no one than this, that he lay down his life for his friends" (John 15:13). That's what Ziba did.

## March 31
### LET HIM CURSE

"... the Lord ... will repay me with good ..."
(2 Samuel 16:12)

Traveler: *David*
Read: 2 Samuel 16:5–14

Not long after I was promoted to senior management, I had to close an office in another city and lay off about 30 people. This was an office I had inherited from a previous manager, who had been promoted even higher. I got to clean up the mess. Of course, as soon as I did the dirty work, then I became targeted by my boss, and I was eventually forced out of the company. He knew I knew the truth.

I have always viewed management not in terms of how many employees work for me, but in how many families I serve. So the task of removing 30 families from my care was intensely painful, even if they had understood the situation, which they did not. I was cursed by everyone involved.

In a similar way, David was cursed by Shimei, a member of Saul's family, who held David responsible for Saul's demise. Shimei did not understand the situation either, but he cursed David with all his heart.

David's response is a good lesson for all of us with distasteful work to do: "Leave him alone; let him curse, for the Lord has told him to. It may be that the Lord will see my distress and repay me with good for the cursing I am receiving today" (2 Samuel 16:11–12).

David knew God used tough circumstances in his life to test his faith and to mature him. He accepted the cursing and the stoning (verse 6), because he believed it was God's will. And he hoped to gain favor in God's eyes by accepting this humiliation.

Do you know someone who dislikes you because of a situation they do not understand completely? How surprising it is to think that God may have actually caused that person to treat you that way. God must think highly of you to ask you to persevere in such a tough position. And if you do, He will repay you with good.

## *April 1*
### EVEN THE BEST OF INTENTIONS

"You have defied the word of the Lord . . ."
(1 Kings 13:21)

Traveler: *The Man of God*
**Read: 1 Kings 13:1–34**

I go on business trips with the best of intentions. By taking books to read and even meditations to write for this devotional book, I plan to use all of my free time for good. But all too often, fatigue from the trip or discouragement from the business dealings of the day leave me in a state of suspended animation, where I don't feel like doing anything. I just can't concentrate on reading or writing; it's all too easy to "veg" in front of the television.

It's encouraging for mere mortals to find that even a man of God can be misled. During the time of King Jeroboam, a man of God came from Judah to Bethel to prophecy against King Jeroboam's practices. The king tempted the man of God to join him for food and drink, but the man of God refused, in accordance with the directions God had given him (verse 10). So far, so good.

But God used another prophet from that town to test the man of God. He was tricked into returning to eat and drink, violating God's instructions. It's not as if he had committed murder or robbery! Today we would call this "entrapment." Later, the man of God was killed by a lion, in punishment for defying the word of God (verse 24).

If a man of God could be fooled so easily, what about us? It's chilling to think that we may be tested as we travel, to see whether we really stick to the word of God. When we don't, and then nothing bad happens immediately, we think we're safe. But the man of God was allowed to finish his refreshment and head home before he was killed. The timing of God's punishment may be delayed only by His great love for us.

Is it time to take stock? What are God's instructions to you before you leave? And are you following them to the letter while you're gone?

## April 2
### ELIJAH AND YOU

*"For the jar . . . and the jug . . . did not run dry . . ."*
(1 Kings 17:16)

Traveler: *Elijah*
**Read: 1 Kings 17:1–24**

The least likely time to start a new engineering consulting business was in 1994, when corporate downsizing was rampant, and unemployment of engineers was skyrocketing. Added to this, the business I'm an expert in was dying rapidly. A consultant in a non-existent market? Why not grow kumquats in a drought?

In the days when Ahab wanted to kill all the prophets of God, God decreed a drought over a period of several years. Elijah, the prophet, hid from Ahab and was totally dependent on the word of God to survive. God ordered Elijah to travel to Kerith Ravine: "You will drink from the brook, and I have ordered the ravens to feed you there" (1 Kings 17:4). But eventually the brook dried up, and Elijah was sent to a widow at Zarepheth, the least likely person to have food and drink during a drought (verses 7–9).

The widow was about to use the last of her food and oil to feed her son; then they expected to die. But Elijah brought a miracle of God: "For the jar of flour was not used up and the jug of oil did not run dry, in keeping with the word of the Lord spoken by Elijah" (verse 16).

The poor market in my business has been like a drought to the industry as a whole, but God has sent me to places where there has been work. My clients have been a little like the widow, thinking they could die soon, but I've been able to help keep them running for awhile. Somehow, God has kept our businesses from running dry.

What about your work? How can you be like Elijah to your customers, finding new ways to remain competitive, to help keep the jug from running dry? Does Elijah's mission to the widow of Zarepheth shed new light on your responsibilities as you travel?

## April 3
### CONFRONTATION

"... Elijah had them brought down ... and slaughtered there."
(1 Kings 18:40)

Traveler: *Elijah*
**Read: 1 Kings 18:1–40**

Blinded in the glare of television lights and distracted by the rudeness of newspaper photographers, I made my report to the board of directors. Suddenly, my client's lawyer jumped up in the back of the room and shouted, "Mr. Chairman, I demand the floor. Your consultant is lying. His optimism is just avoiding the truth. This plant will never work properly. It is doomed. I demand an independent audit conducted by his chief competitor."

It was obvious that this outburst was pre-arranged, and that I was about to be fired and probably sued. Calmly, I gave out the names of my competitors and then endured two months of intense scrutiny by my chief competitor, who had every incentive to make me look bad and to ruin my company.

Elijah had to face Ahab, even though Ahab was killing every prophet of God. There was a showdown on Mount Carmel, where Elijah's credibility was tested against Ahab's prophets of Baal and Asherah—850 of them. But God's power overwhelmed Ahab's false prophets: "When all the people saw this, they fell prostrate and cried, 'The Lord—he is God! The Lord—he is God!'" (1 Kings 18:39). Then Elijah had all Ahab's prophets killed.

My competitor turned out to be not a false prophet, but a man of truth. His report vindicated everything I had said, to the letter. He could find nothing wrong. Of course, this enraged the lawyer even more, and my competitor was fired, not me. And suddenly the unfavorable spotlight of the media shifted from me to that lawyer. He never regained the political clout he had used skillfully for so many years.

Once again, the story of Elijah is so inspiring to business travelers who must persevere on someone else's home field. Do you have tough battles to face as you travel? You need only one weapon: the power of the one God. You could rely on other gods. But, like the prophets of Baal and Asherah, you might get burned.

## April 4
### POSTURE FOR PRAYER

"... but Elijah ... bent down ... and put his face between his knees." (1 Kings 18:42)

Traveler: *Elijah*
**Read: 1 Kings 18:41–46**

Today, with the benefit of satellite telecommunications, we are besieged daily with visual images of disasters around the world, from drought and death in Africa to flood and famine in Bangladesh. These tragic events strike all people equally, with no regard to politics, religion or race. God's people sometimes suffer hardship as much as ungodly people. But what is the response of God's people to such an event?

When God sent a drought during the reign of King Ahab, both evil people and good people suffered. When Elijah overcame Ahab's false prophets, God allowed the rain to fall on Ahab and Elijah alike. But the responses of Ahab and Elijah to the end of the drought were very different.

Ahab's response was to go off to eat and drink, a particularly curious response, since his entire cast of 850 prophets had just been killed (1 Kings 18:40). Ahab lived for the moment; when the crisis passed, it was party time again.

Just like most of American society says today: "Sorry to hear about the bombing in Oklahoma City, but there's nothing I can do. What time do I tee off today?"

"... [B]ut Elijah climbed to the top of Carmel, bent down to the ground and put his face between his knees" (verse 42). He prayed, fervently, humbly. He acknowledged the power of God and waited for Him, rather than eating and drinking with Ahab. Even though Elijah was sorely tested in the next episode, he had a personal relationship with God. Ahab looked stronger at the time, but Elijah's connection with God paid off in the long run.

What is your response? To brush off events that affect us all, or to put your head between your knees in a posture of prayer? To eat and drink when the storm passes you by, or to humble yourself before God? To go about your business, or to wait for the "power of the Lord" (verse 46)?

## *April 5*
### SPECIAL FOOD

> "I have had enough, Lord . . . Take my life . . ."
> (1 Kings 19:4)

**Traveler:** *Elijah*
**Read:** 1 Kings 19:1–8

It started out as a simple business trip; meet a man for lunch in St. Louis, then fly to Richmond for a meeting the next day. But there was fog in St. Louis; we diverted to Kansas City; I missed the lunch appointment; we spent eight hours waiting for fog to lift; the only flight toward Richmond went through Atlanta; a stop in Louisville; another stop in Norfolk; finally arrived in Richmond just before breakfast. Seven cities in twenty hours, a personal record for takeoffs and landings in one day. All on my birthday! The only thing I enjoyed was feeling sorry for myself.

Elijah had a tough trip, too. Running for his life from Jezebel, the wife of Ahab, adrenaline carried him one day's trip into the desert before he collapsed (1 Kings 19:3–5). "I have had enough, Lord . . . Take my life . . ." (verse 4). But an angel came and fed him fresh baked bread and water. Before he laid down again to sleep, the angel fed him again. The food sent by God strengthened him so much that he was able to travel forty days and nights until he rested in a cave at Horeb (verses 7–9).

Somehow, I survived the meeting in Richmond the next day, but I was dead-tired. No angel touched me and fed me special food that would give me strength without sleep. But that was 1983, before I had established a personal relationship with Jesus Christ. Since then, I have been fed many times with special food that has kept me going, no matter how tired I was.

That food was the word of God. Whenever I have taken the time to study the Bible as I travel, I am always energized in unexpected ways. The food of God nourishes me in ways that the best gourmet meal cannot.

How about you? Has an angel touched you with special food lately? Or do you choose to ignore His help and drag through each trip, wondering why you're so tired?

## *April 6*
### WHAT ARE YOU DOING?

"And after the fire came a gentle whisper."
(1 Kings 19:12)

Traveler: *Elijah*
**Read: 1 Kings 19:9–18**

The rush of modern business is intense, but is even more so for those who travel frequently. Business can be exhilarating, like the thrill of making a major presentation or of being invited to special training just before a big promotion. Many Christian business people interpret the press of business as God's affirmation that they are doing what He wants in their lives. That was certainly how I went about my career.

But for most of us, there is a dark side, too. There is pressure to perform well, to put in long hours, to be away from family and community for long periods of time. In the middle of all that activity, we often lose sight of God and don't listen as closely for His will.

While Elijah was fleeing from Jezebel and Ahab, he hid in a cave at Horeb. The Lord spoke to him and asked him what he was doing hiding in a cave (1 Kings 19:9). Elijah explained his difficulty, just as I might explain why I spent the whole weekend fixing a problem at the office. God replied, "Go out and stand on the mountain in the presence of the Lord, for the Lord is about to pass by" (verse 11). Then, in rapid succession, a great wind, an earthquake and a fire came with great power, but the presence of the Lord was in none of these (verses 11–12). The presence of the Lord was in a gentle whisper which followed, quiet and personal (verse 12). Now when God asked Elijah the same question, He had Elijah's full attention and Elijah was given instructions on what to do next in his ministry. (I Kings 19:15–18)

God calls to you in the din, too. Do you really take the time to listen to Him? Or are you too busy looking for him in the cacophony of busyness? God may not appear in the grand things you see, even though He may have a role in causing them to happen. God Himself will communicate with you through a gentle whisper, one you can hear only if you are perfectly still.

## April 7
### SOLVING A TOUGH PROBLEM

> "... Elisha cut a stick ... and made the iron float."
> (2 Kings 6:6)

**Traveler:** *Elisha*
**Read:** 2 Kings 6:1–7

I like to joke, "The difficult I do immediately; the impossible takes a little longer." Yet there's an element of truth in that old paradox, a spirit of never giving up until the right solution is found.

For over a year I worked, trying to fix a pump which prevented a brand new power plant from running, at a loss of over $1 million each week. I tried every problem solving technique I knew. But the pump kept destroying itself, as if it had a personal death wish.

One night I went into the plant after midnight to check some readings on a test we were running. An old man I had never seen before was standing by the pump. Apparently he worked the midnight shift and did not rotate shifts like the other workers. He asked what I was doing. Since it's so easy to chat informally on the "graveyard" shift, I poured out my frustration. He listened briefly, then snorted, "Shoot, I know what's wrong. But nobody listens to me." I told him I'd gladly listen.

He had been on the construction crew and had observed that the pump's foundation was poured improperly. *Great,* I thought. *Here's a man with no education who thinks he saw something that will cost a fortune to dig up and inspect.*

Believing that old midnight millwright was as tough as believing that Elisha could make a lost ax head float: "When he showed him the place, Elisha ... made the iron float" (2 Kings 6:6). God provided the old man to me in the same way He had provided Elisha to the prophet who lost his borrowed ax. With great fear, we suffered the expense and delay of taking the pump off its foundation and discovered "honeycombing" where solid concrete was supposed to be. The old millwright was right. Not long after, the pump was fixed, and I haven't heard from that client in 15 years.

Miracles come in many forms for people of faith.

## *April 8*
## IF WE WERE ISRAEL

"So the Lord . . . removed them from his presence."
(2 Kings 17:18)

Travelers: *The Israelites*
**Read: 2 Kings 17:7–23**

The whole nation of Israel became travelers in exile. It didn't happen quickly, but they tested God's love for them so many times over so many years that He finally gave up on them. American Christians have always felt that God selected us as His children in the modern era. So how are we doing? My guess is that we've had enough time, about 220 years, to disappoint God too. Is our epitaph already written? Consider this adaptation, where I have added italics to change ancient context into modern:

All this took place because the *Americans* had sinned against the Lord their God, who had brought them up out of *religious intolerance by the British*. They worshipped other gods and followed the practices of the nations the Lord had driven out before them, as well as the practices that the *Americans* themselves had introduced. The *Americans* secretly did things against the Lord their God that were not right. From *city to city they built themselves cable television stations in all their towns. They set up New Age book stores and pornography shops on every street corner. They worshipped Mother Earth*, as the nations whom the Lord had driven out before them had done. They did wicked things that provoked the Lord to anger. They worshipped *money*, though the Lord had said, "You shall not do this."

The Lord warned *America* through his prophets and seers . . . They forsook all the commands of the Lord their God and made for themselves a *culture of pleasure*. They bowed down to starry hosts, and *they worshipped Satan*. They sacrificed their sons and daughters to *morally corrupt public schools*. They practiced divination and sorcery and sold themselves to do evil in the eyes of the Lord, provoking Him to anger.

So the Lord was very angry with *America* and removed them from His presence" (2 Kings 17:7–13, 16–18). Isn't it chilling to see how modern American life parallels the fatal position of ancient Israel? (2 Kings 17)

## *April 9*
### TEST OF TRUST

"... if you have come to betray me ... may ... God ... see it and judge you." (1 Chronicles 12:17)

**Traveler:** *David*
**Read: 1 Chronicles 12:1–18**

One of the biggest problems I had in my business career was forming trusting relationships with partners. At first, I had no problem at all trusting people, but that trust was not returned. I was betrayed by ambition on more than one occasion. And as these relationships broke down, I'm sure my partners felt the same way about me.

King David taught me what was missing. After Saul's death David became king and soldiers went to offer their services to him. David said, "If you have come to me in peace, to help me, I am ready to have you unite with me. But if you have come to betray me to my enemies when my hands are free from violence, may the God of our fathers see it and judge you" (1 Chronicles 12:17). Amasai, leader of the men, replied in the Spirit that they were committed to David and to David's God, who would help them.

Until recently I never had the courage to ask for a commitment like that. David asked for a commitment of loyalty to himself, but more importantly in the context of loyalty to God. And the Holy Spirit spoke through Amasai as a sign of God's involvement. A covenant sealed in the name of God, not in the name of men, will last.

My new business partner Bob was the first person I've ever discussed loyalty with. Since he is a passionate Christian it was easy, because our relationship is based on our mutual love for God. I could trust him totally. That's the first time in my life I've felt that way about someone other than my wife. David showed the way, choosing godly men to do God's work.

How are your relationships in business and in other parts of your life? Are they motivated by potential personal gain or by service to God? How would your friends answer? Can you even talk to them about God? Can you read them this story about David without embarrassment?

Take stock.

## *April 10*
### STRANGERS, EVEN AT HOME

"We are aliens and strangers . . ."
(1 Chronicles 29:15)

Travelers: *All People of God*
**Read: 1 Chronicles 29:10–20**

I spent so much time in Columbus, Ohio, in 1984, that I was beginning to feel like a resident. That is, until I shared that feeling with a local resident, who promptly informed me that my acquired Colorado twang labeled me as a stranger the moment I spoke. In God's kingdom, we are never permanent residents on earth; we speak with a spiritual accent that identifies us. We are strangers here until we are called to our true home with Him.

No one had a greater right to claim his earthly home as his kingdom than David, at the point when he had raised money for building the temple in Jerusalem. Imagine what that event would look like today. We can picture David smiling at the ground-breaking ceremony saying, "One small shovel for man, one great kingdom for mankind." But that's not what he said. Concluding a passionate prayer, David said:

> But who am I, and who are my people, that we should be able to give as generously as this? Everything comes from you, and we have given you only what comes from your hand. We are aliens and strangers in your sight, as were all our forefathers. Our days on earth are like a shadow, without hope. (1 Chronicles 29:14–15)

What a morbid thing to say at a celebration! But his words confirm that everyone is a frequent traveler, even if we stay home. All of God's people belong to a different kingdom, a different world. All of us must have faith in motion as we move through this life.

When David said we have no hope, he meant that we have no hope apart from God. And he was acting on faith: "Therefore, God is not ashamed to be called their God, for he has prepared a city for them" (Hebrews 11:16).

Where is your true home and how do you get there? By faith! Read the rest of Hebrews 11. We'll come back to it in proper sequence.

## *April 11*
STARTING OVER

"The Levites even abandoned . . . their property . . ."
(2 Chronicles 11:14)

Travelers: *The Levites*
**Read: 2 Chronicles 11:5–17**

This meditation is a bit apocalyptic. But perhaps the 1995 bombing in Oklahoma City caused me to ask this question: "What if the government of the United States were overthrown?" I never dreamed I would ask a question like that, but I never dreamed that red-blooded Americans would perpetrate the kind of terrorism I thought was reserved for other parts of the world. Not in America! Not bombings by our own people!

The Old Testament stories in Kings and Chronicles indicate what life might be like without a central government. In those days, Kings came and went, most of them evil. Today we get a slight feel for how that would be, with presidential choices that are less than inspiring.

Rehoboam was the son of Solomon. At times he was faithful to God and at times he was not. But when he consolidated Judah under his control, even though Jeroboam led a rebellion against him, Rehoboam followed God's law. It was like a magnet to God-fearing people: "The priests and Levites from all their districts throughout Israel sided with him. The Levites even abandoned their pasturelands and their property and came to Judah and Jerusalem because Jeroboam and his sons had rejected them as priests of the Lord . . . Those from every tribe of Israel who set their hearts on seeking the Lord, the God of Israel, followed the Levites . . . They strengthened the kingdom of Judah and supported Rehoboam son of Solomon three years, walking in the ways of David and Solomon during this time" (2 Chronicles 11:13–14, 16–17).

People actually left everything to go where a leader sought the Lord.

After 220 years of relatively stable government in America, it's hard to imagine leaving everything behind to follow God. And in a century which has produced everything from Charles Manson and Jim Jones to David Koresh, cults are a very real danger. But if America were to collapse, would I have the kind of faith needed to go where a leader was ready to proclaim the God of our fathers?

What would it take for you to start over?

## *April 12*
### PRAYER OF THE POWERLESS

"... there is no one like you ..."
(2 Chronicles 14:11)

Traveler: *King Asa*
**Read: 2 Chronicles 14:2–15**

Successful as music leader of a congregation in California, the last thing David Burns expected was to pick up and move to our church in Colorado. But the Lord's call was extremely strong, and the tough decision was made to leave relative security, venturing into the unknown.

Apparently, God had a test in mind. How else could the subsequent events be explained? Almost as quickly as David uttered his "Yes" to our church, his daughter Sara was struck with a terrible life-threatening illness. Weeks of agony followed, not just for Sara, but for David as well, wondering if he had made the right decision.

David Burns, a messianic Jew who had accepted Jesus Christ not that long before, must have felt like King Asa facing the massive army of Zerah the Cushite (2 Chronicles 14:9). Asa knew where to turn. He prayed, "Lord, there is no one like you to help the powerless against the mighty. Help us, O Lord our God, for we rely on you, and in your name we have come against this vast army. O Lord, you are our God; do not let man prevail against you" (2 Chronicles 14:11). The Lord struck down Asa's foe. He did the same for David Burns.

Because of David's dilemma, our church reached out over the miles with cards, letters and hours of phone calls. Loving relationships were born among people who had never met. The Holy Spirit connected David to our church in beautiful ways that could not have taken place without Sara's illness. Prayers for Sara lit up God's switchboard — small people praying to help a powerless young lady against a mighty army of disease. Then Sara's illness suddenly disappeared, and the family was able to move to Colorado, three months late, but infinitely richer in trusting God for all things.

Is your faith strong enough to do what David Burns did? If you feel powerless or under attack, remember the Burns family, and how God delivers the powerless from the mighty.

## *April 13*
SAFE STREETS?

"In those days it was not safe to travel about . . ."
(2 Chronicles 15:5)

Traveler: *Azariah*
**Read: 2 Chronicles 15:1–19**

Arriving at my hotel in downtown Los Angeles one warm evening in the 1970s, I decided to take a walk before turning in for the night. It was about 10:00 p.m., and I walked around central Los Angeles for a half hour or so, enjoying the city and the relative quiet of the hour. It never occurred to me to worry about my safety.

Twenty years later I wouldn't venture out at night for a walk even in a small town, let alone in a big city! What has happened?

As the moral character of our nation has eroded alarmingly, we have tried to answer with more police, tougher laws, curfews and other social programs to protect our great society. But it is all doomed to failure unless we turn to the one approach which can save us, the same approach King Asa used.

> The Spirit of God came upon Azariah son of Oded. He went out to meet Asa and said to him, "Listen to me, Asa and all Judah and Benjamin. The Lord is with you when you are with him. If you seek him, he will be found by you, but if you forsake him, he will forsake you . . . be strong and do not give up, for your work will be rewarded." (2 Chronicles 15:1–2,7)

Asa simply turned to God and took strength in the battle against lawlessness. Our National Day of Prayer is a good start for turning to God. But until our leaders truly humble themselves in seeking God, we will continue to decay. Asa took action, but not by adding more police. Instead, he removed all idols and repaired churches, called for major revival, took oaths of loyalty to God, fired public officials who worshipped Satan and personally led a godly life as an example to the people. "All Judah rejoiced . . . They sought God eagerly, and he was found by them. So the Lord gave them rest on every side" (verse 15).

America has mourned its current state of moral decline. When is the last time we rejoiced? King Asa shows us how.

## *April 14*
## RISE AND FALL

". . . those whose hearts are fully committed . . ."
(2 Chronicles 16:9)

Traveler: *Hanani the Seer*
**Read: 2 Chronicles 16:1–13**

Think of someone who fits the description of King Asa, who was a very good king for awhile, returning his people to fearing God, making reforms which brought relative peace for several years. Yet Asa could not be satisfied forever with relying on the Lord, even though God had delivered him from the Cushites. Eventually, Asa took power into his own hands and made a treaty with the enemy, which angered God. He was chastised by a seer named Hanani, who said, "For the eyes of the Lord range throughout the earth to strengthen those whose hearts are fully committed to him. You have done a foolish thing, and from now on you will be at war" (2 Chronicles 16:9).

Asa rose to power by trusting God. He died in misery (verse 12) because he did not continue in his faith. Is it any wonder why we see turmoil in life? Even good people fall back on their own wisdom, or lack of it, and fail eventually.

So, did you think of anyone like King Asa? How about sports figures who have fallen? Or political leaders? Even religious leaders? What about you and I? No matter how hard we try, even if we have a period of truly trusting God, we tend to fall back to our sinful ways, only to repent and try again. Is it hopeless?

Jesus Christ knew the nature of humanity, too: "He did not need man's testimony about man, for he knew what was in a man" (John 2:25). It is hopeless if we say we believe in Christ, but our hearts are not fully committed. Our hearts are capable of all sorts of evil; only the Holy Spirit can come in and overpower our humanity. There is no such thing as part way. Either our hearts are committed, or they are not.

Today is the day when you can take the step. Stop right now and pray: O God, that's right. I haven't been fully committed. Come into my heart. In Jesus' name, Amen.

APRIL

## *April 15*
### HIS OFFICIALS

> "They taught throughout Judah . . . taking the Book . . ."
> (2 Chronicles 17:9)

Travelers: *Jehoshaphat's Officials*
**Read: 2 Chronicles 17:1–11**

During a break in an important meeting in Chicago, my client asked how my new consulting business was going. He wondered if being on my own was tough after all those years with an established company.

Since my client is a Christian, I quoted Jesus: "And do not set your heart on what you will eat or drink; do not worry about it. For the pagan world runs after all such things, and your Father knows that you need them. But seek his kingdom, and these things will be given to you as well" (Luke 12:29–31). Then I asked him how it felt to be part of God's plan, since he had given me the assignment that had brought us to Chicago.

King Jehoshaphat sent his officials throughout Judah to teach the word of God. Not only did it affect his own people: "The fear of the Lord fell on all the kingdoms of the lands surrounding Judah, so that they did not make war with Jehoshaphat" (2 Chronicles 17:10). Even the Philistines brought gifts to make peace.

It's hard to imagine our government sending its officials out to teach the Bible. But as I contemplated how wonderful that would be, I realized that you and I are officials of another kingdom, the kingdom of God, and we have been sent out by our King to teach His law to those we encounter. In fact, non-Christians are as affected by biblical values as Christians. And just as work has been given to me by some very unreligious people because they trust me, so can we, as a traveling business community, bring peace to our land by sharing our true hearts. People respond when they are told that work and money are secondary to the pursuit of God. They don't always understand it, but they always respect it.

Are you one of God's officials? Are you a teacher of God's Law? Can your witness make a difference in bringing peace and prosperity? Perhaps this will help you look at your next trip a little differently.

*April 16*
SECURITY COUNSEL

"... they came from every town ... to seek him."
(2 Chronicles 20:4)

Travelers: *The People of Judah*
**Read: 2 Chronicles 20:1-30**

What would it be like if Billy Graham became president of the United States? How would he deal with international crises as they arise?

In real life, our president is surrounded by military advisers and congressional leaders who keep abreast of each development in a crisis. It all goes on behind closed doors, especially in the early days, before the public is aware that something is wrong. When the crisis breaks into the open, American men and women are often put in harm's way to solve it. And as a nation, we begin to pray for their safety, usually with a feeling of insecurity and helplessness. Things feel out of control because the crisis is well along before we ever know about it.

The Bible offers a different model. When King Jehoshaphat was threatened by a major invasion, he "resolved to inquire of the Lord, and he proclaimed a fast for all Judah. The people of Judah came together to seek help from the Lord...." (2 Chronicles 20:3–4). Instead of political spin control and secret plotting of strategy, this king opened it up to the people to fast and pray. "All the men of Judah, with their wives and children and little ones, stood there before the Lord ... Then the Spirit of the Lord ... said, '... the battle is not yours, but God's'" (verses 13 and 15).

Imagine President Graham declaring a fast! Imagine people stopping where they are, or even coming to Washington, to pray with contrite hearts! Imagine our leaders on their knees in prayer. After a while, President Graham stands up and says, "I now have peace in my heart. Thank you for coming to pray with me. Here is how we will handle the crisis." Does that give you chills? It does to me!

Does this little dream bring to mind anything you'd like to know about the heart of our future leaders? Will they be brave enough to humble themselves? Are you willing to support them with fasting and prayer?

## April 17
### PROFIT . . . OR PROPHET?

"... the Lord sent prophets to the people to bring them back to him ..." (2 Chronicles 24:19)

Travelers: *Prophets*
**Read: 2 Chronicles 24:17–25**

The Old Testament is full of stories where God sent messengers—prophets—to warn the people that He was displeased. In the time of King Joash, God became extremely angry with Judah and Jerusalem because they had once again abandoned the faith of their fathers: "Although the Lord sent prophets to the people to bring them back to him, and though they testified against them, they would not listen" (2 Chronicles 24:19).

It's hard to imagine how those people could be so hard-hearted when they had true prophets of God shouting at them. How did those prophets look? Did they dress differently than other people, or was it what they said that set them apart? We do know that they were not welcome, and in some cases they were killed for their messages.

If we had that kind of easily recognizable prophet in our day, we'd listen, right? The problem is, God doesn't seem to make 'em that obvious anymore. Or does He? Martin Luther King comes to mind as a modern day prophet who preached nothing more than the love of Jesus Christ, and he was killed for it. Other modern prophets might include James Dobson. He is alive, but his opposition to the 1995 Beijing Women's Conference and other anti-family issues has made many enemies. His "stoning" has been more political than actual. And what about ex-coach Bill McCartney, the founder of the Promise Keepers men's' movement? His declaration, based on biblical truth, that homosexuality is an abomination of God raised howls of outrage. And that's just in America. In other countries, God's prophets face real death for telling the truth.

So maybe God's prophets are just as visible today as they were centuries ago. And maybe God is just as mad as He was then. As a nation, we certainly have refused to listen. We're too busy with TV and surfin' the net to pay attention.

How about you? As a business traveler, are you too busy making a profit? Think about this: Could it be you who God wants to be a prophet? Are you conducting yourself as God's emissary would?

## April 18
### HORTON OR HEZEKIAH?

"... and God heard them, for their prayer reached heaven ..."
(2 Chronicles 30:27)

Travelers: *Pilgrims to Jerusalem*
**Read: 2 Chronicles 30:13–27**

As individual travelers, we are scattered across the land, just as the Israelites were many times in their history. Many of us fear God as individuals, and our healthy respect for Him brings us a proper sense of priorities and usually some measure of success (compare King Jotham in 2 Chronicles 27:6). But just as the Israelites were not united as a nation, we operate as individuals, flung far and wide. We are not united in a single, powerful prayer to God for our nation. We know God hears our personal concerns and that He protects us as we go, but can He hear us as a nation?

When Hezekiah became King of Judah after the disastrous reign of his father Ahaz, he set about unifying Israel and Judah and restoring the Temple. He concluded his efforts with the grandest celebration of the Passover since the time of Solomon, an awesome two-week party! It was only when the entire nation had come together after decades of mutual hate that their unified prayer reached heaven, and God "healed the people" (2 Chronicles 30:20). Note carefully what God heard. Not millions of individual prayers, but a single unified prayer. Singular, not plural.

This reminds me of the children's book by Dr. Seuss, *Horton Hears a Who,* where it took every last citizen of Whoville, right down to the tiniest child, to shout loud enough to be heard by Horton. I believe, as does Bill McCartney, that God is waiting for a prayer of unity from us—all of us, especially within the Christian community. Until we truly reconcile and destroy all barriers between us, we will be just like Israel and Judah, perhaps even to the point of another civil war. We must celebrate what we have in common until ethnic, theological and other walls come tumbling down.

Are you part of that prayer as you travel? Do your actions unify or separate? Are you too busy to offer another "voice" along the way?

## *April 19*
A RING IN THE NOSE

". . . the Lord was moved by his entreaty . . ."
(2 Chronicles 33:13)

Traveler: *Manasseh*
Read: 2 Chronicles 33:1–14

Frequent travel can become frequent drudgery, especially if you repeat the same route, time after time. Once, I was required to stay in the same budget motel for three months straight, one of those units where every room is exactly the same. I swear the walls started to move in and the little window got smaller each day. I went through my daily routine as if I had a ring in my nose, pulled along like an ox in a stupor by an unseen task master.

It never occurred to me that my misery might have been caused by an angry God who wanted to shake me out of my lethargy as a believer. Was He trying to tell me that I had a responsibility to reflect His love and to act more like a Christian during this assignment?

King Manasseh paid no attention to God's warnings about breaking the law, so Manasseh was taken prisoner and bound with shackles; they even put a hook in his nose and led him to Babylon. Imagine the humiliation. But in his misery, he cried out to God and humbled himself before God. In an amazing turn-around, ". . . the Lord was moved by his entreaty . . ." (2 Chronicles 33:13) and delivered him back to Jerusalem and to his kingdom.

Manasseh was not a nice person! Yet God's love for his children is so strong that He can't wait to forgive us, if only we will humble ourselves before him and turn from evil.

I doubt you're as bad as Manasseh. I don't think I was quite that bad either. But are there really degrees of good and bad in God's eyes? No matter how big or small our distance from God, He wants only one thing: for us to humble ourselves before him and seek His face every day.

It's funny how the motel room looks bigger and brighter when we do!

## April 20
### REAL HELP

> ". . . I took courage and gathered leading men . . ."
> (Ezra 7:28)

**Traveler:** *Ezra*
**Read: Ezra 7:11–28**

In founding Oasis Hospitality International, I felt that "the hand of the Lord my God was on me" (Ezra 7:28). My first reaction was the same as Ezra — to gather some leading men around me for support and assistance. But as I write this devotion on September 3, 1995, almost two years after the founding of Oasis, something has been missing. Ezra has provided the answer today.

Venturing out in faith is tough. It's easy to say we'll rely on protection from the Lord, but in reality there are clear dangers along the way. Ezra found that relying on worldly protection can be embarrassing as well as quenching to the spirit of God's call: "I was ashamed to ask the king for soldiers and horsemen to protect us from enemies on the road, because we had told the king, 'The gracious hand of our God is on everyone who looks to him, but his great anger is against all who forsake him'" (Ezra 8:22). Can't you just feel Ezra's knees shaking? Can't you hear him thinking, "Oh, boy, here we are ready to set out on this great adventure, and I've given up all protection. We're dead meat."

But Ezra had a greater fear, which I too have underestimated over the past two years. That was his fear of God, if he didn't trust in His protection (see 2 Chronicles 15:2, for example). Ezra's response was immediate. The very next verse jumps off the page at me today: "So we fasted and petitioned our God about this . . ." (Ezra 8:23). Ezra realized that it's not just the people you gather around you, but how you collectively express total dependence on God. His answer came quickly: "The hand of our God was on us, and he protected us from enemies and bandits along the way" (Ezra 8:31).

I've worked with some great people in bringing Oasis this far. But we haven't fasted and petitioned God to show the way.

Is your prayer life a passing convenience, or a passionate communication?

## *April 21*
### NEW TOWN, NEW TASK

"So they began this good work."
(Nehemiah 2:18)

Traveler: *Nehemiah*
Read: Nehemiah 2:11–18

For many years I had the privilege of visiting hundreds of small towns across America. As a consultant working for small municipalities, I visited each town to perform a study or help with a problem of some kind. But I felt that knowing only the engineering aspects of the problem was not enough. I needed to know the people and how they felt about their town.

So before I made my first appearance at Town Hall or anywhere official, I would spend an hour or two just walking the main streets of the town. It was never clear to me why I did that. It just seemed that I was able to perform better when I had touched a little something within the town's soul.

Nehemiah had that same feeling. When God chose him to rebuild the wall of Jerusalem, he didn't just dive into the work blindly. He stayed three days, apparently getting to know the city. Then he surveyed the damage, cataloguing the work needed on each of the gates. Then, when he went to the officials to tell them why he had come, he had a sense of passion about the work: "You see the trouble we are in: Jerusalem lies in ruins, and its gates have been burned with fire. Come let us rebuild the wall of Jerusalem, and we will no longer be in disgrace" (Nehemiah 2:17).

Even though Nehemiah was really a visitor, since he had lived in exile in Babylon, he observed that the task involved them all. He didn't say, "You see the trouble you are in." He said, "You see the trouble *we* are in." That's the sign of a Christian business person adopting customers' problems as their own to help improve their quality of life. That's what made me a good consultant. Like Nehemiah, I went to those towns because God called me there, and that made me become part of them.

What work do you do? Do you take the time to make it God's work? Do you perform as God would have you perform? Do you care about the people you contact?

*Faith in Motion*

## *April 22*
### ODD JOBS

"... you have come ... for such a time as this?"
(Esther 4:14)

Traveler: *Esther*
Read: Esther 4:1–17

Have you ever wondered why God asked you to do the job you're doing? Whether it is a tough job and you're questioning your ability to hang in there, or it's mundane and you feel as if your life is being wasted, imagine how tough Esther's odd job was.

Esther was taken into King Xerxes' harem and had to please the king in every way. She must have wondered why God would put her through this. But she did her job so well that she became queen. As her "stock" rose in the king's court, however, her uncle Mordecai never let her forget who she was.

Later, Esther was in the right place to expose the conspiracy of Haman, who planned to execute all Jews. She had to risk her life by asking the king to stop Haman, without being summoned by the king first. So despite her high position, Esther had to decide how to prepare for this crisis. God had asked her to save her people.

Esther sent this message to her uncle: "Go, gather together all the Jews who are in Susa, and fast for me. Do not eat or drink for three days, night or day. I and my maids will fast as you do. When this is done, I will go to the king, even though it is against the law. And if I perish, I perish" (Esther 4:16).

That's how to prepare to do God's work if you're uncertain. Gather your people, fast with them and prepare to take on the task. God doesn't necessarily want you to perish, but only to be so dependent on Him that you put your welfare in His hands, in faith.

The theme of these Old Testament stories is total reliance on God's will and blessing. Time and time again, these heroes approached God with reverence and awe. Have we lost that? How might we apply it today? Who are the people you can count on to support you in this way?

## April 23
### SATAN ROAMS

"... roaming ... and going back and forth ..."
(Job 1:7)

**Traveler:** *Satan*
**Read: Job 1:1–12**

Satan is a frequent traveler. That puts us very close to him. And he has so much to chose from to use against us. If you have never done so, read *This Present Darkness* by Frank Peretti, to get an idea of Satan's tirelessness.

To tell the truth, I hated the story of Job until very recently. It's one thing to pray for God to protect me from evil. It's quite another to think that God might allow Satan free reign with everything I have. How could God do that? Yes, Job was up to the task, but am I? Are you?

The thought of Satan fluttering around me is depressing. In fact, as this is written I have been living through an adventure which only Satan could conjure. And at first I handled it very badly, probably worse than Job would have.

When we moved into a new home recently, the phone company cut off all three of my business lines and refused to restore them for several months. Without warning, they essentially put me out of business. This isn't as bad as what Job went through, but it certainly is a serious situation. The question is, "Did Satan attack, or did God allow this to happen?" Perhaps both!

In the early days of this crisis, I was extremely angry and depressed. I yelled at the phone company people every day, trying to convince them that my business was in jeopardy. Of course, I reached many more voice-mail touch-tone menus than actual human beings. But as the weeks passed, and as I came across the book of Job in writing devotions for you, I began to laugh. I had never before understood Job's experience nor why God would allow such a thing to happen. Now I understand completely. As long as I try to be captain of my own ship, I am vulnerable to Satan's roamings. Only when I learn to let go, even in a storm, and let God control the situation am I free of Satan, who cannot touch me without God's permission.

I have no idea when I'll get phones again. But this experience has made me a happier person. How's that for a transition?

*Faith in Motion*

## *April 24*
## FRIENDS OF JOB

"I am angry with you and your . . . friends . . ."
(Job 42:7)

**Travelers:** *Job's Friends*
**Read: Job 42:7–17**

There may actually be something worse than personally going through an experience like Job, who was tested by Satan, with God's permission. God was never angry with Job; in fact, God loved him intensely. But God hated what Job's friends did. It might have been worse to be Job's friend than to be Job himself, because God became very angry with Job's friends.

Job's friends gathered around during his trials and wanted to offer sympathy. But it came out as judgment, and it must have hurt Job deeply. Worse yet, Job's friends blamed everything on an angry God who must have judged Job for something he had done wrong. No one knew what that might have been, but their belief that God would do such things to his children ignored the immense love of God.

Our pastor and his wife, Bill and Jan Oudemolen, are among the most righteous people I have ever met. Yet God has allowed them to remain childless, a burden that is almost unbearable at times. Jan's health is sometimes frail, and I'm sure it would be easy in the midst of painful illness to ". . . curse God and die" (Job 2:9). Yet Bill and Jan remain faithful, not understanding why, but always trusting in God's plan.

As friends who love them dearly, we might be tempted to say things like, "God kept them childless so that our congregation could be their family." How crass! Imagine how that kind of comment hurts! We cannot know all God's purposes. Luckily, Bill and Jan pray for us just as Job prayed for his friends. Without those prayers we would be lost.

Whether trouble comes to you or to a friend, don't try to understand it intellectually. God wants you to accept it as part of His plan. In every case, you are far richer afterwards than you were before. And your understanding of what it means to be "rich" will be different than it was before.

## *April 25*
### COUNSEL OR COUNCIL?

"... like a tree planted by streams of water ..."
(Psalm 1:3)

Traveler: *Any Person Walking Through Life*
**Read: Psalm 1:1–6**

A "council" is any group of decision makers performing a task. Your church, your local amateur sports association and your business are all councils in a way. Wherever you go, you are probably involved in councils of various types.

But to receive "counsel" means to be given deep, serious advice on how to approach a problem. Seeking counsel means to approach someone wiser and ask what you should do.

So it seems inevitable that we will be involved in councils throughout our lives. But Psalm 1 is telling us that a council can turn into wicked counsel. If so, flee!

I walked and worked in the council of a company for fifteen years. I was even elected to serve on its managing council. It was a high honor, and I began to walk in the counsel of the senior members of that council, who had been involved for many years.

But I discovered that their counsel was humanistic, not fearing of God. The decisions they made were on behalf of their own financial well-being, putting many people out of work needlessly. They saw management as privilege. I saw it as service, as an advocate for feeding families.

> Blessed is the man who does not walk in the counsel of the wicked.... He is like a tree planted by streams of water, which yields its fruit in season and whose leaf does not wither. Whatever he does prospers. (Psalm 1:1,3)

In 1993, I began to realize that the "stream" which had nurtured my business growth for many years had become polluted. I began to wither in that council's counsel, and I did not prosper physically or spiritually. So I walked away from a huge income, virtually guaranteed employment and a fat retirement. I started over in the counsel of godly people.

Are your roots healthy? Are you prospering or withering? Does the counsel you walk in please God?

## *April 26*
HEAVYWEIGHT

"... you are a shield around me, O Lord ..."
(Psalm 3:3)

**Traveler:** *David*
**Read: Psalm 3:1–8**

Due to family commitments, our 1995 family vacation featured a drive from Colorado to New York to North Carolina and back to Colorado, almost 5,000 miles. Since our car had almost 90,000 miles on it, I decided to rent a car for the two week trip. A quiet prodding in my spirit led me to rent the biggest car I could find—a Cadillac Coup de Ville. Rental prices weren't that much more than for a smaller car, and we'd have more room to stretch out in as we went. I also felt that the car's size made it safer. It would provide a shield around us.

There is a better shield than a heavyweight Cadillac, and we took Him on our trip, too: "But you are a shield around me O Lord" (Psalm 3:3). The Psalm doesn't say God is like a shield. It says He *is* my shield. He goes on the road with me.

As we headed west from Asheville, North Carolina, for the long trip home, we knew from television reports that we were going to cross the path of Tropical Storm Erin, which was heading north from Louisiana. The encounter was consummated in Memphis. After twelve long hours of driving, I was tired. The storm reached its peak just as we approached the giant bridge on I-40, crossing the mighty Mississippi.

I have never seen it rain so hard. In snow it's called a whiteout. I guess in rain it's a washout. Cars were strewn everywhere along the highway, victims of "hydroplaning." But our heavyweight Caddy motored through the water without a hitch, because of its weight and advanced braking system, which was activated many times. It rained so hard that we never saw the river. But on the other side, the storm suddenly ended: "From the Lord comes deliverance" (Psalm 3:8).

God is a frequent traveler. He goes on the road with you. He is your shield, literally. A heavyweight.

## April 27
### TURN AROUND

> "Turn, O Lord, and deliver me . . ."
> (Psalm 6:4)

**Travelers:** *David's Enemies*
**Read: Psalm 6:1–10**

It's been eighteen months since I left my senior management post with a large firm. Although I left on my own, there was no question that I would have been run out of the company very soon. I could handle that.

What I couldn't handle well was the silent treatment I received from everyone, from partners to employees. No one said thank you for fifteen years of hard work. Not even a best wishes card arrived. Just silence.

At first my ego kept me going, along with the excitement of starting my own business. But after a year, I began to slip into depression. It just hurt so bad to receive no appreciation for having started a whole new business line and the millions of dollars of revenue it brought to the company. No one had rejected the profit. They just rejected me.

That's how David felt as he ran from his enemies: "My soul is in anguish. How long, O Lord, how long?" (Psalm 6:3). He did not doubt God. He knew he had to go through some difficult testing and he questioned whether God would finally deliver him. In faith, David knew that when the time was right, God would turn and smile on him.

Last week I had an unexpected call from an ex-employee I haven't heard from since I left the company. He said, "You know, I just realized that I never thanked you for all you did for me. You hired me, you trusted me, and you allowed me freedom. I never realized how valuable that was until you were gone. Thanks!" Oh, man, talk about deliverance. All I needed to know was that I had been a good leader. And God finally turned, after a long quiet spell to give me that comfort.

If you're fleeing from your enemies (and I hope you are) remember that God is not the enemy, even if he allows you to be tested in a time of loneliness. Wait for Him. Trust Him. He will deliver you: "All my enemies will be ashamed and dismayed; they will turn back in sudden disgrace" (Psalm 6:10).

## April 28
### STRUTTING HIS STUFF

"... keep us safe and protect us from such people forever."
(Psalm 12:7)

Traveler: *God*
**Read: Psalm 12:1–8**

In the mid-1980s, I had a client who was powerful and arrogant. He stepped on people for pleasure, especially women. No one dared suggest harassment; he was too scary to confront. This man could get anything he wanted by asking. There was always someone around anxious to make him happy and receive favors in return. He was the epitome of the psalmist's description: "The wicked freely strut about when what is vile is honored among men" (Psalm 12:8). He was the most vile man I ever met, yet he was honored by those around him.

I recently ran into this man when I returned to his city after ten years. I almost did not recognize him. Unshaven, glazed eyes, alcoholic, divorced, pathetic. Ten years younger than me, he looked much older. His house of cards had fallen and he had lost everything since I had last heard from him. Now he was a bouncer in a cheap bar.

The amazing thing is that I worked for this man for two years. I didn't just work for him; I was with him continuously, up close, too close. What I saw him do was appalling. But by the grace of God, I managed to avoid contamination. When he disappeared in New Orleans on a three-day binge, I could have gone along, but I was never less tempted in my life. He tried very hard to corrupt me, yet my ethics seemed to give him an anchor during the sober times.

What was it that protected me? God Himself, on the move: "'Because of the oppression of the weak and the groaning of the needy, I will now arise,' says the Lord" (Psalm 12:5).

Ours is an active God, anxious to protect us if we will let Him. He rises up and takes on the wicked. Sometimes his judgment is a long time in coming, but He judges nevertheless. When you feel totally isolated, as if "... the faithful have vanished from among men ..." (Psalm 12:1), remember that God is not sitting back watching.

He will arise and protect you.

## *April 29*
### OUR ULTIMATE DESTINATION

"Who may live on your holy hill?"
(Psalm 15:1)

**Travelers:** *Everyone*
**Read: Psalm 15:1–5**

Every one of us, not just business travelers, is on a journey toward the final destination of living with God. But not everyone will make it. Some of us will lose the directions we were given. We won't remember how to get there.

But God wrote a map and it's fairly easy to read. Carry the map with you, through life or through your business trip. It's called Psalm 15. That's the map.

What does it take to live on God's holy hill?

Walking blamelessly
   Doing what is righteous
      Speaking the truth
         Speaking no slander
            Doing no wrong to a neighbor
               Casting no slurs


Despising vile men
   Honoring those who fear the Lord
      Keeping the truth even when it hurts
         Lending money without usury
            Accepting no bribes against the innocent


"He who does these things will never be shaken" (Psalm 15:5).

## *April 30*
## THE PATH OF LIFE

"You have made known . . . the path"
(Psalm 16:11)

Traveler: *David*
**Read: Psalm 16:1–11**

There are two ways to tour Canyon de Chelly in northeastern Arizona. The tour operated by the U. S. Parks Service uses primarily college-educated, Anglo-American guides who point out the cliff dwellings and other historical points of interest from a geological perspective. But the tour run by the Navajo Nation offers an entirely different view. To the Navajo guide, the land is holy and the spirits of his people still reside where they were massacred by the U. S. Army a century ago. He takes tourists to places the "white" tour never goes. The experience in the canyon depends on the guide.

The path of the business traveler is as wide as the wing-span of a Boeing 747. It leads around the world to destinations both humble and exotic. It has no limits. It contains endless opportunities for good and for evil. The experience you have depends on which guide you choose. Wouldn't you rather have the Guide who addresses the spiritual realities and knows the special pathways?

Psalm 16 points out the path from a Godly perspective. First: "Apart from you I have no good thing" (verse 2). If it's not of God, forget it.

Second: ". . . the saints . . . in the land . . . are the glorious ones" (verse 3). Seek out godly people as you go. They are everywhere, but not always where you expect.

Third: "The sorrows of those will increase who run after other gods" (verse 4). Stay away from those who worship worldly things. Their trouble is only beginning, even though they seem so happy and successful.

Fourth: "The boundary lines have fallen for me in pleasant places" (verse 6). Stay within the limits of God's law; obedience is surprisingly enjoyable.

Fifth: "You have made known to me the path of life; you will fill me with joy in your presence, with eternal pleasures at your right hand" (verse 11). There is a path of eternal life along which God will guide you. Or, you can choose the path of death.

## May 1
## HIGH PLACES

"... he enables me to stand on the heights."
(Psalm 18:33)

**Traveler:** *David*
**Read: Psalm 18:1–36**

Recently, we moved from a home in a valley to a new residence just a mile away but a thousand feet higher up. At the old house, deer were our regular companions, coming down out of the hills for water from a nearby stream or for food during snowy weather. In the valley they were usually docile, quietly passing by at dawn or dusk. Rarely did they move quickly, only when something scared them. Even more rarely did antlered bucks venture that close to civilization.

At the new house, which is perched among giant red rocks and steep slopes, we see an entirely different side of the same deer. The valley is where they travel; the high places are where they live. One evening we saw a buck, a doe and two fawns frolicking on the hillside, chasing each other at blinding speed, bounding on all fours, oblivious to the steep slope and slippery rocks. What a contrast from their wary vigilance down in the valley.

As a business traveler, you go down to the valley for food and water, too. And you are always on the lookout for evil. When deer are frightened, they flee in a flash, because God gave the physical tools to do so. It's not so easy for you; often business travel puts you right in the middle of a tough situation. You need another form of protection.

King David identifies your protection in Psalm 18: "To the faithful you show yourself faithful, to the blameless you show yourself blameless, to the pure you show yourself pure, but to the crooked you show yourself shrewd. You save the humble but bring low those whose eyes are haughty ... with my God I can scale a wall" (Psalm 18:25–29). The tool God built into you for our protection is faith in Him. Only then are you saved from the dangers you encounter in the valley.

As soon as possible, read *Hinds Feet In High Places,* by Hannah Hurnard. It's based on this psalm and it will inspire you.

## May 2
### WHO IS THE ENEMY?

"I pursued my enemies . . . I crushed them . . ."
(Psalm 18:37–38)

Traveler: *David*
**Read: Psalm 18:37–50**

Reading the Old Testament can be tricky. Throughout these pages I have compared my business enemies to David's enemies or any of Israel's enemies. There is value in that, because we must know of God's strength in times of adversity.

But we can get carried away with that approach, too. In Psalm 18, David exults over God's deliverance of David from those who wanted to kill him: "I pursued my enemies . . . I crushed them . . ." (Psalm 18:37–38).

There is one very important distinction between David's experiences and ours. David lived hundreds of years before the birth of Jesus Christ. His accountability to God was very different than ours. David was required to fulfill the Law of Moses, and during the time covered by Psalm 18, he did just that. But Christ brought something more. When asked what the most important commandment was, Jesus replied, "The most important one . . . is this: 'Hear, O Israel, the Lord our God, the Lord is one. Love the Lord your God with all your heart and with all your soul and with all your mind and with all your strength.' The second is this: 'Love your neighbor as yourself.' There is no commandment greater than these" (Mark 12:29–31).

I would paraphrase that to say, "Love your business enemy as yourself." That's a standard David never had to meet. Loving your enemies that way means praying for them and loving them even when they hate you. It's easier to crush them than to love them. That's Christ's standard.

So who is the enemy? Satan! "Put on the full armor of God so that you can take your stand against the devil's schemes. For our struggle is not against flesh and blood, but against . . . the spiritual forces of evil in the heavenly realms" (Ephesians 6:5).

Your business enemies are not your enemies at all. They are potential members of your family. Jesus Christ calls you to take a stand against the devil, not to crush those who might suddenly see the light of God's love because of you!

## May 3
### THE GOOD SHEPHERD

"Surely goodness and love will follow me . . ."
(Psalm 23:6)

Traveler: *David*
Read: Psalm 23:1–6

One of the pleasures of writing these devotions as we walk through the Bible is the anticipation of coming across passages which are most familiar. Having squeezed special meaning for travelers out of so many stories, it's fascinating to stumble at last into familiar territory and see what new insight awaits there. Such is the case, for most of us, with Psalm 23. If you memorized it as a child, like I did, you may have never paused to think about it in the context of travel. I think you'll find that it is one of the best travel psalms.

- Travel can be tiring: "He makes me lie down in green pastures" (verse 2)
- Travel can be confusing: "He leads me beside quiet waters" (verse 2)
- Travel can be complicated: "He guides me in paths of righteousness" (verse 3)
- Travel can be scary: "I will fear no evil, for you are with me" (verse 4)
- Travel can require sacrifice: ". . . my cup overflows" (verse 5)
- Travel conflicts with home life: "I will dwell in the house of the Lord forever" (verse 6)

No matter what challenges travel brings your way, God is there, like a good shepherd, close by, watching over you, fixing each problem. The rewards for letting Him care for you are awesome: "I shall not be in want" (verse 1). "He restores my soul" (verse 3). "Goodness and love will follow me all the days of my life" (verse 6)

That's a pretty packed psalm for a little kids' verse, isn't it?

## May 4
### THE ULTIMATE ITINERARY

"Who may ascend the hill of the Lord?"
(Psalm 24:3)

Traveler: *David*
**Read: Psalm 24:1–10**

This one may not seem as familiar as Psalm 23, but to music lovers it is.

Chances are that when you make travel plans, you work with a travel agent. Or perhaps you make your own reservations through an on-line computer service. Eventually, every trip ends up with an itinerary which lists where you are going, how you will get there and where you will stay. Each trip is like a small slice of life. It has a birth, a finite life and an end point when you arrive home. But it all starts when you discover that you must go somewhere, and you plan out your itinerary carefully.

As I've said many times in this book, life is one long journey, too. Do you have an itinerary for this longer journey? Do you know where your final destination is? Do you know how you're going to get there? Do you know where you'll stay along the way, and when you will arrive?

My prayer is that your destination is the "hill of the Lord" (verse 3). Whether you are able to ascend it depends on how well you planned your itinerary. If you planned it according to Psalm 24, you may indeed stand with God: "He who has clean hands and a pure heart, who does not lift up his soul to an idol or swear by what is false . . . Such is the generation of those who seek him" (verses 4 and 6).

Now comes the familiar part. Assuming you have chosen the right itinerary, what will you see when you get there? Sit back, close your eyes and listen to Handel's Messiah: "Lift up your heads, O you gates; be lifted up, you ancient doors, that the King of glory may come in. Who is this King of glory? The Lord strong and mighty . . ." (verses 7,8).

Plan carefully. Jesus Himself waits to greet you on arrival! The ticket is cheap, too—one way.

## May 5
ARE YOU PERFECT?

"... though he stumble, he will not fall ..."
(Psalm 37:24)

**Traveler:** *David*
**Read: Psalm 37:18–40**

For a long time, I thought that, although I was not perfect, I was much closer to it than a murderer or a thief or a cheat. As a result, I really didn't understand how badly I needed Jesus Christ, who died for my sins. Truly evil people needed him worse than I did. Come on, I'm not that bad!

In fact, that's exactly what many Christian churches teach: "Jesus loves me, I'm not sad, for the Bible tells me I'm not bad. Little ones to him belong; they are weak and I'm not wrong." Okay, it's a stupid rhyme, but I was taught to rationalize scripture in the light of reason—human, flawed reason. It was many years before I could see how evil I really am.

Jesus said, "What comes out of a man is what makes him 'unclean.' For from within, out of men's hearts, come evil thoughts ..." (Mark 7:20–21) and every kind of evil action imaginable. In Jesus' list, slander, arrogance and folly are right there with sexual immorality, theft and murder. Evil is evil. There are no degrees. Oswald Chambers says, "... if we stand on our own rights and wisdom, at any second an eruption may occur in our personal lives, and we shall discover to our unutterable horror that what Jesus said is appallingly true."[4]

The key is not to get down on yourself, but to understand that Psalm 37 is for you, too, even if you haven't done some really bad things. You have still stumbled in the eyes of God; just admit it and give your situation to Him. Not only will the Lord uphold you with His hand and keep you from falling (verse 24): "He will make your righteousness shine like the dawn, the justice of your cause like the noonday sun" (verse 6).

What a promise! All you have to do is admit what God already knows.

## May 6
### SOLID ROCK

"... and gave me a firm place to stand."
(Psalm 40:2)

Traveler: *God*
Read: Psalm 40:1–17

An old friend called. I had not heard from him in two years. We had worked together very closely at one time, but we had drifted apart when I left the company. I could tell he had something on his mind. After some small talk, I simply asked him how he was, and he began to pour out his heart to me.

Business was bad and getting worse, he said. He wanted desperately to quit, but he couldn't because he still had three young children at home and needed to work until they go to college. Since he started his family fairly late in life, he will be in his sixties when that happens. Despite the fact that he is now on the Board of Directors and makes lots of money, it is never enough for his lifestyle. He is stuck and can't get out.

He said to me, "Boy, you're lucky. You've left the company. You don't have to work for anyone anymore. You're going to school, and you have your ministry for frequent travelers. You really know where your life is going. I sure wish I had that kind of direction."

If he only knew I have never worked harder in my life! If only he knew I put in more hours now than I ever did working in corporate America! But what he saw was my happiness. I wasn't complaining to him about my work, because I am doing it for the right reasons now. I am working for God, even when I am working for men.

I tried to explain that to him: "I waited patiently for the Lord; he turned to me and heard my cry. He lifted me out of the slimy pit, out of the mud and mire; he set my feet on a rock and gave me a firm place to stand" (verses 1, 2). My friend could not understand what religion had to do with it. Why would I make life decisions on any basis other than money? Yet he could see plainly that I was standing on a rock and he was mired in mud.

Are you standing or sinking?

## May 7
### CONFERENCE CALL

"When can I go and meet with God?"
(Psalm 42:2)

Traveler: *Sons of Korah*
**Read: Psalm 42:1–11**

My office window frames a rocky crag that towers hundreds of feet above. Whenever I am involved in a long telephone call, I lean back in my desk chair, prop my feet over the corner of the desk and look up the mountain slope as I talk and listen.

Yesterday, I was involved on a conference call with several associates on the east coast. We had been talking about a serious report we're writing together when I asked for a "time out." I was away from the phone for two or three minutes. When I returned, my friends wondered humorously whether I had answered nature's call for relief or nature's call for a donut (they know me very well).

But I told them, "I never left the room. In fact, I never put down the phone. I just wanted to watch a magnificent six-point buck moving down the mountain toward the stream below. That's the call of nature I answered." They thought it was very weird that I would interrupt serious business to watch a deer.

What my friends didn't understand is that my "call of nature" is really a "call of God." It is a thirst so strong that I will interrupt business to get just a sip of Him. That's what makes my days so enjoyable—the freedom to rest in Him even briefly: "As the deer pants for streams of water, so my soul pants for you O God. My soul thirsts for God, for the living God. When can I go and meet with God?" (Psalm 42:1–2).

When is the last time you had a conference call with God, during the day? Will you answer his call when He presents himself in a surprising, unplanned moment? Or does He need an appointment with your executive assistant? Go and meet with God today. You'll be amazed how your secondary business, that of making a living, will be suddenly revitalized.

## May 8
### THE TRUE PILOT

"... to him who rides the ancient skies above ..."
(Psalm 68:33)

Traveler: *God*
**Read: Psalm 68:1–20**

Rolling rumble. Free fall. Big bump. Pounding pulse. Nausea. Cold sweat. Arms numb. Heart attack?

No, panic attack. Even after twenty-five years and two million miles as a passenger, my deeply buried fear of flying had broken through. Moments later, I recovered. But I was humiliated.

Fear of flying may haunt you, too. You know that bad things can happen when you fly. And every thunderstorm reminds you about wind shear. But avoiding airplanes is not an option. Your job depends on travel, so you endure each turbulent down-draft in quiet desperation. The Apostle Paul had his "thorn in the flesh" (2 Corinthians 12:7). You and I have ours.

I confided in a close friend that a fear of flying was beginning to harm my health. He thought for a moment, put his hands on my shoulders and drawled, "You know all those buttons they put in the arm rest of your airplane seat? I've pushed every one of those li'l things 'til my fingertips were raw, and never once did I fly the airplane. All you get from those buttons is music." Then he looked into my soul and said, "Try trusting the pilot." The true Pilot.

Who really controls the sky? Not an airline pilot and not an air traffic controller. It is God. He is the one who "... makes the clouds his chariot and rides on the wings of the wind" (Psalm 104:3). It is God "who rides the ancient skies above, who thunders with mighty voice" (Psalm 68:33). Even those menacing "dark clouds [are] under his feet" (Psalm 18:9).

Now as I fly, the bounces and jolts are insignificant. I look out and see God's chariot in each cloud. And the same wind that transports God on His mighty missions lifts my plane and carries me home.

## May 9
### FRIDAY NIGHT FLIGHTS

"Your procession has come into view, O God . . ."
(Psalm 68:24)

Traveler: *God*
**Read: Psalm 68:24–35**

Trying to get home from a big city on a Friday night might be the most dehumanizing form of travel. Friday night flights might as well be the Friday night fights. People are often grumpy and rude, stressed out from long business meetings, traffic jams, security checks and overbooked aircraft. This, folks, is a mission field. How we act as Christians in this kind of situation can make the difference in someone's life. Our peacefulness and even joy during the Friday night crush can cause someone to take notice. Someone might wonder what we see that is so different from what they see.

Assuming you've experienced the kind of abuse I'm referring to here, I'll guess you'd agree that a sense of joy is often lacking. Wouldn't it be great if the experience could be turned into the Friday night procession? What if the airport looked like God's procession, rounding the security check point and heading down the concourse: "In front are the singers, after them the musicians; with them are the maidens playing tambourines. Praise God in the great congregation; praise the Lord in the assembly . . ." (Psalm 68:25–26).

Yeah, right.

But think again. To bring joy into a bad situation, God's procession doesn't have to look exactly like the one depicted by David. It can be one of attitude; wheat coexisting with chaff. It can be something you start, right there in your three-piece suit: "But thanks be to God, who always leads us in triumphal procession in Christ and through us spreads everywhere the fragrance of the knowledge of Him. For we are to God the aroma of Christ among those who are being saved and those who are perishing" (2 Corinthians 2:14–15).

If Friday night stinks, what kind of sweet fragrance can you offer? What kind of aroma can you waft through the area? A simple kindness to the most obnoxious traveler can fill the air with joy. And it can be multiplied into a parade as it is observed by others, the saved and the perishing alike.

# *May 10*
## FOOTPRINTS IN THE SAND

> ". . . though your footprints were not seen."
> (Psalm 77:19)

**Traveler:** *Asaph*
**Read: Psalm 77:1–20**

Some travelers' meditations are best borrowed from their original source. Such is the case of the poem "Footprints." It has become a beloved theme for paintings, needlework and other devotional tools:

> One night a man had a dream. He dreamed he was walking along the beach with the Lord.
>
> Scenes from his life flashed across the sky and he noticed two sets of footprints in the sand; one belonging to him and the other to the Lord.
>
> When the last scene of his life had flashed before him, he recalled that at the lowest and saddest times of his life there was only one set of footprints.
>
> Dismayed, he asked, "Lord, you said that once I decided to follow you, you'd walk with me all the way. Why, at the troublesome times of my life, the times I needed you most, would you leave me?"
>
> The Lord replied, "My precious, precious child, I love you and I would never, never leave you. During your times of trial and suffering when you saw only one set of footprints—That was when I carried you."[5]

I hope these words buoy your spirits today. When your trip seems unending and your work hardest, you are not alone: "Your path led through the sea, your way through the mighty waters, though your footprints were not seen" (Psalm 77:19). God is there leading and carrying you, whether or not you can see His footprints.

## May 11
## FOREIGN GOD

"... you shall not bow down to an alien God."
(Psalm 81:9)

**Travelers:** *The Israelites*
**Read: Psalm 81:1–16**

While considering this psalm of David's chief priest (see 1 Chronicles 16), I was traveling again to Connecticut. As the trip progressed, I tried to observe how many times I was delivered from evil. Or putting it the other way around, I watched how many times things went as planned. The airplane flights were safe, my hotel room was waiting for me when I arrived, my client liked my work very much (when he could have disliked it), the rental car company brought me a new set of keys within an hour after I lost the first set (how embarrassing!), and blessing of blessings, I did not catch the flu when everyone I encountered along the way was coughing and sneezing. Deliverance!

Asaph implies that we deprive ourselves of God's continuous blessing, even though we know that He is constantly rescuing us: "You shall have no foreign God among you.... But my people would not listen to me.... So I gave them over to their stubborn hearts...." (verses 9, 11, 12). That made me wonder: what kind of foreign gods am I tempted to follow? Just being aware of God's deliverance is not enough if I anger Him with divided loyalties.

Then I realized my foreign god is me! I spend most of my time worrying about my own comfort, my schedule, my budget, my appointments, my stuff! Even as I thought about deliverance on that last trip, it was all in the context of me. Is it any wonder that life is such a hassle? By focusing on me, I have allowed God to give me up "... to follow [my] own devices" (verse 12).

How about you? How often has God delivered you? Do you worship yourself? It's not too late to change. God's promises are awesome: "If my people would but listen to me ... how quickly I would subdue their enemies ... you would be fed with the finest of wheat; with honey from the rock I would satisfy you" (Psalm 81:13,16).

## May 12
### PILGRIMAGE

"They go from strength to strength . . ."
(Psalm 84:7)

Travelers: *People on Pilgrimage*
**Read: Psalm 84:1–12**

When I get several business trips lined up before me, covering several weeks in a row, I begin to dread them and to concentrate on all the things I will miss while I'm gone, like family activities, Bible studies with friends and sports events. My senses become dulled and I go into suspended animation, feeling less, so that I hurt less.

This kind of behavior is not only stupid, it's not biblical.

The question is, "Where am I going, anyway?" Or, "What is the purpose of my trip?" Since I'm so short-sighted, I answer with the obvious: the purpose of the trip is to call on a client or to work in a plant or to prepare a report. Strictly business. Get it over with as soon as possible so I can go home. Then, I'll be happy.

But God's purpose for my trip is different. He has an entirely different frame of reference. To God, my trip is only one short leg of a much longer journey, a pilgrimage to see God Himself. It's a matter of perspective, which is hard to master in the midst of a December East Coast swing.

The psalmist has the answer: "Blessed are those whose strength is in you, who have set their hearts on pilgrimage. As they pass through the Valley of Baca, they make it a place of springs; the autumn rains also cover it with pools. They go from strength to strength, till each appears before God . . ." (Psalm 84:5–7).

"Baca" could be translated either "weeping" or "balsam trees," and it was probably figuratively used for an arid stretch devoid of refreshment. It, too, was a matter of perpsective. Travelers chose to see in it springs, rains and pools, because their hearts were set on the bigger goal. They understood that their trip was only one small part of their pilgrimage that ends in the presence of God.

Do you focus on uncomfortable physical conditions you encounter along the way? Or do you transform them, going from strength to strength on your lifelong pilgrimage?

## May 13
## KNOW FEAR

"... that I may fear your name."
(Psalm 86:11)

**Traveler:** *David*
**Read: Psalm 86:1–17**

You've probably seen kids wearing tee shirts that proclaim in big letters, "No Fear." I'm just distant enough from that generation that I'm not sure where these shirts come from nor why some company thought they were cute enough to market. But I do know the effect they have.

Kids today are being taught that they make their own reality; that it's okay if something is right for them even if it's wrong for someone else. The only thing to fear is a narrow mind; anything goes. Life is a sport; just do it.

Fortunately, I get to see another group of kids who go to a Christian school and whom I have the honor of serving as their baseball coach. One of them wears a tee shirt inscribed with the words "Know Fear—Psalm 86:11." This kid is not a wimp. In fact, he's more macho than most kids. But he has his priorities in order. He has learned that when he fears God, *then* he fears nothing else, including bigger older kids on the opposing team. That kind of confidence is unstoppable.

I'm not sure most of us have learned that lesson. As adults, we see how tough the world is and we become fearful. There's just so much that can go wrong. But that's a sign of a divided heart: one part knowing God and one part fearing the world. King David knew this same feeling and he knew where to go to get it fixed—in prayer: "Teach me your way, O Lord, and I will walk in your truth; give me an undivided heart, that I may fear your name" (Psalm 86:11).

It's a paradox. Fear so that you won't fear. But asking God to undivide your heart solves the puzzle. An undivided fear of God yields an undivided confidence that God has overcome the world! And He has: "In this world you will have trouble. But take heart! I have overcome the world" (John 16:33).

Take (an undivided) heart!

## May 14
### TERROR OF THE NIGHT

"... no disaster will come near your tent."
(Psalm 91:10)

Traveler: *God*
**Read: Psalm 91:1–16**

These pages have chronicled the difficult departure I had from the engineering partnership to which I belonged. Writing these devotions has helped to heal me from the emotional damage I suffered. Through the love of God, my family and friends, I have tried to focus away from those trials and onto other important biblical lessons for travelers.

But I must return once more to that situation with a tragic epilogue. Just before I left the firm we elected a new managing partner. He was chosen because of his outstanding consulting skills, commitment to quality, outgoing personality, non-stop energy, all in a package of relative youth, which would carry the firm far into the future. In short, he had it all—a beautiful wife, family and home. The all-American boy.

I recently learned that at the peak of what the world calls a successful career, he killed himself. Checked out. Walked away. What a loss! Why?

I won't speculate as to how he came to the edge of his personal crisis, but I do know that he came to the brink of terror in the night and he could not face it. What makes it tougher is that he was a Christian. I'm comforted by that because, despite taking his own life, I believe God has forgiven him; he was a very good man and I understand what that company could do to people.

But what happened in the middle of the night? It seems clear that he did not dwell "... in the shelter of the Most High ..." nor "... rest in the shadow of the Almighty" (Psalm 91:1). Instead of avoiding "... the pestilence that stalks in the darkness ..." (verse 6), it took him. He had read these words but did not claim them. And disaster struck.

Read verses 9 through 16 now. Read them again. *Read them again!* Please don't give up when trouble comes! There is always another way to go under the protection of His wings! Walk away from that bad situation, but don't walk away from life!

"With long life will I satisfy him and show him my salvation" (verse 16).

## May 15
### LIKE JOSEPH

"... he sent a man before them ..."
(Psalm 105:17)

**Traveler:** *Joseph*
**Read: Psalm 105:1–45**

I never compared myself to Joseph until I read this psalm. Unlike Joseph, I was not the victim of treachery (Genesis 37), but I was sent into exile, traveling in strange places for a very long time. And like Joseph, I was blessed by "Pharaoh," that is, my non-believing clients who trusted my values and faith.

What I never considered before was the possibility that God sent me out before you frequent travelers, to prepare a way for you: "The Lord made his people very fruitful . . ." (Psalm 105:24). I didn't understand the assignment any more than Joseph did. But God's people—you travelers—are coming to where I have been, and I have tried to provide some measure of comfort across these pages. If Joseph had not spent years merging into Egyptian culture, he could never have helped them in their time of need. If I had not spent so many years traveling, I would not understand how you feel.

The beauty of this psalm, though, lies in what came after Joseph served God. It was God who delivered Joseph's people, who fed them during famine, who led them out of Egypt, who made them fruitful. Not Joseph.

Nor will it be me who makes you fruitful. It will be God. As He confronts you right now with realization of the blessings He has poured out on you, what do you think it means to be fruitful? To earn lots of money and move up the corporate ladder? To send your kids to the very best colleges? Perhaps that is part of God's blessing. But I think those things follow only after your recognition that God always remembers his people—always.

Reflect that knowledge of God "... with rejoicing ... with shouts of joy" (verse 43). It's in your joy, when no one else expects it, that God is truly honored. That's when you're the most fruitful.

## May 16
### GOOD NEWS, BAD NEWS

"He will have no fear of bad news . . ."
(Psalm 112:7)

Traveler: *"Good"*
**Read: Psalm 112:1–10**

You have heard the old line when someone says, "I have some good news and I have some bad news." You are probably more familiar with bad news than most people, because you so often get bad news about flight delays, usually in half-hour intervals. You know the routine: "Ladies and Gentlemen, the maintenance department is working on the aircraft and we will have more information in half an hour." Then another half hour, then another. Meanwhile, you're told not to leave the area because the plane could take off quite suddenly.

As soon as the airline employee begins such an announcement, you know it's bad news. Don't you just dread it? Wouldn't it be wonderful if we never had to dread bad news? Can you imagine being so "together" that nothing bothers you? Psalm 112 shows how.

It turns out that some travelers are not people. Some travelers are actually concepts: "Blessed is the man who fears the Lord, who finds great delight in his commands . . . Good will come to him who is generous and lends freely, who conducts his affairs with justice" (Psalm 112:1,5). So "good" actually "travels" and helps God's people. How does this happen?

When I get bad news of a flight delay, the last thing I think of is God and His commands; all I want to do is get out of Chicago! But this psalm suggests that if I concentrate on God, something good will happen. Not only will good come to me, there's more: "Surely he will never be shaken . . . He will have no fear of bad news; his heart is steadfast, trusting in the Lord" (verses 6 and 7).

Wow! Imagine being so consumed with God that bad news cannot cause fear! The psalm teaches that if something bad happens to a person consumed with God, it must be for good reason; trust and obey with a secure heart.

Can you do that? I'm sure going to try during my next trip or any time bad news comes!

## May 17
### REAL MEN DON'T

"For you, O Lord, have delivered . . . my feet from stumbling . . ." (Psalm 116:8)

Travelers: *You and I*
**Read: Psalm 116:1–19**

Real men don't ask for directions. Or so I am told, frequently. It's a common theme in comic pages and other sources of humor about modern life. To tell the truth, I've always been a little rankled by the derogatory tone used to criticize the natural competitiveness of men. Yes, we can make a game or a competition out of almost anything. And yes, we carry it too far all too frequently. But I have always been convinced that without some sense of adventure, our minds would go soft and we would become noncompetitive—as in incompetent.

Recently, I was given some bad directions to a school where my son was scheduled to play basketball. Although I was in the right neighborhood, I couldn't find the last cross street where the school was. It took every ounce of concentration to keep my bearings and get us to a main street where I *could* ask for directions. But while I was lost, I enjoyed the challenge just a little bit. Instead of criticizing me, my wife commended me for solving the problem with my built-in compass.

If I had not asked for directions at the right time, though, all my competitive instincts would have failed, and we would still be out there driving around. It's quite all right to enjoy a competitive challenge, but it's even more important to know when you're overmatched.

In Psalm 116, David shares how it feels to be totally overwhelmed. And he does the right thing: he pours out his heart to the very best direction Giver there is: "O Lord, save me!" (Psalm 116:4). And God gives directions that deliver the lost.

If you're feeling lost, and it's easy to feel that way in the midst of a long business trip, ask for directions. Real men—and real women—go to the Source of all knowledge. God keeps you from stumbling, so that you ". . . may walk before the Lord in the land of the living" (Psalm 116:9).

## May 18
CENTER PIECE

"What can man do to me?"
(Psalm 118:6)

Travelers: *You and I*
**Read: Psalm 118:1–29**

Suddenly the cash was gone and I had to borrow several thousand dollars to pay my business expenses. And that did not include my own salary, which I could not pay for the second month in a row. Failing business? It depends on how you look at it.

My business is totally dedicated to God. If it lives, it lives to God; if it dies, it dies to God (see Romans 14:8). Whether my business dies or survives, it belongs to God. So then how does God define success?

Oddly, the tougher my cash flow situation has become, the more confident I have become. That's because I believe God is teaching me to truly trust Him with daily decisions and not to think too far ahead. If I were rolling in money right now, I might be distracted by that success. If the business survives, there is no question that the glory will be His, not mine.

Psalm 118 says, "Open for me the gates of righteousness; I will enter and give thanks to the Lord . . . The stone the builders rejected has become the capstone; the Lord has done this, and it is marvelous in our eyes" (Psalm 118:19,22,23). I am trying to enter the gate of righteousness by giving thanks to the Lord for guiding me, no matter what happens. In total surrender to Him, I have placed God as the center piece in my company's foundation.

Even though this page is being written in a hotel room charged to a credit card with no cash to back it up, I trust that God will move those who owe me money to pay—soon. But having taken the time to set my priorities straight, it really doesn't matter what happens. "What can men do to me" (verse 6) if I fail financially? God will open another door.

Now I can cry with the psalmist, "O Lord, save us; O Lord, grant us success" (verse 25). And I know how God defines success. Do you?

## *May 19*
### MEMORIZE THIS

"How can a young man keep his way pure?"
(Psalm 119:9)

Travelers: *You and I*
**Read: Psalm 119:1–16**

You may not be young, and you may not be a man, but take the time to memorize this and you will never be without success as you travel:

How can a young man keep his way pure?
By living according to your word.

I seek you with all my heart;
do not let me stray from your commands.

I have hidden your word in my heart
that I might not sin against you.

Praise be to you, O Lord; teach me your decrees.
With my lips I recount all the laws that come from your mouth.

I rejoice in following your statutes as one rejoices in great riches.
I meditate on your precepts and consider your ways.

I delight in your decrees;
I will not neglect your word.

(Psalm 119: 9–16)

Take as many days as you need to memorize these priceless words. Then, get ready for a great adventure as we devote nine straight days to the most amazing psalm in the Bible.

## May 20
### GOD'S GROOVE

"I run in the path of your commands . . ."
(Psalm 119:32)

Travelers: *You and I*
**Read: Psalm 119:25–32**

Only a mechanical engineer could find a rubber belt conveyor inside this psalm. But that's the joy of writing this book. God is everywhere I go. And I look forward to the day when you start sending me *your* stories of God's presence as you travel and work.

Today, I visited a power plant in Florida, to look at a newly designed conveyor system. By "sandwiching" material between two rubber belts, the conveyor squeezes and presses its cargo so that it can go up a much steeper incline than a normal conveyor. This design results in smaller plants and reduced cost, because less steep conveyors take up much more space.

But all conveyors must be aligned properly. Have you ever tried to re-roll a roll of paper towels or gift wrapping paper (okay, toilet paper, too)? Rolling up a baseball infield tarpaulin is another example. It's hard to keep the material aligned on the roll. Conveyors are the same way. If not carefully aligned, they will gradually slide to one side of the pulley and either be torn up or slip off. It takes a very skilled technician to properly align a conveyor so it doesn't run off its pulleys.

Conveyors are just like us. If we are properly aligned by the Master Technician, we won't run off our guides: "I run in the path of your commands, for you have set my heart free" (Psalm 119:32). By running in the path of God's commands, it would seem that we lose our freedom. Not at all! By allowing ourselves to be properly controlled and aligned, our hearts are set free. There is no greater freedom.

Does your life become so hectic that you begin to feel out of control? Try thinking of yourself as a conveyor, running in a path set and aligned by God. Don't just run. Run in a groove, God's groove. And watch your heart soar up higher inclines than you could with your old design.

## May 21
### PLEASE DON'T SEND ME TO...

"I will speak of your statutes before kings..."
(Psalm 119:46)

**Travelers:** *You and I*
**Read: Psalm 119:41–48**

In giving my business to God to use as He wishes, surrendering financial matters is only part of the challenge. God may also *send* me where I don't want to go. If you've ever heard the Christian song "Please Don't Send Me To Africa," you know what I mean. As much as I have struggled while traveling across America all these years, I have dreaded even more the thought of going overseas. Yet that is exactly what God seems to be preparing me for, although my song may be "Please Don't Send Me To Chechnya." Parts of Africa don't sound as bad as other war-torn places!

Psalm 119 is amazing, because it seems to take us gradually to deeper and deeper levels to understand one simple truth: obeying God's commands. It becomes apparent that God expects our obedience in every situation, not just in convenient ones. Yesterday we looked at keeping on-track, maintaining alignment in the regular run. Today we look at the extraordinary. Not only must I get into God's groove every day; I must also be prepared when God takes me out of that groove for His purposes.

Right now I'm looking at business opportunities in Chechnya, El Salvador and Pakistan. That's enough to make your blood "Kurdle." (That's a very deep pun, hopefully not too irreverent for a devotion). It's scary. But Psalm 119 gives me the guidance I need to persevere. By following God's precepts I avoid looking like the "Ugly American." All cultures appreciate and respect a man of God. Like a smile, God's precepts are multi-cultural. Americans who honor God and family are respected everywhere. That's why I can "walk in freedom" (verse 45) when I do international work and why I can speak to kings without being "put to shame" (verse 46).

Focusing on God makes me much less afraid about where He will send me. Are you ready for what God has in store for you?

## *May 22*
## THE THEME OF YOUR SONG

"... the theme of my song wherever I lodge."
(Psalm 119:54)

Travelers: *You and I*
**Read: Psalm 119:49–64**

As this longest of psalms takes us ever deeper into understanding God's precepts, I am challenged, wondering what is "... the theme of my song wherever I lodge" (Psalm 119:54). Too often, I allow myself to become isolated, avoiding contact with other hotel guests. Isn't that an odd confession for one who founded a ministry to frequent travelers? I've talked to other Christian leaders who feel the same way. I'm so busy giving to people during the day; just let me alone for awhile. I'll use the time to pray and seek God and write devotions, just as I'm doing now.

But God seems to be saying something else in this part of Psalm 119: "I am a friend to all who fear you, to all who follow your precepts" (verse 63). Well, I am anything but a friend to people I encounter at the hotel. I just want to be alone. And God says that's bad. Perhaps I end up feeling so lonely because I have the wrong theme for my song.

There are so many ways I could be a good "citizen" of the place where I lodge. Instead of ordering room service, I could go to the restaurant frequently, or greet the housekeeping staff instead of ignoring them, or even tell the manager about Oasis Hospitality.

Last night, in response to this prodding, I went down to the hotel bar, a place I have doggedly avoided for a long time, because I once drowned my sorrows there. But as a disciple of Christ, I see it differently now. Immediately I was drawn to an African American brother who was obviously miserable. I encouraged him and listened to his problems.

Isn't that what Jesus Himself did? Didn't he reach the people where they were, even at the risk of being called a wine-bibber: "It is not the healthy who need a doctor, but the sick. I have not come to call the righteous, but sinners" (Mark 2:17). That was the theme of Jesus' song wherever He lodged, and I pray that it can become yours, too.

Be a friend.

## May 23
### SOAK AND SCRUB

"Before I was afflicted . . . now I obey . . ."
(Psalm 119:67)

**Travelers:** *You and I*
**Read: Psalm 119:65-80**

In the early 1980s I was traveling a great deal and hating it. As I have indicated before, I numbed some of the pain with alcohol. It was my own little medicine, a private affair. I wasn't an alcoholic, and no one would notice what I did by myself. Or so I thought until I took my annual physical.

Studying the results of blood tests, my doctor asked, "You don't drink much alcohol, do you?"

"No," I lied.

He said, "Great! Then I must congratulate you on all the exercise you must be getting! Your cholesterol is extremely low, and there's only two ways to do that: alcohol or exercise." He said it with such cheer that I'll never know whether he was a great actor, or I actually had him fooled.

That was the first indication that I had strayed too far. I was extremely fortunate to get this polite early warning before a more serious affliction came about. Immediately, I recognized the signal and ". . . now I obey your word" (verse 67). God used my affliction to teach me more about His precepts (see verse 68).

Are there places in your walk where you do not obey God's word entirely? Of course there are, because we are all imperfect. Take the time right now to soak yourself in Psalm 119 and find the places where God might allow affliction for the sake of deeper understanding of His word. But keep in mind that just soaking is not enough.

When I was a little boy, I thought just getting into the bath tub constituted taking a bath. But when I got out, the dirty places I had not scrubbed were more obvious than before I got in, and I was dispatched back quickly to do a more thorough job. Let this psalm be like that for you. Soak and scrub in the word until all the dirty places are washed clean.

# May 24
## UNFINISHED PRODUCT

"Though I am like a wineskin in the smoke . . ."
(Psalm 119:83)

Travelers: *You and I*
**Read: Psalm 119:81–104**

Have I reached the point yet where I think of nothing but God and His precepts? Not even close. I honestly cannot imagine being that good at it, until I die. How could I, with all the distractions of modern life? Maybe if I became a monk in Tibet, but not in the U. S. of A. How could this psalm demand such perfection?

The answer, of course, is that God does not expect me to be perfect: "To all perfection I see a limit; but your commands are boundless" (verse 96). No one can be perfect, but everyone can take comfort that God is perfection.

So where is the psalm leading us now? "Though I am like a wineskin in the smoke, I do not forget your decrees" (verse 83). A wineskin in the smoke is a wineskin that has not yet been fully prepared for use. It must be smoked to give it toughness and flexibility, so that it will last and protect the wine. If I am like a wineskin in the smoke, then I know I am not perfect, but I am being prepared for service. If the wine is the word of God, then I must go through a period of isolation and treatment before I am fit to carry that precious word to others.

What am I training for? "Let your compassion come to me that I may live . . ." (verse 77). I am as dead as the skin before smoking if God does not hang me in the smoke and patiently teach me His wisdom. But once I receive God's compassion, I can be the receptacle of that passion for giving to others: "May those who fear you turn to me, those who understand your statutes" (verse 79). Only in receiving God's grace can I pour it out to others.

Is the psalm preparing you, too?

## May 25
### WHEN LIGHT IS DARK

*"Your word is a lamp to my feet . . ."*
(Psalm 119:105)

Travelers: *You and I*
**Read: Psalm 119:105–128**

"Light has come into the world, but men loved darkness instead of light because their deeds were evil" (John 3:19). The Bible symbolizes evil as darkness; when we are saved by Jesus Christ, we come into His light. But how do we detect that which appears to be light but which is really darkness?

There are so many examples in daily life of true evil; it's not hard to see the darkness in such things as child abuse and violence. But what about other facets of modern life that don't seem so obviously evil? Much of modern life seems light: advances in medical science, Hubble telescope pictures that seem to affirm the infinity of God, improvements in the environment and so on.

I believe that God's good is happening right along side of Satan's evil in this world. But if I become infatuated with technology and allow it to set the course of my life, I have strayed off of God's path: "Your word is a lamp to my feet and a light for my path" (verse 105). It's not that all other things are bad; it's that I still need to look to God to determine my path. So light can become darkness if not used the right way.

Recently, I got up in the middle of the night to use the bathroom in my hotel room. This room was especially dark, and I had to turn on the bathroom light to see. But when I turned that light off, my eyes could not adjust quickly enough, and I whacked my shin on a cabinet, trying to feel my way back to the bed. The light was good when it was on, but it did not light my path back to the bed after I turned it off.

Are you blinded by modern light and bruising your shins as you feel your way? God's light is like moonlight. It may not seem bright at first when compared to the glare of civilization. But if you take the time to adjust your spiritual eyes to God's word, it lights your path clearly and beautifully, like the light of a full moon.

## May 26
### A DIFFERENT THORN

"... let no sin rule over me."
(Psalm 119:133)

Travelers: *You and I*
**Read: Psalm 119:129–152**

How can I ever convey the power of this psalm? Surely no other passage in the Bible addresses the same subject from so many perspectives! "Turn to me and have mercy on me, as you always do to those who love your name. Direct my footsteps according to your word; let no sin rule over me" (verses 132 and 133). Here we see the overpowering love of God, not to perfect people, but to those who fail. If we love His name, He turns to us, *always!*

If the study of this psalm has caused you to feel that you can never be good enough to receive this kind of love, consider the Apostle Paul. No one messed up more before he became a Christian, but after that he was nearly perfect, right? Wrong! "To keep me from becoming conceited because of these great revelations, there was given to me a thorn in my flesh, a messenger of Satan, to torment me. Three times I pleaded with the Lord to take it away from me. But he said to me, 'My grace is sufficient for you, for my power is made perfect in weakness" (2 Corinthians 12:7–8).

You'll never know exactly what Paul's thorn in the flesh was. And I believe God did not reveal it intentionally. I believe that Paul's thorn was your thorn and my thorn. Whatever plagues you today is no worse than what plagued Paul. And God says it's okay—not the sin, but the acknowledgment that the sin shows how weak you are. And in your weakness is God's perfection.

God's grace is sufficient for you! You don't have to be perfect! Just accept the fact that you are weak. If Paul could be weak, you can be weak. It's okay. In recognizing your weakness, no sin will ever again rule over you.

God's got it, not you.

## May 27
### AND IN CONCLUSION . . .

"Seek your servant . . ."
(Psalm 119:176)

Travelers: *You and I*
**Read: Psalm 119:153–176**

My first trip to a lake to go swimming was almost my last. I was only four years old, but I remember what happened that day very clearly.

The lake my parents chose to swim at was very nice, because it had a concrete bottom, much like a swimming pool. Beyond a rope at the "deep" end, the concrete ended and the mud bottom took over. But for little kids, the "shallow" end was good because it was easier to keep from slipping. The water was only about three feet deep at the shallow end, but then at the age of four, *I* was only about three feet deep. I remember straining to keep my head above water even as I waded in for the first time. I had a panicky feeling from the start, because my light body wanted to float in the water, which made it hard for me to maintain my balance.

My parents were nearby, but they couldn't watch me every second. The pool was very crowded, and people were jostling each other for swimming space. Suddenly, I was under water. Someone had dived into the water, creating a tidal wave that knocked me down. I couldn't breathe, and I couldn't stand back up. Then, a big, strong hand grabbed me by the neck and pulled me out, coughing and sputtering, but no worse for the wear. It was my father. He was watching more closely than I thought and saw me go under. What seemed like an eternity to me as I fought for air was really only a second or two. My father never lost sight of me and knew when I disappeared under the surface.

You have a Father who watches you just as diligently if you slip and fall. If you do not forget His commands, He will constantly seek you. He does not stand far off, hoping you figure out that you have strayed. He *seeks you out!* Doesn't that make you feel special? Isn't that a marvelous end to such a special psalm?

## May 28
### WHERE HELP COMES FROM

"... the Lord will watch over your coming and going..."
(Psalm 121:8)

Travelers: *You and I*
**Read: Psalm 121:1–8**

Chien Lee was both coming *and* going. He thought he was just going—on an airplane from Denver to Springfield, Missouri, that is. I was also going to Springfield that day—in Massachusetts. Here's how we ended up sitting next to each other.

I arrived at the Denver airport and learned that my flight was going to be an hour late. With a grudging shrug, I pulled out my Eugenia Price novel and hunkered down. A different flight was in the final stages of boarding at my gate, and several people rushed on at the last second, heading for Springfield, Missouri.

Later my plane arrived and I settled into my aisle seat. Just before the doors were closed, an Oriental man came rushing in and collapsed into the seat beside me. I was enjoying my book so much that I scarcely acknowledged him.

An hour after takeoff, my seat neighbor asked in a thick Chinese accent, "I from California. Never been Springfield before. What weather like?"

I answered hospitably, "New England is usually cool in the fall, but very pretty." He replied, "New England? Never heard Missouri called New England..."

Then it hit me. His flight from California had arrived late and he had missed his flight to Springfield, Missouri, the one I had watched depart. But as he ran up to the gate with a ticket for Springfield, no one had checked to see *which* Springfield, because our flight was indeed heading for Springfield. The poor man was on his way to Massachusetts instead of Missouri, and he was going to miss his mother's emergency surgery entirely. I tried to console him as best I could until we parted.

If you look to the airlines for help, you'll end up in the wrong city, like Chien Lee. If you look to the hills, or to nature in general, you'll end up in the wrong place, too. Psalm 121 tells you where to go for help: "My help comes from the Lord ... The Lord will keep you from all harm..." (Psalm 121:2, 7).

Are you looking in the right places?

## May 29
### ESCAPING THE SNARE

"We have escaped . . . Our help is in the name of the Lord . . ."
(Psalm 124:7–8)

Travelers: *You and I*
**Read: Psalm 124:1–8**

As the flight I mentioned yesterday descended into Springfield, I didn't notice how bad the weather was. I vaguely heard the pilot power up the engines and I noticed once when we took a big dip during final approach. But I was too busy comforting Mr. Lee to notice what was happening. It turns out that God was very busy comforting me.

Not until I left the airport terminal did I realize it was raining horizontally. A "Nor'easter" had struck and the wind was well above 60 miles per hour. That explained the screaming engines and the bumpy approach; I didn't give it another thought, until the next morning.

I turned on the news and learned that a jet landing just minutes after my plane had been caught in a down-draft, clipped trees and a radar tower and had barely made it down safely. There had been an engine fire, and all the passengers had to flee for safety, sliding down the chutes with bare feet into the teeth of the storm (shoes must come off in such an emergency). There, but by the grace of God, might have been I.

"If the Lord had not been on our side . . . the torrent would have swept over us, the raging waters would have swept us away" (Psalm 124:1,4,5). How amazing that I came to this psalm the day after that experience. God not only delivered me from a terrifying landing, but He chose to lead me to a place in His word that promises protection: "Our help is in the name of the Lord, the Maker of heaven and earth" (verse 8).

Indirectly, He is also the Maker of airplanes. At least the ones that are on Israel's side. He doesn't promise physical safety for every airplane. But He does promise that we will escape ". . . like a bird out of the fowler's snare . . ." (verse 7).

Are *you* on Israel's side?

## May 30
## SEEDS TO SOW

"Those who sow in tears will reap with songs of joy."
(Psalm 126:5)

Travelers: *You and I*
**Read: Psalm 126:1–6**

Consulting must be the ultimate profession for trusting God, especially when you're a small, upstart company with very little extra money in the bank. When a big assignment comes along and I work very hard, the financial compensation can be enjoyable. But for every great assignment, there's a period of drought and uncertainty. It can be very frightening not knowing when that next job will come. Big companies always use that time to do some marketing or research, so employees keep getting paid. In small companies, if there's no work, there's no pay.

As this is written, I've not had a paycheck in two months. Oddly, I'm drawing closer to God during this time, not farther away.

My friend and pastor Brian Boone recently preached a great sermon on the Lord's Prayer (Matthew 11:2–4). He observed that Jesus says, "Give us each day our daily bread" (verse 3), not "Give us each year our annual bread." Brian pointed out that when the Israelites received manna from heaven, they only received enough for one day at a time. In fact, when they tried to store it up, it rotted (Exodus 16:20). Today we are so taken up with strategic planning and long-term financial goals, we forget what the Lord taught us.

Consulting has been the perfect reminder. There are days when I think I should give up my own business and go back to work for a salary. If that's what God wants, I'll do it. But if God wants me out on the edge, demonstrating how to live by faith each day, that's what I must do.

Are you looking for your annual bread? Or are you out sowing in tears, not knowing where you find fulfillment? Remember, this is not just about physical food, but spiritual health as well: "He who goes out weeping, carrying seed to sow, will return with songs of joy, carrying sheaves with him" (Psalm 126:6).

What seeds are you carrying to sow as you travel? If they're God's seeds, you'll be returning with songs of joy!

## May 31
### SPIRITUAL AERODYNAMICS

"... your right hand will hold me fast."
(Psalm 139:10)

Travelers: *You and I*
**Read: Psalm 139:1-24**

It's a bleak December dawn in Connecticut. Even before I open the drapes of my hotel room, I know a storm has blown in during the night. I can hear the wind whistling through the inadequate heater which can't overpower the chill.

Peeking out, I am greeted by low, gray scudding clouds. The world seems asleep, even dead, any semblance of green long gone. I think the world may be hiding from this morning. I wish I could.

Across the parking lot is a group of trees, stripped bare by the season. At the very top of the tallest tree is a large bird, probably a hawk. Supporting him is a fragile branch whipping in the gale. The hawk moves with it, swinging wildly from side to side, maybe ten feet each way. I can't imagine what it would be like to be at the top of that tree in this storm.

But the hawk is perfectly serene. While his lower body adjusts automatically to the swinging motion, his head remains almost perfectly still, able to spot his prey far below. No wonder the eagle became our national symbol of power and strength!

The hawk seems to have the confidence that someone cares about him: "You discern my going out and my lying down . . . you hem me in . . . where can I flee from your presence . . . If I rise on the wings of the dawn, if I settle on the far side of the sea, even there your hand will guide me, your right hand will hold me fast" (Psalm 139:3,5,7,9–10).

Perhaps you need to renew that kind of confidence before you go out today. Psalm 139 seems specially aimed at travelers. Take time right now to read it three times aloud, slowly. Let the words sink in. Feel the peace of God flow over you with perfect spiritual aerodynamics. Be as attuned to His care for you as the hawk is to its prey in a gale. You are even more ". . . fearfully and wonderfully made" (verse 14) than the hawk!

## *June 1*
## DYING OF THIRST

"Show me the way I should go, for to you I lift up my soul."
(Psalm 143:8)

Travelers: *You and I*
**Read: Psalm 143:1–12**

Recently, I flew from West Palm Beach, Florida to Atlanta and then from Atlanta to Chicago. I was in the air, including an air traffic control slowdown, for over five hours, from seven o'clock in the morning until after noon. I had checked out of the hotel before the restaurant opened, assuming breakfast would be served on the plane. I had forgotten I was living in the 1990s! When I asked about food on the second flight, the attendant replied rudely, "This is the new order, buddy. Bring your own food." By the time I got off the plane in Chicago, late for my meeting because of the air traffic delay, I was not only starving, but extremely thirsty. I should have planned better.

As we go through our daily chores, especially when we're away from home, do we need to plan better to bring along spiritual food? Even if we take along our Bibles, do we really seek the Holy Spirit to guide us every step of the way? No. Most of us are too distracted.

Oswald Chambers, in his devotional book *Daily Thoughts for Disciples*, (Discovery House, 1994) for December 15 calls this kind of living "ante-pentecostal," where the prefix "ante" is Latin for "before": "We think ante-pentecostal thoughts, the Holy Spirit is not a living factor in our thinking; we have only a vague impression that He is here." That is so true—we know about the Holy Spirit but we don't act like He is with us.

As a result, we are like David, feeling lost and seeking the right way to go: ". . . no one living is righteous before you . . . I spread out my hands to you; my soul thirsts for you like a parched land" (Psalm 143:2,6).

Do you feel spiritually thirsty? It's because you're human. Plan to take some water with you next time—water the world can't provide you. Take along the water of Jesus Christ: ". . . streams of living water will flow from within" (John 7:38).

## June 2
### THE BEGINNING OF WISDOM

"...let's swallow them alive..."
(Proverbs 1:12)

Travelers: *You and I*
**Read: Proverbs 1:1–33**

In the months that followed my departure from my old company, I received numerous phone calls testing the waters for potential legal action against that company. The temptation toward revenge was enticing. An age discrimination suit would have been easy, whether or not the company actually acted illegally. Sympathetic juries are common.

Enticement is everywhere in modern business. For the quick-thinking, computer-savvy and market-smart, there is always a big deal to do, another company to buy, a competitor to gobble-up. This is not to say that doing business is bad, or that we should not compete in a free market. But this first proverb tests our motives: are we out to innovate products and services which improve the quality of life for God's people, or do we simply want to be the biggest fish in the pond? How easy is it for us to be enticed for reasons which are unwise and do not honor God?

The language of this proverb can still be heard in business circles today: "Let's lie in wait...waylay some harmless soul...swallow them alive...get all sorts of valuable things... fill our houses...share a common purse" (Proverbs 1:11–14). Do you like the smell of business blood? Do you love the thrill of the hunt? Do you tingle when a competitor makes a mistake and you close in for the kill? If so, consider God's view.

God says "...their feet rush into sin...lie in wait for their own blood...waylay only themselves..." (verses 16, 18). Worst of all, everyone else can see what they are up to: "How useless to spread a net in full view of all the birds!" (verse 17). Those who would entice you into a quick kill might actually succeed for a short while, but: "Such is the end of all who go after ill-gotten gain; it takes away the lives of those who get it" (verse 19).

If you feel enticed as you travel through life, step back and ask how God would view the opportunity. There's nothing wrong with a good profit, unless it comes from greed and ill-will. Examine your motives each day and fear God (verse 7) as you go. That's the beginning of wisdom.

## *June 3*
## DREAMER OR SCHEMER?

"... lean not on your own understanding ..."
(Proverbs 3:5)

Travelers: *You and I*
Read: Proverbs 3:1–6

I'm a dreamer. On my good days, I believe God made me that way; I get some really great ideas for businesses and ministries. But on other days, I feel that all I do is dream and never accomplish anything concrete and worthwhile. On good days, I see God in all I do; on bad days, I see only me.

For over twenty years I have had a burden to create a product that would eliminate the ugly black smoke and smell from diesel engines. Actually this desire goes back over forty years, to my childhood in Cleveland, Ohio, where fresh fallen snow turned black overnight from dirty air. In my adult years in Denver, Colorado, I have watched air quality deteriorate, because of the huge truck and train fleets which are so vital to commerce in the West.

But every time I try to design the idea I've had, I begin to feel foolish for having such a grand scheme. My confidence wanes, and I postpone it a little longer. Am I the one who does the postponing? Or is it not yet time according to God's plan for me?

Not long ago I felt frustration over this uncertainty. No more: "Trust in the Lord with all your heart and lean not on your own understanding; in all your ways acknowledge him, and he will make your paths straight" (Proverbs 3:5–6). The proverb doesn't say to think about God when it's convenient, just on my good days, but with my entire being. That includes times when I may not understand what God is doing. But when I trust Him completely, then my paths will become straight.

It could be that God wants me to keep consulting and traveling until I finish this book. Then perhaps He wants me to create an air pollution control device. Or maybe something else I haven't even dreamed of yet. Instead of feeling frustrated, now I feel liberated!

Are you leaning on your own understanding of things or God's?

## June 4
### SOURCE OF WISDOM

"Do not be wise in your own eyes..."
(Proverbs 3:7)

Travelers: *You and I*
**Read: Proverbs 3:7–18**

If this Proverb is true, then I'm off to a very good start. Because I don't feel very smart when it comes to building a business. I'm a good consultant in my own special way, but what I seem to know the most is how little I know.

Setting up accounting systems, marketing and especially finance overwhelms me. Should I borrow money or not? Does God want me to grow a big business? How will I ever learn enough in the information explosion age to compete? From a business perspective, I am certainly not wise in my own eyes. Where do I start?

Proverbs 3 gives me all the information I need: ". . . fear the Lord . . . shun evil . . . honor the Lord with your wealth . . . do not despise the Lord's discipline . . . blessed is the man who finds wisdom . . . her ways are pleasant ways, and all her paths are peace" (Proverbs 3:7,9,11,13,17).

So I've started well by fearing the Lord, shunning evil and honoring Him with my tithe. Nor have I despised Him for His discipline. But now I must ask, "What is wisdom?" Am I pursuing it? What can I do to find it? Go back to school?

I know that wisdom, as perceived by the world, is academic education and computer literacy. But I'm just not sure about wisdom on the Internet! There is, of course, tremendous information available in cyberspace today. Is that wisdom? Or is raw information to wisdom what noise is to music? A recent letter to the editor in *Newsweek* lamented, "I pity the next generation, who will never know the joy of curling up by a warm fire with a classic novel." Instead, their eyeballs will pop with the visual stimulation of the latest CD. That's not wisdom.

What does wisdom mean to you? Does it start with God? And where does He send you to get it? Will you go? If you're not feeling at peace, the proverb suggests you haven't found it yet. Take some time right now and read the book of Proverbs. It's about wisdom and much more. And ask yourself what it would take to find the kind of peace that wisdom brings.

## June 5
### MORE ON WISDOM

"Then you will go on your way in safety, and your foot will not stumble . . ." (Proverbs 3:23)

Travelers: *You and I*
**Read: Proverbs 3:19–35**

Proverbs 3 may be one of the richest passages in the entire Bible, right up there with Psalm 119. Yesterday I asked, "What is wisdom?" Today, the proverb answers: "My son, preserve sound judgment and discernment, do not let them out of your sight . . ." (Proverbs 3:21). Judgment and discernment. What are they? I think sound judgment and discernment both have to do with considering the consequences before acting. A big part of that is prayer, including God in the decision-making process.

When I founded my own business, I found that the days were long and the work hard. I had no regrets, because I truly enjoyed working for God as my boss. But I also knew that if my partner Bob could join me in the business, maybe I'd get a day off or even a vacation at some point.

It would have been easy to borrow money and bring Bob right on board. But Bob didn't have clients who would give him work automatically like I did. By sitting down and estimating how long we could carry Bob on salary without his bringing in any work, we quickly realized that we'd be broke in a matter of weeks. We considered the consequences and decided to wait until a good paying assignment came along.

It was eighteen long months. And it seemed to us as if it would never happen. But God was part of our daily waiting process, and finally the assignment came and Bob was able to join the company—profitably.

That's sound judgment and discernment. They are not easy to practice. But the proverb tells us how to know when we are exercising them correctly: ". . . when you lie down, you will not be afraid . . . your sleep will be sweet" (verse 24).

Ah, sweet sleep! How's yours today? If it's pretty restless, consider asking God to show you the areas where you're not showing sound judgment and discernment. Ask Him right now. And sleep good tonight.

## June 6
## LINDA'S JOY

*". . . like the first gleam of dawn, shining ever brighter . . ."*
(Proverbs 4:18)

Travelers: *The Righteous*
**Read: Proverbs 4:1–27**

It was a day full of apprehension, full of unknowns: Orientation Day at the University of Northern Colorado (UNC). The day had finally come to set my daughter free. And to make matters worse, I hated conducted tours of any kind. But I had to endure a tour of the campus, as a good dad.

From the moment she entered the room, our tour guide was different than others. She simply lit the place up with boundless enthusiasm and *joy!* In fact, that was her middle name—Linda Joy Warriner. Out of the hundreds of student tour guides we could have drawn, we were given Linda Joy, who erased my apprehensions in about ten seconds. As we walked, she had us laughing and joking as if we had known each other for years. And despite the fact that UNC is a state school, Linda Joy let us know the secret of her joy—she was a Christian.

Our daughter went on to great success at UNC, and I almost forgot that wonderful orientation day, until a new teacher showed up at my son's Christian school three years later. Irony of ironies, it was Linda Joy! Even more peculiar, she became the spiritual advisor for my son's sophomore class. Now both my kids have been blessed by one whose path ". . . is like the first gleam of dawn, shining ever brighter till the full light of day" (Proverbs 4:18).

Take a minute and think of someone in your life who lights up a room like Linda Joy. I don't mean just from physical beauty, but because of his or her path of righteousness.

Now ask yourself how people react when you enter a room. If the daily worries of the world drag you down, you probably reflect that countenance to others. But deep inside is the joy of righteousness, waiting to be released like the dawn. Take time right now to ask God to dust you off. Ask Him to forgive you for whatever causes you to absorb light instead of reflect it. And don't be surprised tomorrow when someone says, "Wow! What happened to you? You look radiant today!"

## June 7
### WALKING WITH INTEGRITY

> "... but he who takes crooked paths will be found out."
> (Proverbs 10:9)

**Travelers:** *You and I*
**Read: Proverbs 10:1–14**

I was vulnerable and everyone knew it. Having just moved to a new state to conduct a construction project, I bought a new home in that state, and retained my home in Colorado. The last thing I could afford was to get fired early in the assignment and be stuck with two homes and no job. That's exactly what they threatened.

My client was an agency of the state government, and I arrived just before a gubernatorial election. The race was close, and the incumbent was scrambling for survival. He needed money, and he had the organization—big party politics—to get it. The call went out for a $2,500 plate dinner to honor the governor, and everyone who was anyone was expected to attend, that is, donate.

All the other consultants working there advised me that if I wanted to stay, I'd better ante up. If I didn't, the governor would make a clean sweep, and I'd be gone before I ever got started. Even my own company's management thought it was a good idea. I refused. If I was going to go down, it would not be by intimidation from a big, political machine. And what if the incumbent lost? Better to work hard and stay clean: "The man of integrity walks securely, but he who takes crooked paths will be found out" (Proverbs 10:9).

That fall, the incumbent won, narrowly, and life went on. Nothing bad happened to me because of my failure to contribute, and my work became extremely valuable to the client. But the next year, an investigative reporter for the local paper started a series of articles on campaign contributions to the governor. He uncovered a whole series of illegal contributions. Among them were every major consulting company working for the state at that time, except one—my company.

Ten years later, I am the only one of the original group still working for that client. New governors have come and gone, but they still retain me for my expertise.

God's travel words give you a better perspective for decision-making, don't they?

*Faith in Motion*

## *June 8*
### EXPECTING FAILURE

"What the wicked dreads will overtake him..."
(Proverbs 10:24)

Travelers: *You and I*
Read: Proverbs 10:15–32

For many years I worked for a man who expected everyone around him to fail, and they usually did. His master was the dollar and his only goal was to be independently wealthy. He openly flaunted each new purchase—boats, homes, cars—and then convinced each person working for him that if he failed, he would lose his wealth. But his fear of losing wealth led to losing almost everything else—family, friends and colleagues.

I have often wondered how many people die of illnesses they expect to contract. The mind has tremendous power over the body, and I would guess that we can invite our own demise by worrying about something until it actually happens that way.

I never thought of that as being wicked, but God says it is: "What the wicked dreads will overtake him; what the righteous desire will be granted" (Proverbs 10:24). The difference is fear versus faith.

Do you fear illness or failure or perhaps something else that is too private to say aloud? If so, that very thing can be heard rumbling toward you from behind, like an avalanche thundering down a steep mountain slope; you cannot outrun it. But have you tried giving those fears to God? Can you turn your fear into *desire* for God's deliverance?

As this is written, my business is undergoing a severe challenge. I fear that it is going to fail, and yesterday I expressed that fear to my family instead of declaring my faith that God will work it out. I missed an opportunity, and I infected those closest to me with fear. Nice going! Today I must rectify that.

Are you wicked or righteous? How do you know the difference? By how you respond to the challenges that come your way. If you respond in fear, as I did, God is not pleased. But if you respond in faith, transforming that fear into faith that God will grant your wish, it will be granted.

Then nothing but God's love will overtake you.

## June 9
### PEER PRESSURE

"... but a companion of fools suffers harm."
(Proverbs 13:20)

Travelers: *You and I*
Read: Proverbs 13:1–25

We were freshmen in high school, all six of us. We had grown up together on the same street and now we were in high school together. We were cool.

Every Monday night we all walked up the street to the school to attend "Key Club," a youth organization sponsored by Kiwanis International. Unfortunately, as much as we learned during those meetings about community involvement, our conduct outside was less than respectable.

Our favorite activity was long-range snow-ball-throwing, at any target far enough away to make it a challenge. If the target was moving, all the better. Hidden by a big bush in front of the school, we could fire at unsuspecting vehicles, much like a quarterback leading a wide receiver with a long pass. These were innocent snowballs, with no stones in them.

Usually when a car was hit, the brake lights came on momentarily, but the startled driver would quickly move on, not knowing the source of the loud *thump*. One night, after a spectacular hit on a taxi, the target actually stopped in the road for a few moments. We cowered behind the bush until the taxi moved on.

A few minutes later it was time to go home. As we emerged from our cover, there was the taxi, waiting for us. In panic, we headed for the back alleys. But every time we emerged onto a street, he was there! Finally he cornered us, jumped out of the cab and came at us with a knife. He stopped only when he realized that there were six of us. Screaming that he'd kill anyone who nailed him again, he left.

Our snowball-throwing ended forever that night. We had each been a "... companion of fools" (Proverbs 13:20) and we knew we had almost "... suffered harm" (same verse).

Are there times when you've been a companion of fools? Did you grow up before you suffered harm? Today, focus on the bright side of this proverb: "He who walks with the wise grows wise ..." (same verse). With whom do you walk?

## June 10
### INTERNET ANONYMOUS

"A simple man believes anything..."
(Proverbs 14:15)

Travelers: *You and I*
**Read: Proverbs 14:1–35**

Most people know about Alcoholics Anonymous, an organization for alcoholics. And we know of many other addictions: nicotine, sex, sports. But Internet Anonymous hasn't started up yet. It will.

It astounds me how people jump into the latest fads without thinking about the potential cost. Our society must be desperate for entertainment. We'll even max out our credit cards if necessary to be involved in a fad. But a proverb offers warning to all who would jump in with both feet: "A simple man believes anything, but a prudent man gives thought to his steps" (Proverbs 14:15). What does it mean to be prudent?

When video games first came out, my kids begged me to have their own. But I took a watchful pose until I saw how other kids were reacting to them. The result? Every kid I knew who got a video game became addicted to it. They wanted to do nothing but play video games. If my kids were invited over to play, all they played was video games. Which of course made my kids want them even more.

Finally, when we thought our son was old enough, we bought him one game. He couldn't put it down. Until he had the game mastered and he became a little bored with it, he would sneak chances to play it, even when his time-limit had expired. And that was only one game! But at least we had learned beforehand the dangers of video games and had some rules in place to manage by. That's being prudent.

There are so many choices in life where you can be simple and believe that the world offers no consequences to a new fad, or you can be prudent and think about the potential drawbacks. The latest example is the Internet. Are you diving in head first, to get all that information out there in cyberspace? Or are you wondering, as I am, where all this will lead? I'm not saying it's bad. Just think it through. Be prudent.

## June 11
### UPWARD PATH

"... to keep him from going down to the grave."
(Proverbs 15:24)

Travelers: *You and I*
**Read: Proverbs 15:1–33**

One of the great frustrations during my many years of business travel was my inability to pursue additional education. Over the years, I have had a burning desire to go back to school. Whether to get a master's in engineering, study theology or even just learn the arts, it doesn't matter. That unfulfilled desire has been there for almost three decades. Travel and business schedules made it impossible.

But if I can find the time to write this book, there must be a way. And now there is. Yesterday I wrote about being prudent with technology. Today I must balance that with awe for the university extension programs that are being done by video tape. What a wonder! I can't carry a video machine around with me when I travel, but I could certainly take courses for consumption when I'm home. But will I? Apparently I no longer have an excuse!

How does my path of life look? Flat, leading from one airport to another? Or upward, finding creative ways to learn? "The path of life leads upward for the wise to keep him from going down to the grave" (Proverbs 15:24). Frankly, it's been pretty flat, and I can see my skills eroding in an increasingly competitive world. That's not very wise.

How can you make your path of life lead upward? Start with reading your Bible every day, first thing. It alone gives you a thirst for wisdom and knowledge. What else can you be reading as you travel? Is it the latest Harlequin romance or Tom Clancy novel? Or can you develop a reading program that really takes you up the incline to greater wisdom? How about an extension degree program? The sheepskin itself may not be so important. What counts is the rigor of a program that stretches your mind—upward.

A program that keeps you out of the grave.

## June 12
### ARE YOU SURE THIS IS THE WAY?

"... nor to be hasty and miss the way."
(Proverbs 19:2)

Travelers: *You and I*
**Read: Proverbs 19:1–29**

Too bad I didn't read this proverb before setting out that day in 1965: "It is not good to have zeal without knowledge, nor to be hasty and miss the way" (Proverbs 19:2).

I had plenty of zeal for being with Sue that day. We had met that summer at church youth camp, and this was our first real date, driving to downtown Cleveland for a youth leaders' meeting. How hard could it be to drive ten miles or so from the suburbs into the city?

At that time, the Interstate Highway system was fairly new and freeways were not yet a common fact of life, especially to a 16-year old with a new drivers license. No one in my family knew much about freeways either, so there was no coaching before I left.

As we headed out in my shiny, high-riding '53 Plymouth, I was with my gal, and the road was not what I noticed. When we came to the freeway interchange from I-271 to I-90, I took the exit ramp deftly, without paying much attention. We drove. We talked. And talked. Our zeal for being together exceeded our knowledge.

After an hour or so, Sue wondered when we might arrive, because it was almost time for the meeting to start. Right then, I spotted a mileage sign: "Erie 10." Erie! Pennsylvania? I had taken the exit ramp to I-90 East, not I-90 West, and we were now about 80 miles away from our destination!

As a veteran traveler, you know the perils of hastiness and of not having the right directions to guide you. But how about in your personal life? Are you proceeding with zeal or knowledge? What is the way you are trying to follow? Don't miss The Way, God's way.

By the way, we arrived two hours late to the meeting. But Sue married me anyway.

## June 13
### WHERE IS GOD?

"How then can anyone understand his own way?"
(Proverbs 20:24)

Travelers: *You and I*
Read: **Proverbs 20:1–30**

Knowledge *about* God is different than *knowing* God. The former represents so many people I know who call themselves Christians. When a crisis comes into their lives, they end up asking, "How could a loving God do this to me?" So many churches teach the Bible like a text book, not a relationship book.

My friend Bill lost his important job with a giant aerospace company a few years ago. He was devastated and went into deep depression. I tried to help him through it by sharing meals frequently and just being there for him. Eventually, he asked me not to visit him anymore, because my faith in God, my *personal relationship* with Jesus Christ, did nothing to help him get a job. He was offended when I asked him to trust God; he did the opposite and rebelled against Him. He asked, with tears in his eyes, "How can I trust someone who does such bad things? If God were real, these things would not have been allowed to happen to me. My wife is my God, because she loves me so much!"

Proverbs 20:24 says, "A man's steps are directed by the Lord. How then can anyone understand his own way?"

Thanks to growing up in a Christian home, I have always believed that God directs our steps, but that sometimes it is very difficult to understand the way He takes us. As I look back, every difficult time in my life has had a purpose, and in obedience to God, I grew stronger as a result of difficult times. Why couldn't I convince Bill of this? Perhaps I'll never know. Perhaps I'll get another chance. Perhaps God will use someone else to reach him.

Do you know God? Do you go to Him every day and talk? Do you pour out your heart to Him, asking for understanding when you have none? Can you learn to ask "How far would you like me to go?" instead of "Why?"

Know God.

## June 14
### LET'S DO DINNER

"Do not join those who . . . gorge themselves on meat . . ."
(Proverbs 23:19)

Travelers: *You and I*
**Read: Proverbs 23:1–35**

Rarely is the business day over at 5:00 p.m. when I'm traveling, especially if I travel with co-workers. The business dinner has long been a time of mixing socializing with serious business. I have always felt obligated to be hospitable and go along, even when I'd rather read quietly in my room.

Other devotions in this book have focused on the damaging effects of too much alcohol, but this is the first one that identifies the dangers of gluttony, or eating too much. The two certainly go together. A couple cocktails before dinner not only enhance the appetite, but impair one's ability to use common sense. When I asked my chiropractor friend why my heart pounds so hard after a late dinner, he said, "Mixing sugar and caffeine has the same effect on your heart as mixing alcohol with jet fuel. It's explosive."

That got my attention.

Now when I'm asked to go to a late dinner, I rarely order an entree. It's amazing how a salad or just an appetizer will carry me over to the next day, without feeling like a stuffed pig, apple in mouth. And I make sure that if there's one glass of wine, that there is never a second one.

I've noticed something else, too. More business is transacted at dinner than just the formal meeting agenda. Character judgments of strength and weakness are made which can affect one's career for years to come. Again the proverb warns us: "Listen, my son, and be wise, and keep your heart on the right path. Do not join those who drink too much wine or gorge themselves on meat, for drunkards and gluttons become poor, and drowsiness clothes them in rags" (Proverbs 23:19–21).

If you've ever eaten too much too late, consider the adverse health effects. But also consider that more may be happening around the table than you realize, if you're too drowsy or preoccupied with food and drink to notice. The business day doesn't end at 5:00 p.m.

## June 15
## CHARGE!

> ". . . the simple keep going and suffer for it."
> (Proverbs 27:12)

Travelers: *You and I*
Read: Proverbs 27:1–27

If you're ever caught playing golf in a thunderstorm, legend has it that you should take a one-iron out of your bag and hold it high over your head. Even though this might attract lightning, it won't, because "even God can't hit a one-iron!"

Great joke. Bad advice, especially in the mountains of Colorado.

I grew up in the Great Lakes area where thunderstorms are fairly predictable. You can see the storm coming from far off, and it almost always starts raining before the lightning comes close enough to pose a threat. If you're a golfer, there's usually plenty of time to take cover. My guess is that the humid air of summer dampens the tendency of lightning to strike until a heavy shower is underway, which provides a "conductor" to the ground.

Not in Colorado. During the summer, the air can be extremely dry, with humidity below 20% and sometimes below 10%. Every afternoon, thunderclouds build up over the mountains, fueled by cooler air and melting snow at higher elevations. As these clouds drift eastward over the lower elevations, you can see rain falling from the clouds, but the rain often doesn't reach the ground. It evaporates in the intense dry heat closer to the ground. The result is a "dry thunderstorm."

When a dry thunderstorm is in the area, lightning can strike instantly, with no warning whatsoever. A cloud can appear harmless, and it's hard to quit playing golf when it's not even raining. It's embarrassing to "chicken out" when others want to keep going. "The prudent see danger and take refuge, but the simple keep going and suffer for it" (Proverbs 27:12). Many a Colorado golfer has paid with his life for his bad judgment.

How about in business and travel? Are you brave enough to take refuge when you see danger, or are you too macho to back off a dangerous situation?

Be prudent. Don't just "charge" off. Don't get struck by lightning.

## June 16
### THE ONLY ONE

"Who has gone up to heaven and come down?"
(Proverbs 30:4)

Traveler: *Jesus*
**Read: Proverbs 30:1–33**

The most wonderful parts of the Old Testament are when Jesus was identified long before He actually came to earth. Agur, son of Jakeh, did not know he was speaking of Jesus when he cried: "Who has gone up to heaven and come down? Who has gathered up the wind in the hollow of his hands? Who has wrapped up the waters in his cloak? Who has established all the ends of the earth?" (Proverbs 30:4).

But Jesus was there when God established the ends of the earth: "He was with God in the beginning" (John 1:2). Jesus was there as God fashioned creation: "The earth is the Lord's, and everything in it, the world, and all who live in it; for he founded it upon the seas and established it upon the waters" (Psalm 24:1–2). Jesus was there beside God throughout all of Old Testament history, waiting to make His entrance.

After He came to earth, He identified Himself as the only one who answers Agur's question: "No one has ever gone into heaven except the one who came from heaven—the Son of Man" (John 3:13). And by traveling into heaven after coming from heaven, He saved us: "But to each one of us grace has been given . . . When he ascended on high, he led captives in his train . . . He . . . is the very one who ascended higher than all the heavens in order to fill the whole universe" (Ephesians 4:7–10). Jesus is the only one who travels like that.

Jesus is the source of wisdom sought so fervently in Proverbs. Agur seemed to know God, since he prayed to God in verse 7. But he also seemed to know there was more to God—his Son. Agur said, "I am the most ignorant of men . . . I have not learned wisdom, nor have I knowledge of the Holy One" (Proverbs 30:2–3). He cries across the centuries, "What is his name and the name of his son? Tell me if you know!" (verse 4).

Do you know the name of God's Son? Do you tell others that you know the answer?

## June 17
### THE THIRST FOR JESUS

"... during the few and meaningless days he passes through like a shadow ..." (Ecclesiastes 6:12)

Travelers: *You and I*
**Read: Ecclesiastes 6:7–12**

I love the book of Ecclesiastes! It reminds me of that great gospel song, "Oh, How I Love Jesus," except that this book sounds more like "Oh, How I *Need* Jesus." Ecclesiastes sets the Old Testament apart from the New, and Christianity from other religions. A person can know of God, feel His power and His sovereignty, but also feel His distance. Without the personal Savior, all of life seems humdrum, useless.

This book reads as easily in the 1990s as it did centuries ago: "All man's efforts are for his mouth, yet his appetite is never satisfied ... This too is meaningless, a chasing after the wind" (Ecclesiastes 6:7,9). Such a skeptic! Do you know anyone like this writer? They are everywhere today: "For who knows what is good for a man in life, during the few and meaningless days he passes through like a shadow?" (verse 12). Such a thirst for beauty. And the answer lies so close at hand.

In all my previous trips to Washington, DC, I hated trying to get around the area, because of the traffic and congestion. Watching a taxi's meter tick off dollars while sitting still in a traffic jam left me feeling like a meaningless shadow in an indifferent city. That's how the writer of Ecclesiastes felt. Passing through like a shadow. Does anyone care?

But on the day I wrote this devotion, I took my first ride on the Metro, Washington's sparkling subway system. I'd never had the nerve to try it before, but felt compelled on this particular day. It is sleek, modern, *fast*, and even has automated ticketing, complete with a refund window if you buy too much ticket. The employees are courteous and anxious to answer any questions. What a difference! In a rocketing whoosh under the Potomac, my trip did not feel meaningless.

Finding Jesus is like discovering the Metro. Life takes on meaning. Are you even more thirsty for the New Testament now, after reading Ecclesiastes? I hope so. We're getting closer!

## June 18
POOR ME!

"A fool's work wearies him . . ."
(Ecclesiastes 10:15)

Travelers: *You and I*
**Read: Ecclesiastes 10:1–20**

I never thought of myself as a fool, but this one worries me. My work has always wearied me. What have I been doing wrong? "Even as he walks along the road, the fool lacks sense and shows everyone how stupid he is" (Ecclesiastes 10:3). Has my fatigue betrayed an Old Testament lack of faith? Yes.

When I worked for a big company, it was easy to justify staying in the nicer hotels, living the jet set life to the hilt. I have been known to change hotels because I felt certain hotel chains were "beneath" me. Poor me! I worked so hard and traveled so much; didn't I deserve a little comfort? But those physical trappings did nothing to ease the pain of my Old Testament relationship with God. I can see now that I was tired for a different reason. I was focusing on physical comfort instead of spiritual comfort.

Part of running my own company has been to learn to trust God daily, no matter what the circumstances. That includes staying at cheaper hotels and renting cheaper cars. It has also included a budding personal relationship with Jesus Christ. And guess what! I'm learning that the tougher the circumstance, the better I feel about relying on spiritual comfort instead of physical. I'm actually laughing when things get a little lowly.

Tonight is my third night in a dingy, smelly, worn-out "used-to-be" hotel in Arlington, Virginia. I must have insulted my travel agent to earn the right to stay here; I'm not sure. Just two years ago, I would have refused. It is truly lacking. In fact, I can't even receive an Oasis fax here at night; they have to lock up the fax machine to make sure it doesn't get stolen!

But since I am so far from a good restaurant, I've ordered pizza or brought back a deli sandwich each evening. No need to worry about wasting the evening watching television; they don't even have cable! Instead I have spent the last three evenings writing devotions for you. And I'll bet I won't be wearied at all tomorrow! Praise God!

## June 19
### GROUND ZERO FOR CHRISTIAN TRAVELERS

> "Here am I. Send me!"
> (Isaiah 6:8)

**Traveler:** *Isaiah*
**Read:** Isaiah 6:1–13

Who am I to fantasize that I can run a Christian ministry? How dare I even think of following what the likes of James Dobson (Focus on the Family), Bill Bright (Campus Crusade for Christ), Bill McCartney (Promise Keepers), and a host of other incredibly good Christians have done? How can an engineer with no formal ministry training or experience expect to cut it in the difficult world of para-church ministries? Isn't the competition for charitable dollars intense and growing more so each day?

In just over two years, our fledgling ministry has raised less than $1,000 from the general public. The message hasn't gotten out, and no one seems to understand the need for faxing devotions to people in their hotel rooms. To date, every major publisher has turned down proposals to publish this devotional book, saying, "Well-written, but there's no market."

Should I quit? Did I fail in God's calling to me back in 1981?

Isaiah met God in much more spectacular fashion than I did. Yet he felt just as inadequate: "Woe to me! . . . I am ruined! For I am a man of unclean lips, living among a people of unclean lips . . ." (Isaiah 6:5). Isaiah expected to die because he had seen God and was unworthy. But then an angel touched his lips and took away his sin (verses 6 and 7). Then God asked, "Whom shall I send? And who will go for us?" (verse 8). And the newly cleansed Isaiah leaped: "Here am I. Send me!"

Isaiah never knew Jesus personally. So when Jesus did for me what the angel did for Isaiah, taking away my sins, I too was cleansed and called by God to go out in His name.

And so are you. This is the mother of all travel devotions. God sends us out, warts and all, to reach His people. Remember, God's strength is made perfect in our weakness (2 Corinthians 12:9). Will you cower in a corner when God speaks to you? Not if your sins have been atoned for by Jesus Christ. You'll shout, "Send me!"

*FAITH IN MOTION*

*June 20*
YOUR TRUE MISSION

"If you do not stand firm in your faith, you will not stand at all."
(Isaiah 7:9)

Traveler: *Isaiah*
Read: Isaiah 7:1–25

The human purpose for any business trip seems quite obvious. Whether it's a meeting with a client, a problem solving assignment at a manufacturing plant or a training session, your mission is usually clear when you leave. But what is your true mission in God's eyes? Might He have something else for you to do?

When people ask me what I do for a living, as they always do on airplanes, I like to say, "I'm a Christian on temporary assignment as a consulting engineer." That response never fails to start an interesting discussion. Non-believers seem to respect my true mission as much as believers. And my true mission is to interact with people I encounter, telling them that there is hope is the world. So many people seem to have no hope at all.

Isaiah was sent out by God, with the most important announcement the world has ever heard. He warned King Ahaz that his loss of faith would result in the loss of his kingdom: "If you do not stand firm in your faith, you will not stand at all" (Isaiah 7:9). Then God gave a sign through Isaiah that would change the world forever: "The virgin will be with child and will give birth to a son, and will call him Immanuel" (verse 14).

Every time I see these words I am astounded. They were written almost 700 years before the actual event took place! Ahaz was given a choice: believe in God's power by standing firm in faith, or fall. Ahaz chose to fall.

That's the same mission you are given today: to tell people to stand firm in faith or fall, not only as individuals, but as a nation. As a frequent traveler you rub elbows with some of the most influential people in the world. Your true mission is to tell them that their choice is the same as Ahaz's choice 2,700 years ago.

Now, is your trip just another business trip, or does it have a higher purpose? To whom will God lead you today to deliver His message?

## June 21
### IS PEACE A MIRAGE?

"My people . . . my handiwork . . . my inheritance."
(Isaiah 19:25)

Travelers: *Those on God's Highway*
**Read: Isaiah 19:23–25**

In the 1940s, it was impossible to imagine a united Europe where England, France and Germany, among others, would share a common market and currency. Yet today that peace has come about, despite evil attempts to tear it apart. In the 1990's, it was even harder to imagine Jews, Arabs and Palestinians sitting down together in peace, yet it happened, despite radical fringe attacks to prevent it. Oddly, the assassination of a Jewish leader by his own people seems to have brought these factions together, in grief. We are witnessing things today that seemed inconceivable such a short time ago.

If Isaiah could predict the birth of Christ over 600 years in advance, couldn't he also have predicted events taking place today? How could he even have known about Yassir Arafat and the Palestinian displacement from their homeland? Yet he wrote: "In that day there will be a highway from Egypt to Assyria. The Assyrians will go to Egypt and the Egyptians will go to Assyria. The Egyptians and Assyrians will worship together. In that day Israel will be the third, along with Egypt and Assyria, a blessing on the earth. The Lord Almighty will bless them, saying, 'Blessed be Egypt my people, Assyria my handiwork, and Israel my inheritance" (Isaiah 19:23–25).

Unthinkable just a few years ago! True today! I visited the World Bank in Washington, DC, recently and observed the most wonderful collection of people, from every corner of the earth, all working together in one place for the good of all people. I could see Isaiah's words being acted out!

But what about Bosnia? It's terrifying to see the Nazi death camps repeated there today. It's so easy to conclude that true world peace is a mirage. Put out one fire, it just flames up somewhere else. It's so easy to lose hope.

But there *is* an answer. Isaiah proclaimed God's universal love for all people. If Israel, the Arab states and the Palestinians can come together, then anything is possible. Not through human action; we muddle it up every time. Trust God's plan and His timing.

## June 22
### WALKING IN THE WAY

"... your name and renown are the desire of our hearts."
(Isaiah 26:8)

Travelers: *All Believers*
Read: Isaiah 26:1–21

Our mission as Christians is to become a point of light in a dark world. We know of a future world when all will be light; when Jesus will return to claim His people. Everything will change. But until then, it's up to us to be like torches of love in a dark cave.

We send faxes to travelers each night at their hotels, with one of these devotions attached. They are a great help to travelers, but they also have a side benefit. I've been fascinated to see how I am treated at the front desk of a hotel when I am receiving an Oasis fax every day. You see, there's nothing less private than a hotel fax. You can be assured that your fax has been read by at least one, if not more, hotel personnel before it is given to you. So it's pretty humorous to see the look of surprise on a staff person's face when a devotional fax comes through instead of the typical business fax.

Many hotel personnel have asked me about Oasis. Others have waived the charge for receiving faxes, without permission to do so. Still others have introduced me to the hotel manager. Even non-believers respect what we are trying to do: "The path of the righteous is level; O upright One, you make the way of the righteous smooth. Yes, Lord, walking in the way of your laws, we wait for you; your name and renown are the desire of our hearts" (Isaiah 26:7–8).

Isn't it great to be recognized by hotel people as one who walks in the way? They don't always understand you, but they do respect you. And they welcome the peace you bring into their establishment.

As Oasis travelers are refreshed and encouraged, they take on a special glow that effects other people: "... let your light shine before men, that they may see your good deeds and praise your Father in heaven" (Matthew 5:16).

## June 23
### A DARK AND STORMY NIGHT

"... and you ... will be gathered up one by one."
(Isaiah 27:12)

**Traveler:** *The Lord*
**Read: Isaiah 27:1–13**

Any devotee of the comic strip "Peanuts" by Charles Schulz can tell you that all good stories begin with the title above. For decades we've watched Snoopy begin his best-selling novel with those immortal words!

Well, for my story, I must tell you that it *was* a dark and stormy night. So stormy, in fact, that I chose to take the train from Hartford, Connecticut to Washington, D.C., instead of flying on a puddle-jumping commuter flight. With sixty mile per hour winds and temperatures right at freezing, I knew the potential for ice on airplane wings.

My train that night became the perfect metaphor for the Christian life. As the storm raged outside, it was warm and cozy inside the train. And unlike the airplanes I frequent, this train was uncrowded. Who ever dreamed of leg room where your knees don't dimple the seat back in front of you? I had a great Christian novel with me that evening. As the hours went on, my smile got bigger. I felt as if I had been delivered by God, Himself.

At some point during the trip, I got up and walked back toward the snack car, to get some food. Yes, unlike today's airlines, Amtrak still serves real food! The snack car was at the end of the train, so I had to walk through three other cars to get there. One car was completely empty, except for one man. He had the car entirely to himself! As I passed by, he looked up with a smile of total contentment.

Have you ever realized that God sees you exactly like the man with an entire car to himself? In the crush of business and travel, it may not always feel that way. But Isaiah foresees a time when God will be looking just for you: "In that day the Lord will thresh from the flowing Euphrates to the Wadi of Egypt, and you, O Israelites, will be gathered up one by one" (Isaiah 27:12).

That threshing will go from Seattle to Miami and from Los Angeles to Kennebunkport! All aboard!

## *June 24*
## ABOVE THE DIN

> "This is the way; walk in it."
> (Isaiah 30:21)

Travelers: *The Israelites*
**Read: Isaiah 30:15–22**

Frequent travel is about noise. Noise makes it hard to seek God's presence. Once upon a time I could usually find a quiet nook in any airport, where I could pull out a good book and read, oblivious to the crowd passing by. Now, almost every gate area is near a television blaring out airport news and shopping channels.

Aboard the plane, jet engine noise, safety demonstrations, frequent flyer program advertisements and well-lubricated ski clubs are all noisy. So are rental car buses, taxis and big city traffic. Even the hotel. Most heating/air conditioning units make lots of noise all night, turning on and off. And some of my most heart-stopping moments have been from doors slamming down the hall at 2:00 a.m..

Noise everywhere. How can you get some peace? Isaiah says: "In repentance and rest is your salvation, in quietness and trust is your strength, but you would have none of it" (Isaiah 30:15). If it's too noisy to read, shut your eyes for a few moments and pray. Isaiah suggests that the place to start is repentance. Take a short time to review areas where you have not honored God during the day; it will have an amazing effect on your ability to tolerate the noise around you. Peace comes in admitting that you are no better than those around you.

Even in the middle of chaos, a quiet prayer of repentance brings rest, trust and strength. Instead of fleeing from it in indignation (verses 16, 17), turn it over to God: "Yet the Lord longs to be gracious to you; he rises to show you compassion" (verse 18).

If you do seek God above the din, a surprising thing will happen: "Whether you turn to the right or to the left, your ears will hear a voice behind you, saying, 'This is the way; walk in it'" (verse 21).

## *June 25*
## GOING FOR HELP

"Woe to those who . . . do not look to the Holy One . . ."
(Isaiah 31:1)

**Travelers:** *Those Not Seeking God*
**Read: Isaiah 31:1–9**

I thought I was pretty hot stuff. My mother refused to tell me what I had scored on my childhood IQ test, because she felt the knowledge could make me conceited. Good idea, but that only made me *more* cocky—I figured my IQ must be really high if she wouldn't tell me. (Mom, if you're reading this, it's okay to tell me now!) I got good grades in high school and college, but not great grades, because I was a little too lazy to learn the right way to study for tests.

In business I quickly learned that moving ahead was based not only on what I knew, but who I knew. Distasteful as it is, looking back over 30 years, I realize I was a born politician with a personality that could win "friends." Coupled with an upbringing which demanded respect for my elders, I moved up quickly, more because of my personality than my credentials. I thought I was pretty unique.

Then I ran into a book, *The Corporate Steeplechase,* (Facts on File, New York, 1984) by Dr. Srully Blotnick (isn't that a great name?). The subtitle of the book is *Predictable Crises in a Business Career.* It's based on an overwhelming data base which tracked thousands of individuals through each decade of their careers.

The book was about me. Like innumerable other young people, I had sacrificed knowledge and wisdom in my quest to get ahead. By the time I had reached my early forties, my knowledge base was becoming obsolete; my foundation had eroded away. Blotnick's book predicted the whole thing.

So did Isaiah: "Woe to those who go down to Egypt for help. . . who trust in the multitude of their chariots and in the great strength of their horsemen" (Isaiah 31:1). "Return to him you have so greatly revolted against . . ." (verse 6). Instead of going to God for help, I trusted in the chariots and horsemen of the politically-motivated within my company.

Where do you go for help?

## June 26
## TO A DEGREE

"His bread will be supplied, and water will not fail him."
(Isaiah 33:16)

Traveler: *The Righteous Person*
**Read: Isaiah 33:1–19**

The prophet Isaiah has strong words for those who avoid big sins: "He who walks righteously and speaks what is right, who rejects gain from extortion and keeps his hand from accepting bribes, who stops his ears against plots of murder and shuts his eyes against contemplating evil—this is the man who will dwell on the heights, whose refuge will be the mountain fortress" (Isaiah 33:15–16). Thankfully, very few of us would ever consider such serious acts as lying, extortion, bribery, murder and conspiracy. These words imply big crimes, organized crime stuff, headlines and media madness. Thank God I'd never do any of those things.

Oh, really? How far is a little white lie from full-blown dishonesty? How far is a clever negotiating ploy from extortion? How far is accepting a small favor from bribery? How far is character assassination from true murder? And how far is repeating a nasty rumor from contemplating evil?

Isn't a small lie the same as a big lie? Isn't a little extortion the same as organized crime? Isn't any form of bribery still bribery? Murder and conspiracy, too? And we've all done at least some of those things at least in some small way.

Not a pretty picture is it? Everyone needs to take a closer look in the mirror, during this time of down-sizing and massive layoffs. Every one of us probably deserves worse than we get. But it's not too late to start over. Isaiah gives the guidance: walk righteously, speak what is right, reject unfair gain, turn away from favors, plug your ears to rumors and close your eyes to anything ungodly.

Have you bemoaned the loss of the so-called "American dream?" We lost it ourselves. But there is a better way. If we accept it, God promises, through the prophet, that we will always eat and drink (verse 16). And ". . . your eyes will . . . view a land that stretches afar" (verse 17).

Buy into the "Godly dream" instead. What a view!

## *June 27*
### FREQUENT TRAVELER'S MISSION STATEMENT

"... sorrow and sighing will flee away."
(Isaiah 35:10)

Travelers: *The Redeemed of the Lord*
**Read: Isaiah 35:1–10**

I've pointed out many times in these devotions that God's purposes for your travels may be very different from your own or those of your employer. But those purposes do not conflict with each other. In fact, focusing on God's purpose for your travel makes your secular work go all that much better. Keeping your eye on the far horizon is always the best way to navigate.

When I was about ten years old, I got a new bicycle which had, of course, new tires. The tires made neat patterns on the street when I rode through a puddle. One day, I splashed through a small lake purposefully, then rode along with my head down, hypnotically watching tire tracks on cement.

POW! I ran right into the back bumper of a parked car. In those days, bumpers were bumpers, and in this case the bumper won. The front wheel of my new bike looked like what we'd call "Pac-Man" today. And the bruises on my body looked worse.

Do you travel with your head down, thinking only about sales goals or other business matters? How about looking out to God's horizon: "Strengthen the feeble hands, steady the knees that give way; say to those with fearful hearts, 'Be strong, do not fear; your God will come . . . he will come to save you'" (Isaiah 35:3–4). In other words, who can you help while you're traveling?

When God is with you, great things can happen: "Then the eyes of the blind will be opened and the ears of the deaf unstopped. Then will the lame leap like a deer, and the mute tongue shout for joy" (verses 5 and 6). Maybe not literally, but your touch might change someone's attitude, and that's like opening the eyes of the blind.

And something else will happen. Your regular work and travel will never seem mundane or routine again. You'll be living God's purpose and traveling on His way (verses 8 through 10).

## *June 28*
## LEAD, FOLLOW OR GET OUT OF THE WAY!

"... he gently leads those that have young."
(Isaiah 40:11)

Traveler: *God*
**Read: Isaiah 40:1–11**

Isaiah 40 has some very important passages. Verse one is used as a major part of Handel's "Messiah." And verse three is quoted by Mark, in describing the ministry of John the Baptist in advance of the arrival of the Messiah, Jesus Christ (see Mark 1:2). But for travelers, there is another section which may be as important: "He tends his flock like a shepherd: He gathers the lambs in his arms and carries them close to his heart; he gently leads those that have young" (Isaiah 40:11).

What I remember most about my Grandpa Walters was how I could climb up into his lap any time I wanted. He was a recovered alcoholic with only an eighth grade education, so he didn't spout any great words of wisdom. And I don't recall him reading stories to me, although he may have. What I remember is that he was there for me. He held me and loved me, and I knew it. A generation later he cried at my daughter's baptism. He was like a gentle shepherd to me.

It's not hard to picture God picking up a small lamb and carrying it close to his heart. We've probably all seen paintings of Christ doing exactly that. Very peaceful, very lovely. But my guess is that any aggressive, savvy business person would not appreciate being called a sheep. It's just not very macho. Sheep are commonly considered to be weak and helpless, while business people must be strong self-starters, bold, in control of the situation. Survival of the fittest, not the cuddliest and woolliest. Sheep follow, for heaven's sake; they don't *lead!*

Be honest, though. Wouldn't it be nice if you didn't have to carry all that worldly weight around on your shoulders? Just once, wouldn't you like a wise master to take you by the hand and show you the way? Wouldn't it be great not to go it totally alone this time? Isaiah is telling you that's exactly what happens when you go with God. He gently leads you. He loves you and you know it.

## June 29
## MY COMPLAINT

"... those who hope in the Lord ... they will run and not grow weary" (Isaiah 40:31)

Travelers: *You and I*
**Read: Isaiah 40:12–31**

As I get older, my body is beginning to complain about traveling. Because of the physical abuse I have heaped on it during my life, and because of hereditary traits I can see my father struggling with, my body has begun to fight back when I ask it to sit immobile in an airplane seat for three hours or more.

I bring this up not to ask you to feel sorry for me, but rather to make a point about spiritual and physical growth. Because of bad circulation, I can look forward to a sore back and swollen ankles every time I take a trip. Doctors say, "Get used to it." Or stop traveling.

Until that is possible, I've got to learn how to manage the discomfort: wear loose-fitting clothes, get up and move around more frequently, sleep better in those comfortable hotel beds and eat a better diet. Those things are up to me. However, no matter how much conventional wisdom I employ, the laws of physics and old age will prevail eventually.

But there's another way:

> Why do you ... complain, O Israel, "My way is hidden from the Lord; my cause is disregarded by my God?" Do you not know? Have you not heard?... He will not grow tired or weary, and his understanding no one can fathom. He gives strength to the weary and increases the power of the weak. Even youths grow tired and weary, and young men stumble and fall, but those who hope in the Lord will renew their strength. They will soar on wings of eagles; they will run and not grow weary, they will walk and not be faint. (Isaiah 40:27–31)

So it's not up to me. It's up to God. What I have to do as I travel is focus on His goodness and the fact that He knows my condition. When I trust Him, my physical limitations are manageable. As a doctor once told me, the body and the heart *are* connected.

Believe in God's grace. Soar, run, walk.

*June 30*
PERSONAL TRAINER

"I am the Lord . . . who teaches you what is best . . ."
(Isaiah 48:17)

Travelers: *You and I*
**Read: Isaiah 48:17–22**

Yesterday, I finally confessed to my doctor that my right elbow was really hurting. I hate that. I've never been a good patient, and I'd rather live with the pain and hope for natural healing than take corrective action. It was easier when I was young. Now, I have to admit that I'll need help to heal, if I'm going to pitch batting practice this coming spring.

When the doctor touched the swollen tendon in my elbow, the pain made me yelp. But that was only the beginning. I thought he was my friend, but I'd have never known it as he deeply massaged until I couldn't take any more. Then the dreaded words: "Come back in two days. We'll be sharing this kind of closeness for a long time to come."

Doctor Greg *is* my friend. And he knows I want to work out with my high school baseball team more than anything else. So he must hurt me to heal me. He is my personal trainer.

I have another Personal Trainer, and I have listened to Him very reluctantly, too: "'I am the Lord your God, who teaches you what is best for you, who directs you in the way you should go. If only you had paid attention to my commands, your peace would have been like a river, your righteousness like the waves of the sea" (Isaiah 48:17–18).

When I was young, I had the chance to listen to God. But I was not always a good student. Yet my Personal Trainer is very patient. He keeps finding new ways for me to learn. Now, I finally realize that I won't heal on my own.

And He loves me enough to know that painful therapy is what I must endure.

Are you ready at last to let your Personal Trainer massage the sore spots in your life? It'll hurt. But imagine your joy when pain you thought you'd live with for the rest of your life suddenly disappears! Peace like a river is only that far away.

## *July 1*
## WHO IS THIS JESUS?

"Surely he took up our infirmities and carried our sorrows . . ."
(Isaiah 53:4)

Traveler: *Jesus*
**Read: Isaiah 52:13–53:12**

If you have come to the fifty-second chapter of Isaiah in this devotional book, but you do not yet have a personal relationship with Jesus Christ—we don't get to study His life of travel until later—here's an opportunity to comprehend the incomprehensible nature of the Son of God. You probably know *about* Jesus. So you know that His story is difficult for the average person to understand. It takes faith to understand it.

Where does a faith like that start? Perhaps in hearing God's own words, spoken through the prophet, concerning His plan for His Son. But these aren't words spoken by a proud papa at the birth of his son. They were spoken *600 years in advance of His birth!* And they are the bedrock of what every Christian believes.

Read Isaiah 52:13 through 53:12 very slowly. Now read the passage again. Let the words soak into your soul: ". . . many who were appalled at him . . . no beauty or majesty to attract us to him . . . despised and rejected by men . . . familiar with suffering . . . took up our infirmities and carried our sorrows . . . crushed for our iniquities . . . punishment that brought us peace was upon him . . . oppressed and afflicted . . . led like a lamb to the slaughter . . . did not open his mouth . . . assigned a grave with the wicked . . . Lord's will to crush him . . . after the suffering of his soul, he will see the light of life . . ."

There. You have just seen a sneak preview of the New Testament, all predicted centuries earlier, all true. Why would anyone suffer such a fate? After reading God's plan for Jesus, wouldn't you expect Jesus to be harsh and gruff? But before this book is complete, you'll discover a Jesus, a frequent traveler like you, who loved everyone around Him, and who still loves you today. He died for you. Do you deserve Him? No.

All it takes is the faith to believe that He wants you anyway. Stop right now and ask God to open a place in your heart for Jesus. If you've never asked that before, or if maybe you've slipped away from Him just a little, this is a great moment, designed by God just for you. Do it now!

## July 2
### FIRST CLASS FOR FREE

> "Come . . . buy . . . without cost . . . the richest of fare."
> (Isaiah 55:1–2)

Travelers: *You and I*
**Read: Isaiah 55:1–13**

"Ladies and gentlemen, your attention, please. If there is a Mr. Beaumont on board the aircraft, will you please ring the call button above your seat?"

Great. Just great. In twenty-five-plus years, I had never been bumped from a flight. Now it looked like it was about to happen. Naturally, it was a Friday night, and I wanted to get home. How come these things never happen on Monday morning out-bound flights?

When I identified myself, a stern-looking flight attendant coolly asked me to gather my things and come to the front of the plane. She was almost rude, but I kept my cool. When we got to the front, she pulled me into the food galley and broke into a wide grin. "Mr. Beaumont, I had to put on a mean face back there so that no one else would question me. We've got an over-booking problem and a man needs to get on this flight desperately. There's only one seat left and it's in first class. Would you be too upset if I asked you to move to first class so this man could have your seat in the back?"

"Why not give him the first class seat, I asked?"

"Because our computer says you're one of our best customers, and, well, he's not very friendly. Would you do me this favor?"

As bizarre as that episode was, Isaiah says that's a normal occurrence for God: "Come, all you who are thirsty, come to the waters; and you who have no money, come, buy and eat! Come, buy wine and milk without money and without cost. Why spend money on what is not bread, and your labor on what does not satisfy? Listen, listen to me, and eat what is good, and your soul will delight in the richest of fare" (Isaiah 55:1–2). If I had reacted angrily when I thought a bump was coming, I probably would not have been given this gift. Thankfully, God's wisdom is better than mine.

A surprise up-grade to first-class was pretty nice. But it can't compare to God's richest fare!

## July 3
### YOU NEVER KNOW WHEN

"... the righteous are taken away to be spared from evil."
(Isaiah 57:1)

Travelers: *The Righteous*
**Read: Isaiah 57:1–13**

Today as I prepared to write this devotion, I remembered one airplane flight that was so turbulent that I actually called quietly to God in fear. I wasn't in panic; I simply wondered if the plane could take that kind of pounding. If not, I needed my Lord near.

He was there with me! I don't know whether the wild ride lasted two minutes or twenty. I was so concentrated on His love that I was mentally transported out of the situation.

Every traveler wonders at times what it might be like to die in a crash. And everyone has wondered why some people die suddenly with so much left undone. Often we hear someone ask, "How could a loving God allow that?"

Isaiah tells us of God's perspective: "The righteous perish, and no one ponders it in his heart; devout men are taken away, and no one understands that the righteous are taken away to be spared from evil. Those who walk uprightly enter into peace; they find rest as they lie in death" (Isaiah 57:1–2). Had my plane crashed, I believe I would have been swept away into instant communion with God. My family left behind would have suffered, but not me, not for long.

It's good that I thought of these things today. Before I had a chance to write them down, I had a doctor's appointment which was intended to be a routine check-up. It turns out I have skin cancer. Today has been interesting. Tomorrow is unknown.

My reaction? Total peace. Whether it's airplanes or some other surprise, we never really know what God has in mind. But we do know that He cares about His children, deeply and compassionately. I never dreamed I'd react this calmly to bad news. That's the power of God's love.

Never fear for a true believer in God, regardless of what happens. Only fear for those who do not believe. It is not rest they find at the end.

## July 4
### E. T. PHONE HOME

"... your iniquities have separated you from your God ..."
(Isaiah 59:2)

Travelers: *You and I*
**Read: Isaiah 59:1–15**

Rick Stookey, a member of my Monday morning men's Bible study, turned the tables on me recently and sent *me* a devotional fax while I was traveling. Here's what he shared with me:

"Pastor Bill [Oudemolen] mentioned in his sermon last Sunday a heart condition called the 'E. T. Syndrome (ETS).' With my background in pharmaceutical sales and critical care nursing, you can imagine how I perked up my ears to learn about this heart ailment. According to Pastor Bill, 'E. T. Syndrome' refers to a heart that is 'Easily Turned' from focusing on God. Imagine my surprise when I not only learned about a heart condition I had never heard of before, but discovered I actually suffer from this terrible malady.

With the daily stresses of life, ETS, as it is sure to become known, can become a chronic condition. But there is a treatment available: daily fellowship with our God through His word and through prayer! Daily doses of this treatment can keep this syndrome under control. But if we start missing our doses of communion with Him, this syndrome will surely reappear.

So take your medicine, Larry. And I'll take mine."

There is no easier time to contract ETS than during frequent travel. Do you have ETS? If you're a human being, the answer is yes. Read Isaiah 59:1–15 right now. The language is pretty strong, and you may not feel that you are as bad, or that your heart is as easily turned, as described in Isaiah's condemnation of Israel. But one sin is not smaller or larger than another in God's eyes. Unless you're perfect, you've caught it. Don't try to dodge it. Don't be in denial, just as you might be after learning you have a serious physical disease. This is worse. Accept it.

Now make a determined effort to be healed. Take your medicine and control your symptoms.

## July 5
### WE'RE ENGAGED!

"... so will your God rejoice over you."
(Isaiah 62:5)

**Travelers:** *The Israelites*
**Read: Isaiah 62:1–12**

Isaiah's prophecies leave us with an incredible sense of waiting for the Messiah, Israel's salvation. I have that same sense of waiting, even yearning, to finally complete the Old Testament and begin the New—the story of the Messiah and the story of your personal Savior, the one who gives you what Old Testament Israel gave up. The primary traveler is Jesus Christ, the model for us all.

Isaiah gives us a hint, like a sneak preview before the feature film: "Coming soon to a theater near you!" This is no Rhett and Scarlett. This is better. Why? Think about who the superstars are in *this* picture. There are two.

The first is a Savior. Better than that, He is your Savior: "See, your Savior comes! See, his reward is with him, and his recompense accompanies him'" (Isaiah 62:11). That Savior is Jesus Christ, whose arrival was foretold by Isaiah hundreds of years before it happened. That's a traveling Savior, my friend. He has come for those who believe. We don't have to go to Him.

But who is that co-star right there with Him? Why it's you! "... You will be called Hephzibah ... for the Lord will take delight in you ... As a young man marries a maiden ... as a bridegroom rejoices over his bride, so will your God rejoice over you" (verses 4–5). In Hebrew, "Hephzibah" means "my delight is in her." So this personal preview shows that there's a wedding coming and you're the bride!

So how does it feel to be engaged? And how does it feel to be a bride? Some men may have a problem with this image: "I'm not puttin' on a white dress for Anyone!" Fine. Use a white suit. The point is not man and woman. It is God rejoicing over His loved one, who makes Him as happy as a newly married couple.

## July 6
### WHOM SHALL WE BLAME?

"Why, O Lord, do you make us wander from your ways . . . ?"
(Isaiah 63:17)

Travelers: *You and I*
**Read: Isaiah 63:7–19**

Back in the 1970s, comedian Flip Wilson portrayed a character he called Reverend Leroy. Whenever Reverend Leroy was caught doing something un-reverend-like, he would say, "Da devil made me do it!"

In Isaiah's time, Israel was being punished for its repeated failure to live according to God's way. God simply turned His back on the nation and disaster came in waves. They found a unique person to blame for their failures—God Himself: "Why, O Lord, do you make us wander from your ways and harden our hearts so we do not revere you? Return for the sake of your servants . . ." (Isaiah 63:17).

Aha! If God is so all-powerful, then it must be God that allowed them to stray! And many people use the same reasoning today: "It says so right here in the Bible! Let's blame God!"

Not so fast. Go back and look a little before that: "He said, 'Surely they are my people, sons who will not be false to me'; and so he became their Savior. In all their distress he too was distressed, and the angel of his presence saved them . . . he lifted them up and carried them in the days of old. Yet they rebelled and grieved his Holy Spirit. So he turned and became their enemy and he himself fought against them" (verses 8–10).

Did God *make* the Israelites wander from his ways and *cause* them to harden their hearts, or did they *choose* to rebel against Him and He *allowed* them to wander? If you read only verse 17, you can try to blame God, just like Reverend Leroy blamed the devil. But if you read the Bible as a whole, taking a lifetime to seek its true message, you know whom to blame.

If you've wandered from God's way, and we all have, don't blame God. Just accept responsibility. Suddenly, you won't be trying to discover where God has gone. He'll come back to you in a rush!

## July 7
### IMAGINE THAT!

"... an obstinate people ... pursuing their own imaginations ..." (Isaiah 65:2)

Travelers: *You and I*
Read: Isaiah 65:1–5

In 1960, I could not have imagined how my life would be affected by computers. Who can describe the incredible technological leaps of the second half of the twentieth century? In 1960, we still had typewriters, carbon paper, erasers, graph paper, t-squares and triangles. We never imagined a world of the Internet, laser and digital copy machines, word processors, spread sheet software and computer-aided design drafting.

One thing our times have never lacked is imagination. If you can imagine it, build it! There are no limits to what science can accomplish. Technology will solve all the problems of humanity. Surely God has blessed our nation!

We Americans truly believed, even as I was growing up after World War II, that we were the recipients of God's blessing: "I revealed myself to those who did not ask for me; I was found by those who did not seek me. To a nation that did not call on my name, I said, 'Here am I, here am I'" (Isaiah 65:1). Old Testament Israel fell because of its failure to obey God, and America was right there to pick up the promise. We were the ones with a "manifest destiny." At least that's what I was taught.

But somewhere along the line, we too found a new God, the God of technology, the product of our imaginations. And now we are just like the ancient Israelites, listening to the rest of Isaiah's message and realizing that our doom too may be near: "All day long I have held out my hands to an obstinate people, who walk in ways not good, pursuing their own imaginations ... Such people are smoke in my nostrils ... I will measure into their laps the full payment for their former deeds" (verses 2, 5, 7).

Is your imagination good enough to picture what God can do to an obstinate nation? It's not that technology is bad; it's that it has become God. How long do we have before our time, like Israel's, is up?

Please pray for our nation!

## July 8
### FOREIGN GODS

"I love foreign Gods, and I must go after them."
(Jeremiah 2:25)

Travelers: *The Israelites*
**Read: Jeremiah 2:23–25**

We know that the Israelites began to worship foreign Gods, some of whom were called the "Baals." Jeremiah compares their behavior to that of female camels and donkeys in heat (Jeremiah 2:23–24). This reference almost needs to be rated "PG-13," parental guidance suggested. What kinds of foreign gods do we have today that could elicit that kind of response?

There are many, of course, and each of us has addictions, some worse than others. But how far are any of us from such a compulsive addiction to something that we can't keep from pursuing it?

Take television. I am amazed how addicted people are to watching videos, no matter what the circumstances. On airplanes, just as we break through the clouds into the glorious blue yonder, a flight attendant asks us to lower our window shades so that the in-flight movie can be seen better. You can get a video any time at home; why shut out such glorious sunshine high above the storms below? I pompously judge these folks as seriously addicted to a foreign god.

But don't ask if I'm ready to give up watching the Denver Broncos, Denver Nuggets and Colorado Rockies on television. My response is even more conditioned than those video freaks on the plane! "Read a good book," I tell my kids, but only on nights when there's not a game on, okay? Look, I don't watch every game that's on television; only the Denver ones, except of course for my alma mater Michigan State; oh, and the University of Colorado and Colorado State University sports. There's usually one evening a week somewhere when I'm not watching one of them, so how can you say I'm addicted?"

I know I should cut down. But I don't want to! Is it really so bad? "It's no use! I love foreign gods, and I must go after them" (verse 25). And that's just television! Let's not talk about money, power and a host of others.

## July 9
### AVOIDING A STALL

"Return, faithless people; I will cure you of backsliding."
(Jeremiah 3:22)

Travelers: *The Israelites*
**Read: Jeremiah 3:6–25**

I was studying Jeremiah 3 as my plane taxied out for takeoff from Washington, D.C. The plane was very full, so it took awhile to lumber down the runway, reach the proper air speed and lift off. As the landing gear lifted into the belly of the plane and its aerodynamics improved, it picked up speed and flew me home, powered by jet engines that propelled me forward, allowing the wings to lift.

What would have happened if that plane had done what the Israelites did during the time of Jeremiah, backsliding away from God? It would not have been able to fly. Backsliding in aviation is called going into a stall. If there is not enough air flowing over its wings for lift, a plane falls crazily to the ground. There is no cure for a stall in flying.

God told the Israelites: "'How gladly would I treat you like sons and give you a desirable land, the most beautiful inheritance of any nation. I thought you would call me 'Father' and not turn away from following me. But like a woman unfaithful to her husband, so you have been unfaithful to me, O house of Israel,' declares the Lord. A cry is heard on the barren heights, the weeping and pleading of the people of Israel, because they have perverted their ways and have forgotten the Lord their God" (Jeremiah 3:19–21). It sounds like there was no cure for their backsliding, either, after all they had done wrong. Condemned.

But God, to the very end, waits for His children to see the light. He told them: "Return, faithless people; I will cure you of backsliding" (verse 22).

So there is a cure! But it requires a response on our part: "Yes, we will come to you, for you are the Lord our God" (verse 22).

What does backsliding mean in your life? If that's too old-fashioned of a word, how close are you to stalling because you are losing the flow of God's Spirit across your wings?

## July 10
## CROSSROADS

"... ask where the good way is, and walk in it ..."
(Jeremiah 6:16)

**Travelers:** *The Israelites*
**Read: Jeremiah 6:16–21**

I live close to the intersection of two major highways. At any hour of the day, tourists can be seen pulling off the side of the road, poring over maps, trying to figure out which way to go. The reason for their confusion is sad but true. US-285 is a major north-south artery, but at our local crossroads, it is heading east-west because of a bend around metropolitan Denver. Likewise, C-470 is supposed to be an east-west connection, but it points north and south at its intersection with US-285.

So, you can go west on US-285 North and turn north on C-470 West. Or should you go south on C-470 East? Where the heck is Colorado Springs? I got confused just trying to write this, and I negotiate that intersection every day!

The crossroads of life can be just as confusing. In the modern business world, you can be working an intelligent five-year plan for developing, marketing and producing a new product, only to have new technology render your product obsolete overnight. Crossroads.

Or your job can be eliminated with no warning, after a sudden merger or sale of the company. Crossroads. Where do I go now? "This is what the Lord says: 'Stand at the crossroads and look; ask for the ancient paths, ask where the good way is, and walk in it, and you will find rest for your souls" (Jeremiah 6:16).

If you choose to take your next steps without asking for help, you're doomed. But if you seek the ancient path, that is God's will for you, He will lead you to the good way. And you will find rest from the stress of facing the crossroads: "Now listen, you who say, 'Today or tomorrow we will go to this or that city, spend a year there, carry on business and make money.' Why, you do not even know what will happen tomorrow ... Instead, you ought to say, 'If it is the Lord's will, we will live and do this or that'" (James 4:13–15).

That's the ancient path.

## *July 11*
### BACKWARD OR FORWARD?

". . . day after day, again and again I sent you my servants the prophets." (Jeremiah 7:25)

Travelers: *The Prophets*
**Read: Jeremiah 7:1-29**

The biblical prophets were frequent travelers. They roamed the land, spreading the true message of God—his power, majesty, commandments, love and judgment. Through Jeremiah God pointed out that His prophets were not just an occasional burst, but sources of continuous guidance: ". . . but I gave them this command: Obey me, and I will be your God and you will be my people. Walk in all the ways I command you, that it may go well with you. But they did not listen or pay attention . . . They went backward and not forward. From the time your forefathers left Egypt until now, day after day, again and again I sent you my servants the prophets . . . They were stiff-necked and did more evil than their forefathers" (Jeremiah 7:23-26).

Day after day. Do you think God stopped sending prophets after the time of Jeremiah? Probably not. Can you think of people from modern times who were prophets of God? Martin Luther King? Billy Graham? Bill McCartney (Founder of Promise Keepers)? A thousand others would come to mind if you thought about it very long.

Day after day, again and again. Who else might be a prophet? *You.*

Keep in mind that biblical prophets, and modern ones for that matter, did not just begin speaking the word of God from birth. There was a definite time of maturing and living before an appearance from God, who used them to speak to His people. With the exception of Jesus (and He is higher than a prophet in my book), did the prophets of old *know* when they were small children that they would become prophets? That's a good, little research project.

But what is to prevent us from wondering if you might be a prophet, one who is waiting for your time to hear from God? If you travel frequently and have the word of God firmly planted in your heart, how far are you from shouting out God's truth?

Hopefully, not far.

## July 12
### THE OASIS HOTEL

"Oh, that I had in the desert a lodging place for travelers . . ."
(Jeremiah 9:2)

Traveler: *God*
**Read: Jeremiah 8:22–9:6**

Where is the nicest hotel you have ever stayed? If you're like me, you'd say that most hotels are very much the same. The budget hotels are a little cheaper, a little noisier and a little less elegant. The big hotel chains have more cable television channels and better room service. But they all seem very impersonal. Not the kind of places that make me *want* to return, even if I were on vacation.

While you're pondering whether you have a favorite hotel, ask yourself what the qualities of your ideal hotel would be. This is an important question, because the potential of Oasis Hospitality International may include developing a unique type of hotel for travelers.

The closest thing to perfection I've ever seen is the Glen Eyrie conference center in Colorado Springs, Colorado. The Glen is an old castle, with elegantly decorated rooms and a first-class dining room serving the very best of food. The scenery and the beautiful castle itself are spectacular, but that's not what makes the Glen so ideal. I think it's the way you can be totally alone if you wish, or you can mingle with other guests who are Christians (the Glen is owned and operated by the Navigators, a Christian organization). It's the combination of the physical amenities *and* the people that make it such a memorable place to visit.

Too bad there aren't more places like that where business travelers could go regularly. Even God Himself wished for such a place: "Oh, that I had in the desert a lodging place for travelers, so that I might leave my people and go away from them, for they are all adulterers and murderers, a crowd of unfaithful people" (Jeremiah 9:2).

God sought a haven from the "madding crowd," and so do we as frequent travelers. How about designing a new chain of hotels as we go along in this book, adding a biblical perspective for design features that would make it unique among hotels? Think about it.

## July 13
### TURNING THE TABLES

"... how can you compete with horses?"
(Jeremiah 12:5)

**Traveler:** *Jeremiah*
**Read: Jeremiah 12:1–17**

For years, my job was to scout out our competition and to know what their latest strategies were. Of course, their jobs were the same, to analyze and dissect what we were doing. It was always a little humorous to watch us work at the same professional conferences. We were in a race for business, and we wore each other out in the process.

In fact, there were times when neither of us was selected for a new project because our bitterness carried over into our sales presentations, and our potential clients were disgusted. I hated lowering myself to that level, and I hated how the competition was often dishonest. I lost several jobs by not retaliating in kind. Like Jeremiah, I asked, "Why does the way of the wicked prosper? Why do all the faithless live at ease?" (Jeremiah 12:1).

God answered Jeremiah, "If you have raced with men on foot and they have worn you out, how can you compete with horses" (verse 5)? In other words, if all I do is wear myself out worrying about why bad people prosper, I'll never move beyond petty jealousy. To compete with horses requires a completely different approach.

Recently, I attended a conference where I brought along a whole new outlook on doing business. Before I left home I spent time quietly listening for God's direction for my business. Then I simply chose to forget about the competition and to focus on doing my very best. I totally ignored the opposition. I drove them crazy. I was so clear on God's direction that I didn't care what they did or said, true or false. It didn't matter. My compass was set and the customer was my sole focus.

I was ready for a horse race.

Do you let the bad guys run you ragged? Is the game played according to their tempo, not yours? Step back from the situation, seek God's guidance and compete with horses.

## July 14
### GOD'S DOWNSIZING

> "Let them go!"
> (Jeremiah 15:1)

**Travelers:** *The Israelites*
**Read: Jeremiah 15:1–4**

If you haven't been caught in a staff reduction yet, there's a very good chance you will be in the future. If you're on top of the world now, you may not be later. But if you're down now, you'll be surprised how fast you recover. Life feels like a yo-yo, but most people I know have found ways to survive, even though they end up on paths they would not have chosen, nor could they have foreseen.

What would it be like if you were called in to the boss's office and told that you would be laid off, that your job was being eliminated, and that the boss would make sure that you never got another job as long as you lived? You would be permanently black-balled. You would be without hope. Even appealing to higher levels in the company would be fruitless. Isn't that an awful thought? What might you have done to receive that kind of condemnation?

When God reviewed the "personnel files" of the people of Israel, here's what he concluded: "They greatly love to wander; they do not restrain their feet. So the Lord does not accept them; he will now remember their wickedness and punish them for their sins" (Jeremiah 14:10).

Yes, we've sinned, so give us a few demerits and we'll get on with life, okay Lord? Look, no one's perfect, so show some mercy.

But the question is, does God have a limit? Is there a place where He will simply give up on us? All we do is repent briefly and go right back to sinning. Well, God does have a limit, and he reached it with Israel: "'Even if Moses and Samuel were to stand before me, my heart would not go out to this people. Send them away from my presence! Let them go'" (Jeremiah 15:1)! And God black-listed them to death, the sword, starvation and captivity (verse 2).

Dismal isn't it? It doesn't have to be (see Jeremiah 26:12). God seeks only a change in heart, a permanent change. Tell God you're sorry today. And mean it.

## July 15
### ENDLESS JOURNEY

"I will enslave you to your enemies in a land you do not know..."

(Jeremiah 17:4)

**Travelers:** *The Israelites*
**Read: Jeremiah 17:1–10**

Yesterday I received a call from one of the most frequent travelers in the Christian Travelers' Network. He gave me not only his itinerary, but also a prayer request. His prayer was that his company find him a project close to home very soon; commuting to Chicago every week for over a year was taking its toll on his family and himself. He sounded depressed.

Virtually every frequent traveler I have ever met has encountered that feeling. When a new project starts, the euphoria of winning the project overshadows the inconvenience of traveling, and usually the anticipation of career advancement numbs the reality of the length of the assignment. But then, inevitably, desperation sets in. Missing one or two kid's school events isn't so bad, but missing an entire year of them will earn you nothing but scorn from those who love you the most. It's tough. Tensions rise. Even the most faithful families endure with considerable pain.

During a long assignment, you can identify with how the Israelites felt when God told them: "I will enslave you to your enemies in a land you do not know, for you have kindled my anger, and it will burn forever" (Jeremiah 17:4). Have you ever felt that God must be very angry with you to cause you and your family to suffer through long separations? Do you feel as if you've been put into exile?

Well, it's not just a traveler who kindles God's anger. Because we are human, we can anger God without moving an inch. And we can be enslaved to enemies right at home. Enemies like television, sports, lust, greed, power, money. God allows us to become enslaved to them if we turn our hearts from Him. The land we do not know can be the land we know the best. The land we desire is a healthy relationship with Him, regardless of our physical surroundings.

"This is what the Lord says: '... Blessed is the man who trusts in the Lord ... He will be like a tree planted by the water ... It has no worries in a year of drought ...'" (Jeremiah 17:5, 7, 8). How deep are your roots?

## July 16
### GOD'S CLAY

"So turn from your evil ways . . . and reform your ways and your actions." (Jeremiah 18:11)

Traveler: *Jeremiah*
Read: Jeremiah 18:1–23

My wife Sue is a professional seamstress. She sews everything, from minor alternations to wedding gowns. Over the years, I have often "visited" her sewing room to find her tearing up her work and starting over. I once asked her, "Isn't it discouraging to keep destroying something you've created?"

"No," she answered, "It's got to be done right, or it's not worth doing at all. The joy comes in seeing the garment fitting perfectly because of the corrections I've made along the way." She has to tear down to build up.

God sent Jeremiah to visit a potter. As Jeremiah watched the potter destroy a pot with a small flaw, God said: "O house of Israel, can I not do with you as this potter does? Like clay in the hand of the potter, so are you in my hand, O house of Israel. If at any time I announce that a nation or kingdom is to be uprooted, torn down and destroyed, and if that nation I warned repents of its evil, then I will relent and not inflict on it the disaster I had planned" (Jeremiah 18:6–8).

If you had been the garment Sue was sewing, you'd have no control over whether you would be torn apart. If you were a pot in the making, it would not be your fault if there was a flaw in your make-up. And as a human being, you didn't choose your sinful nature. But unlike the garment or the pot, you have the free will to *choose* whether you will be given over to disaster or saved from extinction: "So turn from your evil ways, each one of you, and reform your ways and your actions" (verse 11).

It's easy to say, "Hey, I'm not so bad. At least I'm not a robber or a murderer!" True, but each of us has many reasons to fear the things we have done wrong in our lives and we need to ask God's forgiveness. When is the last time you did that?

Whose clay are you?

## July 17
### LEADER OF THE PACK

> "I will surely save you out of a distant place . . ."
> (Jeremiah 30:10)

**Travelers:** *The Israelites*
**Read: Jeremiah 30:1–10**

Not now! It was snowing horizontally, and the temperature was well below zero. On the Minneapolis Christian radio station they were advising people to stay indoors, out of wind chill factors howling to sixty below. I had to drive sixty miles to the airport. And now my rental car windshield wipers had quit working.

Salt spray white-washed my windshield, despite the chill, but I knew I had to keep going. To stop on the side of the highway might mean getting stuck, and people die in conditions like that. The road was covered with dangerous icy ridges, between salt spots, making traction treacherous, but I realized that the faster I drove, the fewer cars could pass me and further spray-up my windshield. I prayed aloud the entire drive that God would help me make the right decisions, balancing between dangerous speed and a dirty window.

It's times like that when I know how little control I have, and how God can do anything He wants with me. Instead of getting scared, I am awed by the strength and mental power He gives me if I ask. Such was the case that frigid winter day.

Like the Israelites, I do not deserve salvation on my own: "I will discipline you but only with justice; I will not let you go entirely unpunished . . . because your guilt is so great and your sins so many" (Jeremiah 30:11,14). But God also said, "I will surely save you out of a distant place . . ." (verse 10). Why would He do that?

Make no mistake, God wants you to be saved. He waits and waits for you to turn from your own evil heart to Him. At the instant you do that sincerely, He is there. It takes leadership on your part to make it happen: "Their leader will be one of their own; their ruler will arise from among them. I will bring him near and he will come close to me, for who is he who will devote himself to be close to me?" (verse 21).

Will you be the leader God saves from a distant land?

## July 18
### BE LIKE EFFY

"After I strayed, I repented . . ."
(Jeremiah 31:19)

Traveler: *Ephraim*
**Read: Jeremiah 31:18–22**

I just figured out why more people don't follow God's ways! God needs a catchy marketing theme and jingle! God identified a role model for us to follow, a guy named Ephraim. But who can grab any press with a name like that? Earvin Johnson adopted the name "Magic." And Michael Jordan shortened his name to fit the glitzy ad campaign "Be Like Mike." Yeah, today you gotta have some pizzazz!

Ephraim was the second son of Joseph, and he received a very special blessing from Jacob (Genesis 48:19). But they never changed his name to "Effy," so he never got much press in the Bible. That is, until Jeremiah came along.

When God pointed to the kind of repentance that would free Israel from captivity, he pointed toward Effy as a model: "After I strayed, I repented; after I came to understand, I beat my breast. I was ashamed and humiliated because I bore the disgrace of my youth" (Jeremiah 31:19). But when God heard this confession, His heart immediately poured forth: "Is not Ephraim my dear son, the child in whom I delight? . . . Therefore my heart yearns for him; I have great compassion for him . . ." (verse 20).

Are you not God's son or daughter, too? Isn't God just waiting until you have full understanding of true repentance? Can't you sense Him so near, perhaps with tears rolling down his cheeks, hoping that this is the moment you will truly return to Him?

Don't be like Mike. Don't be like Magic. God waits patiently with this promise: "I will lead them beside streams of water on a level path where they will not stumble . . . Set up the road signs; put up guideposts. Take note of the highway, the road that you take. Return . . ." (verses 9 and 21). Be like Effy!

## *July 19*
### WHAT TO PRAY FOR

". . . you made a fatal mistake when you sent me . . ."
(Jeremiah 42:20)

**Traveler:** *Jeremiah*
**Read: Jeremiah 41:16–42:22**

Most of us have heard the old saying, "Be careful what you pray for; you may get it." The saying is biblically correct. We tend to pray for what we want, not what God wants. If we open our hearts far enough, we may get what God wants, and that may come with some surprises.

For example, someone might pray for his job to stop requiring so much travel. That prayer might be answered by losing the job altogether. Or another might pray for a new home, which comes with a higher payment and longer working hours. Still others pray, "Lord, if you'll get me out of this mess, I'll do whatever you say for the rest of my life." Oh, really?

We haven't changed very much from the Israelites, who wanted to keep God near enough to fend off big disasters, but not so close as to cramp their style of life. When they tried to flee to Egypt from captivity in Babylon, they went to Jeremiah and begged, "Pray that the Lord your God will tell us where we should go and what we should do" (Jeremiah 42:3). God answered through the prophet, "If you stay in this land, I will build you up and not tear you down; I will plant you and not uproot you, for I am grieved over the disaster I have inflicted on you" (verse 10).

But they went on to Egypt anyway. Even though God had said exactly what He would do (that is, He answered their prayers), they fled to Egypt. Jeremiah replied, "O remnant of Judah, the Lord has told you, 'Do not go to Egypt.' Be sure of this: I warn you today that you made a fatal mistake when you sent me to the Lord your God and said, 'Pray to the Lord our God for us; tell us everything he says and we will do it. . . .'" So now be sure of this: You will die . . ." (verses 19,20,22).

Be careful what you pray for.

## July 20
### EASY TARGET

> "Arise and attack a nation at ease, which lives in confidence . . ."
> (Jeremiah 49:31)

Travelers: *The Babylonians*
Read: Jeremiah 49:28–33

This devotion was written on a day in December, 1995, when I was supposed to be working. I had spent quite a sum of money to come to Washington, D.C. to make business contacts in the government. But the government was shut down. It was the first day of the great budget showdown, and all but one of my appointments was canceled.

The budget showdown was the first attempt in modern history to force the nation to balance its budget. That is, the government was being asked to spend what it took in, not the billions in excess which have made us the largest debtor nation in the world. Sadly, the showdown ended with yet another agreement to raise the debt ceiling and borrow more money. But at least, to many Americans, the realization struck home that we cannot continue on this path much longer. At least a line was drawn. At least we showed a sense of repentance for our long legacy of fiscal foolishness.

Israel's moral and spiritual decline had caused it to become lax, and its departure from obedience to God had left it vulnerable to attack: "Nebuchadnezzar, king of Babylon has plotted against you; he has devised a plan against you" (Jeremiah 49:30). And what was the plan? "Arise and attack a nation at ease, which lives in confidence" (verse 31). Israel was an easy target. It fell.

Is America an easy target? Not with our strong military, you say. But what plan is being devised against us? As the world's police force for defending freedom, how long will it take us to be spread too thin, on too many humanitarian missions? And what happens if, just at the wrong moment, the world's financial markets collapse? What happens if all that huge debt gets called in at a moment when our expenses are high?

We'll fall. We're an easy target, too.

And you? Are you an easy target personally? Satan lives by the same strategy as Nebuchadnezzar. Are you at ease, living in confidence on your own strength?

## July 21
### AMERICA IN EXILE?

"Do not lose heart . . . when rumors are heard in the land . . ."
(Jeremiah 51:46)

**Travelers:** *The Israelites*
**Read: Jeremiah 51:36–53**

Israel was in exile in Babylon for a very long time. During that time, God gave Babylon power over Israel, even though Babylon was itself an evil nation. God's mission was to teach His children a lesson. But when the time came to free Israel, God brought disaster down on the Babylonians. They, too, lost God's favor.

Is it possible that America has been in exile without ever leaving home? Our country was founded as a haven for religious freedom; most of the founding fathers were devout Christians. But in the twentieth century, during our lifetimes, things have changed dramatically. I read recently about a young girl who was given a zero grade on a term paper about the life of Jesus Christ, while papers on Satanism and witchcraft were allowed. Even more amazing, the U. S. Supreme Court refused to hear her protest. The true America has been in exile since 1954, when prayer was banned in the schools.

Christians in America are much more like the Israelites in Babylon than we want to imagine. And that's exactly what should give us tremendous hope! The book of Jeremiah ends on a shockingly upbeat note after such an agonizingly long prophecy of doom. Like a parent who ends the punishment of a misbehaving child with a giant hug, God says that it's over: "Come out of her, my people! Run for your lives! Run from the fierce anger of the Lord. Do not lose heart or be afraid when rumors are heard in the land; one rumor comes this year, another the next, rumors of violence in the land and of ruler against ruler. For the time will surely come when I punish the idols of Babylon; her whole land will be disgraced . . . Then heaven and earth . . . will shout for joy over Babylon . . ." (Jeremiah 51:45–48).

Violence in the American Babylon may be economic, not physical. But the rumors are there for exiles to note.

## July 22
### THE DAYS OF OLD

"... all the treasures that were hers in the days of old."
(Lamentations 1:7)

Travelers: *The Israelites*
**Read: Lamentations 1:1–9**

I can point to the exact moment when the company I worked for turned from the path of prosperity to destruction. The good people still working there must wonder every day about the treasures they once had. The company was highly profitable, with a great work environment where people cared about each other. But that was lost, probably forever, because those in power instituted subtle but sure changes in values. Only with the perspective of time is the picture so clear.

The writer of Lamentations (probably Jeremiah) also had a historical perspective on the fall of Jerusalem: "In the days of her affliction and wandering Jerusalem remembers all the treasures that were hers in days of old. When her people fell into enemy hands, there was no one to help her. Her enemies looked at her and laughed at her destruction" (Lamentations 1:7).

Will we look back on American history with the same kind of regret? I'm thinking of a bombed-out hulk of a government building in Oklahoma City. Are the seeds of our destruction budding within? We always thought the Commies would do us in. Satan is more clever than that.

Look in the mirror. The bad news is that the enemy is within. The good news is that it's not too late to do something about it. The enemy within is the same enemy that plagued the Israelites. We have walked away from God's teaching even farther than they did. But now is the time to recognize that we have been deceived: "Do not be deceived: God cannot be mocked. A man reaps what he sows" (Galatians 6:7). And a nation reaps what it sows.

Yet God waits for us with open arms, if only we will see what has happened before it is too late. He yearns for us to return to Him.

When we look back over time, will it be with regret or relief?

## July 23
### NO COUCH POTATO

> "... while I was among the exiles ... the heavens were opened ..." (Ezekiel 1:1)

Travelers: *Ezekiel and God*
**Read: Ezekiel 1:1–14**

In my thirty-third year, the first month on the twenty-first day, while sitting on an airplane during three years of almost continuous travel, God gave me the vision to start a ministry for frequent travelers. I did not receive this message while sitting at home behind a desk. I was out among those who travel, and I felt what you feel. God asked me to comfort you and encourage you. Eventually, the Christian Travelers' Network was formed for this purpose.

Ezekiel, the prophet received a similar calling: "In the thirtieth year, in the fourth month on the fifth day, while I was among the exiles by the Kebar River, the heavens were opened and I saw visions of God" (Ezekiel 1:1). Ezekiel was out among the people he was called to serve.

The introduction to the book of Ezekiel in my NIV Bible says, "Nowhere in the Bible are God's initiative and control over all creation expressed more clearly and pervasively than in Ezekiel . . . God's total sovereignty is also evident in his mobility. He was not limited to his temple; he can respond to his people under any circumstance."

God is a frequent traveler. God is not a couch potato, lounging in some heavenly setting, far from the action, ruling things with hand signals to messenger angels.

Two days ago at breakfast, my family prayed for God to put a hedge of protection around me as I went off to a series of meetings. At lunch in one of Denver's finer restaurants, I nearly swallowed an inch-long sliver of steel that had cork-screwed from a faulty can opener into the marinara sauce. Something—or Someone—kept me from swallowing that mouthful. I could almost feel God right beside me at that moment.

How do you think of God? If He seems distant to you, take time while you are out among the "exiles" and look for His message. He is closer to you than you can imagine. And He provides infinite strength at moments when you need Him most.

## July 24
## OVERWHELMED

"... I sat among them for seven days—overwhelmed."
(Ezekiel 3:15)

Traveler: *Ezekiel*
**Read: Ezekiel 3:1–15**

Every big city has its share of panhandlers. As a Christian, I have always struggled with how to treat them. But I have never encountered them in such great numbers as in Washington, D.C. I have no idea why this is the case, but a walk down any of Washington's busiest streets becomes a gauntlet of people, God's people, asking for money. To me, it is overwhelming.

Not all spiritual experiences are sweet, but all have purpose. Ezekiel's assignment was not fun: "The Spirit then lifted me up and took me away, and I went in bitterness and in the anger of my spirit, with the strong hand of the Lord upon me. I came to the exiles who lived at Tel Abib near the Kebar River. And there, where they were living, I sat among them for seven days—overwhelmed" (Ezekiel 3:14–15).

I feel anger and bitterness too when I encounter panhandlers. These feelings are not directed at them, but at their situations. What caused them to become exiles from society? Which ones are truly in need? Which ones are just lazy beggars?

Two things become apparent. First, it is not my job to judge each one. And second, I have never taken the time to stop and spend time among them, to try and understand their plight. I am always too busy, running from meeting to meeting, from train to plane.

Notice that Ezekiel spent seven days among them. Job's friends spent seven days with him in silence, trying to understand the depths of his suffering (Job 2:13). Joseph observed a seven-day mourning period for his father (Genesis 50:10). And the people of Jabesh Gilead fasted seven days after the Philistines killed Saul (1 Samuel 31:13).

Perhaps there is a way to understand panhandlers. That would be to spend seven days among them. That would not be a sweet experience. Neither is the word of God easy to apply. Think about it. What does God really expect of us in ministry?

## *July 25*
### A PROMISING RETURN

"... I have been a sanctuary for them in the countries where they have gone." (Ezekiel 11:16)

Traveler: *God*
**Read: Ezekiel 11:1–15**

If you travel frequently on business, you probably long for the day when it will end and you can stay home for good. I have met very few people who have traveled for more than ten years and still enjoy it. That's why the experiences of the Israelites in exile are helpful to us. We can share how they felt, how they longed to return home and how God was working His plan for them, even though it took a long time to come true.

Through the prophet Ezekiel, we see God's long term plan: "... Although I sent them far away among the nations and scattered them among the countries, yet for a little while I have been a sanctuary for them in the countries where they have gone ... I will gather you from the nations and bring you back from the countries where you have been scattered, and I will give you back the land of Israel again" (Ezekiel 11:16–17).

God has a purpose for our travel. More than that, He has been a sanctuary for us wherever we have gone. What is a sanctuary? I think of a church, a place of worship. I think also of a place of protection, like a wildlife sanctuary. So God is with us as we carry out His plan, using our circumstances to bring us closer to Him in personal worship. And He provides us protection while we are learning about Him.

This message is specially important as more and more of us are required to travel internationally just to keep our jobs. If you think Hoboken was tough, wait until Ho Chi Minh City!

Best of all is God's promise to bring His people home. Are you wondering when your current assignment will end? Take heart. Use this time wisely to connect personally with God while you are being protected by Him in a "foreign" situation. When the time is right, He will give you back your land. That land may be your heart, which will then be totally aligned with His purposes, for the rest of your life.

## July 26
### FLOURISHING IN A FLEABAG

"I dry up the green tree and make the dry tree flourish."
(Ezekiel 17:24)

Traveler: *Ezekiel*
**Read: Ezekiel 17:1–24**

I saw an advertisement last week for a new generation of hotels for business travelers. The concept is to make new hotel rooms much more conducive to work. Brighter lighting, extra phone lines, fax machine, printer, data link—maximizing a person's connectivity with the Internet and the home office. Better working conditions mean more productivity, right?

They are missing something that's as old as time. That is, the need for rest and spiritual refreshment. Sure, there are times when a report must be worked on at night. But not everyone can work eighteen hours a day, not if they want to live beyond the age of fifty.

Of course, the new business hotel concept is only a nineties marketing variation, and the ideas come from business travelers themselves. And certainly working hard in your room is better than the distractions of cable television and the hotel bar.

But recently, I discovered a different way to spend my time. I was stuck in a very tired, old place with no television, no room service, no restaurant, no bar, not even pictures on the wall. The lighting would have made Abe Lincoln's firelight seem bright. It was more like a jail cell than a hotel room. To make matters worse, I didn't have a car. I thought I was trapped.

Guess what. With no distractions, I propped up a pillow, pulled out my Bible, and wrote over fifty of these devotions in two evenings, where I normally average no more than two a day.

God said, "All the trees of the field will know that I the Lord bring down the tall tree and make the low tree grow tall. I dry up the green tree and make the dry tree flourish" (Ezekiel 17:24). My room was very dry. And it flourished.

Hotels can be trees, too. How's that for market analysis?

## July 27
### TO THE FRONT OF THE LINE

"... their hearts are greedy for unjust gain."
(Ezekiel 33:31)

Travelers: *God's People*
**Read: Ezekiel 33:21–33**

Dark clouds scudded across an angry sky, cutting off the Washington Monument below its pointed pinnacle. Wind whipped the flags above the shivering crowd waiting in the taxi line at the train station. A steady rain fell—no, flew—horizontally. Nasty.

I stood in line about thirty minutes, slowly working my way to the front. But in the nation's capital, there are those who cannot tolerate the thought of waiting, of standing in line like a common person. I watched as one young couple at the back of the line became very agitated. The man hissed, "This is ridiculous! I don't care what that starter says up there. There's got to be a better way!" Someone advised him, "Look, there's plenty of cabs in line; it'll only take a few minutes and you'll be on your way." But he snarled and dragged his wife, and all their baggage, out from under the limited shelter offered by the station into the storm to hail a cab.

The Israelites were an impatient lot, too. And they would not listen to God's guidance to "stay in line." God told Ezekiel, "My people come to you, as they usually do, and sit before you to listen to your words, but they do not put them into practice. With their mouths they express devotion, but their hearts are greedy for unjust gain" (Ezekiel 33:31). Can't you hear them yelling, "There's got to be a better way!"

But God said, "When all this comes true—and it surely will—then they will know that a prophet has been among them" (verse 33).

As my taxi, which I had patiently "earned," pulled away from the station, I saw that couple huddled on a nearby corner, waving at one taxi after another, as each one splashed by and got in line with the other taxis at the train station. The man and his wife were thoroughly soaked and every driver in town seemed to know that they had tried to gain unjustly.

Do you just listen to God's words, or do you put them into practice?

## July 28
### SHEPHERD OR SHEEP?

> "Should not shepherds take care of the flock?"
> (Ezekiel 34:2)

Travelers: *The Israelites*
Read: Ezekiel 34:1–31

I have wasted more evenings than I can count in hotel rooms over the years. After a hard day's work with a customer, all I want is a hot shower, an edible meal, a good book and a good night's sleep. I take good care of myself. But I have always been conscious of the amount of time spent "vegging out."

The tendency to "cocoon" inside a hotel is even greater today, because there is increasing danger outside. Twenty years ago a nice evening walk around the neighborhood was exhilarating. Today, you might be a target. Better to be a good sheep and stay in the fold.

But I know Christians who spend their first ten minutes, after arriving at the hotel, scanning the Yellow Pages to find a local church with a worship service that evening. They have a thirst for being with God's people that overcomes any concerns about safety. And they are always richly blessed by touching the community, even though they are strangers. They are shepherds, always caring for the flock.

Ezekiel pointed out that Israel's ultimate doom came because its leaders, its shepherds, abandoned their flocks, caring only for themselves: "Woe to the shepherds of Israel who only take care of themselves! Should not shepherds take care of the flock? You eat the curds, clothe yourselves with the wool and slaughter the choice animals, but you do not take care of the flock" (Ezekiel 34:2–3).

I'm not sure I have all the answers for frequent travelers who have the potential to be the shepherds—leaders—of our land. But I do know what God expects: "You have not strengthened the weak or healed the sick or bound up the injured. You have not brought back the strays or searched for the lost" (verse 4).

How can we, as a community on the move, reach the weak, sick and injured? How can we seek the lost? I'm not sure. But I know how not to do it. That's by worrying only whether there's an extra portion of pepperoni on my room service pizza.

## July 29
### DEM DRY BONES

"... it was full of bones."
(Ezekiel 37:1)

**Traveler:** *Ezekiel*
**Read: Ezekiel 37:1–14**

In 1980, we had lived in our house in the southwestern quadrant of metropolitan Denver, for four years. When we first moved to this house, we thought it was "out in the country," miles from anywhere, surrounded by rolling hills, a few lakes and streams and a great view of the mountains to the west. But in a very short time, the area became a beehive of activity with tens of thousands of new homes, schools and the biggest shopping mall west of the Mississippi.

I was part of a group of people who saw that this booming area was badly in need of new churches. And we set about founding a new one to serve a population that rapidly grew above 100,000 people. It was as if God had set us in that area for that purpose. For the next five years, development of that church consumed every spare moment.

Ezekiel, the prophet was carried along in the spirit of God and set down in a valley of dry bones: "The hand of the Lord was upon me, and he brought me out by the Spirit of the Lord and set me in the middle of a valley; it was full of bones . . . Then he said to me, 'Prophesy to these bones and say to them, "Dry bones, hear the word of the Lord! This is what the Sovereign Lord says to these bones: I will make breath enter you, and you will come to life"'" (Ezekiel 37:1,4–5).

Ezekiel was first carried along by God's spirit. Then God set him down in a valley of death and asked him to breathe life into the opportunity he saw in front of him. God set us down in a place where His new church could breathe life into a new community.

What situation is God trying to put you down into that appears like dry bones, devoid of life, but which could be brought alive by your involvement? Are you being carried along in God's spirit so that He can show you His valley of dry bones?

Seek Him now. Opportunity awaits.

## July 30
### JUNK FOOD

> "But Daniel resolved not to defile himself with the royal food and wine . . ." (Daniel 1:8)

Traveler: *Daniel*
**Read: Daniel 1:1–17**

My son's basketball team was playing in a small town a good distance away. Sue and I often find some fast-food nearby and bring it to the gym for dinner. Small town: no restaurants near the school. But when some other fans from our school brought in hot dogs and soft drinks, we learned that there was a convenience store about five miles away. With growling stomachs, we sprinted to the store to grab something before the game started.

Since the convenience store had the only supply of hot food within miles, their hot dogs were gone when we got there. So, in a fit of pique and revenge against the standards of decency and good diet, I selected a tall can of cheese flavored potato chips, a 32 ounce cola, and, to top it off, a chocolate candy bar. I'm sure my wife was silently making funeral arrangements, suspecting this "meal" would be my last.

The book of Daniel is the perfect guide for godly conduct while traveling. During Israel's exile, Daniel was selected by Nebuchadnezzar to serve in the king's palace, learn the language and literature of the Babylonians and to eat the best that the King had to offer. The King planned to "re-culture" the Jews. "But Daniel resolved not to defile himself with the royal food and wine . . ." (Daniel 1:8) and he found a sympathetic official who wanted to help Daniel and his three friends. Daniel said, "'Please test your servants for ten days: Give us nothing but vegetables to eat and water to drink' . . . At the end of the ten days they looked healthier and better nourished than any of the young men who ate the royal food" (verses 12,15).

"To these four young men God gave knowledge and understanding of all kinds of literature and learning" (verse 17). Do you resolve not to defile yourself when you travel, or do you feel sorry for yourself like I did? Could you be missing out on God's wisdom?

## July 31
### NEED A FOURTH?

"... the God we serve is able to save us..."
(Daniel 3:17)

Travelers: *Shadrach, Meshach, Abednego and an Angel*
**Read: Daniel 3:1–30**

Few of us have ever been tested for our faith as severely as Shadrach, Meshach and Abednego, who were thrown into a fiery furnace for not worshipping King Nebuchadnezzar. But we've all been tested much more subtly. Daniel's friends refused to worship the king. Do we refuse to worship other gods?

These three men chose to defy the king with no hesitation: "If we are thrown into the blazing furnace, the God we serve is able to save us from it, and he will rescue us from your hand, O king. But even if he does not, we want you to know, O king, that we will not serve your gods or worship the image of gold you have set up" (Daniel 3:17–18). They had no assurance that they would not die in the fire! They knew the matter was up to God and they knew right from wrong.

Now who are the travelers in this story? Not only Shadrach, Meshach and Abednego: "'Look! I see four men walking around in the fire, unbound and unharmed, and fourth looks like a son of the gods . . . servants of the Most High God, come out! Come here!'" (verses 25, 26). The men walked out of the fire totally unharmed. And the king said, "'Praise be to the God of Shadrach, Meshach and Abednego, who has sent his angel and rescued his servants! They trusted in him and defied the king's command and were willing to give up their lives rather than serve or worship any god except their own God'" (verse 28). The angel of God was the fourth traveler and he came to those who trusted God.

Today, do you try to rationalize shades of gray rather than the black and white of what's right and what's wrong? Are you willing to die for what's right? Are you trusting God? If you think you've been challenged before, are you ready for when the fire gets *really* hot?

## *August 1*
### THE BIGGER THEY ARE . . .

"And those who walk in pride he is able to humble."
(Daniel 4:37)

Traveler: *Nebuchadnezzar*
**Read: Daniel 4:1–37**

The bigger they are, the harder they fall. This old saying was never more true than for King Nebuchadnezzar. And I'm wondering, as I write in early 1996, if it won't also prove true for the Republican Party.

Nebuchadnezzar was warned in a dream interpreted by Daniel that unless the king acknowledged that heaven ruled the earth, he would lose his kingdom and his sanity, and live like a wild animal. It happened. Nebuchadnezzar crowed about his "mighty power and . . . the glory of my majesty" (Daniel 4:30). Immediately God took it all away, and for a long time the king wandered in insanity. Then one day, his senses returned and he glorified God. His testimony is so powerful in the first person: "Now I, Nebuchadnezzar, praise and exalt and glorify the King of Heaven, because everything he does is right and all his ways are just. And those who walk in pride he is able to humble" (verse 37).

In November, 1994, one of the great political victories of modern times was won by the Republican Party, destroying a Democratic machine that had been in power for almost half a century. The people had had enough, and they wanted change. The keys to power were handed to the Republicans.

But instead of consolidating power by accomplishing badly needed change in our government, they turned on each other, numerous candidates clawing at each other for the right to dethrone the current president. In just a few short months, they went from the most successful political coup in American history to a bunch of back-stabbing, negative mud-throwers. With the presidential election still nine months away, the American people have already snorted their disgust. Me, too, a lifelong Republican. I don't know how the election will turn out. At this writing, that's not important. What's necessary now is to point out what happened, independently of the results. Pride got in the way of service.

Do you walk in pride? Think back over the last week. Were there times when you could have responded to a situation with humility?

## August 2
### ANGEL TRAFFIC CONTROL

"Gabriel . . . came to me in swift flight . . ."
(Daniel 9:21)

**Traveler:** *Gabriel*
**Read: Daniel 9:20–27**

Whenever I can, I listen to Air Traffic Control (ATC) as I fly. I love the unique language controllers and pilots use to communicate with each other. Their professionalism has often amazed me during stormy weather over Chicago. But now we read that the system is getting old and out-dated, with more frequent breakdowns of 1960's vintage equipment. The government has moved too slowly to modernize the system and many feel that serious problems lie ahead. That's a chilling thought for all frequent fliers.

I have listened to events when a plane has lost its radio and ATC worked feverishly to re-establish contact with the plane on emergency frequencies. It would be a scary feeling to be flying in traffic and lose contact with ATC. And there's another kind of ATC—Angel Traffic Control. It could be even worse to lose contact with this protective system. Yet most of us are in greater danger of being lost on God's radar than on Air Traffic Control radar.

Daniel was always tuned in. The way he maintained contact is important for all of us to learn: "While I was speaking and praying, confessing my sin and the sin of my people Israel and making my request to the Lord my God for his holy hill—while I was still in prayer, Gabriel, the man I had seen in the earlier vision, came to me in swift flight . . . and said to me, 'Daniel, I have now come to give you insight and understanding. As soon as you began to pray, an answer was given, which I have come to tell you, for you are highly esteemed'" (Daniel 9:20–23).

Something made Daniel's radar signal so strong that Gabriel glided in on instruments as soon as Daniel began to pray! That signal was confession. If you feel far from God, or if you wonder why an angel hasn't come to you personally, take a look at how you pray and whether you truly confess your sins and those of our nation.

Are you held in high esteem by Angel Traffic Control? If not, your signal can always become stronger. Fix it today!

## August 3
### END TIMES

"Multitudes who sleep in the dust of the earth will awake . . ."
(Daniel 12:2)

Traveler: *Daniel*
**Read: Daniel 10:1–12:4**

I have seen frequent travelers perpetrate some of the strangest acts on fellow travelers. From smashing packages in overhead bins to cutting into line to cursing overworked flight attendants, I have never understood the arrogant attitude of some people. But then maybe I do. Maybe they believe that how they treat others doesn't matter, since they'll never see them again anyway. After all, what are the odds of bumping into a stranger you've offended a second time?

Whether you ever see that person again is not the point. It's amazing how few people realize the immortality of their actions. As bad as it would be to encounter that offended person on a future flight, there is another kind of encounter that would be far worse: "Multitudes who sleep in the dust of the earth will awake: some to everlasting life, others to shame and everlasting contempt. Those who are wise will shine like the brightness of the heavens, and those who lead many to righteousness, like the stars for ever and ever" (Daniel 12:2–3).

Can you imagine being reminded of those deeds you committed on fellow travelers for all eternity? Why don't more people take the eternal implications of their actions seriously? There is a common misconception that perhaps Christians will indeed be resurrected in an afterlife (and maybe they even deserve something good for their faith), but nonbelievers will just go to sleep peacefully at death and that's it. Just quiet oblivion. No afterlife, no accountability. Blackness. You live your life, I'll live mine. No harm, no foul. No penalty shots at the end of the game.

Wrong. For those trusting God: "As for you, go your way till the end. You will rest, and then at the end of the days you will rise to receive your allotted inheritance" (verse 13). But others will rise to receive their allotted everlasting contempt.

If you have regrets over how you've treated others in the past, God waits with armed outstretched for you to confess to Him and to heal you. You have so much to inherit!

## August 4
### DON'T LOOK DOWN!

> "Though you soar like the eagle . . . from there I will bring you down." (Obadiah 1:4)

Travelers: *Edomites*
**Read: Obadiah 1:1–21**

An old saying goes like this: "He who dies with the most toys wins." I don't think so. Instead, I believe that life has a way of balancing out, that God gives us each opportunities to succeed and fail. How we come out depends on the battle between our free will and our willingness to depend on Him in faith.

Not too long ago, I was a very powerful business executive in a fairly large company. Not too long after that, I came crashing out of favor with the "big-wigs" of the firm. Then, for awhile my own consulting business flourished. Recently it has staggered in the wake of two major project cancellations. Tomorrow, who knows? Through it all, my faith has become stronger as has my relationship with my family. God has provided, in ways I could not have expected.

Last week, *two* of my friends came to me reporting probable bankruptcy proceedings. Both are good men who, by the world's standards, did not "deserve" what has happened. They are also wonderful Christians and radiate a faith that makes it clear they won't be taking their financial assets, or lack thereof, to heaven.

Another friend recently avoided economic disaster by the skin of his teeth. Today, while I'm struggling, his business has turned around, and he's flying high. Praise God! And he does!

If you're doing extremely well today, enjoy yourself, because it may not last. That's hard to say, because I am a die-hard optimist. But I'm convinced that tough times happen for a reason: "'Though you soar like the eagle and make your nest among the stars, from there I will bring you down,' declares the Lord" (Obadiah 1:4). The reason is just to make sure you haven't forgotten who put you up there in the first place.

And if you're down right now, the trips are adding up and the orders aren't, take heart! Stay the course and watch for a fresh breeze beneath those eagle wings of yours.

## August 5
### NOT GOOD

> "But Jonah ran away from the Lord . . ."
> (Jonah 1:3)

**Traveler:** *Jonah*
**Read:** Jonah 1:1–17

There is a humorous, secular myth that the presence of a man or women "of the cloth" can bring protection even to those who do not believe. Everyone who travels frequently has seen a nun or priest board an airplane, after which someone whispers, "Guess we don't have to worry about this plane crashing!"

It's a good thing those non-believers never read about the trip Jonah took: "The word of the Lord came to Jonah, son of Amittai: 'Go to the great city of Ninevah and preach against it, because its wickedness has come up before me.' But Jonah ran away from the Lord and headed for Tarshish. He went down to Joppa, where he found a ship bound for that port" (Jonah 1:1–3).

God called Jonah; he fled, and God kept pursuing him. So hard, in fact, that Jonah's ship was engulfed in a terrifying storm. When the sailors discovered that Jonah was running from God, they threw him overboard to save themselves. And the storm stopped. Jonah's calling hadn't kept the ship safe; he had brought it disaster. The non-believers recognized God's power more than Jonah did!

It never occurred to me that if I avoid God's calling, I could bring bad things down on those around me. I've always looked on God as my Great Protector in an evil world. It seems clear that God expects more from His children than from those who do not yet know Him. And it seems that He is not beyond scaring the spaghetti out of everyone to get our attention. An old commercial proclaimed, "It's not nice to fool Mother Nature!" Well, it's not good to run from God's calling, either!

Fortunately, it wasn't too late for Jonah. After spending three days in the belly of a huge fish, Jonah was ejected. We can almost see him wiping his brow in relief: "Jonah obeyed the word of the Lord and went to Ninevah" (Jonah 3:3).

Has God called you to something you've been avoiding? Think about all those around you, if you keep running.

## August 6
### SOMETIMES GOD SMILES

> "... act justly ... love mercy ... walk humbly ..."
> (Micah 6:8)

Travelers: *You and I*
Read: Micah 6:1–8

We spend lots of time complaining about what's wrong with the world. There are plenty of wrongs to choose from. But every once in awhile, something happens that makes God smile. Such an event happened here in Denver recently.

Within hours of the announcement that the Oklahoma City bombing trial was being moved to Denver to assure a fair trial, thousands of people all over the city thought first about the Oklahoma families who would now have to spend weeks or months far from home if they want to attend the trial. Others, of course, began rubbing their hands together with glee, calculating the money they can make from this windfall invasion of international media. But local agencies were swamped with calls from people volunteering every imaginable form of hospitality to help those families. The calls came from every sector—believers and nonbelievers alike. They came from people with big hearts, who may be closer to God than they realize (see Mark 12:28–34).

This event proves that all people know right from wrong, justice from injustice, love from hate. God wrote His laws on every heart: "He has showed you, O man, what is good. And what does the Lord require of you? To act justly and to love mercy and to walk humbly with your God" (Micah 6:8). A society that puts these principles into action might save itself from the kind of wrath Micah proclaimed.

If the people of Denver can reach out to the people of Oklahoma City with such passion, I wonder if the people of Denver will learn to reach out to the people of Denver. There's a sort of romance to taking up the task of helping the bombing victims' families. But we have plenty of bombed-out souls right in our own back yard.

How can you take Micah's teaching to heart right where you are today? Don't wait for a big media event.

## August 7
### CLEAN SWEEP

"... they sweep past ... guilty men whose own strength is their god." (Habakkuk 1:11)

Travelers: *The Babylonians*
**Read: Habakkuk 1:1–11**

Corporate downsizing in the 1990s has been accompanied by a major upswing in the stock market. As one national news magazine put it, Wall Street loves corporate killers. Investors apparently believe that cutting jobs makes a healthier company.

There are days when cancer patients feel good, too. We must ask how long this trend can continue before all the jobs have gone overseas and only the stockholders thrive.

Habakkuk wondered the same thing as he watched his homeland desecrated by strangers: "How long, O Lord, must I call for help, but you do not listen? Or cry out to you, 'Violence!' but you do not save? Why do you make me look at injustice? Why do you tolerate wrong?" (Habakkuk 1:2). He got a shocking answer straight from God: "Look at the nations and watch—and be utterly amazed. For I am doing something in your days that you would not believe, even if you were told. I am raising up the Babylonians, that ruthless and impetuous people ... they sweep past like the wind and go on—guilty men, whose own strength is their god" (verses 5,6,11).

God not only allowed the Babylonians to rise, He caused it! Israel deserved what it got because of its repeated disobedience. But when calamity came, they couldn't understand why God was so nasty.

We're the same way. God allows the ungodly to rule until we learn something, no matter how long that takes or how tough it gets. He wants us to trust in Him completely. When we do, we will be like new: "The Sovereign Lord is my strength; he makes my feet like the feet of a deer, he enables me to go on the heights" (Habakkuk 3:19).

If you've never read Hannah Hurnard's book, *Hinds Feet in High Places*, read it now. It's about overcoming handicaps, ones that God uses to cause a clean sweep in your heart.

## August 8
### POCKET HOLES

"... to put them in a purse with holes in it."
(Haggai 1:6)

Travelers: *You and I*
**Read: Haggai 1:1–15**

As you bustle about, ask yourself if you have enough material wealth. Most Americans would say "No," especially in these days of such uncertainty. Today it's time to take stock of your lifestyle: "Now this is what the Lord Almighty says: 'Give careful thought to your ways. You have planted much, but have harvested little. You eat, but never have enough. You drink, but never have your fill. You put on clothes, but are not warm. You earn wages, only to put them in a purse with holes in it'" (Haggai 1:5–6).

Those are very convicting words to me. As a small business owner, I am always worrying about where the next project will come from—but have I planted the kind of opportunities that can be harvested, or have I become lazy in business development?

It's Girl Scout Cookie season as I write this—I eat, but I never have enough! As I work in my home office, I always carry a cup of coffee or a glass of water around, drinking but not having my fill. Why? And I never feel good about my clothes, always feeling out of style. I earn pretty good wages, but my pockets are definitely full of holes. My money flows easily for entertainment; not so easily for building our new church.

Haggai penned his prophecy to encourage returning exiles to rebuild the temple in Jerusalem. God had to dry up their crops to get their attention: "... while each of you is busy with his own house" (verse 9). Finally, the people were stirred and obeyed.

Haggai talked about the physical temple. Our challenge is to respond just as faithfully to building the spiritual one, the Kingdom of God.

As you approach the end of the Old Testament, give careful thought to your ways. Are you ready to harvest for God? Are you hungry and thirsty for Him? By working a little harder, can you be warmer with fewer clothes? Can you save up spiritual treasures where they once slipped by?

Jesus is coming! Are you ready?

## August 9
### BY CONTRAST

"Shout and be glad . . . be still . . ."
(Zechariah 2:10, 13)

**Traveler:** *God*
**Read: Zechariah 2:1–13**

Is there anything quite like a high school basketball game between two arch rivals? Rooting for either team is a roller-coaster of ups and downs. One moment the home crowd is roaring its approval while the visitors are quiet. Instantly the tide turns. The visitors come back with a brilliant pass assisting an easy lay-up. Their fans erupt in ear-rattling hullabaloo, and the home crowd sits down. Briefly. Back and forth it goes.

In close games, it goes right down to the wire, like the game I attended last night. The home team won by two points after an incredibly hard-fought battle, which both sides deserved to win. But in the end, only one side was shouting and celebrating; the other side left quietly.

As our study approaches the end of the Old Testament, we've lived through all of Israel's trials and failures. We anxiously await the travel stories of the New Testament. A bridge is found here, in Zechariah and Malachi. Even though God punished Israel severely, He never lost His passionate love for His children. And when they returned to the Promised Land after the exile, He poured out His vision for what they could become. He also made it very clear that the nations He had allowed to rule Israel would soon suffer terribly for having abused His people.

Zechariah confirms that there will be winners and losers: "'Shout and be glad, O Daughter of Zion. For I am coming, and I will live among you,' declares the Lord . . . 'Be still before the Lord, all mankind, because he has roused himself from his holy dwelling'" (Zechariah 2:10–13). In the end, God's people will be shouting gladly. God's enemies will be silent. And the traveler in all this is God Himself. Don't you love the verb "roused?" Our God is not passive!

If you're feeling beaten and punished by God, take heart. First, remember that it is your actions that lead to sin and pain, not God's. Second, remember that He loves you beyond words. Stay faithful. You will shout for joy! Soon!

## *August 10*
### WHAT IS THAT SMELL?

"... dressed in filthy clothes as he stood before the angel."
(Zechariah 3:3)

Traveler: *Jesus, the Branch*
**Read: Zechariah 3:1–10**

Try jumping on an airplane immediately after spending a full day climbing around a hot, dusty, stinky garbage processing plant. When clothes absorb odor, they retain it for a long time. I never knew whether to tell those sitting near me exactly what they were smelling or to assume their ignorance was bliss.

My sin smells that bad and even worse to God. And I can't run from it any more than I could separate myself from my aromatic jeans on the airplane. That's why Zechariah is such a book of hope. In a vision, Zechariah saw the high priest Joshua dressed in filthy clothes, standing before an angel. Joshua represented the sin of the Israelites. And Satan was right there accusing him. But God said, "Is not this man a burning stick snatched from the fire?" (Zechariah 3:2).

Are we not all singed by the devil's wiles and temptations? You bet we are! But God said to Joshua, and He says to us: "See I have taken away your sin . . . If you will walk in my ways and keep my requirements, then you will govern my house and have charge of my courts, and I will give you a place among these standing here" (verses 4,7).

What follows is how God will do the trick: "I am going to bring my servant, the Branch . . . and I will remove the sin of this land in a single day" (verses 8,9). The "Branch" refers to the prophecy of Isaiah 4:2, which was written over 200 hundred years before Zechariah. The Branch is Jesus Christ, whom we will meet soon in these pages, face to face.

By the way, even after a hot, steamy, soapy shower, the smell of garbage stays in my nostrils for a while. By my own will, all the scrubbing in the world can't get me clean. Thankfully, a much stronger Cleanser is used on my heart.

So much for my dirty laundry. How about yours? Only the Branch can clean you entirely.

## *August 11*
WHO IS YOUR KING?

". . . Your king comes to you, righteous and having salvation . . ."
(Zechariah 9:9)

**Traveler:** *Jesus the King*
**Read: Zechariah 9:9–17**

In modern America, it's hard to imagine what it would be like to have a king, a monarch, a single person who rules over all. Our democracy is diametrically opposed to such a concept. Our forefathers fled from the King of England, in search of religious freedom. So what would it be like to have a king?

My king would be responsible for protecting me and for keeping peace in the land. In return, my very life would belong to him. He could tax me, induct me into the military, even tell me what to believe. If he was not a benevolent king, he could make my life miserable. I can imagine good kings and bad kings. What would a good king be like?

A good king would provide for me and guarantee eternal safety from evil. He would not tax me unfairly; in fact a great king would not tax me at all. And instead of telling me what to believe, he would be so gracious and kind, righteous in fact, that I would want to be like him, rather than be required to think like him. And I think my good king would not be arrogant. He would be wise beyond measure, but not flaunting riches and excess. He would drive a common man's car, not a Rolls Royce. My king would care for me so much that he would spend time with me, working right beside me, teaching and counseling me, wanting me to succeed, not feeling his political power threatened in any way, almost as if his power came from God.

I think I've found my Good King: "See, your king comes to you, righteous and having salvation, gentle and riding on a donkey . . . He will proclaim peace to the nations. His rule will extend from sea to sea . . ." (Zechariah 9:9). My King is coming soon. He is riding a donkey! Or is that an old Volkswagen bug?

FAITH IN MOTION

## August 12
ROBBING GOD

"Bring the whole tithe . . ."
(Malachi 3:10)

Travelers: *You and I*
**Read: Malachi 2:17–3:18**

This devotion is a little like Christmas Eve. It's the last one in the Old Testament, and we await the coming of the greatest traveler, Jesus, with great excitement. The New Testament feels like a brightly wrapped Christmas present sitting under the tree, beckoning. We can hardly stand the anticipation, waiting until we are allowed to open it.

What would it be like on Christmas morning if your father suddenly said, "Sorry, you can't have the present I've prepared for you. You don't deserve it." That's the kind of warning the prophet Malachi gave to the Israelites:

> "Ever since the time of your forefathers you have turned away from my decrees and have not kept them. Return to me, and I will return to you," says the Lord Almighty. "But you ask, 'How are we to return?' Will a man rob God? Yet you rob me. But you ask, 'How do we rob you?' In tithes and offerings. You are under a curse—the whole nation of you—because you are robbing me. Bring the whole tithe in the storehouse, that there may be food in my house. Test me in this," says the Lord Almighty, "and see if I will not throw open the floodgates of heaven and pour out so much blessing that you will not have room enough for it." (Malachi 3:7–10)

What is a tithe? The ancient root of the word means "tenth." Traditionally, a tithe has been interpreted as one-tenth of one's earnings. God warned the Israelites that failing to give the entire tithe was robbing God; robbing Him meant forfeiting indescribably wonderful blessings.

The modern focus on tithing is usually about money and giving to the church. But I think God has something more in mind. He is asking if you have dedicated enough of *yourself* to Him. Or perhaps you are holding something back. Not your money; your heart. Do you love Him? Do you want Him to give you the Gift?

Step forward. Offer yourself to Him. And watch the floodgates of heaven open through the travels and teachings of His Son, Jesus Christ.

## August 13
### SON-RISE

"We saw his star . . . and have come . . ."
(Matthew 2:2)

**Travelers:** *Wise Men*
**Read: Matthew 2:1–12**

I have always marveled at God's sunrises and sunsets. On certain days of the year, with just the right weather conditions, the colors are breath-taking. These events pass in just a few moments, but I feel as if God has reached down and touched me.

From my perch in the Colorado mountains, I've seen moon-rises and even moon-sets, shimmering momentarily atop the peaks like the cherry on a sundae. Once, I captured on film a moon-set, framed by bright crimson mountains reflecting a colorful sunrise on the other side of the sky, all framed by a rainbow. I wept that day as a gentle rain shower washed me in God's splendor.

There was another kind of "rise," even more beautiful than any other. It was a star-rise, unique in history: "After Jesus was born in Bethlehem in Judea, during the time of King Herod, Magi from the east came to Jerusalem and asked, 'Where is the one who has been born king of the Jews? We saw his star in the east and have come to worship him'" (Matthew 2:2). That star-rise was so spectacular that it caused some very wise men to leave everything and travel to find its source, which they already knew was the birth of a king.

How did the Magi know the significance of the star-rise? They used their specially honed sense of natural astronomy to recognize when something special had happened. Exactly how they knew it was because of the birth of the king of the Jews is not certain, but we can guess that they were aware of Balaam's prophecy centuries earlier: "I see him, but not now; I behold him, but not near. A star will come out of Jacob; a scepter will rise out of Israel" (Numbers 24:17).

Wisdom. The Magi pursued it relentlessly. They were rewarded with the most spectacular "rise" in history.

Wisdom. Are you seeking it everywhere you go? There are many sunrises, sunsets, moonrises and moonsets. There was only one Son-rise.

## *August 14*
### WONDER OR WISDOM?

> ". . . having been warned in a dream . . . they returned . . . by another route." (Matthew 2:12)

**Travelers:** *The Magi*
**Read (again): Matthew 2:1–12**

One of the guiding principles of my life, especially at times when I'm making decisions prayerfully, has been: "You'll never know unless you try." Without God directing my path, making decisions on that basis represents reckless abandon. But if wisdom and prayer are combined, all the excitement of life awaits. On more than one occasion, I've plunged ahead with a major life-changing experience, knowing only that I had trusted God and would not regret later that I had not tried.

The Magi knew from the stars that a momentous event had occurred. They apparently had wealth, wisdom and power. To leave all that and venture out onto the open road in search of the star must have taken great courage. But they were overcome with the desire to experience first-hand an unprecedented wonder.

They went. They met Herod. And Herod tried to manipulate them to locate this threat to his throne. But then something even more amazing happened: "And having been warned in a dream not to go back to Herod, they returned to their country by another route" (Matthew 2:12). Picture Herod waiting, waiting, and finally realizing he's been stood up!

Had the Magi never ventured out, they never would have encountered the treacherous Herod. Neither would they have been blessed by a warning directly from God. Nor would they have seen the Christ child in person. They would have wondered for the rest of their lives what they had missed by not going.

Have you ever wondered what it would be like to have God reach down and keep you from making a bad decision? Wouldn't life be easier if He talked to you like He did to the Magi? Well, He does! But you'll never know about it unless you venture out in faith toward that unknown task He has given you. If you don't respond, you'll always wonder what might have happened.

God was there for the Magi. He's there for you, too.

## August 15
### DREAM OR DIRECTION?

"... an angel of the Lord appeared in a dream ..."
(Matthew 2:19)

**Travelers:** *Joseph, Mary and Jesus*
**Read: Matthew 2:19–23**

My wife and daughter have dreams that would make Alfred Hitchcock afraid to take a shower. Their tortuous tales are generated in the subconscious realm by recent events in their actual, physical lives. As with most dreams, multiple events get all mixed up in the mind, and the resulting dream is often hilarious fodder over the breakfast table. I won't embarrass either of them by sharing examples, other than to confirm that, in her dreams, my wife is still trying to get out of college, almost thirty years after she actually graduated; "they" just won't let her out!

For some reason, I dream much less frequently, or perhaps I just sleep more soundly and don't remember them when I wake up. But when I do have a dream, it's usually a nightmare. At first, I really didn't pay much attention. A bad dream is just that, and then I wake up. But the story of Jesus' father made me think again.

Imagine what it would have been like for Joseph: "After Herod died, an angel of the Lord appeared in a dream to Joseph in Egypt and said, 'Get up and take the child and his mother and go to the land of Israel, for those who were trying to take the child's life are dead'" (Matthew 2:19–20). There was no CNN Headline News in those days. How else could Joseph have known that the coast was clear? Wouldn't it be wonderful to have that kind of connection with God?

While pondering my own dreams, I realized that nightmares often came when I was doing something wrong in my life. The dreams caused me to take stock and make changes; then I went back to sleeping like a rock. Was I receiving clear warnings from God through the dirty filter of my humanity? "Now we see but a poor reflection as in a mirror; then we shall see face to face. Now I know in part; then I shall know fully, even as I am fully known" (1 Corinthians 13:12).

Should you pay a little more attention to the ways God may be speaking to you?

## *August 16*
### WHAT'S WRONG WITH THIS PICTURE?

"... it is proper ... to fulfill all righteousness."
(Matthew 3:15)

**Traveler:** *Jesus*
**Read: Matthew 3:13–17**

Ted Williams. To any baseball fan, the name inspires awe. The "Splendid Splinter" was the last man to hit "400" for a whole major league season. Even in his last at-bat before retirement, he hit a home run. I had the privilege as a young boy to see him destroy my beloved Cleveland Indians.

Today, Ted Williams is known as perhaps the greatest guru of hitting. Modern-day hitters are sometimes invited to meet with him. An invitation to meet with him means as much to a player as an Academy Award to an actor; maybe more. Such was the reaction of the Colorado Rockies' pitcher Dante Bichette, in 1996. His gaze was nearly star-crossed when he returned from his "audience" with the great one.

Imagine now that the tables were reversed and Ted Williams was invited by Bichette, and that Williams stated that it was only proper that Bichette find time in his busy schedule for Williams. Crazy, right? The student is not greater than the teacher? Then consider this: "Then Jesus came from Galilee to the Jordan to be baptized by John. But John tried to deter him, saying, 'I need to be baptized by you, and do you come to me?' Jesus replied, 'Let it be so now; it is proper for us to do this to fulfill all righteousness'" (Matthew 3:13–15). These are the very first words spoken by Jesus in the Gospel of Matthew. What's wrong with this picture?

Nothing. Baptism means confessing your sins, but Jesus had none to confess. So there must be something more here. It's humility, and it is the very foundation of Christ. If the very Son of God could be humble enough to submit to an earthly baptism, and in the process give honor to the man who paved the way for Him, then true humility is the first and foremost model of Christ-like behavior.

Are you better than Jesus Christ? Probably not. So why not begin right now to ask Him for humility which matches His own?

## August 17
### '-AHOLIC FROLIC

"... led by the Spirit ... to be tempted by the devil."
(Matthew 4:1)

Traveler: *Jesus*
Read: Matthew 4:1–11

There are lots of "'-aholic's." Workaholic. Alcoholic. For me, it was "chocaholic." Temptation lurked everywhere. Just waft the aroma of semi-sweet in my direction and stand back. Nature took its course. I could down one of those giant Hershey bars (with almonds) during the first three innings of a baseball game and wash it down with a Coke. At restaurants, dinner was defined as "that which stands in the way of dessert," preferably triple-chocolate-decadent-delight.

Suggesting that I gave in to temptation is like discovering that birds fly. That's what makes the story of Jesus' temptation by Satan so amazing. If you have trouble understanding the intensity of His temptation, just imagine being tempted for forty straight days by whatever is your most knee-buckling weakness, with nothing to console you. It had to be agony: "All this I will give you..." (Matthew 4:9).

Note two things. First, Satan finally gave up (verse 11). He packed it in, probably with a hiss, and left. No fanfare, no lightning bolts, just gone. Second, as soon as Satan left, angels rushed in to care for Jesus (see tomorrow's devotion).

In my case, being much weaker than Jesus, I had to develop a potentially serious heart condition, which is triggered by too much sugar and caffeine—translated chocolate—to get my attention. Now temptation has left me entirely, because I did not enjoy waking up at night thinking I was having a heart attack. Total resistance to temptation, as demonstrated by Jesus, is a much better approach!

Are you under severe temptation? Is temptation everywhere you turn? Resist it, my friend! Resist it again and again! The experience of God's only Son proves that Satan will give it up if you dig in your heels just when you feel weakest. How could you feel weaker than Christ was after forty days? Color Satan gone!

You can do it!

## August 18
### WHAT IS AN ANGEL?

*". . . and angels came and attended him."*
(Matthew 4:11)

Travelers: *Angels*
**Read (again): Matthew 4:1–11**

In the two years since I became self-employed, Satan has tempted me numerous times with doubt about how the bills will get paid when the cash flow slows down. As this is written, I have no idea what I'll be doing next month. Bowing to temptation, I have even sent out a few resumes to prospective employers, "hedging my bets" if things turn bad.

Jesus, on the other hand, didn't give in, even a little. It was Satan who quit.

Is a need for refreshment and encouragement created after Satan walks off the job? Jesus must have been completely exhausted after His temptation that makes anything we could face look easy. Angels quickly filled that role for Him. Have you ever asked what an angel is, or how you would recognize one? Try this: "Are not all angels ministering spirits sent to serve those who will inherit salvation?" (Hebrews 1:14).

Angels are the tools in God's tool kit. Some may actually look like people with wings. But just as a screwdriver is very different from a socket wrench, I believe angels come in any spiritual form God chooses. My angel has been in the form of my wife's attitude toward self-employment. Twenty years ago, she would have cowered on the ledge overlooking our financial security; today she has the prayer-cement of absolute certainty that God is in control. Even when I have given in to temptation and expressed doubt, she has never wavered. That is a ministering spirit. That is an angel.

If you've been wavering lately, Satan is delighted. He can keep on raising doubts in your heart. But if you reach deep-down within yourself one more time and usher that devil out the front door, an angel will be waiting to greet you in the silence that follows. I don't know what form the angel will take, but I'll stake my life on the fact that help is very, very near. So near you can almost feel it.

## *August 19*
### MAGNIFICENT MAGNETISM

"At once they left their nets and followed him."
(Matthew 4:20)

Travelers: *Jesus, Simon, Andrew, James and John*
**Read: Matthew 4:18–22; Mark 1:16–20; Luke 5:2–11; John 1:35–42**

Looking up from my computer screen, I see a man striding down the street. I know most everyone in the neighborhood. This man is a stranger. Oh, great! He's heading up my front walk. He's ringing the door bell. Another salesman. Sorry, buddy, I'm not buying.

Opening the door with a swift dismissal on my lips, I stop short. This man is unlike anyone I've ever seen. His eyes penetrate my soul. I am speechless. I stare, dumbfounded. The man says, "Come, follow me, and I will make you a fixer of people instead of power plants."

Without pausing even to close the door, I go.

Imagine the kind of magnetism it would take for me to suddenly drop what I'm doing and leave home with a man I've never met. It seems every bit as impossible as the story of Jesus calling his disciples: "At once they left their nets and followed him" (Matthew 4:40). Later, they were even willing to die violently for Him.

Ah, but they were probably single and their fishing businesses were probably doing badly. What did they have to lose? If they'd had families to support, they wouldn't have left so quickly, right? Sorry. Simon had a mother-in-law (Mark 1:30), so he must have been married. And James and John left their old father right there in the family fishing boat, high and dry (verse 22). Today these guys would be chased by the authorities for neglect. Dopey flower children in the 1960s followed cult leaders almost that quickly, but not respectable, employed adults!

What would you do if Jesus came knocking on your door? Would you know Him? Would you go? Is your current travel one way of going with Him? I hope so.

## August 20
### SPREADING STANDARD

"... go and be reconciled to your brother ..."
(Matthew 5:24)

Travelers: *You and I*
**Read: Matthew 5:21–26; Luke 12:54–59**

It was the first morning of our new men's bible study group. Six of us sat in a small circle, squirming uncomfortably. After exchanging small talk for a short while, we decided to share prayer requests. Gary, the most mature member of our group, expressed a burden for calling an old friend with whom he had not talked since an argument, nine years ago. It took courage for Gary to share that ache.

Dave, the least experienced Christian in the group, immediately responded that failed relationships are poison, and he intended to "stay in Gary's face" every week until Gary made the call. Gary found it hard to pick up the phone. Every Monday morning Dave's first words were directed right at him: "Did you make the call?"

"No, but I'm getting closer."

Sometimes it's frequent travel inside our hearts that's required. Jesus sets a higher standard, one that's very tough to meet: "Therefore, if you are offering your gift at the altar and there remember that your brother has something against you, leave your gift there in front of the altar. First go and be reconciled to your brother; then come and offer your gift" (Matthew 5:23–24). Anger is as bad as murder (verse 22). Calling someone a fool is as bad as cursing them. And not resolving an argument means your gift is not welcome to God, according to Jesus' higher standard.

As the weeks went on, Dave's persistence had a bigger benefit: each of us began to remember calls we should make, too. None of us were exempt from Gary's type of hesitancy. Slowly, each of us began reporting that we had made a call and rekindled a relationship. Finally, Gary came through. The call had been made, and we had a great celebration!

There was a great celebration in heaven, too. Jesus sets tough standards, but they spread good everywhere! Is there a trip you need to make in your heart? Is there a call you need to make?

## *August 21*
### GETTING IN SYNCH

> "... deliver us from the evil one."
> (Matthew 6:13)

**Traveler:** *Jesus*
**Read: Matthew 6:9–13; Luke 11:2–4**

One of the great privileges of my life has been to participate in bringing huge, new electric generating units on line. There is something extremely satisfying about working hard for months-on-end to provide light and heat to homes and businesses. However, if the generator is not connected properly, disaster can result.

Our electricity is called "alternating current," because it is actually generated in waves, with a positive peak of electricity followed by a negative wave. Too complicated? Picture a tug-of-war game, with two sides pulling equally on opposite ends of a rope. First one side moves ahead; then the other side pulls them back. That's actually how electricity flows, back and forth, sixty times every second—so fast you never know there's anything there but a strong voltage and current to light bulbs and drive motors.

When a new generator is turned on, it must be "synchronized" with the rest of the electric system it's feeding. That's so that all the positive pulses of electricity occur together. If the generator is connected "out of synch," the positive pulses oppose the negative ones, and an explosion can occur.

In the Lord's prayer, Jesus teaches how to get in synch with God. God will not forgive your sins until you forgive the people who have offended you: "Forgive us our debts, as we also have forgiven our debtors" (Matthew 6:12). Sounds easy. It isn't. But failing to truly forgive those who have hurt you is the same as connecting a generator out of synch. The energy is going in the wrong direction at the wrong time, and the result can be explosive.

If you feel susceptible to temptation and to the wiles of Satan, spend more time with the Lord's prayer. Delivery from temptation and from the Devil will only happen when you have practiced forgiveness. Who in your life comes to mind right now as you read this whom you have not forgiven?

Now is the time! Let it go! Get in synch!

## *August 22*
WORRY WART?

"... seek first his kingdom ..."
(Matthew 6:33)

Traveler: *Jesus*
**Read: Matthew 6:25–34; Luke 12:22–31**

It was a perfect spring morning for flying home from Connecticut. Warm sunshine, a light breeze, not a cloud in sight. Problem was, my flight wasn't scheduled until late that evening, and the weather prediction was not good.

All day I watched as clouds began to build, and temperatures began to drop. Automatically, my mind went to my least favorite thought: early spring warmth, pushed out by a late winter cold front, often creates ideal icing conditions along the East Coast. In short, I began to worry. Not consciously, but it was there in the back of my mind.

When I got to the airport, I learned that my flight was going to be late—bad weather—of course. So I sat down to write devotions for this book. "But seek first his kingdom ..." (Matthew 6:33) was the next scripture subject. As the plane taxied to the end of the runway, the storm arrived in force. The pilot decided to blast his way through it. Normally, this kind of situation, as related in earlier parts of this book, would have terrified me. But I said, "Okay, Jesus, I'm seeking your kingdom right here and right now. I'll give the worry to You."

It was probably the wildest climb-out I've had in years. But I had my eyes closed, deeply involved in a passionate talk with Jesus. That's right, talk. I could not be heard above the roar of the engines, so I kept right on praising Him aloud, seeking Him any way I could.

Suddenly it was over. I opened my eyes, looked around and confirmed by the wild looks on faces all around that indeed it had been a rough ride. But I was fine. No pounding heart or other symptoms which I had displayed in the recent past. Why? Because I sought God's kingdom first, in the form of a personal conversation with my Lord. It was a major victory.

Next time you feel worry, seek the kingdom instead.

## *August 23*
FALSE FRUIT

"... false prophets ... come to you in sheep's clothing ..."
(Matthew 7:15)

**Traveler:** *Jesus*
**Read: Matthew 7:15–20**

He was a very nice young man. That's why I didn't realize the trap until it was too late. Earlier I had helped this man by raising some funds within my company to buy a new computer for his alternative high school class. Two years later he was calling to set up an appointment to "return the favor." He had an idea that would raise money for our hospitality ministry. So I agreed to meet with him.

Thirty seconds into the meeting it was obvious I had been suckered into a presentation by a home products marketing organization, one of those get-rich-quick programs. By becoming a distributor of their products, I could make lots of money and donate it to Oasis. But that wasn't all. He wanted me to give him our ministry's membership list so he could market products to all our members!

I was speechless. How could anyone be so desperate that he would ask a friend to betray the sacred confidence of Christian ministry to sell soap? When I refused as politely as possible, he didn't even know how to stop selling. As I left the restaurant, he was still pleading with me.

Jesus said, "Watch out for false prophets. They come to you in sheep's clothing, but inwardly they are ferocious wolves. By their fruit you will recognize them. Do people pick grapes from thornbushes, or figs from thistles?" (Matthew 7:15–16).

I don't feel that my friend had become a wolf. He is a very committed family man, a good Christian and very bright. But a company that brainwashes young people to sell so desperately makes them look like sheep in wolves' clothing. Their fruit is money, not lost souls. And they are in danger of another kind of meeting: one where Christ Himself says, "Every tree that does not bear good fruit is cut down and thrown into the fire" (verse 19).

What kind of fruit are you bearing today?

## August 24
### SINGED SINNER

"Not everyone . . . will enter the kingdom of heaven . . ."
(Matthew 7:21)

Traveler: *Jesus*
Read: Matthew 7:21–23

When I was in third grade, our house was on the edge of a big ravine. It was paradise for a little boy, because I could explore the "jungle," beyond parental oversight, while still remaining close enough to hear the call for dinner.

As boys are prone to do, my friends and I started playing with little fires down in the gully. Harmless, really, there was nothing there that could burn down. But little boys don't understand the greater implications of such experimentation.

One evening, when I hustled home in response to Dad's whistle—the shrillest east of the Mississippi—Mom was finishing preparations for dinner. Her back was toward me as I walked in. Without even turning around, she asked, "Have you been playing with fire?"

"No," I lied.

Slowly she turned around, gazed at me for a moment, and said, "Go look in the mirror."

To my horror the mirror reflected what I could not hide: the complete absence of eyebrows and eyelashes. Mom had smelled the smoke even before she turned around to look at me. I had gotten too close to the fire, in more ways than one.

My facial hair grew back quickly, but the lesson was burned into my heart then and there: God knows our true hearts even when we try to fool someone else. "Not everyone who says to me, 'Lord, Lord,' will enter the kingdom of heaven, but only he who does the will of my Father who is in heaven" (Matthew 7:21).

Childhood deceptions seem innocent from the distance of several decades. But adult ones carry much greater danger. If you're doing something right now that is fooling people, now is the time to give it up. Think it through. You aren't fooling God. Are you willing to risk the most chilling words in the Bible: "I never knew you" (verse 23)?

God is even more loving than Mom. He waits with open arms to hear you give up that sin.

## *August 25*
### HEAVENLY HUMBLE

"... many will come ... and will take their places ..."
(Matthew 8:11)

**Traveler:** *Jesus*
**Read:** Matthew 8:5–13; Luke 7:1–10

If you met him today, you would never know that he served hard time in prison. Once he forged checks and embezzled money from his employer. Now he spends all his free time, and I mean every available moment, reading his Bible. He's studying to become a pastor. And he's going to be a very good one. Because he was on the outside of God's kingdom, realized how weak and sinful he was, and gave his heart to Jesus Christ right there in prison. What an inspiration he is today!

My friend Greg is much like the Roman centurion who encountered Jesus in Capernaum. This soldier sought help for his paralyzed and suffering servant. He knew he didn't deserve anything from such a man as Jesus: "Lord, I do not deserve to have you come under my roof. But just say the word, and my servant will be healed. For I myself am a man under authority, with soldiers under me. I tell this one, 'Go,' and he goes; and that one, 'Come,' and he comes. I say to my servant, 'Do this,' and he does it" (Matthew 8:8–9).

While the Jewish leaders walked around flaunting their knowledge of the law, here was a man who knew nothing and deserved nothing. Jesus made it clear that His kingdom would become full of centurions, not scribes: "I tell you the truth, I have not found anyone in Israel with such great faith. I say to you that many will come from the east and the west, and will take their places at the feast with Abraham, Isaac and Jacob in the kingdom of heaven. But the subjects of the kingdom will be thrown outside ..." (verses 10–12).

The original subjects were the Israelites, but those who do not believe in Jesus will be cast aside. Many upright and proper people who call themselves Christians will be cast aside, too, because their actions do not fit their words. But my friend Greg will be there, sitting next to the centurion, at the greatest of all feasts.

Will you be there?

## August 26
## NOW OR NEVER?

"Follow me . . ."
(Matthew 8:22)

Traveler: *Jesus*
Read: Matthew 8:18–22: Luke 9:57–60

What does "now" mean? Well, it doesn't mean later. Does "now" mean this minute? Or perhaps tomorrow in comparison to next year? Or as soon as I can arrange my affairs? What did Jesus mean when He said: "Follow me, and let the dead bury their own dead" (Matthew 8:22)?

Today, so many decisions require careful thought, especially travel decisions. Get the best air-fare. Find the bargain rental car. Make sure the frequent flier points get assigned to the right account. Confirm meeting times, places and agendas. Do your homework!

What would it be like to just go? Go now, this very minute? Don't even shut the door behind you.? It wouldn't be easy following Jesus: "Foxes have holes and birds of the air have nests, but the Son of Man has no place to lay his head" (verse 20). His disciples found the courage to drop everything they were doing and follow. Others wanted to get their affairs in order before leaving. Jesus implied that unless we follow Him this instant, we're probably not following Him at all.

But it's not as impossible as it sounds. The call of Jesus to follow is not just a physical calling; that was true when Jesus actually physically walked the earth. But since His death and resurrection, His call is a matter of the heart as much as a physical one. Yes, some of us are called to literally pick up and go, such as missionaries. But it's just as valid to respond to that urgency in your heart.

Whatever situation you're in, you can change it in a heartbeat by committing to following Him in your heart, from the inside out. That decision is no easier than physically leaving the front door open and walking out. But it is just as important.

Now is the time to get up earlier and read your Bible every day. Now is the time to volunteer to help the homeless. Now is the time to tutor and mentor a disadvantaged student. That's what it means to follow Him now. Not later.

## August 27
### FEAR OR FAITH?

"... his disciples followed ... 'Why are you so afraid?'"
(Matthew 8:23,26)

Travelers: *Jesus and the Disciples*
**Read: Matthew 8:23–27; Mark 4:36–41; Luke 8:22–25**

We'd been on the island of Kauai for a week when we decided to try a whale watching excursion out along the Napali Coast. I should have known that this would be no ordinary experience when I saw tee-shirts for sale which read, "I survived the Napali Coast."

If you've ever seen an abandoned surf board get thrown from wave to wave, you know how the ocean treats a zodiac raft in heavy seas. After a rough ride out to the Napali Coast, we anchored in a cove and snorkeled for awhile.

Suddenly, the boat's pilot yelled, "Everybody back to the boat! A storm's coming, and we need to get off this coral reef, fast!" Within minutes the storm hit. For two hours we were thrown from the top of twenty foot waves, slammed down at the bottom of a swell, then launched to the top again for another free-fall. I got scared when I realized that as each wave approached, the pilot made sure he new where my son was. Mitch was only seven and was easily the youngest in the boat. The pilot's body language made it clear that if we went overboard, he would save my son.

But what would I do about my wife and daughter? None of us were good swimmers, and the razor-like coral reef was only yards away.

We could have used Jesus at that point. When His boat full of disciples got caught in a storm, He asked them, "You of little faith, why are you so afraid? Then he got up and rebuked the winds and the waves, and it was completely calm" (Matthew 8:26). No such calm came over our boat.

But Jesus was there. At one of the most helpless moments of my life, I gave my family to Him, because I had no control over the outcome. Eventually, we got back to shore, battered but safe. And I had learned that there's more than one way to calm the waves.

## August 28
## DRIVING DEMONS

"He said to them, 'Go!'"
(Matthew 8:32)

Traveler: *Jesus*
Read: Matthew 8:28–34; Mark 5:1–17; Luke 8:26–37

The Bible leaves us with the impression that there were many demon-possessed people in Jesus' day. Today, we don't seem to have that many. Occasionally we become aware of someone gone mad, but Hollywood has probably given us more demonic characters than are actually found in normal life. So, have things changed since Jesus' time?

I'm not so sure. Is it possible that most of us are possessed by demons, but that we just don't foam at the mouth? (Although some rush-hour drivers I've seen come close.) If this is true, then Jesus is much closer to throwing out demons in modern life than we think.

What if, for example, we are possessed by a demon which causes our lives to feel out of control? Most of us have felt that way at one time. Have we ever treated that condition like a demon and just asked Jesus to cast it out?

Yesterday, that's exactly what we did. Sue and I decided to take the day, when both of us should have working, and go to the Colorado Rockies baseball game. Now, it's easy enough to play hooky. But our prayer was that we would not feel guilty about taking time to just be together and have some fun.

Once when Jesus encountered demons, they were so strong that they asked to be cast into a herd of pigs. We can almost see a wry smile on Jesus' face as He agreed to the request: "He said to them, 'Go!' So they came out and went into the pigs, and the whole herd rushed down the steep bank into the lake and died in the water" (Matthew 8:32).

Even after twenty-seven years of marriage, I can say yesterday was one of the most wonderful days I have ever spent with my wife, because we asked Jesus to cast out our demon of guilt. We could almost hear oinks, splashes and gurgles.

Jesus still casts out demons today. Have you asked Him?

## *August 29*
TAXING TALE

"... and Matthew got up and followed him."
(Matthew 9:9)

Travelers: *Jesus and Matthew*
Read: **Matthew 9:1–9; Mark 2:14–17; Luke 5:27–32**

Let's say that I've got a big new business venture to form, people to hire, products to make, and finance to arrange. This is going to be really big. But I need people I can depend on for my corporate management slots, people with special skills: a couple PhD's, a Harvard MBA, great engineering talent, a banker, someone with good marketing experience. And beyond their professional skills, I want people of the highest integrity, because so much will be riding on their decisions. They must be honest, hard-working, diligent and faithful.

Where do I go to find such people? Well, let's see. First, I'll go to our local tavern. There's some guys who are there every night without fail. They're certainly loyal! Then there's that friend of a friend who just got out of jail. I'm sure he's been rehabilitated and probably needs a job, so I'll make him the company treasurer. And I met a guy hawking tickets outside the Denver Nuggets' arena. I'm not sure where he got all those tickets, but he must be a pretty good marketing man.

Absurd, right? No, I'm not forming some big business venture, but what if I was? Is this how I'd go about choosing my top talent? Nope. But it's how Jesus looked as He chose his disciples. He chose men who were not qualified, had bad attitudes, poor education and at least one who was probably downright dishonest.

Matthew. A tax collector. For the Romans. The enemy. How strange. How did Jesus know this was the right man? How did Matthew know in an instant that he should follow Jesus? Something special must have happened to Matthew when Jesus looked into his eyes. Matthew just *knew!* Jesus said simply, "Follow me' ... and Matthew got up and followed him" (Matthew 9:9).

You are probably not a liar and a cheat, but I'm guessing you're not perfect, either. Would you recognize the power in Jesus' gaze if He came to invite you? Well, He's doing just that every day. Look into His eyes. Don't look away. Don't be ashamed. Just do what Matthew did.

## August 30
### MISSION OF MERCY

"Go and learn..."
(Matthew 9:13)

Traveler: *Jesus*
**Read: Matthew 9:10–13; Psalm 104:3; Hosea 6:6**

I was working on this passage one evening on an airplane when it became so bumpy I couldn't write. In previous pages I've described how I now treat these events as opportunities to close my eyes and talk personally with Jesus. We had a particularly long chat that evening.

When I opened my eyes, I realized that the lady next to me was looking at me, her eyes wide with fear. Nervously, she said, "How can you write when the plane is bouncing like this?" I replied, "I can't. You didn't notice that I had my eyes closed."

Then I took a risk. I added, "I was praying, not just out of fear for safety. You see, I've learned a great secret about bumpy flights. Have you ever read Psalm 104:3?" I handed her my Bible, opened to the right place and watched as a smile slowly softened her face. I said, "Sometimes chariot rides are bumpy, but I like the Guy that's driving." After that, we had a delightful discussion, and I learned that her family was in the middle of moving, tearing up roots, and there was great stress in her life. For a few moments I had helped her relax.

This episode shows the priceless opportunity we have as frequent travelers. We're not always behind a desk in an office, stuck in the same routine day after day, like the Pharisees who had nothing better to do than watch for Jesus to break a rule. We're out there, touching people. Jesus quoted God through the prophet Hosea: "I desire mercy, not sacrifice" (Matthew 9:13). Jesus also said, "Go and learn what this means..."

What does it mean to give mercy? I think it's helping people in this turbulent world. Nothing fancy, just good ol' personal touch. What kind of sacrifice is not so pleasing to God? The kind that keeps you locked into a ritual that tries to define righteousness just by repeated action. Like going to church without faith and love.

Give me a bumpy airplane ride any day, if I can demonstrate God's mercy.

## *August 31*
HEALTH AND HEALING

"... a woman ... came up ... and touched ... his cloak."
(Matthew 9:20)

**Traveler:** *Jesus*
**Read: Matthew 9:18–26; Mark 5:22–43; Luke 8:41–56**

Over the years, my wife developed allergies to dairy products, sugar and corn, in addition to suffering through some tough hormone imbalances. My nickname for her is "Saint Sue," because it takes a saint to watch my son and I eat ice cream and cake while she can't have any. She has assured me that the streets of heaven are paved with Snickers Bars.

Recently, she decided she wasn't going to accept the implication that she would spend the rest of her life in martyrdom. If that is God's will, fine. But what if there were opportunities for improving her health that she had not tried? What if she challenged conventional wisdom and stepped out in faith, combining new knowledge with faith? Are doctors always right?

There was another woman who decided the same thing. She didn't just have allergies. She had been bleeding non-stop for twelve years! Can you imagine what that must have been like? But she challenged the conventional: "Just then a woman who had been subject to bleeding for twelve years came up behind him and touched the edge of his cloak. She said to herself, 'If I only touch his cloak, I will be healed'" (Matthew 9:20–21).

She was, the instant she touched Jesus.

Saint Sue has entered the field of herbal medicines, natural stuff designed by God, not man-made medicines. Like many other people, she has begun to suspect that our culture is saturated in artificial chemicals which are poisoning our bodies. She's learned so much that she's now helping others, including me. And some of her problems have disappeared. Not all of them yet. But she believes Jesus will look at her, too, and say, "Take heart, daughter ... your faith has healed you" (verse 22).

How strong is your faith? Strong enough to believe that just by coming near Jesus, He will heal you? Have you given Him the chance?

## September 1
### SITCOM SILLINESS

"... send out workers into his harvest field."
(Matthew 9:38)

**Traveler:** *Jesus*
**Read: Matthew 9:35–38**

Some things don't change. As Jesus went all over the countryside teaching, preaching and healing, he encountered some very disturbed people: "... he had compassion on them, because they were harassed and helpless, like sheep without a shepherd. Then he said to his disciples, 'The harvest is plentiful but the workers are few. Ask the Lord of the harvest, therefore, to send out workers into his harvest field'" (Matthew 9:36–38). If Jesus were to walk into your community today, wouldn't He see the same thing? Families harassed on every side with job, money, schedule and parenting problems? Don't a lot of people seem like sheep without a shepherd?

A number of years ago, we turned off the television on weeknights, primarily to ensure that homework got done. Now with older kids and a good degree of maturity on their part, we'll occasionally turn on a special program. And of course, between all the beer and soap commercials, the networks pitch their sitcoms endlessly. We just sit there scratching our heads. Do people really watch that stuff, welcoming sex and violence into their homes like old friends? Every night? Week after week? Why? Aren't they like sheep without a shepherd? Aren't they just using sitcoms to escape from real life?

I know this will step on some toes; don't forget I watch too many sports programs, which is just as stupid. But I want to issue a challenge. Which are you, sheep or shepherd? Television can provide good entertainment occasionally. But are you addicted to certain brain-numbing, dumbing shows? Do you watch to learn, or just to get a cheap thrill? And doesn't one small relaxation of your standards of decency lead to another—and another?

Jesus Christ is calling you to be a worker in the harvest field of souls for His kingdom. Hopefully, these pages have convinced you to leave the television off in your hotel room. Now, can you leave it off at home, too?

## *September 2*
## CLOSE ENCOUNTERS

> "As you go, preach the message, 'The kingdom of heaven is near.'" (Matthew 10:7)

Travelers: *The Twelve*
**Read: Matthew 10:5–8**

What does the word "near" mean? Just how near is near? What does Jesus mean when He says, "Go rather to the lost sheep of Israel. As you go, preach this message, 'The kingdom of heaven is near.'. . . Freely you have received, freely give" (Matthew 10:6,7,8).

Sue and I live in a rather large ranch-style house. Now that the kids are grown up, we spend much of our days rattling around in the house alone, just the two of us. Over the years, Sue has taught me the fine art of wearing slippers, so we seldom hear the sound of footsteps on the hard tile and carpeted floors. We probably need to wear Swiss cow bells. That's because we're constantly surprising each other by popping into a room, with no warning. Sue jumps so much when this happens that I remind her I'm the guy who lives with her; remember me?

That's "near." Up close and personal. The kingdom of God is so near, so close, that if you turn around, its presence might startle you. That's the message Jesus told His disciples to preach. Not very complicated. Not rocket science.

Jesus also told them not to spend their time preaching to Gentiles or Samaritans, those who were not familiar with the Old Testament God, but rather to the lost sheep of Israel. That is, to those who had the tradition and the forewarning of the kingdom of God.

Today, the Christian church in America represents the lost sheep of Israel. We are the ones who have lost track of how near the kingdom of God is. Until we can become united in the name of Christ, until we can preach the message of the kingdom, until we can ". . . heal the sick, raise the dead, clean those who have leprosy, drive out demons . . ." (verse 8) we are facing the same kind of destruction that Israel faced.

How near is near? God's kingdom is so near it surprises us, but are we acting like it? The problem is us.

## September 3
### TRUE HOSPITALITY

"Whatever town or village you enter, search for some worthy person . . ."(Matthew 10:11)

Travelers: *The Twelve*
**Read: Matthew 10:11–14; Mark 6:8–11; Luke 10:4–12**

From the moment God gave me the vision to found Oasis Hospitality International, I have been fascinated by Jesus' words in this passage of scripture. I am convinced that Christian frequent travelers are sent out by Christ, even as the disciples were sent out, first the twelve, and later seventy-two. But adapting Jesus' instructions to modern travelers is not easy.

There are so many differences between our modern culture and that of ancient Israel; there are also some interesting parallels. Is our culture so different that it eliminates the kind of hospitality Jesus described? He said, ". . . search for some worthy person there and stay at his house until you leave" (Matthew 10:11). But how can we do that today, when safety and security are such a problem? Or is it that we as Christians have lost something that can be regained? I think it's the latter. Things weren't terribly safe in Jesus' day, either.

In *The Hospitality Commands,* we find that "These first Christian teachers and evangelists were not a well-financed band of travelers who could regularly afford institutional lodging, so they depended on the generous hospitality of Christian people . . . there were few acceptable places in which Christian travelers could stay. Inns were notoriously immoral, filthy places."[6]

Today, Christian travelers can more frequently afford hotel lodging and inns are usually clean. But they can be just as immoral. And we no longer have a way of gathering together during travel to spread the gospel of Jesus Christ. (Read Strauch's book.) How can the Christian Travelers Network help revive true hospitality? Will you join us? Will you make the effort to identify yourself to other members of the Network? Will you help search for that worthy person?

## September 4
### DID I SAY THAT?

> "... You will be brought before governors and kings ..."
> (Matthew 10:18)

Travelers: *The Twelve*
**Read: Matthew 10:17–23; Mark 13:11–13; Luke 21:12–17**

I always park in or near the same place at the airport, so that I never have to worry about finding my car. If you think that sounds strange, you're not a frequent traveler, and you've never had to distinguish one week from another over, say, eight straight weeks of traveling. Let's see, did I park on Level 2, or was that last week?

So I always park on the end of a row, along the same aisle, so it doesn't matter whether the car is in Row B or Row Q. I always walk right to it, along that aisle. One night, well after midnight, I straggled along that same familiar aisle, dead-tired from a long week away. As I approached my car, I saw something under my windshield wiper. It was a parking ticket. What?

While I had been away, the city had repainted the parking lines, very craftily eliminating the last space on the end of the row—*my* space! I got the ticket because I hadn't moved my car—hard to do long distance. I wasn't going to take this one sitting down. I decided to go to court for the first time in my life.

Now traffic court is not the same as a persecuted Christian being dragged before a judge in a foreign country. But it serves a point. Jesus said, "But when they arrest you, do not worry about what to say or how to say it. At that time you will be given what to say, for it will not be you speaking, but the Spirit of your Father speaking through you" (Matthew 10:19–20).

I prepared for my day in court very carefully. I had facts, figures and even some library research. When my turn came, I began my defense eloquently; Perry Mason would have been proud. But before I finished my second sentence, the judge interrupted me and said, "Case dismissed." I just stood there stunned. He didn't even hear the part about the parking lines being painted over.

God's promises are true. Believe them.

## *September 5*
### BLESSINGS IN DISGUISE

"When you are persecuted in one place, flee to another."
(Matthew 10:23)

Travelers: *The Twelve*
**Read: Matthew 10:21–31; Mark 13:11–13; Luke 12:2–9**

The passages in Matthew 10 and Mark 13 deal with Christ's descriptions of the end times, when God's judgment will come upon the earth and the Son of Man will come in power and glory. The times just prior to that cataclysmic event will be very tough, including persecution and treachery: "Brother will betray brother to death, and a father his child; children will rebel against their parents and have them put to death. All men will hate you because of me, but he who stands firm to the end will be saved" (Matthew 10:21–22).

We had been active members of the same church for almost twenty years. But in 1990, our new youth pastor, a big, gruff, Peter-like guy, suggested that one youth meeting a month involve Bible study. The youth advisor and chairman of the church's board had wanted only social activities for youth. And he did not like the pastor's lack of "polish."

A quiet campaign began against the pastor, and before anyone realized what had happened, the youth pastor was crucified in the professional sense and sent packing. They even evicted him from the parsonage!

I tried all sorts of mediation, but nothing worked. The Spirit had fled that place, and so did we. I have never experienced a more painful time, leaving a church and friends whom we loved. We had to stand firm. There was no choice.

We fled to an independent Bible church which was devoid of denominational power plays. God's word rang true there. Both Sue and I realized that while we had always known *about* Christ, we had never come face to face in a personal relationship *with* Him. We were actually born again and became new believers! None of this could have happened if the ugly dismissal of the youth pastor had not come first.

Blessings often come as a direct result of persecution. Don't be afraid to flee.

## September 6
### GET A LIFE

"... anyone who does not ... follow me is not worthy of me."
(Matthew 10:38)

Travelers: *The Twelve*
**Read: Matthew 10:37–42; Luke 17:33; John 12:25**

As I sit here writing devotions, my consulting business is coming apart at the seams. Not because I've done anything wrong. I'm just an expert in a dying field, or at least one that is going dormant for the foreseeable future. If consulting engineering was my life, I'd be miserable, perhaps even distraught. Certainly many of my friends in this industry are. They have nowhere to turn.

I see it differently. I feel that I'm on the verge of discovering unimaginable treasure. I see this as answer to prayers for direction. Our culture jokes, "Get a life!" Jesus says, "Whoever finds his life will lose it, and whoever loses his life for my sake will find it" (Matthew 10:39). So, do I pursue my new life under my own power, launching a job search for a lower paying job with dead-end potential, or do I lose my life to God, who will find it for me again?

The answer lies in the previous verse: "... anyone who does not take his cross and follow me is not worthy of me" (verse 38).

I have many options. I can go back to engineering school and get a master's degree. I could get a master's in business administration, or even a law degree. That's the advice I've gotten from some of my closest friends. But only God knows my heart, and He has placed in me a burning desire to follow Christ. I don't even know what that means, yet. I do know that He will show me the way. He will find my life for me.

As I talk to travelers in the Christian Travelers' Network, I find that many struggle with where their lives are going. Those who traveled frequently for many years suddenly change and stay home. Those that get to stay home for awhile often get sent out again, perhaps as part of a promotion. Secular life goes on, unpredictably. But those who live by giving up their lives to Christ find indescribable peace.

And that's the key to getting a life.

## September 7
### THE PLOT SICKENS

> "Aware of this, Jesus withdrew from that place."
> (Matthew 12:15)

Traveler: *Jesus*
Read: **Matthew 12:14–21**

When my son Mitch was in sixth grade, he was ridiculed, not only by kids in his class, but even by the teacher. Everyone laughed as he struggled. Maybe his teacher never heard of the word "encouragement."

Mitch's mother was very aware of this and withdrew him from that place. I argued that he would be forced to encounter the real world sooner or later. She pointed to his obvious decline in school performance because of emotional damage.

Even Jesus was not one to encourage persecution before His appointed time on the cross. He knew the established religious leaders hated him, and He knew they wanted to kill Him: "Aware of this, Jesus withdrew from that place" (Matthew 12:15).

The secular world is fond of saying, "Don't take it personally." Well, how else are you supposed to take it? Amateur psychologists call it paranoia, and certainly it is if you think everyone is out to get you. But the fact is, there's a time to pull-up and run. People can sometimes plot against you. It may be God's way of urging you to move on. As the Kenny Rogers song says, "You've got to know when to hold . . . and know when to fold."

Thank God I listened to my wife when the time came for us to fold Mitch's attendance at that school. We enrolled him in a Christian school, and he went from nearly flunking in a school with no standards to a B-plus average in a school that is extremely tough academically.

Have you ever been set up? Have you ever lost a battle that just wasn't fair? If so, "Consider it pure joy, my brothers, whenever you face trials of many kinds, because you know that the testing of your faith develops perseverance" (James 1:2–3). Ask for God's guidance. Then, if necessary, withdraw, not to lick your wounds in solitude, but to pick up the next exciting chapter in your life, which God has planned.

## September 8
### HANDLING HELL

*". . . seven other spirits more wicked . . . go in and live there . . ."*
(Matthew 12:45)

Traveler: *Jesus*
**Read: Matthew 12:43–45; Luke 11:24–26**

"I can handle it." Those are the famous last words of an addict. It's bad enough when someone has a habit that is difficult to break. But it's even more painful to watch when the habit has been cleanly broken for a period of time, and then the addict "falls off the wagon."

I fell off the ol' Conestoga just recently. I got to the Hartford airport on a Friday evening, ready to hustle home after a long week on the road. But a storm blew in, and my flight was delayed. In a fit of self-pity, I bought my favorite candy. I intended to munch a few pieces while waiting and then stash the rest of the quarter pound in my briefcase for future enjoyment. Yeah, right.

Once a chocaholic, always a chocaholic. Even though I knew exactly what my heart does when given a straight shot of caffeine and sugar, I kept on munching as the flight delay got longer and longer. Soon the bag of candy was gone, and I topped it off with a Classic Coke. My heart raced so fast, it almost beat the plane home.

Why did I do that? I know better. I had not had a binge like that in several years. Once again, Jesus provides the answer: "When an evil spirit comes out of a man, it goes through arid places seeking rest and does not find it. Then it says, 'I will return to the house I left.' When it arrives, it finds the house unoccupied, swept clean and put in order. Then it goes and takes seven other spirits more wicked than itself, and they go in and live there. And the final condition of that man is worse than the first. That is how it will be with this wicked generation" (Matthew 12:43–45).

That describes my actions perfectly. Was Jesus referring to a generation long ago, or perhaps to all generations who don't take total trust in Christ seriously? There's only one way to get rid of an addiction: give it to Jesus. The Holy Spirit is the only power strong enough to keep your house clean all the time.

## *September 9*
## WEEDS OR WHEAT?

"... While everyone was sleeping, his enemy came ..."
(Matthew 13:25)

Traveler: *Jesus*
Read: Matthew 13:24–30; Jeremiah 12:1

One of the great mysteries of life is why good things always happen to bad people and bad things happen to good people. Jeremiah certainly knew all about that: "Why does the way of the wicked prosper? Why do all the faithless live at ease?" (Jeremiah 12:1). Fortunately, Old Testament darkness gives way to New Testament light.

When the construction job I have referred to numerous times in this book turned sour, the contractor brought in an old, wizened veteran of many battles to dig the company out of its hole. This man's job was not to get the job done right, but to get out of the contract any way he could. My job was to assure the owner that he was getting it done right.

Clashes were inevitable. But this man established new standards of dishonesty and deceit. For almost a year, he came to public board meetings and lied about his company's progress and their commitment to quality work. I had no choice but to confront him in the glare of the media. Gladiators in the pit. The "Romans" had a ball watching us.

New Testament light was on my side: "... while you are pulling up the weeds, you may root up the wheat with them. Let both grow together until the harvest. At that time I will tell the harvesters: First collect the weeds and tie them in bundles to be burned; then gather the wheat and bring it into my barn" (Matthew 13:29–30). I knew that if he could lie so easily to us, he was probably lying to his management, too. Harvest time would come for him, too.

It did. He got burned in a very different way. When his management learned what he had been doing, he was assigned to a new job, far, far away, and the company then stood behind its obligations at a cost of tens of millions of dollars. How far away did my weedy friend get sent?

Siberia. I'm not kidding. Siberia. It's so cold there, it burns.

## September 10
### HIGH-RISE

"... so that the birds of the air come and perch in its branches."
(Matthew 13:31)

Traveler: *Jesus*
**Read: Matthew 13:31–33; Mark 4:30–32; Luke 13:18–21**

Once upon a time, far up in the mountains, a pine cone fell from the top of a majestic, blue spruce tree. The pine cone was harvested by a man who works for a garden nursery. The pine cone gave up one very special seed, which was planted at the nursery. In time, it sprouted into a baby blue spruce. It was nurtured over several years, and eventually it grew to four feet tall. That was in 1968.

A house was being built that year. The new owner came to the nursery and bought this very special little blue spruce tree. He planted it right by the front door, right outside the big picture window. The blue spruce tree really liked it there.

Why was that blue spruce tree so special? Because fifteen years later, I bought the house and it became my blue spruce tree. It was about thirty feet tall by then, perfectly straight, and stretching ever upward toward the deep blue Colorado sky.

We had a perfect view into the blue spruce tree from our picture window. It was so close that we felt as if we were part of the tree, yet the glass kept us from startling the birds that lived in it. Early in the morning, just before sunrise, we could gaze into the tree and never see a bird, but as dawn approached, the tree came alive with life, a dozen different kinds of birds waking up and breaking out in song. It was a high-rise for birds, a model of diversity.

It's no wonder Jesus described the kingdom of heaven as a small seed becoming a giant tree: "Though it is the smallest of all your seeds, yet when it grows, it is the largest of garden plants and becomes a tree, so that the birds of the air come and perch in its branches" (Matthew 13:32). Something so tall, so invincible even to heavy spring snowstorms, so spacious, so secure to trusting creatures.

What is your vision of the Kingdom of heaven? More importantly, are you as trusting as the birds who live in my blue spruce tree?

## September 11
### TRASH OR TREASURE?

"... then in his joy went and sold everything he had ..."
(Matthew 13:44)

**Traveler:** *Jesus*
**Read: Matthew 13:44–52**

Could you live on $365,000 per year? Would you believe more than that is thrown away in the garbage every day?

My engineering career was built around burning garbage to make electricity. Burning it sounds much easier to do than it really is. Throughout the 1970s and 1980s, many companies got into the business. The most successful took the whole mass of garbage, threw it in the furnace and threw away the ash that was left.

But one group of men saw more in the ash than trash. Not everything in garbage burns, not even after recycling. There are valuable metals like copper and zinc which Pat Mahoney and his company believed could be recovered profitably. Everyone else thought it would be too expensive to process the ash; Pat stayed at it year after year.

Finally, a process was developed that worked. And it contained a huge surprise. They discovered that for every 2,000 tons of trash they burned, the ash contained an average of $1,000 in cold, hard cash, coins thrown away in a disposal-oriented society. That's $365,000 a year!

Jesus described the kingdom of heaven this way: "... like a treasure hidden in a field" (Matthew 13:44). Or like treasure hidden in a trash pile.

As you travel, it's easy to see how the world resembles a trash pile of bad attitudes, immorality, crime and poverty. But hidden by that very unattractive exterior is the greatest treasure imaginable—God's children, whom you encounter everywhere.

There is treasure just waiting for you to discover it. When you find God's kingdom, and it's everywhere if you look hard enough, don't stop there. Both the man who found treasure hidden in a field (verse 44) and the merchant who found one pearl of great value (verses 45–46) absolutely had to possess the treasure. Capture it with all your heart. It's priceless.

## September 12
### SNORKELING SNAFU

"Take courage! It is I. Don't be afraid . . . Come."
(Matthew 14:27,29)

Travelers: *Jesus and the Disciples*
**Read: Matthew 14:22–31; Mark 6:45–51; John 6:15–21**

I am a notoriously bad swimmer, but when I go to the ocean it's much easier because of the salt water. I can float almost effortlessly. In Hawaii I began to experiment with snorkeling; what a great way to see God's kingdom under water. Tropical fish among the coral reefs are indescribably beautiful.

On New Year's Day, 1994, I spotted a little cove along a stretch of beach. The waves were higher than usual, but people were out swimming. I swam out maybe fifty yards toward the reef and started snorkeling, keeping the reef between me and the open sea for protection. Wrong! Without warning I was smashed by a wave breaking *over* the reef, and then by another. I panicked and swam as fast as I knew how to get away from the reef.

But now I was perhaps two hundred yards away from the beach, and the undertow was pulling me out farther. I no sooner thought about cramping-up than I started to do exactly that. I could see my wife reading a book on the beach, so close, yet so far, but I couldn't get the snorkel mask out of my mouth to yell to her.

That's how Peter felt: "'Lord, if it's you . . . tell me to come to you on the water.' 'Come,' he said. Then Peter got down out of the boat, walked on the water and came toward Jesus. But when he saw the wind, he was afraid and, beginning to sink, cried out, 'Lord, save me!' Immediately Jesus reached out his hand and caught him. 'You of little faith,' he said, 'why did you doubt?'" (Matthew 14:28–31).

If I hadn't panicked, I could have floated long enough to free my mouth and yell for help. But my lack of faith almost got me drowned. There was only one other person on that end of the beach that morning—an off-duty paramedic! He spotted me and yanked me out.

*Seeing* Jesus from afar in your life isn't enough. You must trust Him with everything to keep from sinking.

## September 13
### GUNG HO

"If a blind man leads a blind man, both will fall into a pit."
(Matthew 15:14)

Travelers: *The Pharisees*
Read: **Matthew 15:1–20; Mark 7:1–23**

I'm not sure where the term "gung-ho" originated, but I know what it meant in 1966. On college campuses across the land there were those who hated the war in Viet Nam and those who were "gung-ho" patriotic and committed to serve their country no matter what. I was in the latter group, the son of a proud World War II vet who had done his duty despite tremendous personal sacrifice.

I enrolled in Reserve Officers Training Corps (ROTC), knowing that when I graduated I would have to serve at least four years active duty. That was a more attractive alternative than getting drafted. But my drill instructor made me begin wishing I hadn't chosen ROTC at all. He drilled us relentlessly, hour after hour, far beyond the military's requirements. Complaining only made it worse. The guy was a little Hitler with a death wish.

For punishment of even the tiniest infraction, he would make us stand at attention for three hours at a time. Guys would faint and hit the floor face first, "sissies" according to our leader. So I learned how to bend my knees slightly to keep them from locking up. As a result, the lower disks in my back were permanently damaged. To this day I can't stand up very long without severe back pain. Why did he do that? What good did it do?

Jesus warns of "gung-ho" religious leaders who snuff out faith with rules: "Every plant that my heavenly Father has not planted will be pulled up by the roots. Leave them; they are blind guides. If a blind man leads a blind man, both will fall into a pit" (Matthew 15:13–14). My leader was blind. And it turns out that my country was blind, too. We all fell into a pit in those days.

God chose to deliver me from Viet Nam, by the discovery of my one deaf ear. I'll never know why I was saved, and so many others were lost. My tears pour out again as I remember the insanity of it all!

What kind of leader do you follow?

## September 14
### STAGE WHISPER

"... the disciples forgot to take bread."
(Matthew 16:5)

Travelers: *Jesus and the Disciples*
**Read: Matthew 16:1–12; Mark 8:11–21**

Over the years of traveling, I have learned to become more patient, more tolerant. I try to express the love of Christ in difficult situations and to spread a little light in the darkness. But there's one area I simply haven't conquered—airplane food.

For years I have joked about "mystery chicken." The mystery was how I could keep giving back my brick of moisture-deprived chicken—untouched, only to have the same piece served to me on the very next flight, over and over again for years, or so it seemed. Today, things have advanced to the point where I'd gladly take the chicken; getting fed at all is a miracle now.

See what I mean? I could make a living as a stand-up comedian just doing gigs about airplane food.

But I stand accused by Jesus of being the wrong kind of yeast: "Be on your guard against the yeast of the Pharisees and Sadducees" (Matthew 16:6). Whoever sows the seeds of discord, however quietly, is not a true Christian, but a fake. Have I ever taken the time to actually *thank* God for that greasy cheeseburger that dripped all the way down my sleeve when I opened the tin foil? No, I didn't feel very thankful. How totally disrespectful to a God who holds my plane up in the sky!

Being the wrong kind of yeast is one of Satan's best tools. You don't have to stand up and shout in protest. That would be uncivilized and far too obvious. A simple stage whisper of dissatisfaction will do very nicely. A well-placed look or sigh which feeds on the frustrations of another person can be enough to incite a riot. Things are bad enough without making them worse just for comic relief.

The disciples forgot to bring bread on their trip. What kind of bread do you take on your trips? The yeast of discontent, or the Bread of Life?

## September 15
## DENIAL

"If anyone would come after me, he must deny himself . . ."
(Matthew 16:24)

Traveler: *Jesus*
Read: Matthew 16:24–28; Mark 8:31–9:1; Luke 9:22–27

Sitting in my office today, I ponder the relevance of Christ's instruction: "If anyone would come after me, he must deny himself and take up his cross and follow me. For whoever wants to save his life will lose it, but whoever loses his life for me will find it" (Matthew 16:24–25). What does denial mean? How do I lose my life in order to gain it?

Just now a great wind has begun pounding our house, a frequent event on clear spring days along the eastern slope of the Rockies. Today the wind is reaching at least sixty miles per hour. A tiny sparrow just dropped into the aspen tree outside my window, looking ruffled, seeking safe haven from the wind. A leafless aspen doesn't appear to be the best selection, but it may be its only choice.

The sparrow set out this morning to pursue its dreams. But when the wind hit, it denied its natural desire to fly free and sought out my tree for refuge. As the wind intensified, I thought for sure it would be blown from the tree. But it merely faced *into* the wind and hung on. It probably wasn't as much fun as flying along several hundred feet up in the air, but the sparrow had chosen safety over expanding his self esteem.

Humans are supposedly smarter than birds. But this illustration came to me because of two humans, in the last two weeks, who chose to fly into bad weather, choosing belief in their own power over denial and common sense. Both Jessica DuBroff, the seven-year-old child pilot, and Brook Berringer, quarterback of the National Champion University of Nebraska football team, died. Had they chosen to lose that day's flying time, they would have found themselves flying again in the future.

Christ's concept of denial isn't as negative as it's made out to be. It means recognizing that God is more powerful than man, just as nature is stronger than small airplanes. Losing your life to God and following the cross of Christ means life, not death. Denial actually means fulfillment.

## September 16
### SEEING THINGS DIFFERENTLY

"Jesus . . . led them up a high mountain by themselves."
(Matthew 17:1)

Travelers: *Jesus, Peter, James and John*
**Read: Matthew 17:1–13; Mark 9:2–13; Luke 9:28–36**

Taking up your cross and following Jesus, as we studied yesterday, means seeing things differently. If you take a hike up a mountain with a friend, chances are your friend will not change into anything unusual. But if your Friend is Jesus, things will seem different indeed: "After six days, Jesus took with him Peter, James and John the brother of James, and led them up a high mountain by themselves. There he was transfigured before them. His face shone like the sun, and his clothes became as white as the light" (Matthew 17:1–2).

Years ago, I was driving across the rolling hills of southeastern Ohio, well after midnight, to meet Sue for a quick weekend at her parents' house. Her college was in Kentucky, mine in Michigan, so this weekend was precious. I was driving fairly fast, considering the hilly, narrow two-lane road.

Off in the distance I saw a single small, faint light. I studied it for several seconds, trying to decide how far away it was. *Whoosh!!* Without warning it passed by the right side of my car and vanished. With stampeding heart I realized that what I had thought was a bright light far away was actually a tiny reflector on an Amish horse-cart just a few yards ahead. Only God knows how I avoided plowing into the cart.

Things aren't always as they appear. When you follow Christ, you begin to see that angry traveler you encounter as a sad soul who needs more love in his life. Your family becomes your greatest treasure, rather than a drain on your finances that prevents you from buying that sports car. And long-time feuds become opportunities for reconciliation.

The Apostle Paul, who knew something of miraculous transformations, wrote: "Now we see but a poor reflection as in a mirror; then we shall see face to face. Now I know in part; then I shall know fully . . ." (1 Corinthians 13:12).

Are you ready now to see things differently through Christ?

## September 17
### CHINOOK

"... you will never enter the kingdom of heaven..."
(Matthew 18:3)

**Traveler:** *Jesus*
**Read: Matthew 18:1–5; Mark 9:33–37; Luke 9:46–48**

February is a month of change in Colorado. It gets extremely cold when an arctic front passes through, but temperatures can suddenly rise seventy degrees within an hour. That breathtaking change is accompanied by a powerful wind known as a "Chinook." And oh, what a blow! Chinooks usually blow directly from west to east, turning narrow mountain passes and valleys into wind tunnels. And they create severe turbulence above the mountains as they go.

One February, I took off with my family for a San Diego vacation, right into the teeth of a Chinook. The flight was so rough that an off-duty professional pilot sitting next to my four-year-old son gripped the armrests with white knuckles. The look on his face was all I needed to absorb his fear. Even though the plane was a powerful Boeing 727, it felt as if there was a contest between plane and nature, and the Chinook was about to win.

Above the engine noise and loud rattling, as the plane bounced around, was another sound. It was laughter. Uncontrollable, side-splitting, can't-get-a-breath, giggly, mirthful, contagious laughter. It was my son. He wasn't on a fearful journey through treachery and danger. He was on the roller coaster ride of his life! Soon everyone in the cabin was laughing with him.

Why did my son see it so differently? Because he was a small child. How did he change a bunch of terrified adults into a party spirit? By trusting the plane with child-like faith. How can you change the world from fear to a party spirit? By taking on the same kind of child-like faith: "I tell you the truth, unless you change and become like little children, you will never enter the kingdom of heaven ... whoever humbles himself like this child is the greatest in the kingdom of heaven" (Matthew 18:3–5).

The kingdom of heaven exists right alongside the kingdom of people. Which will you choose?

## September 18
## WRONG TURN

"... will he not leave ... and go to look for the one that wandered off?" (Matthew 18:12)

Traveler: *Jesus*
**Read: Matthew 18:12–14; Luke 15:4–7**

Many frequent travelers in rental cars have seen a part of Newark, New Jersey they didn't know existed. The Newark airport is not located right on an Interstate highway. It is close by, but not close enough. And confusing road signs can guide you down under a big bridge, not over the top of it as you intended.

To make matters worse, your rental car is as obvious down there as a bright, red flashing light. Your Pontiac Grand Am with the big green, yellow or red rental agency sticker on the windshield, is a target.

Target for what? The windshield washer corps, of course! In the neighborhood under the bridge, traffic lights are green for about five seconds, and red for what seems like hours. While you are motionless in traffic, entrepreneurial teenagers with buckets and squeegees work their way down the line, offering to wash your windshield. Yes, your windshield is spotless, having left the rental car wash less than five minutes ago. Five bucks gets it *cleaner* and also allows you to pass down to the next block where the whole scene is repeated again. At times like that, you feel lost, really lost. Not only geographically, but socially. And you wish someone could come and just pluck you out of that situation. Alas, no one is there.

Not true. There is one who is there when you need Him: "What do you think? If a man owns a hundred sheep, and one of them wanders away, will he not leave the ninety-nine on the hills and go to look for the one that wandered off? ... In the same way your Father in heaven is not willing that any of these little ones should be lost" (Matthew 18:12, 14).

It's your choice. Be a big boy and fend for yourself down under the bridge. Or accept Christ as your Shepherd with child-like faith. The "little ones" Christ describes are those who change and become like little children, who enter the kingdom of heaven (verse 3).

## September 19
### HOW TO BE PERFECT

"... go, sell your possessions and give to the poor ... Then come, follow me." (Matthew 19:21)

Traveler: *A Rich Young Man*
**Read: Matthew 19:16–30; Mark 10:17–30; Luke 18:18–30**

This is one of my favorite passages of scripture. It deals with an extremely important facet of human nature, and the passage is often misused.

Modern society is all about the pursuit of perfection, human perfection. Science can solve all our problems, extend life, bring unimaginable material wealth and lead to peace on earth. We seek the perfect body, the perfect mate, the perfect car, the perfect house, the perfect vacation, and on, and on.

Christians, too, seek to become perfect. Most of us identify with the man who asked Jesus, "Teacher, what good thing must I do to get eternal life?" (Matthew 19:16). This man had never committed murder, adultery, theft, nor testified falsely. And neither have most of us. But like him, we also feel that there is more that we need to do to achieve eternal life, to please God, to be perfect.

Many people read Jesus' reply as the final word on perfection: "If you want to be perfect, go, sell your possessions and give to the poor, and you will have treasure in heaven. Then come, follow me" (verse 21). They stop reading right there and say, "Well, I guess that's how I'll become perfect. Jesus said so." But read on. Is selling everything and giving to the poor all it takes to become perfect? No. Jesus was pointing out to that particular man, what roadblock stood in his way. But you could be the poorest person on earth and still not be perfect. Why? What's missing? As I said, read on.

The disciples "... were greatly astonished and asked, 'Who then can be saved?' Jesus looked at them and said, 'With man this is impossible, but with God all things are possible'" (verses 25, 26). In other words, you can't become perfect for all the tea in China without God. Whether you're rich, poor, educated, unschooled, Christian or pagan, you must seek God.

The point isn't just about material wealth. It's about what's blocking you from total dependence on God.

## September 20
### IT'S NOT TOO LATE

"You also go and work in my vineyard."
(Matthew 20:7)

Traveler: *Jesus*
**Read: Matthew 20:1–16; Romans 7:7–25**

Almost everyone has heard of the great novelist James Michener. One of the most productive writers of our time, his books are often based on exhaustive research and detail about his subject. How could he have so much time to write so many books? It's even more astounding to learn that James Michener began writing at the age of forty-one! He had many years of other experiences before he sat down to write.

You might say that James Michener found a whole new kingdom when he began to write, something he never imagined was possible. Did he ever wonder if he was too old when he started? Even though he was last, in terms of starting age, he became first in terms of writing success.

The kingdom of heaven is the same way. Jesus keeps coming to look for us, just as the landowner went to the marketplace to find workers for his vineyard (Matthew 20:1). Those hired early in the morning were guaranteed a day's wage. But so were those hired at noon, middle of the afternoon and late afternoon. "About the eleventh hour he went out and found still others standing around. He asked them, 'Why have you been standing here all day long doing nothing?' 'Because no one has hired us,' they answered. He said to them, 'You also go and work in my vineyard'" (verses 6–7).

When the time came to pay the workers in the vineyard, they all got the same amount of pay. Isn't that unfair? Jesus says no: "'Don't I have the right to do what I want with my own money? Or are you envious because I am generous?' So the last will be first, and the first will be last" (verses 15–16).

There is no one more generous than God. He reaches out time and again, inviting you into His kingdom. Do you fear it's too late, because of all the sin in your life? Wrong! It's not too late.

It wasn't too late for James Michener to start writing. And it's not too late for you to accept Christ's invitation into His kingdom. Pray right now and accept the invitation!

## September 21
### MISTAKEN IDENTITY

"... the Son of Man did not come to be served, but to serve ..."
(Matthew 20:28)

Traveler: *Jesus*
Read: Matthew 20:20–28; Mark 10:35–45

I had been reading this passage of scripture just before getting onto an airplane, so I decided to see if I could learn what it would be like to serve instead of being served.

Going down the jetway to board the plane, an elderly man was having trouble navigating the awkward slopes, and I offered to take his bag so he could balance himself. Then I followed him to his seat, stored his bag and helped him get seated. By this time other people were entering the plane, and I had no trouble finding people to help, mostly shorter people who struggled to store their bags overhead. Opportunities were everywhere for helping. I never noticed all these things when I was concerned only with myself. I was having great fun!

Maybe it was because I had seen so many flight attendants do it, but I offered pillows to those who were getting seated nearby. Smiles all around, jovial conversation. Finally someone asked me for a cup of water. I answered that they would have to ask a flight attendant for that. They were surprised to learn that I was not a flight attendant.

It was a case of mistaken identity. A joyful case. All I had done was practice the teachings of Jesus: "You know that the rulers of the Gentiles lord it over them, and their high officials exercise authority over them. Not so with you. Instead, whoever wants to become great among you must be your servant, and whoever wants to be first must be your slave—just as the Son of Man did not come to be served, but to serve, and to give his life as a ransom for many" (Matthew 20:26–28).

Opportunities to serve are everywhere, especially when you travel. Why not see if you can be mistaken for someone else? Try to make someone think, "Surely no one would be that nice unless they were being *paid* for it!"

## September 22
NOTHING SPECIAL

"Immediately they received their sight and followed him."
(Matthew 20:34)

Travelers: *Two Blind Men*
**Read: Matthew 20:29–34; Mark 10:46–52; Luke 18:35–43**

Last night I was sitting at a Colorado Rockies baseball game when a very young boy toddled down the aisle behind his mother, carrying something in his hat. As he bumped down stairs that were pretty big for his pudgy legs, he dropped a small packet. It looked like a little bag of coffee sweetener, and I didn't think much of it. But after he went about ten more steps down toward the field, he suddenly realized he had dropped something. I had forgotten how something not very special to an adult can be very, very special to a little boy. He began to cry as he discovered his loss.

I jumped up out of my aisle seat, grabbed the dropped packet and ran it down to the little boy, who promptly produced the biggest smile I've ever seen. His mother stood behind him with a cup of coffee. The boy had been given a "big boy's job" of carrying his mother's sweetener back to their seats. It was a very important job to him. And he looked at me as his hero. He was so cute, even the people along the aisle who saw what had happened gave him and me a little applause.

That's how Jesus' ministry was, too. He didn't go out of His way to change people's lives. He did it wherever he ran into them, on the streets: "As Jesus and his disciples were leaving Jericho, a large crowd followed him. Two blind men were sitting by the roadside, and when they heard that Jesus was going by, they shouted, 'Lord, Son of David, have mercy on us!' . . . Jesus had compassion on them and touched their eyes. Immediately they received their sight and followed him" (Matthew 20:29, 34).

And that's how your ministry can be as you travel. If God calls you to be a missionary in a far off country, then by all means go. But until then, He calls you to touch people wherever you happen to be. Nothing special? Wrong! Changing the life of some stranger who has never experienced the love of God is as special as it comes!

## September 23
### FRUITLESS FOLLY

"Seeing a fig tree by the road, he went up to it . . ."
(Matthew 21:19)

Traveler: *Jesus*
Read: Matthew 21:18–22; Mark 11:12–14, 20–24

I have always wondered what the fig tree did to deserve the fate it received at the word of Jesus. It sat there along the road, growing and minding its own business. Mark tells us it wasn't even the season for figs. But when Jesus wanted food, He expected the fig tree to have fruit, whether it was the right time of the year or not. He was so disappointed when it didn't that he cursed the tree, and it withered up. I presume it died quickly.

I have come to believe that the fig tree represents something in our own lives. The world offers so many forms of "food" for the spirit. That new car will get you the girl. That new house will finally solve all the problems you had with the old one. Once you get that promotion, you'll have fewer people to boss you around. More money, more prestige, finally a little reward for all those years of hard work. Each of these kinds of "food" stands beside the road of your life, like a fig tree guaranteeing refreshment.

There's only one problem. For a Christian, the big rewards don't come until we first seek the kingdom of God, through faith in Jesus Christ. Until we do that, it's the off-season for fruit. And we find that the new car has transmission trouble, the new house has a leaky basement, and the promotion brought an ulcer instead of the good life.

So it's perfectly all right to curse your fig tree, just as Jesus did. Make it wither. It had no value to you anyway. There's other more valuable food just down the road. Sure you're hungry, but have faith: "I tell you the truth, if you have faith and do not doubt, not only can you do what was done to the fig tree, but also you can say to this mountain, 'Go, throw yourself into the sea,' and it will be done. If you believe, you will receive whatever you ask for in prayer" (Matthew 21:21–22).

If you pray and believe, you will receive the right kind of fruit.

## September 24
## CHANGELESS

"For many will come . . . and will deceive . . ."
(Matthew 24:5)

Traveler: *Jesus*
**Read: Matthew 24:1–5; Mark 13:1–6; Luke 21:5–8**

In 1969, I made a very conscious career decision to enter the electric power industry. I enjoyed the concept of utility service as a parallel to Christian service—helping people with their needs. And I reasoned that if all else were to fail, there would always be a need for electricity. Therefore, there would always be a need for mechanical engineers like me.

Who could have imagined that within thirty years, the electric power industry would become deregulated, creating a free-for-all for lawyers, bankers, accountants and other business experts, for almost everyone but mechanical engineers in the power field? Technical development and innovation has moved into the realm of electronics and computers. And the failure to provide a cohesive, national renewable energy policy has pulled the rug out. Mechanical engineers with a power specialty have become a commodity, a dime a dozen. What once was a highly respected branch of the profession has devolved into journeyman status.

So, you're in telecommunications, and that's as big as the industrial revolution was one hundred years ago? True, it's hard to imagine where all of it could end. But it will end. It will change. And I hope you haven't put your faith in it.

Whether it's hula hoops or power plants or the Internet, ask yourself if you can imagine a point where your hot business could end. Make sure you are using it as food provided by God and not as the core of your faith—in humanity—rather than in God: "I tell you the truth, not one stone here will be left on another; every one will be thrown down . . . Watch out that no one deceives you. For many will come in my name, claiming, 'I am the Christ,' and will deceive many" (Matthew 24:2,4–5).

God put us here to live abundantly, but not so much so that we forget Him and worship technology. I'm actually very happy my career has changed. I can't even keep up with all the things my Boss wants me to do, in the only truly changeless market there is.

## September 25
### AN INVITATION

"... I was a stranger and you invited me in ..."
(Matthew 25:35)

**Traveler:** *Jesus*
**Read: Matthew 25:31–46**

At most major airports, each airline has what they call a "service desk," somewhere out on each concourse, between a couple of gates. The service desks are not the same as the ticket counters out in the main terminal, which are for happy people buying tickets and checking luggage. No, the service desks are for those who have had flights canceled or delayed. They exist to herd all the downtrodden of the travel industry into one area. Although I've never heard an airline employee admit it, I imagine the service desks are situated to keep unhappy travelers from interacting with happy travelers. Sort of a "cuckoo's nest" for the unfortunate.

I have walked past service desks in various airports a thousand times. Either there's no line, which means there have been no recent problems, or there is a huge line, because even one flight cancellation can upset the plans of hundreds of people.

Where might a Christian ministry dedicated to hospitality help? How different are people languishing at the service desk from this: "For I was hungry and you gave me something to eat, I was thirsty and you gave me something to drink, I was a stranger and you invited me in, I needed clothes and you clothed me, I was sick and you looked after me, I was in prison and you came to visit me" (Matthew 25:35–36). With the possible exception of clothing, these needs are all apparent at the service desk! If you think prison is also an exception, then you've never served a sentence at the service desk!

This is the hosting side of hospitality, the "even greater commission" if you're a fellow traveler. What kind of presence should we have at airports? What kinds of things can we do for travelers with special problems? On the highways of Denver, bright yellow "Samaritan" vans assist motorists in trouble, right alongside the police. What does this imply for Christian hospitality in conjunction with the airlines?

I'm not sure I know yet. But I know my heart is moved by the need! What about yours?

## September 26
### PRAY ALONE

"Sit here while I go over there and pray."
(Matthew 26:36)

Traveler: *Jesus*
**Read: Matthew 26:36–46; Mark 14:32–42; Luke 22:40–46**

In our hectic modern lives, it is very difficult to find time to pray. A mother with small children rarely gets a few minutes of quiet time to seek the Lord. And a business person with a large staff and customers spends all his or her time in meetings or on the telephone, not to mention traveling.

Jesus was busy, too. The gospel story records numerous times when crowds followed him everywhere He went. His ever-questioning disciples appeared to pepper him constantly, and there was always a load of healing and preaching to be done. But Jesus knew the importance of getting alone to pray. Even when He was about to be betrayed at Gethsemane, when He must have been filled with turmoil, He stopped, went off alone and prayed: "Then Jesus went with his disciples to a place called Gethsemane, and he said to them, 'Sit here while I go over there and pray.' . . . Going a little farther, he fell with his face to the ground and prayed, 'My Father, if it is possible, may this cup be taken from me. Yet not as I will, but as you will'" (Matthew 26:36,39).

I've found over the years that a small moment can always be found to pray. Especially when things are tough, such as in the middle of a business meeting, I've found that God provides a few seconds to seek His will for the situation at hand. Getting up and walking to the coffee pot on the conference room table or even going to the rest room provides time to pray quickly for guidance, strength and wisdom. Within seconds I've been reminded of a memorized piece of scripture or of Christ Himself, praying in the garden, and I return to the meeting refreshed and alert.

Think back over your last trip. Did you take time to get away by yourself and pray? Prayer makes the difference between doing it your way and doing it God's way. Seek God's will today, in quiet moments, all by yourself. He will deliver time and time again, in the most unexpected ways.

## September 27
### GOING BEFORE

"He . . . is going ahead of you into Galilee."
(Matthew 28:7)

Traveler: *Jesus*
Read: Matthew 28:1–10; Mark 16:1–8; Luke 24:1–10

The word "going" in this passage of scripture may be one of the most exciting travel words ever heard or written. It is an active verb, present tense. It ends in "-ing." It has no end.

This is the word that changed time and space forever, the moment Jesus rose from the dead. First, an angel told the women who visited the grave: "He has risen from the dead and is going ahead of you into Galilee. There you will see him" (Matthew 28:7). Then Jesus, Himself, appeared to the women: "Do not be afraid. Go and tell my brothers to go to Galilee; there they will see me" (verse 10). Jesus didn't just float off into heaven like a ghost. No, he went along their road ahead of them.

As I have traveled over the years, I have always tried to take Christ with me, like putting on the armor of God (Ephesians 6:11). But I never thought before about Jesus actually *going* out before me. If He could go before the disciples to Galilee, He can go before me to Chicago or New York or Mexico City. And I will see Him there, if I take the time and seek His face as I go.

As I write this, I see that I have not taken the time to contemplate the Risen Christ in the present tense, the Christ who is continuously *going*. It's easier for me to think about the Holy Spirit inside me and about God who controls the heavens. But the Risen Christ is always *going ahead*, preparing my way and yours. How exciting, how dynamic!

What are you facing today? A full day of meetings and then a long flight to another destination and more of the same tomorrow? Does it all seem the same after awhile? It wouldn't seem so mundane if you knew that a very special person was going to drop everything and go there to meet you, would it?

Well, good news! A very special person is *going* ahead of you right now to do just that!

## September 28
### THE GREAT COMMISSION

"Therefore go and make disciples of all nations . . ."
(Matthew 28:19)

Travelers: *The Disciples*
**Read: Matthew 28:16–19**

I have had the privilege of meeting and supporting many missionaries. They have served in New Guinea, Kenya, Germany, Philippines, Ecuador and many other countries. These people have taken seriously the Great Commission of Jesus Christ after his resurrection: "All authority in heaven and on earth has been given to me. Therefore go and make disciples of all nations, baptizing them in the name of the Father and of the Son and of the Holy Spirit, and teaching them to obey everything I have commanded you. And surely I am with you always, to the very end of the age" (Matthew 28:19). They have literally staked their lives on this commission.

There's another country that's in need of discipling and baptism. It once was a Christian nation, but it has slid back to the brink of darkness. Today it still has tremendous wealth and power, but how long will that last? Its only hope is in those who would bring the United States of America back to the faith of its founding fathers.

Missionaries are toiling in America, too, sometimes with little recognition. They work in the inner cities and ghettoes, where a vast harvest of wonderful people live, economically depressed, but with hearts that know what it means to trust God in the midst of difficulty. One such effort is the Denver Street School, an alternative high school for kids who have made bad decisions, have paid their debt to society and earnestly want a second chance. Since 1985, Denver Street School has presided over the graduation of dozens of kids, who never would have had a chance to succeed. One day, these graduates may be the ones who take the lead in reconciliation in our cities and among the races. They know how great America can be when everyone gets a fair chance.

Take a moment to pray for missionaries in America. They are stressed and often in danger; they get tired, working long hours for gains that seem to take forever to reach. As you travel, look around for the inner-city programs which snatch victory from the jaws of defeat. That's *your* great commission.

## September 29
## BE AVAILABLE

"They went to Capernaum . . ."
(Mark 1:21)

Travelers: *Jesus and the Disciples*
**Read: Mark 1:21–28; Luke 4:31–37**

Two facts led to a very special encounter. One, I was on a certain flight to Chicago on a certain day, sitting in a certain seat; and two, I was reading my Bible.

Toward the end of the flight, the woman seated next to me asked me if I knew what God looked like. Somewhat startled, I said, "Well not exactly, but I think of Him as my Daddy and of myself as His little boy." She looked troubled and said, "That's what I was afraid you'd say. You looked so peaceful, I wanted to know what made you so. But my father abused me, and to me a father's image is one of terror and hate. How do I find what you have?"

I proceeded to show her about Jesus, who died in abuse for her and for me. She saw past her past to a Savior of light and love. As we walked down the concourse at Midway Airport, she said, "I know that God put you in that seat beside me today. Thank you for showing me the way."

Jesus used chance encounters like that every day of His ministry here on earth. He simply made Himself available to people as He went along: ". . . and when the Sabbath came, Jesus went into the synagogue and began to teach . . . Just then a man in their synagogue who was possessed by an evil spirit cried out . . . 'Be quiet!' said Jesus sternly . . . The evil spirit . . . came out of him . . ." (Mark 1:21–26). Jesus was available, and He drove out demons.

I am no Billy Graham. And I never thought of myself as one who could drive out demons. Now I realize it's not me, but the Holy Spirit working through me that has that power. God used me on that airplane to drive out that woman's demon, which feasted on the hatred of her father.

And God will use you the same way. Just be available as you go.

## *September 30*
### BE AVAILABLE - PART II

"A man with leprosy came to him and begged . . ."
(Mark 1:40)

Traveler: *A Leper*
**Read: Mark 1:40–44; Matthew 8:2–4; Luke 5:12–14**

It's hard to write more than one devotion on the same subject, but not if that subject appears to be a driving theme. And ministering to those we encounter as we travel may indeed be the definition of "Faith In Motion." I don't think you can read the Gospels, especially the Gospel of Mark, without a profound appreciation for what Jesus did for those He encountered. There were no planned tours with advance publicity teams; no billboards announcing a revival on Saturday night. Just ministry in the streets.

A couple of weeks from now, I will make yet another trip back to Connecticut on regular business. I've been there more times than I can count, staying in the same hotels, eating in the same restaurants, working with the same people, meeting the same old friends for dinner. But I feel convicted by these stories of Jesus' ministry to rethink my next trip. What opportunities will I encounter which I have ignored in the past? Where can I visit that is totally different from my usual stuck-in-the-mud choices of the past?

Jesus encountered hundreds and thousands of people as He traveled: "So he traveled throughout Galilee, preaching in their synagogues and driving out demons. A man with leprosy came to him and begged him on his knees, 'If you are willing, you can make me clean.' Filled with compassion, Jesus reached out his hand and touched the man. 'I am willing,' he said . . ." (Mark 1:39–41).

As He traveled, Jesus visited churches, preached, drove out demons, was filled with compassion and was willing to touch those in need. Not a bad context for any trip. So what does that mean for my trip to Hartford next week? Only that I make myself available to God's leading.

What does this mean for your next trip? Are you willing to reach out in new ways?

## *October 1*
### SABBATH SITUATION

"... as his disciples walked along, they began to pick some heads of grain." (Mark 2:23)

Travelers: *Jesus and the Disciples*
**Read: Mark 2:23–28; Matthew 12:1–8; Luke 6:1–5**

I had been traveling all week—again. Sue had served as single mom, and the kids were tired, too. In fact, our whole family was downright cranky. And getting up early for church was going to make us even more tired.

So I did something rare. On Saturday evening I said, "Let's sleep a little longer tomorrow and then get up and go to our favorite restaurant for brunch. We've just got to get some rest and spend some time together." We had one of the most enjoyable days I can remember.

Later that week, a friend said he'd missed seeing me in church and asked where I'd been. I confessed that we had taken the day off and gone to the mountains for brunch. My friend, who never has to travel on business, looked at me as if I had robbed Fort Knox. He made it clear that skipping church was bad.

It turns out that Jesus got in trouble on the Sabbath, too: "One Sabbath Jesus was going through the grain fields, and as his disciples walked along, they began to pick some heads of grain. The Pharisees said to him, 'Look, why are they doing what is unlawful on the Sabbath?'" (Mark 2:23–24). Jesus pointed out that David had eaten consecrated bread from the temple, when his companions were hungry and in need (verses 25–26). "Then he said to them, 'The Sabbath was made for man, not man for the Sabbath. So the Son of Man is Lord even of the Sabbath'" (verses 27–28).

Honoring God on the Sabbath just might mean giving your family and yourself a break. Don't use this as an excuse to miss church frequently. But when fatigue has the better of you, remember what David did and what Jesus did. They broke the mold to meet a serious need: "Therefore, do not let anyone judge you by what you eat or drink, or with regard to a religious festival, a New Moon celebration or a Sabbath day. These are a shadow of the things that were to come; the reality, however, is found in Christ" (Colossians 2:16–17).

## October 2
### SUITABLE LODGING

"Then Jesus' mother and brothers arrived."
(Mark 3:31)

Travelers: *Jesus' Family*
**Read: Mark 3:31–35; Matthew 12:46–50; Luke 8:19–21**

I received a call from a man who had just been given the choice of being laid off from his job in Denver or of a commute each week to Cheyenne, Wyoming for the next year. It wasn't much of a choice. With five children to feed, he had to go.

His first concern was not where he was going to stay. No, this man was a very serious Christian. He needed to know where there was a church in Cheyenne that had mid-week Bible studies. He'd be home each weekend, but he knew that he needed to find a home away from home, for the long haul between weekends.

"Home away from home" is one way to say it, but "family away from family" is another. Jesus made it clear that as Christians, our families change from a purely biological perspective to a spiritual one: "'Who are my mothers and my brothers?' he asked. Then he looked at those seated in a circle around him and said, 'Here are my mothers and my brothers! Whoever does God's will is my brother and sister and mother'" (Mark 3:33-35).

I believe this is one of the great untapped resources of the Christian faith—connecting with family away from family, finding ways to surround ourselves with God's family as we go. The Christian Travelers' Network hopes to be the vehicle to make that possible.

In the case of this man, who called looking for a church in Cheyenne, we pulled down the Yellow Pages from the Internet for churches in Cheyenne, Wyoming, narrowed down to the type of church he sought, made a few calls and found just what he was looking for. He was welcomed into that fellowship with open arms. It really didn't take much effort on our part. The most important part was his willingness to reach out when he was in need.

If you get sent on a long assignment, what will be your top concern, lodging or family?

## *October 3*
HOMETOWN HERO?

"Jesus . . . went to his hometown . . ."
(Mark 6:1)

Traveler: *Jesus*
Read: Mark 6:1–6; Matthew 13:54–58

Recently, I had one of those days that shakes me to the core. I met a dear friend for coffee, just to chat and catch up with each other's happenings. We talked about families and mutual friends and church events. Soon the conversation drifted to my favorite topic, building biblical hospitality in the modern world, through the Christian Travelers' Network.

My friend listened for awhile. Then he shattered me: "I really wonder if your dream is God's dream. I can see how you're helping a few travelers right here in our local church community. But to spread the network around the world seems impossible. In fact, I don't see you in full-time Christian service at all. I think you're better as a businessman, making lots of money to give to deserving ministries."

Externally I appeared calm and cool. But inside a tornado had been loosed in my thoughts. Was he right? Am I just a pretender? Was the vision I got for the Network really from God, or was it just my ego looking for recognition?

Jesus had a moment, too, when He must have wondered: "Jesus left there and went to his hometown, accompanied by his disciples. When the Sabbath came, he began to teach in the synagogue, and many who heard him were amazed . . . And they took offense at him. Jesus said to them, 'Only in his hometown, among his relatives and in his own house is a prophet without honor.' He could not do any miracles there, except lay his hands on a few sick people and heal them. And he was amazed at their lack of faith" (Mark 6:1–2, 4–6).

But Jesus didn't doubt himself, and He didn't doubt his calling. He moved on.

One of Satan's most effective tools is to use those close to us to discourage us. The answer is to do what Jesus did.

Move on, never losing sight of God's revelation in your life.

## October 4
## BUSY BODIES

"Come with me by yourselves to a quiet place and get some rest." (Mark 6:31)

Travelers: *Jesus and the Disciples*
**Read: Mark 6:30–31**

This is what I love about the Gospel of Mark. While Matthew, Luke and John all have theological viewpoints of what Christ did, Mark seems to just report little human interactions as they were. Mark paints a picture of Jesus that is down to earth, compassionate, caring.

The scene is described in only two verses, and these verses are not found anywhere else in the gospels. But I think they are extremely important because they describe a life-style similar to our own. Jesus sent out the disciples to preach the Good News (Mark 6:7–13). When they returned, they had many exciting things to tell Jesus. "Then, because so many people were coming and going that they did not even have a chance to eat, he said to them, 'Come with me by yourselves to a quiet place and get some rest'" (verse 31).

It doesn't take much imagination to see how that chaotic scene, with lots of people coming and going, parallels our own daily lives. Whether it's airplane flights, meetings, dinner and hotel, or your entire staff demanding to see you when you're back in the office, or chauffeuring four kids to soccer and baseball games, we can identify quite well with that scene.

Jesus took it all in, saw the fatigue on the faces of his disciples, and said, in effect, "Oh, man, you look like you just got run over by a camel!" Jesus was a great leader, and He knew when His troops had had enough. More important than the act of getting away was the disciples' appreciation that their leader cared enough to see their fatigue.

Who is your leader? I hope it's Jesus. He can see that you need a rest. Come away by yourself with Him.

## *October 5*
### WALKING TREES

"I see people; they look like trees walking around."
(Mark 8:24)

**Traveler:** *Jesus*
**Read: Mark 8:22–26**

Here's another of Mark's stories which does not appear elsewhere in the Bible. This time it not only has compassion, but a touch of humor, too. And it teaches a very important point about God's timing.

As he arrived in Bethsaida, Jesus was asked to touch a blind man. "He took the blind man by the hand and led him outside the village. When he had spit on the man's eyes and put his hands on him, Jesus asked, 'Do you see anything?' He looked up and said, 'I see people; they look like trees walking around'" (Mark 8:23–24).

Can't you just see the man squinting? I think this is a funny moment. And joyous. The man was seeing light, but the job wasn't yet complete. I find it fascinating that Jesus, with all His healing power, veteran of many astonishing and immediate miracles, didn't finish the job on the first try. Could it be that He was testing the blind man's faith?

Some missionary friends of ours are back in the United States, raising support. They are wonderful, loving people, but the funding has been agonizingly slow. While talking at a recent gathering about persevering in faith, Becky said, "I know God could end this ordeal in a flash. But sometimes, God takes the bus!"

Yes, God has the power to heal you or end a nightmare quickly, but for reasons known only to Him, He may choose to take the bus, that is, move very slowly. And it can be a very bumpy ride. But hang in there! "Once more Jesus put his hands on the man's eyes. Then his eyes were opened, his sight was restored, and he saw everything clearly" (verse 25).

Jesus' miracles weren't always quick, but they were thorough! The blind man no longer saw what looked like trees walking. Trust Jesus, and one day you will see everything clearly!

## October 6
## SPECIAL ORDER

"This kind can come out only by prayer."
(Mark 9:29)

Traveler: *Jesus*
Read: **Mark 9:14–32; Matthew 17:14–23; Luke 9:37–45**

Continuing with the theme of the past couple days, we come to a story which is reported in Matthew, Mark and Luke, but Mark adds one verse which brings the story to a more personal level.

In all three cases, a boy is possessed by a demon so nasty that even the disciples could not cast it out. Having already experienced the power of healing, the disciples were perplexed. They must have felt like they tried to fire a gun with no bullets in it. In Matthew, the disciples are told they had too little faith to drive out the demon. That's fine, but how can they have enough faith? Matthew leaves it hanging; Luke leaves this question out entirely.

But Mark once again reports what the up-close-and-personal Jesus taught his closest friends: "This kind can come out only by prayer" (Mark 9:29). Aha! The disciples failed the same way we often do, by failing to pray when the problem is the most severe.

Link this now to what the boy's father said to Jesus: "'But if you can do anything, take pity on us and help us.' 'If you can?' said Jesus. 'Everything is possible for him who believes.' Immediately the boy's father exclaimed, 'I do believe; help me overcome my unbelief!'" (verses 22–24).

This may be the most important message I can offer you in this entire book. If you believe but are paralyzed by fear during a crisis, there is only one way out—prayer. Lots of it. The father needed to erase his unbelief by praying for his son. And just as important, the disciples needed to pray fervently to drive out the demon. Oh, man, that's powerful!

Are you in a personal crisis? Surround yourself with prayer warriors and have at it. Do you know someone who's in the battle of their life? Surround them with your prayers. What an awesome responsibility. What an awesome opportunity!

## October 7
### TOP GUN

"... on the way they had argued about who was the greatest."
(Mark 9:34)

Travelers: *Jesus and the Disciples*
**Read: Mark 9:33–35; Matthew 18:1–5; Luke 9:46–48**

Al was the son of a prosperous German merchant, in the 1930s. When Hitler rose to power, Al's family was among those driven out because of their Jewish faith. Al was a teenager when he slipped across the border into Switzerland to escape the Nazis. He never saw or heard from his family again. Somehow he made it to the United States, got an engineering education and then went to Israel, fighting for independence in the late 1940s.

Al knew about electric power plants, and that's what brought us together. From a technical standpoint, Al and I were best friends. We saw problems the same way and enjoyed solving them together. But culturally we could not have been farther apart. And that's where the trouble started.

When we traveled together, Al's habits were the opposite of mine. He liked staying up late, eating big meals and drinking lots of wine—very European. Not surprisingly, early morning was an alien experience to him. I like small dinners, early bedtimes and rooster-crowing get-a-ways. There were several occasions when we missed planes because they were scheduled, in Al's opinion, at too uncivilized an hour. As one who was always proud of being on time, I finally gave up and just left him. He missed the plane, I didn't. His problem, not mine.

Any secular person would have agreed I was right. But not Jesus: "If anyone wants to be first, he must be the very last, and the servant of all" (Mark 9:35). And Paul said, "Let your conversation be always full of grace, seasoned with salt, so that you may know how to answer everyone" (Colossians 4:6). I was neither subservient nor full of grace with Al. And I lost a God-given chance to show him the softer side of the love of Jesus Christ.

Who's that grouchy person in your life? How do you treat him or her? Who is first and who is last?

## October 8
### THE BEST OFFENSE IS A GOOD DEFENSE . . . ?

"One of the teachers . . . came and heard them debating."
(Mark 12:28)

Traveler: *A Teacher of the Law*
**Read: Mark 12:28–34; Matthew 22:34–40**

An evangelist here in the Denver area, named Bill Fay, has a radio program called, "How to Share Your Faith Without an Argument."[7] His ministry came about, at least in part, because he observed that so many good Christian people have trouble sharing their faith, when challenged. Bill has tried to turn around an old sports truism to make it say, "The best defense (of the faith) is a good offense." His approach is brilliant. Where the conversation goes is strictly up to the other person. And it has won many people to know Jesus Christ as their Lord and Savior.

Travelers, as much as anyone, know what it's like to be challenged about their beliefs. A quiet few minutes of Bible reading can be interrupted by a non-believer who can make us feel very uncomfortable. But Jesus shows us that these people may not be so skeptical after all. They may be searching for eternity, and it's up to us to help them find it:

> One of the teachers of the law came and heard them debating. Noticing that Jesus had given them a good answer, he asked him, "Of all the commandments, which is the most important?" "The most important one," answered Jesus, "is this: . . . Love the Lord your God with all your heart and with all your soul and with all your mind and with all your strength. The second is this: Love your neighbor as yourself. There is no commandment greater than these." "Well said, teacher," the man replied. " . . . To love him with all your heart . . . and to love your neighbor as yourself is more important than all burnt offerings and sacrifices." (Mark 12:28–33)

The teacher of the law had a breakthrough because of Jesus' defense. And Jesus knew the man was searching. He said, "You are not far from the kingdom of God" (verse 34). One who, moments ago, had been a skeptic, now found himself in agreement with Jesus.

How's your offense?

## *October 9*
TAKING A STAND

"When they seized him, he fled . . ."
(Mark 14:51–52)

Traveler: *A Young Man*
**Read: Mark 14:43–52; Matthew 26:47–56; Luke 22:47–50; John 18:3–11**

My wife hosted a neighborhood Bible study once a week in our home. It was one of the ways we tried to follow God's leading in reaching out to our community and those we encounter every day. Not long ago, one of the members of the study, who lives just a few doors away, discovered evidence that her estranged husband may have been searching her house when she was not there. With all the current stories of stalking and violent crime, it's no surprise that she became afraid of going home.

She asked me to keep a watchful eye on her driveway. If I saw a vehicle like the one her husband drove during hours when she was at work, she asked me to let her know. I realized that I needed to help, but the task raised some very big questions. What if I did see him at the house illegally? What if he was waiting in the shadows to harm her? What if I did call the police and it's legally none of my business? What if I get sued? What if he comes after me next? This isn't soap opera stuff, folks, it's real. I wanted to flee!

I know what happened to Jesus when His time of trial came. Everybody left him. This story is so profound it is reported in all four of the Gospels. But only Mark puts a distinctly personal side on the story, after the better known part of Jesus' arrest at Gethsemane: "Then everyone deserted him and fled. A young man, wearing nothing but a linen garment, was following Jesus. When they seized him, he fled naked, leaving his garment behind" (Mark 14:50–52). We don't know who the young man was. Some speculate that he was Mark, the writer of the Gospel itself.

I speculate that the young man was me. And you. And every person who has left Jesus by Himself when the going got tough. And just like the young man, when we flee from Jesus, we flee spiritually naked. Our outer trappings don't protect us as much as we think. Satan can spin them off of us in a second.

As your faith in motion grows, will you take a stand for Jesus when asked? Or will you flee naked?

## October 10
### MUTED BY UNBELIEF

"... I have been sent to speak to you ..."
(Luke 1:19)

**Traveler:** *Gabriel*
**Read: Luke 1:8–20**

Zechariah, the priest, and his wife Elizabeth were the ideal pastoral couple: "Both of them were upright in the sight of God, observing all the Lord's commandments and regulations blamelessly" (Luke 1:6–7). Unfortunately, in their old age they were childless, and that was a difficult burden to bear. It's fair to guess that they prayed for children, but for decades there was no answer.

Almost everyone I know has had some burden like that to carry through life, some more personal than others. And many people I know have prayed their hearts out, with no apparent answer.

Zechariah had an encounter with the angel Gabriel, who told him that, at long last, he was to become a father. And what was Zechariah's response? Skepticism: "How can I be sure of this? I am an old man and my wife is well along in years" (verse 18). Sounds like good ol' twentieth century rationalism to me! Gabriel's response? Swift and effective: he struck Zechariah mute, until the day Zechariah's son would be born, "... because you did not believe my words, which will come true at their proper time" (verse 20).

You might respond that, if someone as magnificent as Gabriel got right in your face, you wouldn't be as stupid as Zechariah. You'd recognize God's power immediately and avoid being struck mute by unbelief. If so, then I would ask, when was the last time you were caught in public, proclaiming the Gospel of Jesus Christ? Would anyone accuse you of being too verbose in claiming eternal life through the forgiveness of sins, made possible by Jesus' death on the cross? Are you mute and did not realize it?

You have something even more spectacular than the angel Gabriel, right in your grasp: God's revelation to humanity in the word. That's right, your Bible! Is it possible that you have been struck mute until you believe in the birth of God's promises in your life? Do you really believe God will feed you just like He does the sparrows? Or that He will clothe you more elegantly than the lilies?

## *October 11*
## TIME TRAVELER

"God sent the angel Gabriel to Nazareth . . ."
(Luke 1:26)

Traveler: *Gabriel*
Read: Luke 1:26–38

We've all seen movies like *The Time Machine, 2001 Space Odyssey* and *Star Wars*, where science fiction speculates about what it would be like when humans exceed the speed of light. But at this point in history, all we know scientifically is that the laws of physics are very different on "the other side" of the equation. Nothing works the same. All bets are off. That includes the bets of those who rule the scientific roost. The only one who knows for sure what would happen is not consulted by many true scientists.

Who would expect to find answers to these questions in the Bible? I would, and so should you.

For the most part, the Bible appears to be a long, linear historical account of God's revelation to humanity. There is some repetition, such as when Kings and Chronicles are compared. And there is frequent connection with Old Testament prophecy, as it is referenced in the New Testament. But for the most part, the Bible tells a historical, theological story. Then, when we least expect it, God steps out of chronological history and gives a solid hint as to His transcendence over time and space.

The angel Gabriel is one of those hints. We saw Gabriel many pages ago in this book, in the Old Testament biblical account (Daniel). Then, at the point just before the birth of Christ, he is back again: "In the sixth month, God sent the angel Gabriel to Nazareth . . ." (Luke 1:26). The same Gabriel as centuries before. Gabriel the time traveler.

Without performing an exhaustive search of Gabriel sitings, it's safe to say that Gabriel is a direct indication that God works in strange and wonderful ways, that His revelation cuts across time and space, directly to you today. Think about it. The Bible is not just some story that happened thousands of years ago. It's *also* as current and fresh as your next breath. If Gabriel appeared over the centuries, he could just as easily appear to you, with a message as important as the ones he delivered to Daniel, Zechariah and Mary. Isn't that exciting?

## *October 12*
## TIMING IS EVERYTHING

"... he lived in the desert until he appeared publicly..."
(Luke 1:80)

**Traveler:** *John the Baptist*
**Read: Luke 1:67–80**

During the three years it has taken to write this book, the Christian Travelers' Network has grown only slightly, and making ends meet financially has not been easy. Donations haven't come pouring in, and "Oasis Hospitality" has not become a household word across the nation.

There have been times when people have not understood what the ministry is about, and others have questioned whether it's needed at all. Still others are sure it's a facade for a get-rich-quick scheme, using non-profit status to duck tax liabilities. Even we have wondered if we will ever reach a "critical mass" where the ministry can support itself.

But over these months, we have learned many valuable lessons. Most important have been the ones teaching us what *not* to do. For example, we thought for a long time that we should provide a full spectrum of travel agency services, as an extension of our ministry, both for convenience to our constituents and for fund raising. Recently it has become clear that there is more risk of failure, as newcomers to that profession, than benefit. "Stick to the knitting," as many businesses learn. In our case, that means focusing directly on building the Christian Travelers' Network.

We also learned that building a high-tech fax ministry is much more complicated than we realized. What if we had gotten thousands of responses before we could respond to them? Disaster.

The model of John the Baptist is not only for us, but for anyone: "And the child grew and became strong in spirit; and he lived in the desert until he appeared publicly to Israel" (Luke 1:80). The timing of our development is God's, not our own. He causes us to grow, learn and become strong spiritually. Then He nurtures us outside of the public eye until His timing is fulfilled. Then He turns us loose. If we don't follow His steps, we aren't His.

Don't rush God!

## October 13
### WHERE TO LOOK?

> "Why were you searching for me?"
> (Luke 2:49)

**Traveler:** *Jesus*
**Read: Luke 2:41–52**

Over the many years I traveled frequently, I never had an occasion when my wife tried to reach me and couldn't find me. There were a few times when I forgot to give her my itinerary before leaving, so she had to wait until I called her that evening to find out where I was. Blessedly, no emergencies happened during those times. And she learned that even if there was an emergency, I probably couldn't do much about it anyway, so she didn't try to call me very often, knowing I would call her every night without fail.

As I rose in the ranks of senior management, I began to believe that my staff had spies that followed me around, because they seemed to know exactly where I was. I'd get paged at airports, faxed at hotels and messaged at clients' offices. I reached a peak of thirty-five voice-mail messages in one day (probably more, but that was the capacity of the system). My staff even knew that I get up early in the morning to study, so they would calculate the time difference and call me at 5:30 a.m., even if that was 3:30 a.m. for them.

But the question I never asked until now is, "If they absolutely had to find me, where was the most logical place to look?"

When Jesus was twelve years old, his parents took him to Jerusalem for the Feast of the Passover. When they headed for home, they didn't realize that Jesus had stayed behind, and they had to go back looking for him. "His mother said to him, 'Son, why have you treated us like this? Your father and I have been anxiously searching for you.' 'Why were you searching for me?' he asked. 'Didn't you know I had to be in my Father's house?'" (Luke 2:48–49). If you were going to search for the boy Jesus, there was only one place you needed to look—in the temple.

My staff never looked for me in a church.

Where would someone look for you?

## October 14
## THE GREATER DEBT

"... so he went to the Pharisee's house and reclined at the table."
(Luke 7:36)

Traveler: *Jesus*
**Read: Luke 7:36–50; Matthew 26:6–13; Mark 14:3–9; John 12:1–8**

One of the great strengths of Jesus' time on earth was His willingness to go where people needing salvation were: "Now one of the Pharisees invited Jesus to have dinner with him, so he went to the Pharisee's house and reclined at the table. When a woman who had lived a sinful life in that town learned that Jesus was eating at the Pharisee's house, she brought an alabaster jar of perfume, and as she stood behind him at his feet weeping, she began to wet his feet with her tears. Then she wiped them with her hair, kissed them and poured perfume on them. When the Pharisee who had invited him saw this, he said to himself, 'If this man were a prophet, he would know who is touching him and what kind of woman she is—that she is a sinner'" (Luke 7:36–39).

Ever wonder why the Bible records far more examples of Jesus in fellowship with his opponents than with believers? Jesus never had a home-field advantage. He was always on the visiting team. It didn't matter who or what the circumstances were. He was always ready to teach. And the teaching often came in response to some criticism of his ways. He wasn't afraid to be conspicuous, so that someone new might be brought into the kingdom of God.

When I have traveled I have actually *avoided* invitations to someone's home. As I read this account of Jesus, I feel ashamed. I always have an excuse: too busy, too tired, early flight tomorrow. But what opportunities have I missed? As I look at my growth in Christian belief, I see a disturbing pattern. The more mature I have become in my faith, the less contact I have with the outside world. That's bad.

Jesus used the occasion of his invitation to the Pharisee's house to show that those who are forgiven the most, love Him the most. But I don't spend my time with those who need the most forgiveness. What a shame!

How many invitations do you get? Do you see them as opportunities?

## October 15
### EASY PICKIN'S

"... then the devil comes and takes away the word from their hearts ..." (Luke 8:12)

**Traveler:** *The Devil*
**Read: Luke 8:1–15; Matthew 13:2–23; Mark 4:1–20**

Last night I saw John for the first time in several years. Back in the 1980s, he was an important member of our church. What I remembered the most about John was his four absolutely gorgeous young daughters, ranging in age from one to about six. On Sundays, they were always dressed with lots of bows and lace, and they were the pride of John's life. But John was always a superficial Christian. He was at church because it was expected of him. Any attempt to engage him in serious conversation was rebuffed. The seed of God's word did not appear to be planted very deeply.

We moved away, and I did not see John for many years. When I saw him again, the first thing I asked about was his wonderful family. With downcast eyes, he mumbled that he had left them several years before and married another woman. So dispassionate, so matter-of-fact. I felt like crying. Those girls are in their teenage years now. Where's their dad?

Jesus told a parable about the word of God as seed sown in various places. Some of it falls along a path, where it is trampled and eaten by the birds. He explains it this way: "The seed is the word of God. Those along the path are the ones who hear, and then the devil comes and takes away the word from their hearts, so that they may not believe and be saved" (Luke 8:11–12).

How well-rooted are you? Has God's seed fallen on fertile ground in your heart? Have the roots reached down deep, where they cannot be harmed by "birds?" As you travel, it's easy to be blown around. It's a big world out there. Some things might even look more attractive than other more mundane things at home. Don't be fooled! "But the seed on good soil stands for those with a noble and good heart, who hear the word, retain it, and by persevering produce a crop" (verse 15).

Persevere. And produce fruit.

## October 16
### LOOKING BACK

"... first let me go back and say good-by to my family."
(Luke 9:61)

Traveler: *Jesus*
Read: **Luke 9:57–62; Matthew 8:19–22**

I saw her coming toward me, while she was still quite a distance down the concourse. The airport was very crowded, but she was oblivious to anyone around her. It was like a premonition: collision course.

I was carrying two heavy bags, so I could not pass anyone in the crowd, even though I was trying to make a flight connection. I just had to go where the crowd allowed. Sure enough, she came straight toward me.

I'm sure you've run into someone like her, too. She was walking toward me, but had her head turned, looking back behind her. She was walking one way but looking the other. I don't know if she was looking for someone in the crowd or just fascinated by the sights and sounds of the airport.

*Crunch!* She walked right into me. I said, as kindly as I knew how, "Excuse me!"

She replied, "You really should watch where you're going, sir!" And with a huff, she moved on toward her next encounter.

Leading a part-time life of faith is like walking one way but looking back in the direction you came from. If you look back, you crash. I know. I hesitated for a long time. And I blamed the people I ran into along the way, not realizing it was my lack of commitment that was causing the trouble. But Jesus warns that only a total commitment in His direction will do: "Foxes have holes and birds of the air have nests, but the Son of Man has no place to lay his head . . . No one who puts his hand to the plow and looks back is fit for service in the kingdom of God" (Luke 9:58,62).

Anyone who has plowed a big field or sailed a boat across a big lake can tell you that the only way to move forward is to keep your eyes fixed on a point on the other side. If you look back, the furrows will be crooked, and the boat will be off course.

Which direction are you looking?

## October 17
## CLOSE ENCOUNTERS

> "Go and do likewise."
> (Luke 10:37)

**Traveler:** *Jesus*
**Read: Luke 10:30–37**

At our regular Monday morning prayer group, Dave said he had a prayer request. It was for a very dear friend of his who had become a missionary in Kenya. He and his family had been there only a short while when their vehicle was run off a dirt road by an out-of-control local driver. This was in a remote area, and medical help was not available. Dave's friend was not seriously hurt, but the driver of the offending vehicle was. His friend's pregnant wife had leaped out of their own wreck and rushed to the aid of the man who had nearly killed her moments before. He was badly injured and bleeding profusely.

A few weeks later, in the process of giving birth to their new baby, the wife learned that she had contracted the HIV virus from the man she had saved. Dave's prayer request was that somehow God's will would be done in this terrible tragedy.

Once again, we are struck by how difficult it is to follow Jesus' teachings to the letter. There is no room for anything but self-sacrifice. The Good Samaritan didn't just stop and look at the man who lay beaten and robbed on the side of the road: "He went to him and bandaged his wounds, pouring on oil and wine. Then he put the man on his own donkey, took him to an inn and took care of him. The next day he took out two silver coins and gave them to the innkeeper. 'Look after him,' he said, 'and when I return, I will reimburse you for any extra expense you may have'" (Luke 10:34–35).

To us, Jesus says, "Go and do likewise" (verse 37). Strong words, tough words to live up to. But implied in those words are unimaginable blessing.

Last month, Dave's friends were on furlough from Kenya and he invited me over to meet them. There was a party going on, and some of the biggest smiles I have ever seen. Dave read my look of confusion: this didn't look like a family crushed by tragedy. Then he handed me a piece of paper. It was a hospital lab report, a blood test performed just a few days ago after their arrival in the States.

She was HIV negative. No one could explain the Kenyan blood test.

*FAITH IN MOTION*

*October 18*
PLEASE, DADDY

"... he who seeks finds ..."
(Luke 11:10)

Traveler: *Jesus*
Read: Luke 11:5–13; Matthew 7:7–11

What Marty did for us is only a tiny fraction of what God will do for you.

As my daughter's sixteenth birthday approached, I knew her great love—Broadway. She had appeared in two high school musicals and was a dynamite singer. She played the piano, and strains from all of her favorite musicals wafted through the house every day as soon as she got home from school. I began to dream about taking her to New York to see *Les Miserables* as a very special surprise.

Knowing I had lots of frequent flyer miles made the airline part of the trip easy. But how could I get good seats on her birthday, in New York, when I was in Colorado? I knew you had to be in line at the right time, in New York, and often you must take what you can get rather than pick a certain night.

So in January I called my lawyer friend Marty, in New York, and asked his advice. He confirmed what I already knew. Getting tickets for March 28th would be extremely difficult.

Jesus told a story about how friends might react when presented with a difficult request: "Suppose one of you has a friend, and he goes to him at midnight and says, 'Friend, lend me three loaves of bread, because a friend of mine on a journey has come to me, and I have nothing to set before him.' ... I tell you, though he will not get up and give him the bread because he is his friend, yet because of the man's boldness he will get up and give him as much as he needs" (Luke 11:5–8).

About the end of February I received an envelope in the mail. Two tickets. *Les Miserables*. Tenth row orchestra. March 28th. Marty's secretary had stood in line three days to get them. For my daughter and me.

"If you then, though you are evil, know how to give good gifts to your children, how much more will your Father in heaven give the Holy Spirit to those who ask him!" (verse 13). How much more, indeed!

## October 19
### LOWS AND HIGHS

"Friend, move up to a better place."
(Luke 14:10)

Traveler: *Jesus*
Read: Luke 14:8–11; Proverbs 25:6–7

In the 1970s, Jerry was the kind of manager who is almost extinct today. He was an old World War II bomber pilot who appreciated life and who never took business as seriously as war. What he did take seriously was people, their needs and problems. He made it clear that we were his family and that he would take care of us. Once he even called us all into his office to pray when business got really bad. He knew where to turn, in humility.

Then, at a time when he was slowing down and business was speeding up, Jerry was deemed too old to keep up. He still insisted on doing the payroll by hand on an old accounting sheet, to make sure he had treated everyone fairly. But it took him too long, and some younger managers decided it was time for him to go. So they arranged some things to make him look bad and made sure that senior management was watching. After awhile, the younger guys were in, and Jerry was banished to an early retirement. He was humbled by people who exalted themselves.

Jesus said, "For everyone who exalts himself will be humbled, and he who humbles himself will be exalted" (Luke 14:11).

The man who took over for Jerry got his wish. He is now head of the company, a company which is doing very poorly and which is teeming with strife on the inside. Yesterday I ran into an old friend who still works there. He is being laid off at age 61, rather than being given a decent retirement. The man who took over is still exalting himself at the expense of others. But I believe that he is being humbled on the inside, and the company will soon be humbled completely. A cracked foundation cannot stand forever.

Jerry, meanwhile, is happy and contented in his retirement, honored by a loving wife and family, and not burdened by a failing company. So who's humbled now and who's exalted?

## *October 20*
## SUPER BOWL PARTY

"Go out . . . and make them come in, so that my house will be full." (Luke 14:23)

Traveler: *Jesus*
**Read: Luke 14:16–24; Matthew 22:2–14**

Two days before football's Super Bowl was to be played, my friend Bill called and invited Sue and me to an impromptu party at his house. I was honored to be invited, but one look at Sue's face, and I knew I was in trouble. There were two basic problems: first, she hates football and second, Sunday afternoons have long been reserved at our house for naps, rest and some fun family time in the evening.

Sue was honest. She just didn't want to go. But I was concerned about my friendship with Bill. So I made some very feeble excuses for not attending.

Bill, I imagine, felt just like the man preparing for a great banquet in Jesus' parable: "But they all alike began to make excuses. The first said, 'I have just bought a field, and I must go and see it. Please excuse me.' Another said, 'I have just bought five yoke of oxen, and I'm on my way to try them out. Please excuse me.' Still another said, 'I just got married, so I can't come'" (Luke 14:18–20). My excuses to him probably sounded just as hollow. Honesty on my part would have been a much better solution.

There's another Super Bowl party being planned, though, and this is one I'm sure no one will want to miss. This is the one that Jesus is referring to in the parable of the great banquet. This is God's big party in His kingdom: "Blessed is the man who will eat at the feast in the kingdom of God" (verse 15).

I know Sue won't miss this party. There will be no excuses from her or from me on that day. How about you? You've already been invited by God's word. Have you accepted your invitation? Or have you been making excuses for not believing in the kingdom of God? Jesus makes it clear that God's house will be full regardless. Will you be there?

OCTOBER

## *October 21*
LOST AND FOUND

"... he was lost and is found."
(Luke 15:32)

**Traveler:** *The Prodigal Son*
**Read: Luke 15:11–32**

When I was in the seventh grade, I was already working hard as a newspaper delivery boy. I had a large route and rode my bicycle laden with papers, rain or shine. Recognizing the need for dependable transportation, my parents bought me a new bike. It was nothing fancy, but it looked very nice, and it had a couple of gears on it, which made it much easier to climb a steeply sloped driveway with a hundred papers draped on the back.

I had the bike only a couple days when I came out of school to discover that it had been stolen. Gone. Vanished. Right from the bike rack. Over the next few weeks I mourned for that bike. There was no insurance and no money to buy another one. Some things simply can't be replaced.

In the parable of the prodigal son, Jesus makes the same point. The most valuable possessions to God are not material things, but His children. When one wanders off, He waits patiently for that child's return. If the child discovers the error of his ways and returns to God, there is a giant celebration: "But while he was still a long way off, his father saw him and was filled with compassion for him; he ran to his son, threw his arms around him and kissed him . . . the father said to his servants, 'Quick! . . . Let's have a feast and celebrate! For this son of mine was dead and is alive again; he was lost and is found'" (Luke 15:20, 22, 24).

Eventually the police found my bike, which had been stolen by a jealous classmate. I still remember the joy I felt seeing the officer wheeling it up my driveway. I had thought I would never see it again.

That joy was nothing compared to God's joy when we admit that we haven't been living according to His will, and we come home to Him. You probably haven't squandered your inheritance on wild living. But are there some things that have left you feeling lost and out of touch with God? Now's the perfect time to admit those things to God in prayer. If you do, there will be a very big party in heaven, and you will be the guest of honor!

## October 22
### HALF FULL OR HALF EMPTY?

"... be welcomed into eternal dwellings."
(Luke 16:9)

Traveler: *Jesus*
Read: Luke 16:1–15

Almost everyone knows you can tell an optimist from a pessimist by asking whether a glass of water is half-full or half-empty. As I look over the past year, it would be easy to see my career as half-empty. My area of expertise is becoming obsolete, I've had several projects canceled, and I've lost quite a bit of money in the process. But overshadowing all of that are the opportunities God has given me: helping Oasis Hospitality grow, coaching baseball, spending more time at home with my family and writing this book are just a few. We have managed to stay alive financially; the only bad part is that we haven't made any extra profit.

Interesting. No profit. We ate well. We loved many. We learned in the laboratory of self-employment. And more. In fact, maybe this has been the best year I've ever lived! The glass is definitely half-full and the level is rising! That's because God has used this time to draw me toward Him.

Did you know that corporate downsizing is discussed in the Bible? Look at the parable of the shrewd manager. A manager is about to be laid off because he was inefficient. But before he left, he created good favor with all of his boss' clients, so that when he was out of a job, these folks would be more likely to hire him. Dishonest, yes. Shrewd, yes! Surprisingly, Jesus applauds: "For the people of this world are more shrewd in dealing with their own kind than are the people of light. I tell you, use worldly wealth to gain friends for yourselves, so that when it is gone, you will be welcomed into eternal dwellings" (Luke 16:8–9).

Jesus was no abstract college theologian. His advice works. I have used my friends and associates over the past two years to feed my family (honestly, I might add) while seeking the kingdom of God. I have never felt more secure, even though I have never felt less financially secure: "What is highly valued among men is detestable in God's sight" (verse 15).

Use your worldly position to buy the things that matter—to God. Now *that's* profitable!

## *October 23*
FIRST CLASS OR COACH?

"... the angels carried him ..."
(Luke 16:22)

**Traveler:** *Lazarus*
**Read: Luke 16:19–31**

I remember sitting in the last row of a "stretch" DC-8 a number of years ago. This particular plane was sort of a flying baseball bat with giant wings. It was designed to be flexible and it bounced around a lot. You could look out the windows and watch the wings flap. Or even more disconcerting, you could watch the front of the plane move in different directions than the back. Of course, if you sat up front in first class, you were mercifully unaware of all the flapping going on behind you.

We are all going on one last trip, and when your time comes, I hope it's in first class, not in the back. Each of us will take that trip when we die. Many non-Christians do not believe there will be a last journey; rather there will be nothing, oblivion, peace. Unfortunately, that's not the case. And those that were first class in this life will be in the back, in the next. Or maybe worse; they may have no seat.

Jesus makes it clear that there is an after-life and that everyone goes somewhere. How the rich man went is definitely not the way you want to go: "The time came when the beggar [Lazarus] died and the angels carried him to Abraham's side. The rich man also died and was buried. In hell, where he was in torment, he looked up and saw Abraham far away, with Lazarus by his side. So he called to him, 'Father Abraham, have pity on me. . . .' But Abraham replied, 'Son, remember that in your lifetime you received your good things, while Lazarus received bad things, but now he is comforted here and you are in agony. And besides all this, between us and you a great chasm has been fixed, so that those who want to go from here to you cannot, nor can anyone cross over from there to us'" (Luke 16:22–26).

That chasm is farther across than the wing span of a Stretch DC-8!

## October 24
### GET GRILLED

"The kingdom of God does not come with your careful observation . . ." (Luke 17:20)

Traveler: *Jesus*
Read: Luke 17:20–21

In college at Michigan State University, I didn't have a life. That is, I didn't have a social life. As a full-time engineering student who also worked forty hours per week, all my spare time was spent studying. So I learned to organize my homework such that the easier stuff could be done in the Grill, on weekends.

The Grill was a snack bar in the basement of our dormitory, between the men's and women's sides (yes, I'm so old that men and women were actually separated in those days). The Grill was the social center, with people coming and going in a steady stream. I'd grab a corner table and spend the whole evening working on lab reports and other mundane calculations, while chatting with people as they passed by. I took a great deal of kidding, but it was better than solitary confinement.

So there were two things going on at once: my interior mental process and my exterior setting in the Grill. You might even say that the kingdom of engineering was inside me.

The kingdom of God that Jesus taught about is just like that: "The kingdom of God does not come with your careful observation, nor will people say, 'Here it is,' or 'There it is,' because the kingdom of God is within you" (Luke 17:20–21). You can't observe it from the outside, but you can feel it from the inside. Many people think of the kingdom only as the New Jerusalem (see Revelation). I think it is both!

This devotional is being written as I sit in a coffee shop. At the table next to me is an insurance salesman doing a hard-sell on a potential customer. Just a couple of feet away, the atmosphere is very un-god-like. But here within me, as I talk to you, I know I'm part of the kingdom of God. How paradoxically peaceful!

Look around you right now. Can you sense that the kingdom of God exists right in the middle of other events, actions and situations? It does. It's inside you, growing! Jesus died to give you that gift. Accept it now!

## October 25
### PERSISTENCE PERSONIFIED

"... a widow ... kept coming to him ..."
(Luke 18:3)

Traveler: *A Persistent Widow*
Read: Luke 18:1–8

I don't do it on purpose, but there are times when I am detestably arrogant.

Consider the case of the Fuller Brush Man. Perhaps I can be forgiven for disliking door-to-door salesmen in general, because they often invade my privacy. My ego keeps me from buying anything, even if they have something good. I'm a little easier on kids selling things for school projects, but not very much.

So imagine my surprise when I was reviewing our check register one year, for tax purposes, and discovered that my wife had written several checks to the Fuller Brush Man. You know who he is. He comes to your door too. The consummate professional salesman. He can charm the stripes off a zebra, I thought skeptically.

I asked my wife about him, and she confirmed that she would rather buy routine things like soap and brushes from this man than buy them in the store. Why? Because he is such a nice, persistent man who comes by on a regular basis, always asks about our family and always gives an update on his own wife and children. Surely he doesn't make much money, but he obviously enjoys his work, and well, why not buy something from him?

It often takes a woman's sensitivity to shatter a man's arrogance. She cares about this man, and I realized that's just how God feels about us when we're persistent: "In a certain town there was a judge who neither feared God nor cared about men. And there was a widow in that town who kept coming to him with the plea, 'Grant me justice against my adversary.' For some time he refused. But finally he said to himself, '... because this widow keeps bothering me, I will see that she gets justice, so that she won't eventually wear me out with her coming!' ... And will not God bring about justice for his chosen ones, who cry out to him day and night?" (Luke 18:2–7).

I promise not to judge people so harshly. Do you?

## October 26
### SEEKING AND SAVING

*"For the Son of Man came to seek and to save what was lost."*
(Luke 19:9)

Traveler: *Jesus*
Read: Luke 19:1–9

Yesterday I invited to lunch a man I have known for eleven years. He is a close business associate who lives in another state. Over the years we have become very close friends. But I have known for a long time how empty he is on the inside. Before this visit, I prayed that God would somehow give me a chance, after all these years, to share my faith with him.

Jesus invited Himself over to Zacchaeus's house after spotting him in a tree: "Zacchaeus, come down immediately. I must stay at your house today" (Luke 19:5). Jesus must have felt the same sense of need in Zacchaeus that I did in my friend. As the story in Luke goes, Zacchaeus stood up and repented, without any preaching from Jesus at all. The mere presence of Jesus was enough to convince Zacchaeus that he should change his ways and restore fourfold to anyone he had cheated.

Only moments after my friend sat down for lunch, he said he had just attended a funeral for a close friend and client, who had died suddenly of a heart attack, at a relatively young age. This man left a legacy of caring for people. Everyone knew and loved him, and the church was packed to capacity. Looking somewhat vulnerable for the first time since I'd met him, my friend said, "There won't be many there for my funeral. I just hope someone like you puts in a good word for me with the Big Guy, when my time comes."

And there it was—my opportunity to share my faith. I told him that he has nothing to worry about, if he will just confess to being a sinner and accept Jesus as the one who will "put in a good word with the Big Guy." He didn't accept it right then, but I think he may in the very near future.

Invite yourself to share time with someone in need. You could change his or her life for all eternity.

## October 27
### LET THE STONES CRY OUT

"As he approached . . . the city, he wept over it . . ."
(Luke 19:41)

Traveler: *Jesus*
**Read: Luke 19:28–44**

The April 8, 1996, issue of *Time* magazine features a cover story about the Jesus Seminar, a collection of extremely skeptical "scholars" who have rejected all but a small part of the Bible as non-historical. Neither their credentials as biblical scholars nor their criteria for rejection of biblical text are closely scrutinized in the liberal media. Only their main message is trumpeted: Jesus was a nice guy, but there's been a big mistake about the virgin birth, all those miracles and the claim of resurrection from the dead.

One of the methods used to reject scripture is that if a story is only told once in the four gospels, it must not be true. Such a story is Luke's treatment of Jesus' entry into Jerusalem: "Some of the Pharisees in the crowd said to Jesus, 'Teacher, rebuke your disciples!' 'I tell you,' he replied, 'if they keep quiet, the stones will cry out.' As he approached Jerusalem and saw the city, he wept over it and said, 'If you, even you, had only known on this day what would bring you peace—but now it is hidden from your eyes . . . because you did not recognize the time of God's coming to you'" (Luke 19:39–41,44). This is the only place Jesus is reported to have wept over Jerusalem's pending destruction, so the passage is rejected by the Jesus Seminar.

Who are the "Pharisees" of our day? The Jesus Seminar and skeptics like them. They did not, and they do not recognize the historical time of God's coming to earth as Christ; it is hidden from their eyes.

Their denial is so great that I feel like weeping over my own country now! Our nation, which was founded under the blessings of God, is more vulnerable than "scholars" want to admit. Isn't there a resurgence of communism in Eastern Europe and Asia today? How long until another energy crisis cripples us?

What's that you hear? Is it the sound of stones crying out about America?

## October 28
### ON THE ROAD

"... Jesus came up and walked along with them ..."
(Luke 24:15)

Traveler: *Jesus*
**Read: Luke 24:13–35**

On the road to Emmaus, two of Jesus disciples met Jesus, who walked along with them, "... but they were kept from recognizing him" (Luke 24:16). He had risen from the dead, but they did not realize it yet.

As I think back over my travels, I try to recall people I encountered who could have been Jesus; maybe I was kept from recognizing Him because of my unbelief? There might have been many people like that! But hasn't He walked with me in other, more spiritual ways? Yes, dozens of times, in hundreds of experiences. And I know that because He went on to be with His Father, and in so doing sent me something totally sufficient to let me know that He is there—the Holy Spirit: "I am going to send you what my Father has promised; but stay in the city until you have been clothed with power from on high" (verse 49). We'll read about that in more detail as we go through the Gospel of John.

That's how I know that the resurrection of Jesus Christ is true! Because I know beyond a shadow of doubt that He has sent me the Holy Spirit to guide and protect me, just as He said. I am a changed person, because all my actions, even my bad human ones, are guided by His presence, which is closer to me than breathing. "Blessed assurance, Jesus is mine," confirms the old hymn.

Take some time right now, sit back, close your eyes and think about all the times when God was protecting you and you didn't even realize it. If you've accepted that this guidance could have come only through the resurrection of Jesus, then smile, because the Holy Spirit has been with you continuously.

If you haven't accepted Him, now would be a good time to invite Him in. Don't let this opportunity go by!

## *October 29*
### JUST A LOT OF HOT AIR?

"You hear its sound, but you cannot tell where it comes from . . ."
(John 3:8)

Travelers: *You and I*
**Read: John 3:1–21**

Living in the foothills of the Rocky Mountains, we are accustomed to wind, lots of it. During the summer, hot air rises during the heat of the day, up toward the mountains. Then, at sunset and during the night, the air begins to cool. As it cools, it gets heavier. Just before sunrise "down" in the foothills, the sun has already risen in the high country. This pushes the colder air downward, spilling out of the high country, rushing down the valleys toward us living at lower elevations. We often get a fairly hard gale just as the sun is rising, and the house often shudders in its path.

". . . No one can enter the kingdom of God unless he is born of water and the Spirit. Flesh gives birth to flesh, but the Spirit gives birth to spirit. . . . The wind blows wherever it pleases. You hear its sound, but you cannot tell where it comes from or where it is going. So it is with everyone born of the Spirit" (John 3:5–6,8). What a powerful description!

In the past, I've always read this as if Jesus had said, "So it is with the Spirit." I thought that meant we are observers, and the Spirit moves like the wind, blowing by us. Now I see something different: "So it is with *everyone born of* the Spirit." When I am born again into the Spirit, *I* am like the wind! *I* am blown by invisible forces (God) wherever He wants me to go! Oh, what a difference those extra three words make!

As you are born again into the Spirit, you will feel gentle pressure to move in certain directions, just as the cold air washes down from the mountains each morning. God will use you at Son-rise. People may not understand where you're coming from nor where you're going. But you can no more resist the movement of the Spirit than cold air can flow up hill.

And that's not just a lot of hot air.

## October 30
### LIVING WATER

"... the water I give ... will become ... a spring of water welling up ..."(John 4:14)

Traveler: *Jesus*
**Read: John 4:4–26**

If you visit Pagosa Springs, Colorado, you can see very hot, sulfur-smelly water bubbling to the surface, continuously, never stopping. It's interesting to me that the hot springs are under pressure, down below the ground; that's what keeps them flowing toward the surface. If there was no pressure, cold water from the surface could flow into the ground instead of hot water flowing out. But there is pressure and the hot springs are never contaminated by the outside. Rather, spring water always flows outward, encountering the real world at the surface.

Jesus used the concept of internal pressure in describing what He does for people. He described His ministry as "living water," "... welling up to eternal life" (John 4:14). Welling up is the same as positive pressure pushing toward the surface. It cannot be contaminated from the outside. It can only push outward and cause change as it goes.

What happens when the Spirit reaches the surface is as natural as the Pagosa Hot Springs: "... a time is coming and has now come when the true worshipers will worship the Father in spirit and truth, for they are the kind of worshipers the Father seeks. God is spirit, and his worshipers must worship in spirit and truth" (verses 23–24). The natural result of the living water of Jesus is worship of God, nothing more, nothing less, continuous, unending, no matter where you are.

Do I show evidence that the Spirit is always flowing outward from me, under positive pressure? No. I often allow evil to contaminate the well. So I have a goal—to be a true worshiper, such that the Spirit and truth can be seen flowing from me at all times.

And you? If you feel like the well is dry, stop right now and pray to receive Jesus in your heart. If you know Jesus but the well is capped, get out the pipe wrench, twist off that cap and worship! Spill some of that living water on those around you!

## *October 31*
### TRUE MAGNETISM

"No one can come to me unless the Father . . . draws him . . ."
(John 6:44)

Traveler: *Jesus*
Read: John 6:35–51

There is a restaurant in Rocky Hill, Connecticut, just outside Hartford, that serves the best baby-back ribs I have ever tasted. They've been combining the perfect barbecue sauce with slow-cooked fall-off-the-bone ribs for a very long time. As soon as my client tells me to get on a plane and head for Hartford, I start to salivate. By the time I arrive in town, I'm powerless. I am drawn to this restaurant for a plate of ribs as easily as paper clips leap at a magnet. (I'm in Connecticut as this is written, so guess where I'll probably eat tonight!)

Jesus said, "I am the bread of life. He who comes to me will never go hungry, and he who believes in me will never be thirsty" (John 6:35). So why doesn't everyone who hears of Jesus trust in Him immediately? Because God knows there are skeptics: "No one can come to me unless the Father who sent me draws him'" (verse 44). There must be some sort of spiritual magnetism to draw you to Jesus.

But how does someone know whether the pull is there? "Everyone who listens to the Father and learns from him comes to me" (verse 45). So simply by submitting to God's word and having a spirit of learning, the end result is salvation through Christ. There's nothing secret at all. Either be willing to listen, learn and be saved, or resist submitting in the name of scholarly skepticism and be damned. The choice is simple.

Do you feel drawn to Jesus? If not, take time to listen and learn from God's word. Filter out all the other distractions and concentrate.

You can concentrate that hard when you're reading a novel or preparing for a sales presentation. Now do it when you're exposed to the Truth.

Let yourself be attracted to the Source as God intended.

## November 1
### TURN ON THE LIGHTS

"Whoever follows me will never walk in darkness . . ."
(John 8:12)

Traveler: *Jesus*
**Read: John 8:12–30**

I stayed at a hotel which had a nice formal restaurant. It was obvious that the restaurant was very popular locally, because it was very busy, even on a week night. So I decided to sit down and have dinner there.

The decor was beautiful. Thick carpeting, elegant chandeliers, soft chairs with armrests, live piano music, extremely professional waiters. And the food was even better, capped off with a perfect raspberry and chocolate dessert (my favorite, back in the days when I was allowed to eat dessert). This was *the* place in town.

The next morning, I learned that breakfast is served in the same restaurant. Since it was quite early, I arrived for breakfast as they opened the doors. What greeted my eyes was a major surprise. In the light of day, the restaurant looked very different. Instead of soft lighting from the evening before, the chandeliers were blazing and the window curtains were thrown open, all for the purpose of cleaning-up from the night before. Dirt was everywhere, and I did not enjoy eating breakfast to the accompaniment of an industrial-strength vacuum cleaner. Things were radically different when full light was shed.

Jesus said, "I am the light of the world. Whoever follows me will never walk in darkness, but will have the light of life" (John 8:12). The question for today is, if the full light of Jesus shines on your life, how does it look? Does it look like the restaurant at night, with outer decorations and coverings that appear very nice to the world, but which cover up the true you?

When His light shines, do you look like a dirty restaurant, full of crumbs and litter from the night before? Or do you look like an airy cafe, designed especially for the morning sunlight, with lots of sparkle, green plants and flowers?

Are you walking in darkness or light? If it's a little musty in your corners, fling open the drapes, clean up the dirt and turn on the Light. Full blast.

## November 2
### HOW TO GET HEALED

"So the man went and washed, and came home seeing."
(John 9:7)

Traveler: *Jesus*
Read: John 9:1–12

Why do some people have physical handicaps and others don't? I wondered that when I flunked out of Air Force ROTC; that's when I learned I had a deaf ear. And of course, that's nothing compared to the more severe handicaps many people must bear.

Over the years, as my hearing has declined even more, I have had many embarrassing moments, when I just couldn't hear someone in a crowded room, or I answered a question incorrectly because I missed one word in a sentence. Asking a soft-spoken person to speak louder many times during the same meeting was exasperating. Opposing lawyers used my hearing loss to taunt me, during expert witness testimony.

But my hearing loss also has had many blessings. It sharpened my listening skills to a fine edge. And I became very intuitive and logical. Sentences became like jigsaw puzzles, where I learned how to guess the meaning based on the words I could hear, filling in the blanks for ones I missed. And when success came in the business world, no one could ever say it was handed to me on a silver platter; I had to work extra hard to overcome the handicap.

Jesus gives a stunning answer to those who think that a handicap is some sort of condemnation from God: "As he went along, he saw a man blind from birth. His disciples asked him, 'Rabbi, who sinned, this man or his parents, that he was born blind?' 'Neither this man nor his parents sinned,' said Jesus, 'but this happened so that the work of God might be displayed in his life . . . While I am in the world, I am the light of the world'" (John 9:1–5). Then Jesus proceeded to heal the blind man.

God has not chosen to heal my hearing yet. But He has healed my handicap, the one that keeps me from accepting His infinite wisdom. God is using me so that His work may be displayed in my life. What an honor!

Has God asked you to do something special? Rejoice and be healed!

## November 3
### FOLLOW THE LEADER

"But they will never follow a stranger . . ."
(John 10:5)

**Traveler:** *Jesus*
**Read: John 10:1–18**

Think back over your life and recall all the leaders you've followed.

I remember kids I followed in school, pastors who captured my attention with great preaching, bosses of all shapes and kinds, and friends who believed that life was defined as golf. How many of these leaders were true shepherds? What is the definition of a shepherd?

"I tell you the truth, the man who does not enter the sheep pen by the gate, but climbs in by some other way, is a thief and a robber. The man who enters by the gate is the shepherd of his sheep. The watchman opens the gate for him, and the sheep listen to his voice. He calls his own sheep by name and leads them out. When he has brought out all his own, he goes on ahead of them, and his sheep follow him because they know his voice. But they will never follow a stranger; in fact, they will run away from him because they do not recognize a stranger's voice" (John 10:1–5).

As I look back on all the human leaders in my life, none of them fits the definition of a true shepherd. Most climbed the fence of my life because they wanted something from me. Very few went out before me, risking themselves for my protection. Even fewer talked to me in a way that caused me to recognize their voices as my shepherd.

Only one leader in my life fits the bill. He talks to me and goes out before me today, just as He has all the years of my life—Jesus, my Shepherd. And most amazing of all, whenever I roamed away and got lost, He came to find me, and I knew His voice at once. Even when I was seduced by wolves in sheep's clothing, He came to me and brought me back.

Who is your leader? Does he or she fit the description of a good shepherd? Can you count on him or her to be there forever when you get in trouble? There is only one Good Shepherd. Listen for His voice today.

## November 4
### YOU ARE SPECIAL

"... Jesus arrived at Bethany ... a dinner was given in Jesus' honor." (John 12:1–2)

Traveler: *Jesus*
Read: **John 12:1–8; Matthew 26:6–13; Mark 14:3–9; Luke 7:37–39**

While I was visiting my client and spending the week working for him, he told me that he had accepted a new job, and we would no longer be working together. We had become very good friends, and I wished him well. I hated to see him go, but the new opportunity was better, and he was ready for a change.

Toward 5:00 p.m. that afternoon, he stopped-in and asked if I was busy that evening. I said that I had no plans, and that I'd sure like to buy him dinner to celebrate his new horizon. He said, "No, I want to buy you dinner. I've never thanked you for all the hard work and dedication you've shown over the years."

He took me to his favorite sea-food place, and I had lobster pot-pie that was so good I can still taste it. Was the food that good, or did it taste special because my client's thank-you was so special? I think it was the latter. It's very unusual when a consultant gets thanked for a job well done. Most clients think the "big bucks" are reward enough.

Jesus taught that it's perfectly acceptable to be honored, even though most of us are a bit bashful about it. When Mary poured very expensive perfume on Jesus, Judas chewed her out for not selling the perfume and giving it to the poor. Jesus answered, "You will always have the poor among you, but you will not always have me" (John 12:8).

The statement sounds arrogant at first, but it's not. Yes, you should always help the poor, but if there is someone special in your life, it's also important to realize that you will not always have them around to thank. Have you ever lost someone dear, without the opportunity to communicate how important that person was in your life?

You are special, and I hope your business associates and customers realize that. I hope they honor you one day. And I hope you will sit down right now and call someone who is special to you. Honor that person at a special gathering. Don't delay!

## *November 5*
### GROPING IN THE DARK

"The man who walks in the dark does not know where he is going." (John 12:35)

**Traveler:** *Jesus*
**Read: John 12:20–36**

Chief cook and bottle-washer. You've heard the phrase. I lived it in my college dorm cafeteria, at $1.00 an hour. And that was *before* taxes.

Once, I was asked if I would stay and work Easter weekend. I'd get paid extra. They put me in the bowels of hell, washing pots and pans. The dish pan had a live steam line that heated the water. I was given heavy rubber gloves and an apron to protect myself. If the scalding water ever sloshed inside the glove, it would produce instant burns. But I did my job well.

I was asked to close the kitchen each night and then to open it back up again, at 5:00 a.m. the next morning. At the end of my first day, I hung my rubber gloves and apron on a hook just above the light switch, darkened the place, and left. Next morning, I tiptoed through the darkness, groping for that same light switch. Pushing aside the heavy rubber items, I flicked the switch on and was greeted by a mad rush of thousands of cockroaches, who thought my big gloves were their personal condominium. I'm not sure who was more frightened, them or me. I never went into that kitchen in the dark again. And I tried not to think too much about the food I ate there, for the rest of my college days.

Those roaches remind me of what Satan is like. They're quite comfortable in the dark. If you happen to be in the dark, too, well, good luck. But if you flash on the light, they'll disappear. Other than an initial scary encounter, they're powerless over you.

Jesus said, "Walk while you have the light, before darkness overtakes you. The man who walks in the dark does not know where he is going. Put your trust in the light while you have it, so that you may become sons of light" (John 12:35–36).

Today, are you groping darkly or have you found the Light?

## November 6
### THE TRUE GUIDE

"You know the way to the place where I am going."
(John 14:4)

Traveler: *Jesus*
**Read: John 14:1–14**

"The Meadows? Sure, that's easy. Go out of here and take a left. Then another left. Go through the first light and bend around the park. At the traffic circle, take your second right. Go two lights and turn left. Go past Central Church and keep going until you come by the Colt Gun Factory. Watch for the stop sign and turn left under the bridge. Follow the railroad tracks down to the river and hang a left. You're there."

No joke. Those were the directions I was given by my client, to get from his office in downtown Hartford to the power plant just a mile away. I said, "Can't you give me some street names?"

He laughed, "Nobody knows street names around here, just landmarks! You need a guide?"

Ah, New England. Occupied by automobiles but designed for horse-drawn buggies. If you've never been trapped on a "rotary", by target-shooting local drivers, you don't know the meaning of terror. Yes, I needed a guide.

Life is much like the cobblestone streets of New England. Bumpy, dangerous, terrifying and prone to head-on collisions. Unless you have the True Guide: "Do not let your hearts be troubled. Trust in God; trust also in me. In my Father's house are many rooms; if it were not so, I would have told you. I am going there to prepare a place for you. And if I go and prepare a place for you, I will come back and take you to be with me that you also may be where I am. You know the way to the place where I am going" (John 14:1–4).

I got lost a few times, before I found the power plant. But I have never been lost when I have allowed Jesus, the True Guide, to give me directions.

On whom are you relying today? A local who doesn't know the street names? Or the Guide who not only knows the way, but who takes the time to take you to your destination personally?

## November 7
### THE DOE STOPS HERE

> "I will not leave you as orphans; I will come to you."
> (John 14:18)

**Traveler:** *Jesus*
**Read: John 14:15–31**

My 1964 Nash Rambler could do seventy miles per hour, but only downhill, with a tailwind. It was near midnight and I was pushing that old buggy as hard as the temperature gauge would allow. I had driven the ninety miles from East Lansing, back home to Detroit on a Friday night, only to discover that my parents weren't home. Neighbors said they had left town. Obviously we had mis-communicated. I had no choice but to head back to school.

Well past midnight, on the loneliest stretch I-96 has to offer, a car was passing me, so my view was blocked from the left. Suddenly, a deer leaped over the car that was passing me and landed inches away from the front of my rickety wreck. If this had been a prize fight, they would have called a draw. The doe was killed. And so was my car. Only by the grace of God did the doe miss crashing through my windshield.

There was no one to call. All my friends at school were out of the dorm, and my parents were gone. I've never felt more like an orphan in my life. Finally, hours later at the police station, I roused some guy back at the dorm out of bed, and he reluctantly came to get me.

I wasn't a very good Christian in those days, so it never occurred to me to pray for help. And that's contrary to the teachings of Jesus: "If anyone loves me, he will obey my teaching. My Father will love him, and we will come to him and make our home with him" (John 14:23). That night I didn't feel that anyone was with me.

Here's the better way: "If you love me, you will obey what I command. And I will ask the Father, and he will give you another Counselor to be with you forever—the Spirit of truth . . . But you know him, for he lives with you and will be in you" (verses 15–17).

The buck—or doe—stops with you. Would you rather be an orphan or have an indwelling Friend who is always there?

## November 8
### VINES AND BRANCHES

"... but I chose you and appointed you to go and bear fruit—fruit that will last." (John 15:16)

Travelers: *You and I*
**Read: John 15:1–17**

The previous owners of our house planted two grape vines in the back yard. They were very pretty all summer, but didn't produce any grapes. Over the winter, I was sure they would die, but this spring the vines are alive and well. The question is, what do I have to do to make them bear fruit year after year? I'm no gardener, so I need to ask The Gardener.

"I am the true vine, and my Father is the gardener. He cuts off every branch in me that bears no fruit, while every branch that does bear fruit he prunes so that it will be even more fruitful . . . No branch can bear fruit by itself; it must remain in the vine. Neither can you bear fruit unless you remain in me" (John 15:1–2,4). Not only does Jesus teach me how to take care of my grapevine, He teaches me the true meaning of being a Christian. Nurture the vine, prune that which bears fruit and abandon things that don't work.

So now I understand the real grape vines growing in my back yard. But how does this apply to you and me? First and foremost, stay in the vine. That means stay close to Jesus and obey His commandments. And what are His commandments? "If you obey my commands, you will remain in my love, just as I have obeyed my Father's commands and remain in his love . . . My command is this: Love each other as I have loved you. Greater love has no one than this, that he lay down his life for his friends . . . You did not choose me, but I chose you and appointed you to go and bear fruit—fruit that will last. Then the Father will give you whatever you ask in my name. This is my command: Love each other" (verses 10, 12–13, 16–17).

How do you stay in the vine? Love those you encounter, through sacrifice. How can you lay down your life for your friend today? Are you prepared to obey the command? Are you prepared to receive the blessing?

## November 9
### HOW TRUE IS TRUTH?

"... he will guide you into all truth."
(John 16:13)

**Traveler:** *The Holy Spirit*
**Read: John 16:5–16**

We've all experienced temporary blindness from a flash bulb. The flash is so quick that the effect doesn't last very long. But what's the brightest light you've ever seen?

I was aboard an airplane, cruising at 41,000 feet above sea level, looking out of the window, enjoying the view. The plane went into a turn, rotating my half of the plane upward. Without warning, I looked directly into the sun, with very little atmosphere to protect me. It couldn't have been for more than half of a second, but I have never felt such a burning. And it was an hour before my retina was seeing everything normally. It's a good thing that all the lights I see aren't that bright. I'd be blind. Fortunately, there are natural and man-made filters which keep me from such a direct exposure.

Truth is the same way, although I'll bet you've never thought of it that way. If you were exposed to total, absolute truth, would you be able to stand it all at once? Don't answer that one quickly. Think about it. Could you stare directly into the face of truth and survive? You'd probably have to look away. Jesus was that truth: "I have much more to say to you, more than you can now bear. But when he, the Spirit of truth comes, he will guide you into all truth. He will not speak on his own; he will speak only what he hears, and he will tell you what is yet to come" (John 16:12–13).

If you've ever wished, as I have, that Jesus would just show up right here, right now and perform one of His miracles so that everyone would believe, here is the answer to why that doesn't happen. We couldn't stand it. It would be too much. Instead, faith is a process that takes place over our entire lives, guided expertly by the Holy Spirit, whom we could never have if Jesus had not left us as He did: "It is for your good that I am going away. Unless I go away, the Counselor will not come to you; but if I go, I will send him to you" (verse 7).

Be careful, if you feel like praying for Jesus to come and rescue you right now. That's true truth!

## November 10
### PERFECT FIT

"As you sent me into the world, I have sent them into the world." (John 17:18)

**Travelers:** *You and I*
**Read: John 17:6–19**

With all due respect to the Big Apple, my wife and I felt about as comfortable in New York City as turkeys on the fourth Wednesday in November. We went there to take in a Broadway show and relax a little. There must be some kind of clothing we could wear that would not brand us as tourists, but I've never figured it out. Any New Yorker can look at us for one second and *know* we don't fit in. We felt like targets.

There's a reason for why we feel so much like strangers in this world. When Jesus prayed for his disciples, Jesus addressed His Father: "I am coming to you now, but I say these things while I am still in the world, so that they may have the full measure of my joy within them. I have given them your word and the world has hated them, for they are not of the world any more than I am of the world. My prayer is not that you take them out of the world but that you protect them from the evil one" (John 17:13–15).

So we've been placed in the world; we're going to stay here awhile; we're not well liked, and we need protection from evil. Do we ever!

We were waiting for a traffic light in a massive crowd on Fifth Avenue. I have very good peripheral vision and very bad hearing. And that's exactly the protection God gave me that day. Out of the corner of my eye I saw a heavily bearded man pushing his way through the crowd, directly toward us. He was chanting something under his breath, but I couldn't hear it well enough to be distracted; yet I remained on guard. Suddenly, I spotted a large piece of cardboard that he held in front of him. Just as he bumped into me, I realized what was happening. His hand was already on my wallet when I slammed him in the chest with an elbow uppercut, grabbed Sue's hand, and ran for dear life.

I still had my wallet, and he couldn't catch me because of the crowd. I had been protected.

Are you a perfect fit in the world? I hope not!

## November 11
### CHRISTIANITY 101

"May they be brought to complete unity . . ."
(John 17:23)

**Travelers:** *You and I*
**Read: John 17:20–26**

Over the centuries, we have comprehended much of God's word, at least in part. We understand that we are sinners in need of changed lives, even though we are less than perfect in taking personal action. We know that God is active in the world, even if we don't always understand His timing and His strategy.

We accept that Jesus was born to the Virgin Mary, performed miracles, was crucified and rose from the dead. And we believe in God's grace to forgive our sins through the blood of Jesus Christ, and in eternal life. It's all so beautiful. We anticipate the Second Coming of Christ with great wonder, knowing that the climax will be too wonderful for words.

But there's just one problem. There's one thing that we have not believed, one thing that we have refused to put into practice, one thing flowing from some of the most passionate words Jesus spoke during His life on earth: "My prayer is not for them alone. I pray also for those who will believe in me through their message, that all of them may be one, Father, just as you are in me and I am in you . . . May they be brought to complete unity to let the world know that you sent me and have loved them even as you have loved me" (John 17:20–21, 23).

If this book could have one transcendent message, I pray that it would be to wake us up to realize what incredible failures we have been in response to Jesus' prayer for unity. May I take the risk of rephrasing verses 23 and 24:

> If they are not brought to complete unity, they will not be able to let the world know that you sent me . . . Father, I want those you have given me to be with me where I am, and to see my glory, but how can I bring them to me if they can't love each other, if they cannot join together as one?

How chilling! Are we damned? When will we move toward complete unity?

## November 12
### AGENTS OF CHANGE

> "... you will receive power when the Holy Spirit comes on you..." (Acts 1:8)

Traveler: *The Holy Spirit*
**Read: Acts 1:1–11**

As I moved along in rush hour traffic, bumper to bumper, at about thirty-five miles per hour, I saw him streaking up the entrance ramp, much faster than the column of traffic he was about to enter. About one-hundred yards ahead of me, the entrance lane merged into the right-hand traffic lane. The intruder veered into a small opening between cars and promptly slammed on his brakes. *Screech! Crunch!* He was rear-ended by the car he cut off.

I pulled off the road and dialed 911 to report the accident, giving my name and phone number, since I had witnessed the whole thing. I knew rear-end accidents are almost always blamed on the one in the rear, although in this case, that person never had a chance, because of the reckless driver in front.

About a week later, I received a call from the officer who investigated the accident. He read his report to me, and as I expected, he had given the ticket to the wrong person. When I explained what had really happened, he said he would correct the wrong immediately. He sounded a little pleased; I can imagine that the aggressive driver who barged into that lane was not a very cooperative "victim" of the accident.

As a witness to the accident, my testimony changed the facts as perceived by the police officer. I'm sorry to say that I was probably a better witness in that event than in hundreds of other occasions when my testimony could have changed the world's perception of reality: "... when the Holy Spirit comes on you ... you will be my witnesses ... to the ends of the earth" (Acts 1:8). I have not done very well testifying to the world that they do not have all the facts about Jesus Christ until they admit their sins, put their faith in Him and read God's word.

It would have been a shame for that innocent driver to get a false ticket when I was a witness. Isn't it just as wrong when I fail to share what I've witnessed about God's kingdom? What kind of witness are you? Are you an agent of change with those around you?

## November 13
### A MODERN FLOGGING

"Then they ordered them not to speak . . . and let them go."
(Acts 5:40)

**Travelers:** *The Apostles*
**Read: Acts 5:12–42**

The last time I had seen this man was eighteen months ago, in a court room. He had been on the other side, and his testimony had gone very badly. Mine had gone well, and we had won the case. Now I was sitting in his office for a short meeting on a relatively routine subject.

As he walked into the meeting, he was shaking visibly, red in the face. I thought he might explode. He looked at my client and said, "I'll meet with you any time you'd like, but I will not say another word as long as *he* is with you." We sat in stunned silence for a few minutes and then left. The meeting took place the next day—without me.

It was obvious that he had blamed me for his poor performance and any repercussions that had come out of the court case. But it hurt very badly to see a man so physically affected by something I had done, even though I was right. I pray that this man can find peace, and that rage does not ruin his health.

When we do what is right, as Christians in the business arena, we are bound to be persecuted because we won't fight back. Rather, the apostles showed us how to handle such a public flogging: "They called the apostles in and had them flogged. Then they ordered them not to speak in the name of Jesus, and let them go. The apostles left . . . rejoicing because they had been counted worthy of suffering disgrace for the Name . . . they never stopped teaching and proclaiming the good news that Jesus is the Christ" (Acts 5:40–42).

I asked my client if he thought this blatant rejection of me by the contractor would reduce my effectiveness in future meetings. He said, "Are you kidding? That just shows what a great job you're doing!" I had been judged worthy of suffering disgrace.

That's why the Bible is still so applicable to daily life. Are you judged worthy to suffer? Do you consider it pure joy?

## November 14
### MAY THAT DAY NEVER COME

"Going from house to house, he dragged off men and women . . ." (Acts 8:3)

Traveler: *Saul of Tarsus*
Read: Acts 7:54–8:8

As I pondered this scripture, I wondered what it would be like to be persecuted as severely as the early church was. I thought to myself, "That's probably not going to happen in America."

Then I thought again. During 1996, there were a series of bombings and burnings of churches, primarily in Tennessee, apparently based on racism. So now I should ask, what would it be like to be a member of one of those churches? What would it be like if there was another civil war in America and if anti-church forces dragged us off to prison? Maybe it's not so unimaginable after all. If it did happen, would I stay true to the faith? Would you?

Frequent travelers can probably identify with this part of the story as much as anyone: "On that day a great persecution broke out against the church at Jerusalem, and all except the apostles were scattered throughout Judea and Samaria" (Acts 8:1). We may not be persecuted in the religious sense, but we are certainly scattered all over the landscape every week. In the global market place, that trend will only grow.

My question is, given the fact that we are scattered, what do we do and what do we say while we're away? You'll probably catch me talking more about sports than about anything else. Everyone I meet wants to know more about skiing in the Rockies. Or I talk about the business climate or weather or airline food.

Now compare what the persecuted church did when they were scattered: "Those who had been scattered preached the word wherever they went . . . and proclaimed the Christ . . ." (verse 4). Instead of mourning what they had left behind in Jerusalem, they saw their scattering as opportunity to spread the Good News.

Think over your last few trips. Obviously you can't spend every waking second proclaiming Jesus to someone. But haven't there been missed opportunities along the way? What can you do to improve the percentage of your time devoted to sharing your faith? All by itself, just carrying your Bible in public is a tremendous testimony.

## November 15
### BEWARE THE SORCERER

*"They followed him because he amazed them for a long time . . ."* (Acts 8:11)

**Traveler:** *Philip*
**Read: Acts 8:9–25**

The company where I worked for many years had a fifty-year track record of excellence in advising Wall Street investors on technical projects. The company worked very hard to keep that reputation intact.

One year, a new company was formed by a very brash young man, who announced that he was going to take over our market of working with the investment community. He was very bright and was a marketing genius. Clients flocked to his easy-going personality and listened intently as he told them all the things that his competition (us) was doing wrong. We lost job after job because of this man's talent for talk.

When his studies advanced to the point of needing financing for the projects, however, not one banker would accept the work of this new consultant. He simply did not have the respect that our firm had, and bankers would not risk hundreds of millions of dollars on a newcomer. Finally, he came to us and offered to joint venture on projects, since he was getting so much feasibility work, and we had the reputation for financing.

The early church faced a similar problem. A sorcerer named Simon had a great following in Samaria. He performed many enchanting feats, but when he saw Peter and John cause the Holy Spirit to enter new believers, Simon knew he had encountered the real thing. And he knew he wanted their "market share." "When Simon saw that the Spirit was given at the laying on of the apostles' hands, he offered them money and said, 'Give me also this ability so that everyone on whom I lay my hands may receive the Holy Spirit'" (Acts 8:18–19). Yeah, right. As soon as Simon bought the power, he'd lead good people away like the Pied Piper.

Peter's answer was right on: "May your money perish with you, because you thought you could buy the gift of God with money!" (verse 20). Our answer was the same: you can't buy a good reputation!

Satan takes on many tempting forms. Beware the sorcerer!

## November 16
### A DIFFERENT VACATION

"... an angel of the Lord said to Philip, 'Go South to the road ...'" (Acts 8:26)

Traveler: *Philip*
**Read: Acts 8:26–40**

Our vacation turned out a little different than we planned. Or perhaps it did turn out pretty much as we planned, only by the grace of God.

While we were spending a week in the mountains, I discovered that one of my tires was nearly flat. We had been driving near a construction site the previous day, so I wasn't too surprised. It must have been a slow leak, since it hadn't gone totally flat. So I drove to a gas station, tightened the valve stem and added air. We still had another day before heading home. If it went flat, I'd get it repaired. If it stayed up, it was probably the valve stem.

The next day, the tire was still full of air. But a very strong urging came over me: "Fix the tire." I ignored it, because my rational mind had already set the plan into action. When we headed for home, the tire was still full of air.

The tire stayed full all the way home. The drive included tortuous mountain hair-pin curves, loose gravel and passing big trucks on rural two-lanes. But the morning after arriving home, I walked into the garage and found the tire flat as I-80 in Nebraska.

At the repair shop, I was stunned to learn that the tire could not be repaired. The manager asked how far I had driven on it. When I told him, he face turned white. He said, "Sir, there's a nail imbedded in the *side-wall* of the tire. You could have had a blowout anywhere along that trip!" He could not explain how I made it home without an accident.

Philip was smarter. He went wherever the angel of the Lord told him (Acts 8:26–40). And he changed lives along the way. I was warned by an angel, and I didn't listen. But the whole experience makes me want to try another kind of vacation one day, to get in the car and go where the Spirit guides me. Philip hitched a ride on a chariot and changed a life.

Do you plan things so much that you can't listen to angels?

## November 17
### THE CHOSEN

> "Go! This man is my chosen instrument to carry my name . . ."
> (Acts 9:15)

**Traveler:** *Ananias*
**Read: Acts 9:10–19**

"Are you sitting down?" my friend asked me over the telephone. "Guess who Pat picked as his new Executive Vice President! Your old buddy John Sharp!"

Silence. Increasing pulse rate. Thinking through the implications. I'm dead.

John Sharp had been my client's worst enemy and had dogged me mercilessly through months of confrontations in public. Now he had suddenly switched sides. He had become my client! And now I had to go meet with him face to face. Well, it would probably be over quickly, and surely I'd find other work.

Ananias had a very similar assignment. Jesus Himself came to Ananias and asked him to go and heal Saul, who had been blinded along the road to Damascus. "'Lord,' Ananias answered, 'I have heard many reports about this man and all the harm he has done to your saints in Jerusalem. And he has come here with authority from the chief priests to arrest all who call on your name.' But the Lord said to Ananias, 'Go! This man is my chosen instrument to carry my name before the Gentiles and their kings and before the people of Israel. I will show him how much he must suffer for my name'" (Acts 9:13–16). And Saul, of course, became Paul, perhaps the most amazing of the apostles.

When I sat down in John Sharp's office, his first words were, "I can imagine how you feel. Let me put you at ease. I worked for the other side, and I had to do my job. I hated it, and I hated them. I have always respected how you handled all our dirty tricks. I'm a changed man and you have nothing to fear."

Today, most of my work comes from John Sharp. We've gone into legal battles together, and he knows he can trust me. Do I trust him? Let's just say I trust the Lord, and it's working out fine!

Never forget that today's enemies could be tomorrow's chosen instruments of God. Never burn bridges that God can use for good later.

## November 18
### COACH'S MEETING

> "Your prayers and gifts to the poor have come up . . . before God." (Acts 10:4)

Traveler: *An Angel of God*
**Read: Acts 10:1–48**

It was nearing the end of baseball season. Regular season games are important, but they really just set the stage for the big season-ending tournament. At this point, I sit down with my assistant coaches and take stock. How is each player doing? Who has improved? Who has lost interest? Do we need to make any changes?

This year, all the coaches came to the meeting with the same agenda. We had one first-year player who had quietly worked hard all season, never complaining about lack of playing time, but using practices to show what he could do. The player who had been starting in his position thought he had it made and did not work as hard in practice. He even missed a few practices, which gave the younger player the chance he had been waiting for. All of our coaches knew we had to reward the younger player. He started in the tournament and played very well. The experienced player still does not understand why he was benched.

Coaching decisions are made mostly behind the scenes.

God works this way, too. The story of Cornelius is encouraging to everyone who works in a worldly job, but who always keeps God first: "He and all his family were devout and God-fearing; he gave generously to those in need and prayed to God regularly" (Acts 10:2). One day, in the middle of the day, an angel came to him: "Your prayers and gifts to the poor have come up as a memorial offering before God. Now send men to Joppa to bring back a man named Simon who is called Peter" (verses 4–5).

Cornelius was given a starting job on God's team because he worked hard in practice, praying and giving to the needy, every day. His Coach rewarded him with a major assignment.

Do you practice every day? Does your performance rise up to God as an offering that is acknowledged by God? If not, this may be why your current situation feels like languishing on the bench, collecting pine splinters.

## November 19
### WHAT KIND OF SEED?

"Now those who had been scattered . . . traveled . . . telling the message . . ." (Acts 11:19)

Travelers: *Scattered Believers*
Read: Acts 11:19–26

Recently we had an "alumni" party for my ex-employees, who had been scattered by our company's downsizing two years earlier. Each had stories to tell about working on the "outside." Each had found opportunity, working as a sole proprietor, consulting in the same markets as before. And most of us had shared work with each other, making referrals to clients. All of them agreed that their abilities had been enhanced by the freedom I had given them as employees, to become professionals in their own rights.

You might say that the company blew us off the stem, like dandelion seeds, a bunch of weeds with no value. But instead of weeds, we all produced fruit where we landed. There was quality in those seeds that I had tried to nurture, as their manager.

Scattering can come in the form of religious persecution, as it did after Stephen's ministry: "Now those who had been scattered by the persecution in connection with Stephen traveled as far as Phoenicia, Cyprus and Antioch, . . . telling them the good news about the Lord Jesus. The Lord's hand was with them, and a great number of people believed and turned to the Lord" (Acts 11:19–21). Or, scattering can occur in many different worldly ways.

The question is not whether scattering will occur. It will. The question is what kind of seeds are we? I have no idea how most of the people in my high school graduating class fared in life, probably some better than others. And I don't know where many of the people I worked with twenty years ago ended up. That's because I don't know what kind of seed was planted in them.

But I do know what happens when the seed is Jesus Christ. When that seed is planted and then scattered, it always bears fruit somewhere else. It's easy to spot. Most Christians in one locale are originally from somewhere else. But they never cease sharing the Good News.

When people see you scattered in one place or another, is it obvious to them what kind of seed is planted in you?

## November 20
### HELPING THE BROTHERS

"This they did, sending their gift . . . by Barnabas and Saul."
(Acts 11:30)

Travelers: *Barnabas and Saul*
Read: Acts 11:27–30

Recently, there have been a series of fire-bombings and other attacks on Christian churches in Tennessee and North Carolina. Notice that I describe them as Christian churches, not black churches. To older people, this brings back bad memories of Mississippi, in the 1960s. Will racial hatred never end? What can we do about it?

In the Book of Acts we get many snapshots of how the early church operated as a community. After the persecution of Stephen, a prophet from Jerusalem ". . . predicted that a severe famine would spread over the entire Roman world . . . The disciples, each according to his ability, decided to provide help for the brothers living in Judea. This they did, sending their gift to the elders by Barnabas and Saul" (Acts 11:28–30). The early church was aware of what was happening to their scattered brothers, despite the fact that there were no satellites, computers or telephones. Everyone who traveled carried news of church members located in other places. We can picture a hotbed of verbal reports every time someone arrived in a town.

So what is our response today in the Christian church? We hear occasionally about major denominational annual conferences. And we hear when the church dabbles in national politics, such as the right to life movement or school prayer. But *where* do we hear these reports? Mostly in the media. There is very little discussion between our local church and other churches.

And when we hear of real persecution right here in the United States, what do we do about it? Have we risen up as a unified voice and condemned it? Have we reached down deep, each according to our abilities, and provided help to the brothers who lost their churches? Maybe there has been some local expression of solidarity, but very little has been covered by the national media—no surprise there.

Faith in motion means *putting* your faith in motion. What can you do to promote Christian unity and solidarity as you travel? Does it start, perhaps, with visiting local churches, just so you have news to bring home to your local church? We can't help our brothers and sisters if we don't get to know them first!

## November 21
### SERVING TIME

"... So Peter was kept in prison ..."
(Acts 12:5)

Traveler: *Peter*
Read: Acts 12:1–19

I received a call from a regular member of the Christian Travelers' Network. Thinking he was calling with an itinerary for another trip, I asked jokingly where he was frolicking off to this time. He said, "I'm already there. I'm calling you for prayer."

We pray for our members continuously, but it was a special privilege to be given a specific prayer goal. His job was in jeopardy. He was spending several weeks in a row at the same client's office, trying to close a deal that would save his job and those of dozens of other employees. This man is a serious Christian, so it wasn't as if he had waited until the last desperate moment to pray. But as he sat in his hotel, he remembered that there was another prayer resource as close as our toll-free 800 number.

Times like that can make a person feel as if he or she is in prison. And that's why the book of Acts can be so exciting for people who travel and deal with real problems in the real world. Peter was thrown in prison by King Herod and closely guarded, "... but the church was earnestly praying to God for him" (Acts 12:5). Notice that it was not just Peter's local church, but the church, the whole church, unified.

God heard their prayers and performed a major miracle, allowing Peter to escape (verse 6–19). The power of unified prayer has never been beaten, then or since.

My friend called back a couple of weeks later, from the same city, but this time he was there to sign the contract. His team had pulled off a major victory, and the department was saved. Did his willingness to humbly seek prayer in every place he knew make the difference?

How can you use your current situation to reach out to others, by asking for prayer? How far outside your own little circle can you reach? As you reach farther out, are you planting seeds for future church unity, through shared prayer? Isn't this a good way to serve your time?

## November 22
### AT THE LAST SECOND

> ". . . without a doubt . . . the Lord sent his angel and rescued me . . ." (Acts 12:11)

**Traveler:** *Peter*
**Read: Acts 12:8–19**

The military had always seemed very distant to me. I'm proud of our country's strength, and I believe in a strong defense. But it never got very personal for me. That is, until the man who was about to marry my daughter enlisted.

As the wedding approached, so did the threat of his getting sent to Somalia. None of us will ever forget the sight of an American soldier's body being dragged through the streets of Mogadishu. And that was just before our boy's unit was next in line to be shipped out. A peace-keeping mission had turned ugly. I finally learned what I should have understood long ago: those aren't faceless soldiers; they are our kids, the pride of our lives! It was our darkest hour. My wife got to work the only way she knows how, by mobilizing literally hundreds of prayer warriors

Peter's darkest hour came in prison, when even his closest friends and family gave him up for dead. He was to be put on trial by Herod, and he stood very little chance: "Suddenly an angel of the Lord appeared and a light shone in the cell. He struck Peter on the side, and woke him up. 'Quick, get up!' he said, and the chains fell off Peter's wrists . . . When they had walked the length of one street, suddenly the angel left him. Then Peter came to himself and said, 'Now I know without a doubt that the Lord sent his angel and rescued me from Herod's clutches . . .'" (Acts 12:7,10,11).

In our situation, God moved in two ways. He used the uncertainty of the situation to bring our future son to believe in eternal life; to believe that Jesus died for him. Then, with our precious cargo on board for the very next flight to Somalia, the mission was suddenly canceled, by President Clinton. It was over. No more soldiers went to Somalia after that. God had sent one angel to save our son and another to save all the others involved. I'm as convinced of that as Peter was.

The essence of Christianity is that God will be there in your darkest hour. Trust that.

## November 23
### WHEN TO GO FAST

"So after they had fasted and prayed, . . . they sent them off."
(Acts 13:3)

Travelers: *Barnabus and Saul*
Read: Acts 13:1–3

I participated in my first three-day fast, about two years ago. It was the most incredible thing I have ever been involved with. Each day, as I got physically weaker, I got spiritually stronger and closer to God. It is no wonder to me now, that so many major biblical decisions were made through fasting and prayer. That's how it was for Saul and Barnabas: "While they were worshipping the Lord and fasting, the Holy Spirit said, 'Set apart for me Barnabas and Saul for the work to which I have called them.' So after they had fasted and prayed, they placed their hands on them and sent them off" (Acts 13:2–3). The entire ministry of Saul, who became the Apostle Paul, started out in fasting and worship, cleansing the body to receive direction from the Spirit.

At the end of our three-day fast, our church gathered for worship. There was a unity (there's that word again) among our people, which I had never seen before. We had been struggling with a number of issues that could easily have divided the church. But in that setting, with everyone physically sapped but spiritually alive, those issues took a back seat. I was so moved by this Spirit-led sense of unity that I stood up to quote Churchill: "This is not the beginning of the end. It is the end of the beginning." I felt that there was a parallel between how Londoners felt after bombings and how our church members felt after such divisive issues.

Unfortunately, I got it backwards: "This is not the end of the beginning, but the beginning of the end." Everyone burst out laughing, and if we hadn't eaten something pretty soon, it *would have* been the end! It was my most embarrassing moment, at least until I found another opportunity. But guess what. The Spirit used that, too. People still kid me about how my twisted words were the perfect ice-breaker; the laughter caused much healing that night.

When should you go fast? Fast and pray—always!

## November 24
### BLINDING THE DEVIL

> "Immediately mist and darkness came over him, and he groped about . . ." (Acts 13:11)

Travelers: *Barnabas and Saul*
Read: Acts 13:4–12

My mother was so set against bad language that she would describe a helicopter as a "heckicopter!" But I think I've found a way to curse, to vent all my frustrations, in a way that honors God. How could that be?

Even Peter was susceptible to the devil: "But when Jesus turned and looked at his disciples, he rebuked Peter. 'Get behind me, Satan!' he said. 'You do not have in mind the things of God, but the things of men'" (Mark 8:33). Notice that Jesus was mad at Satan, not Peter. If evil could be found in Peter, it can be found everywhere else, don't you think?

Recently, I was working in one of Atlanta's worst neighborhoods. When I got out of my car at a local chicken place for lunch, I was confronted by a man who wanted money. Not sure whether he was truly needy, I offered him the change in my pocket. He said menacingly, "You've got more than that." There was no one in this neighborhood for me to turn to.

Saul, while traveling on Cyprus met a sorcerer named Elymas who opposed the ways of God: "Then Saul . . . looked straight at Elymas and said, 'You are a child of the devil and an enemy of everything that is right! . . . Will you never stop perverting the right ways of the Lord? Now the hand of the Lord is against you. You are going to be blind . . .' Immediately mist and darkness came over him, and he groped about, seeking someone to lead him by the hand" (Acts 13:9–11). Repeat after me: Saul looked straight at him, spoke to the devil himself and told him he would be blind.

I looked my accuser in the eye and told him to take the change or leave me alone. Amazingly, he did not take the money. I knew I was right because no truly needy person would have passed up what I offered. As I turned my back on him, I cursed quietly, out of ear shot, "Go to hell, Satan!" It felt really good. Now I know where I can curse.

When you encounter an evil person, curse the devil, not the person. Blind Satan. And enjoy it. It's God's work you're doing.

## November 25
### CALL AND ASK

"On the Sabbath they entered the synagogue and sat down."
(Act 13:14)

Traveler: *Paul*
Read: **Acts 13:13–41**

Yesterday, I mentioned the project in Atlanta's inner city. It's a great project because it involves building a recycling facility that will provide jobs for inner city youth and adults. As a man committed to racial reconciliation, I look forward to getting involved in the community. That's because Christians in these areas tend to be *real* Christians—ones whose day-to-day trust in the Lord is much deeper than those of us who always have food on the table and a comfortable room for sleep.

On the same day I encountered the Evil One at the chicken place, I drove a little farther down the street, just to look around. There, just a few hundred yards from the construction site, is a little church.

Paul spotted a church while he was traveling, too: "On the Sabbath they entered the synagogue and sat down. After reading from the Law and the Prophets, the synagogue rulers sent word to them, saying, 'Brothers, if you have a message of encouragement for the people, please speak'" (Acts 13:14–15). How interesting. By visiting the synagogue, Paul and his companions were asked to speak. What an opportunity!

I've wondered how it would be to attend that tiny church in Atlanta, assuming they have a mid-week service. I don't feel comfortable just walking in; I'm not sure I'd even be welcome. But what if I called the pastor and told him why I was there? What if I asked to speak to the congregation about wanting to be part of the community? I'll bet my reception would be great indeed!

This raises an interesting question for Christian travelers. There's always a church nearby. Yet few ever make the effort to visit, especially in the middle of the week. But maybe Paul's model gives you something to shoot for. How about contacting the pastor beforehand and introducing yourself? You could end up with a whole new family!

## November 26
### REJECTION AND JOY

"... they shook the dust from their feet in protest against them and went..." (Acts 13:51)

Travelers: *Paul and Barnabas*
Read: Acts 13:49–52

My wife and I have a friend who is trying to sell her house. Anyone who has ever done so knows the routine. List with a realtor. Make improvements. Hold Open Houses. Obtain feedback. Make more improvements. Sometimes it only takes a few weeks to sell a house. Other times it takes months. Either way it can be nerve wracking.

Last Sunday, our friend's realtor held the first Open House. When it was over, our friend was eager to learn the impressions of those who had passed through. The realtor said, "Well, all in all, it was pretty good. The only problem is that you're going to have to take down all those religious pictures on the walls, especially the one of Jesus. Potential buyers are offended by that." Excuse me?

Paul and Barnabas were greeted with scorn, too: "The word of the Lord spread through the whole region. But the Jews incited the God-fearing women of high-standing and the leading men of the city. They stirred up persecution against Paul and Barnabas, and expelled them from their region. So they shook the dust from their feet in protest against them and went to Iconium. And the disciples were filled with joy and with the Holy Spirit" (Acts 13:49–52). They knew their rejection was because of the political correctness of their day. Instead of wilting under the persecution, you can almost hear them laughing.

Our friend did the same thing. It's hard to say whether taking down the wall pictures would have sped up the sales process. But she said, "I don't want to sell my house to someone who's offended by my own precious property. If it takes longer to sell, so be it." She laughed with great joy, knowing personally the love of her God. Oh, and she changed realtors, too!

Can you turn rejection into joy?

## November 27
### DRAFT DAY

"We must go through many hardships to enter the kingdom of God . . ." (Acts 14:22)

**Travelers:** *Paul and Barnabas*
**Read: Acts 14:21–28**

Every serious basketball player dreams of getting drafted by a professional basketball team. If you are not drafted, it's very hard for you to make it onto a team. And every year there are dozens of young men who declare themselves "hardship" cases, so that they can leave college early and turn professional, using their new-found wealth to support their under-privileged families. I'm sure there are many legitimate cases of hardship. But I'm equally sure that the system is abused, to seduce young men with money. It makes you wonder what the rules are.

I have decided to become a hardship draftee into a league known as the kingdom of God. This league knows the rules and enforces them: "We must go through many hardships to enter the kingdom of God" (Acts 14:22). There is a rule book, known as the Bible. Let's look at its definition of hardship.

First, Jesus says, "In this world you will have trouble. But take heart! I have overcome the world" (John 16:33). Paul, the master of hardship ". . . sent Timothy, who is our brother and God's fellow worker in spreading the gospel of Christ, to strengthen and encourage you in your faith, so that no one would be unsettled by these trials" (1 Thessalonians 3:2–3). And Timothy was taught that ". . . everyone who wants to live a godly life in Christ Jesus will be persecuted, while evil men and impostors will go from bad to worse, deceiving and being deceived" (2 Timothy 3:12–13).

So what are the rules for qualifying for the hardship draft? Persevere in trouble and persecution. It comes with the territory, like practicing basketball skills when everyone else is partying. Be encouraged by preachers of the faith, because Jesus has overcome the world. And recognize that others will seem to get ahead of you in this life, but the godly life in Christ Jesus is eternal. Evil ones will, in God's time, be caught in another kind of draft. A down-draft.

Which league would you like to be drafted into?

## *November 28*
## GROUP DISCOUNT FARE

"Paul wanted to take him along on the journey . . ."
(Acts 16:3)

Travelers: *Paul, Silas and Timothy*
Read: Acts 16:1–5

My son Mitch is getting ready to leave for Monterey, Mexico, for a missions trip. He's going with 33 other high school youth, to help build a dormitory for unwed mothers. Another group from our church is going to Nairobi, Kenya, to work on a homeless children's residence. Still others are going to Jerusalem, for its 3,000th birthday. Summers can be wild in the Christian community.

Each of these trips involves lots of planning, some sacrifice and a huge dose of camaraderie. I've never met a person returning from such a trip who hasn't been exhilarated and changed forever, by exposure to the overpowering needs of others. What a great team spirit emerges from these ventures!

Paul and Silas knew that. As they were traveling to Derbe and then to Lystra, they heard of a young Greek disciple named Timothy. People spoke so highly of him that "Paul wanted to take him along on the journey" (Acts 16:3). Undoubtedly, Timothy made the journey a little easier on Paul and Silas. We can assume that Timothy helped not only with the hard work, but he probably provided some refreshing fellowship as well. Their team was very successful: "So the churches were strengthened in the faith and grew daily in numbers" (verse 5).

My traveling over the years was primarily alone. Even when someone from my company was with me, their interests were different from mine. So I rarely traveled with a group I enjoyed. Now, though, I do travel with a group—spiritually. Almost all the men in my Bible study travel on business, so each week we know who's going to be on the road. We talk about each guy's trip, what the business objectives are and what kind of personal encouragement he needs. Then we pray for each other all week. Upon the traveler's return, we get feedback about how it went for our brother. In this way, we go along as a group!

The group does get a discount fare: the toll of stress and isolation is reduced by the loving of brothers in the Lord. Group travel *is* better! Make sure you have one at home to take along with you.

## November 29
### WHEN NOT TO TRAVEL

"... they tried to enter Bithynia, but the Spirit of Jesus would not allow them ..." (Acts 16:7)

Travelers: *Paul, Silas and Timothy*
Read: Acts 16:6–10

Jeff Hale was traveling on business, as usual. Since the birth of his son Tyler, Jeff had not been home much at all. Tyler had a constant string of ear infections that kept him in pain day after day, night after night. This type of situation will test the mettle of any couple to the breaking point. But when one parent is gone, the stress really builds up.

One Wednesday in New Jersey, Jeff was dreading in advance that his plans called for arriving home in Denver late that Friday, only to leave again for Japan on Sunday. Beth was having a very difficult week, and he wanted to be with her to help. Suddenly, Jeff looked at his co-worker and said, "I think you can handle this situation. I'm going home early." What prompted Jeff's sudden departure from his normal stick-with-it-to-the-end business commitment?

Paul, Silas and Timothy were traveling all over the region of Phrygia and Galatia, "... having been kept by the Holy Spirit from preaching the word in the province of Asia. When they came to the border of Mysia, they tried to enter Bithynia, but the Spirit of Jesus would not allow them to" (Acts 16:6–7). Having been blocked in this way, Paul received a vision concerning where he should go next. It was the Holy Spirit, and Paul's openness to it, that changed their route in mid-course.

Jeff and Beth Hale are two people as open to guidance by the Holy Spirit as anyone I know. What changed Jeff's plans? What sent him home for some extra time with his wife, when she needed him so badly?

How open are you to leading like this? This is not about impulsively calling in sick and taking in an extra round of golf. It does mean having the courage to make life-changing decisions in response to the Spirit's prodding. Jeff's decision meant more to his wife than all the riches in the world.

## *November 30*
### A DIFFERENT KIND OF SABBATH

"... outside the city gate ... we expected to find a place of prayer." (Acts 16:13)

**Travelers:** *Paul's Group*
**Read: Acts 16:11–15**

I do not skip church very often, simply because I can hardly wait to hear what new illumination our pastor will give to each week's scripture. It's like a good sort of soap opera. Even preaching through the book of Jeremiah, I never dreamed anyone could make a book of such gloom and doom so fascinating.

But every so often I get the impulse to forego church. It's usually not premeditated. I get up on Sunday with the intent of going to church, but during my quiet time, the Holy Spirit seems to prod me elsewhere, even if that's nowhere. Of course, many people don't recognize the Sabbath at all. It's just another work day, or an excuse for some worldly fun (hey, I go to Colorado Rockies games on Sundays, too). So the question is, if you feel prodded to do something a little different on a Sunday, especially if you're on the road on a Saturday night stay-over, what's the right approach?

Once again, the travels of Paul and company give us some direction: "On the Sabbath we went outside the city gate to the river, where we expected to find a place of prayer. We sat down and began to speak to the women who had gathered there. One of those listening was a woman named Lydia ... The Lord opened her heart to respond to Paul's message" (Acts 16:13–14). Lydia and the members of her house were all baptized right there. Paul's group set out on that Sabbath first to find a place of prayer. Then they took whatever circumstances the Lord provided. God used them to reach Lydia and her family.

I used one very special Sabbath, after praying in the quiet morning, to just sit and write—to you. I hope that my prodding by the Holy Spirit has been evident as you have read these pages. What a privilege to serve you in this way!

May God bless you in a special way today, knowing how much He loves you! Always start by looking for a quiet place to pray.

## December 1
### PAUL'S PATIENCE

> "Paul entered the synagogue and spoke boldly there for three months..." (Acts 19:8)

Traveler: *Paul*
Read: Acts 19:1–12

What kind of patience would it take to debate the same subject for three straight months? That's what Paul did at Ephesus: "Paul entered the synagogue and spoke boldly there for three months, arguing persuasively about the kingdom of God" (Acts 19:8). Even more amazing, "[h]e took the disciples with him and had discussions daily in the lecture hall of Tyrannus. This went on for two years..." (verses 9 and 10).

For many years I attended numerous professional meetings of the American Society of Mechanical Engineers. At these meetings, technical papers were presented and questions were asked from the floor, directly to the author. For years there was a man who was paid to attend these meetings and to direct the discussions toward one product that his employers were trying to sell. No matter what the subject matter, this man would be the first to ask the author a question, and then he would block anyone else out who wanted to take part. Worst of all, his product was a farce, and everyone knew it. These encounters lasted an hour or so, at each meeting. Often, it took a shouting match to get him to sit down. As much as I hated the disturbances, I respected this man's perseverance. I would have given up long ago.

Imagine if this man had pitched his product for days instead of hours, continuously, week after week. And imagine that he barged into your place of business, uninvited and stayed for two years! That's how many of the local residents of Ephesus felt about Paul. Read further in Acts 19 how a riot started over Paul's teachings!

What incredible patience it must have taken for Paul to persevere day after day, year after year, in the face of overt hatred. But Paul never wavered! Surely many people were won over to Christ, just because of Paul's patience. What a lesson for all of us!

When presenting Christ, be patient and keep at it as long as necessary! Just don't be as obnoxious as the engineer described above.

## December 2
### FINISH WELL

"... I am going to Jerusalem, not knowing what will happen to me ..." (Acts 20:22)

Traveler: *Paul*
Read: Acts 20:13–38

This is a tribute to an old engineer named John Rossie, who finished his life as strongly as he began it, and who went to be with the Lord not long ago. John's engineering talent came from the "old school," as we used to call it. That means he was far more comfortable with a slide rule than with a computer. Old school engineers needed to know almost intuitively whether an answer to a problem was right; there was a great deal of judgment involved. That judgment is lacking today in younger engineers, who think the computer is always right, disregarding the important fact that the computer was programmed by a fallible human.

I can tell you from personal experience, John was right more often than the computer. He had an uncanny ability to smell a wrong solution. Where did he get such insight?

John Rossie received his engineering "training" aboard the battleship New Jersey, during World War II. That was not just an ordinary ship. The New Jersey was involved in many important conflicts in the Pacific theater, most notably the battle of Midway Island. What an amazing story of heroic action and Godly deliverance! If you've never read about Admiral Halsey in that battle, do it this weekend!

So during our years of working together, when John would uncover some intangible but important factor about a boiler problem that the rest of us had missed, we'd always ask, "John, how do you do it?" John's face would become pensive, his mind returning to events we could only imagine, and say wistfully, "You get to know lots about boilers when you're outrunning torpedoes." He wasn't kidding, either.

What do you rely on for that extra insight? Paul knew: "And now, compelled by the Holy Spirit, I am going to Jerusalem, not knowing what will happen to me there. I only know that in every city, the Holy Spirit warns me that prison and hardships are facing me" (Acts 20:22–23). If you feel like that kind of presence is not with you today, Paul can tell you where to get it: "... turn to God in repentance and have faith in our Lord Jesus" (verse 21).

## December 3
### IT IS WELL

> ". . . but the Spirit himself intercedes for us with groans that words cannot express." (Romans 8:26)

Traveler: *The Holy Spirit*
**Read: Romans 8:18–27**

Last week, my wife and I acknowledged for the umpteenth time that, compared to so many folks we know, we don't know what true suffering is. We said it with the full understanding that our situation could change on a moment's notice. True faith is the understanding that, no matter what lies ahead, God is there for us.

Recently, a dear friend and neighbor lost her husband. Because Ralph had lived such a joyous Christian life, his funeral was more like a celebration. But as we sit near his wife in church each Sunday, you can see the pain and loneliness, feelings that we simply have not been exposed to yet.

Paul's letter to the Romans describes eloquently what our friend relies on: ". . . the Spirit helps us in our weakness. We do not know what we ought to pray for, but the Spirit himself intercedes for us with groans that words cannot express. And he who searches our hearts knows the mind of the Spirit, because the Spirit intercedes for the saints in accordance with God's will" (Romans 8:26–27). When the pain is so great that it's even tough to know what to pray for, the Spirit takes over. And I got to see that last Sunday.

We were singing the old hymn "It Is Well With My Soul." With each verse, the congregation's volume crescendoed until we came to the last verse: "And, Lord, haste the day when the faith shall be sight, The clouds be rolled back as a scroll, The trump shall resound, and the Lord shall descend. Even so, it is well with my soul."

As I looked over at our friend, she stood with arms tenderly outstretched, so connected spiritually with her Lord and her husband, it was obvious from her look of joy that the Spirit had interceded for her in a way that words cannot express.

I pray for you that kind of power!

## December 4
### MAY I JOIN YOU?

"I urge you . . . to join me in my struggle . . ."
(Romans 15:30)

Traveler: *Paul*
**Read: Romans 15:23–33**

I want to go along on your trip. May I join you?

You might ask how I could do that. How could I get on an airplane with you and fly to your meeting, and then do the same with someone else? Physically, I can't. And financially, I can't, either! But spiritually, I can support you every step of the way.

I can pray for you the way Paul wanted to be prayed for by the church in Rome: "I urge you, brothers, by our Lord Jesus Christ and by the love of the Spirit, to join me in my struggle by praying to God for me. Pray that I may be rescued from the unbelievers in Judea and that my service in Jerusalem may be acceptable to the saints there, so that by God's will I may come to you with joy and together with you be refreshed" (Romans 15:30–32).

So how can I join you on your trip? First, you should know that I am praying for you. Every morning, when you wake up at the hotel and you're getting ready to meet the world head on, pause for a second and think about someone in Colorado who is praying for you as you go.

I pray for your struggle, whatever it is, big or small. I pray that you may be rescued from unbelievers, wherever you go. I pray that your work may be acceptable, and that many will be blessed by it. And I pray that one day you will come to meet me, with joy, so that together we might be refreshed in the spirit of Jesus Christ.

Oh, and one other thing. Will you join me on my trips in the same way? I think that only another traveler can appreciate what we each face. Your prayers for me are more precious than gold.

God bless you!

## December 5
### WEAKNESS MADE STRONG

"I came to you in weakness and fear, and with much trembling."
(1 Corinthians 2:3)

Traveler: *Paul*
**Read: 1 Corinthians 2:1–5**

Not all legal proceedings take place in a public court room. An arbitration panel meets behind closed doors and has no judge. The panel often is made up of three lawyers—one chosen by each side in a dispute, and one chosen mutually by both sides. Three lawyers means three times as much trouble for an expert witness. After one lawyer finishes with an exhausting list of questions, the second starts in, and then the third. Then the first can come back for more, then the second and third. There are no limits and no judge to sanction unreasonable abuse of the witness. I sat before such a panel, very scared, like waiting for my carcass to be pulled apart by vultures.

That's why the writings of the Apostle Paul are so special. He was not afraid to communicate his human emotions. Sure, God did some mighty things through Paul, but Paul himself was full of fear and self-doubt: "When I came to you, brothers, I did not come with eloquence or superior wisdom as I proclaimed to you the testimony about God. For I resolved to know nothing while I was with you except Jesus Christ and him crucified. I came to you in weakness and fear, and with much trembling" (1 Corinthians 2:1–3). It's all the more powerful a demonstration of the power of the Holy Spirit, when it's through a weak person.

As the lawyer hired by the other side peered down at me, he was cold and calculating. His look could wilt a lily in the rain forest. But as he questioned me, something in my resume caught his eye. He virtually skipped my engineering credentials, coming to a little line at the end, noting that for one year I had attended seminary, taking classes in history and theology. His glowering look softened for just a moment. I think God spoke to him subtly, telling him I was honest. He, even more than the independent arbitrator, went out of his way to hear my side of the story, and we won that dispute.

Where does you credibility come from? Don't be afraid to be afraid.

## December 6
### TIMING IS EVERYTHING

"... wait till the Lord comes."
(1 Corinthians 4:5)

**Traveler:** *Jesus*
**Read: 1 Corinthians 4:1–21**

Earlier in these pages I identified Christian unity as one of the most crying needs of our time. There is another, which I believe blocks Christians from being the servants God intended. And almost every one of us exhibits the tendency.

Judgment.

There is a very fine line between standing up for the values one holds dear and jamming them down someone else's throat. And it seems, the more serious a Christian one becomes, the greater the tendency to judge. Jesus was very clear: "Do not judge, or you too will be judged. For in the same way you judge others, you will be judged, and with the measure you use, it will be measured to you" (Matthew 7:1–2). How can we be agents of light and love when all we do is judge what others are doing? I don't need to cite examples here. Just close your eyes and think back over the last ten conversations you had. I'll bet eight of them involved judging someone. Me, too.

Paul puts the issue in a slightly different light: "So then, men ought to regard us as servants of Christ and as those entrusted with the secret things of God. Now it is required that those who have been given a trust must prove faithful. I care very little if I am judged by you or by any human court; indeed, I do not even judge myself. My conscience is clear, but that does not make me innocent. It is the Lord who judges me. Therefore judge nothing before the appointed time; wait till the Lord comes" (1 Corinthians 4:1–5).

We've been given a secret trust. We're not faithful to it when we judge. Don't even judge yourself. Wait until Jesus returns: "He will bring to light what is hidden in darkness and will expose the motives of men's hearts. At that time each will receive his praise from God" (verse 5).

Take a personal survey this week. Be honest. Count how many times your conversation goes to judging someone, especially when your participation in that conversation gives you social credibility with Christian friends. Now is not the time!

## December 7
### THE PRIZE

"I do not run like a man running aimlessly . . ."
(1 Corinthians 9:26)

**Traveler:** *Paul*
**Read: 1 Corinthians 9:1–27**

I still cry when *The Star Spangled Banner* is played and our flag is raised above the awards podium at the Olympics. For me, it's not about national pride. It's about achievement of an athlete's goals and beating the very best in the world in a spirit of true sportsmanship. I feel the same way when another nation's flag is raised.

As I think back over past Olympics, there seem to be as many memories of failures as of gold medals. Jim Ryan falling in the mile. Dan Jenkins ditto in speed skating—three times! Ben Johnson and steroids. The first U. S. basketball loss to the Russians. I can think of dozens of other tearjerking stories, all amplified by the stunning brevity of a single event, after four years of training.

But as spectacular as the Olympics are on the world stage, they are not the most important competition: "Do you not know that in a race all the runners run, but only one gets the prize? Run in such a way as to get the prize. Everyone who competes in the games goes into strict training. They do it to get a crown that will not last; but we do it to get a crown that will last forever. Therefore I do not run like a man running aimlessly; I do not fight like a man beating the air. No, I beat my body and make it my slave so that after I have preached to others, I myself will not be disqualified for the prize" (1 Corinthians 9:24–27).

Why do you travel? To earn a living? To advance in a corporation? Which race are you in? I hope it's the one that awards a crown that lasts forever. In the real world of business, today's winners are tomorrow's losers; that's just the way the race goes. But if you're in the right race, no amount of training can be too much. The prize is just too important.

Remember, the winners won't be declared until Jesus returns. So be like Paul. Make sure that what you do keeps you from being disqualified.

## December 8
## ONE WAY OUT

". . . he will also provide a way out . . ."
(1 Corinthians 10:13)

Travelers: *You and I*
**Read: 1 Corinthians 10:1–13**

Our little mountain community is nestled in a valley, between two ridges, with roads winding up and down the slopes. For years, my wife and I have enjoyed taking long walks around the area, enjoying ever-changing scenery and wild-life. Quite often we see the same car more than once. On the second or third pass, the car stops, a window opens and a very confused-looking occupant asks, "Can you tell me how to get to the main road?" It's pretty easy to point them in the right direction. You see, there's only one way in and one way out. We have a "closed" road system, designed to ensure that our neighborhood never becomes a major thoroughfare. But it's real easy to get disoriented because of all the curves and hills.

The same is true of temptation: "So, if you think you are standing firm, be careful that you don't fall! No temptation has seized you except what is common to man. And God is faithful; he will not let you be tempted beyond what you can bear. But when you are tempted, he will also provide a way out so that you can stand up under it" (1 Corinthians 10:12–13).

If you're tempted to do something wrong, it's important to realize that you're not the only one to feel that way. Satan is sneaky, but not terribly original. He may approach us in ways he thinks will make us most vulnerable, but he's only got so many cards to play, and they are the same cards he uses on everyone else! I find great comfort in that knowledge alone.

But even more important, God will always provide the way out. It's so important to simply acknowledge God's presence in the middle of temptation. Just say something like, "Oh, Lord, here comes that slice of slime again—you take him in the name of Jesus, okay?"

And guess what. Even though the road seemed terribly complex, all of a sudden you'll get the easiest of directions. There's only one way out to the main road. And God alone provides it.

## December 9
### I WANT THAT

"We always carry around in our body the death of Jesus . . ."
(2 Corinthians 4:10)

Travelers: *You and I*
Read: 2 Corinthians 4:1–18

Frankly, Ken humbled me. Whatever he had, I wanted.

We first met in a Bible study. From week to week, Ken always went out of his way to get more details on any personal prayer request. Later he would be full of questions, seeking more detail, finding more "color" to base his prayers on. Yet whenever it was time to offer his own personal prayer requests, he would only ask to become a better servant. It was very hard to get him to talk about himself.

I just had to learn more about this man, one-on-one. Finally, we arranged a lunch appointment. Ken was very willing to share with me in this different setting. The peace I had sensed came from an anything-but-peaceful background. He had been so rebellious in fact, that he wasn't very comfortable sharing the sordid details. In addition to a very immoral lifestyle, he had lost a business, gotten sued unfairly and filed for bankruptcy. At the end of it all, he found life in the death of Jesus. He was born again and now lives a life of quiet servanthood, helping other people wherever he can.

Ken personifies what Paul described: "But we have this treasure in jars of clay to show that this all-surpassing power is from God and not from us. We are hard pressed on every side, but not crushed; perplexed, but not in despair; persecuted, but not abandoned; struck down, but not destroyed. We always carry around in our body the death of Jesus, so that the life of Jesus may also be revealed in our body" (2 Corinthians 4:7–10). Ken reveals life in Jesus, through the death he lived in his previous life of sin.

Paul quotes Psalm 116:10— "'I believed; therefore I have spoken." And then he describes that sense of peace I found in Ken: "So we fix our eyes not on what is seen, but on what is unseen. For what is seen is temporary, but what is unseen is eternal" (verse 18). The unseen in Ken is his eternal peace with Jesus.

Do people want to know you for what they can see or what they can't see?

FAITH IN MOTION

## December 10
### DIPLOMATIC IMMUNITY

"... the old has gone ..."
(2 Corinthians 5:17)

Travelers: *You and I*
Read: 2 Corinthians 5:11–21

The ancient roots of the word "ambassador" include helper, servant, being sent, and task. Whenever there is news from a foreign country, the U. S. Ambassador is always involved as our highest ranking official in that country. The Ambassador is sent there to represent our country and to perform tasks that enhance the relationship between the two countries.

Foreign ambassadors are treated as citizens of their own countries. They can be expelled from a country, but they cannot be prosecuted for breaking the laws of the countries they work in. I saw this principle at work when I was run-off the road by a poorly trained foreign embassy official driving to our airport. Even if he had caused a wreck, he was protected from jail by diplomatic immunity.

But despite all the spy books and movies we have ingested, leaving us with a negative image of foreign embassies, the positive mission of an ambassador is to work toward reconciliation if there has been a dispute between governments. The ambassador delivers messages to the foreign government, even when military conflict has begun. If there were no diplomatic immunity, a foreign ambassador would be in great peril, and peace would never have a chance.

What does Paul mean, then, when he says, "We are therefore Christ's ambassadors, as though God were making his appeal through us" (2 Corinthians 5:20)? Being an ambassador for Christ means delivering God's message of reconciliation to a culture that is very different from our own. Paul means that we are not citizens of the country we live in, but visitors with a special message of reconciliation—from God: "And he has committed to us the message of reconciliation. We are therefore Christ's ambassadors, as though God were making his appeal through us. We implore you on Christ's behalf: Be reconciled to God. God made him who had no sin to be sin for us, so that in him we might become the righteousness of God" (verses 19–21).

Are you letting God make his appeal through you?

## December 11
### SMALL BUT MIGHTY

"The weapons we fight with are not the weapons of the world."
(2 Corinthians 10:4)

Travelers: *You and I*
Read: 2 Corinthians 10:1–18

Today, our son is a big, strapping, healthy young man. But he started out, in the spring of 1979, as a womb full of trouble.

Because of a serious hormone imbalance, Sue was violently ill throughout the pregnancy. She spent weeks in the hospital on intravenous feeding, her body too weak to manage the battle going on inside. At one point, I began to realize that she could die of a heart attack or some other stress-induced crisis. When healthy, Sue is "five foot nothin'" and little more than a hundred pounds. In the throes of this war, she looked as if she could just disappear, so weak and pale.

One day, when I visited her in the hospital though, her color had suddenly returned, and she was sitting up for the first time in weeks. And she was as mad as I have ever seen her, before or since. "Our pastor was just here," she said, obviously unhappy with the visit. "He told me that it was time to consider aborting the baby to save me. I told him to leave immediately. I will die before I will give up this baby!" And she meant it.

From that point on, she began to improve. The rest of the pregnancy was troubled, but not as bad as what we had been through. And on August 16, 1979, a squirmy, kicking boy was born, his eyes open from the get-go, almost as if he was saying, "Thanks, Mom, for letting me live." *That's* what the abortion issue is really about. Real people. Babies who become real blessings in God's kingdom. Not selfish parents who put themselves first because of discomfort.

I give thanks to God for giving me this small but mighty woman, ". . . who does not wage war as the world does" (2 Corinthians 10:3). And for both of my children, who make my life such a joy.

How do you wage war? Do your weapons have ". . . divine power to demolish strongholds" (verse 4).

## December 12
HOW DARE WE?

"... A field that reaches even to you."
(2 Corinthians 10:13)

Traveler: *Paul*
**Read: 2 Corinthians 10:12–18**

James Dobson founded Focus on the Family, with a burden for families and a small grant for a radio program. Today his ministry touches every aspect of life in America.

Bill McCartney and a friend shared a dream, on a long drive down I-25 one night. This year, Promise Keepers meetings will reach over half-a-million men.

Bill Bright had a vision of a ministry for students. Now the reach of Campus Crusade for Christ defies description, touching young and old alike, around the world. And there are thousands more ministries, with a little less fame but with every bit as much good, reaching everywhere.

So who am I to start a ministry to develop a network of traveling Christians? The sheer magnitude and scope of such a vision is overwhelming, even stupid, some would say. I've already spent lots of my own money, and all we have to show for it is a small, loyal group of constituents. There is very little money left. And not much is coming in. How easy it is to get discouraged!

Wait a minute. Who's in control here? Me or God? If God wants this mission to go forward, He will provide the means. If not, what is that to me? Keep on plugging until He says to stop.

What's that? An incoming fax. From Finland? As in Scandinavia? A visitor from there has just picked up our brochure at the airport and wants to join the network!

Lord, your timing is so amazing! Yes, Lord, I'm listening. Tell Satan to go take a flying leap? Sure, I'd love to. "Our hope is that, as your faith continues to grow, our area of activity among you will greatly expand, so that we can preach the gospel in the regions beyond you" (2 Corinthians 10:15–16). God doesn't say when that expansion will occur. He only asks that our faith continue to grow. Mine sure did when that fax came!

## December 13
### THE TRIALS OF TRAVEL

"... my power is made perfect in weakness."
(2 Corinthians 12:9)

Traveler: *Paul*
Read: 2 Corinthians 12:1–10

The floor was now the ceiling. Jerry Schemmel was hanging upside down, still strapped in by his seat belt. Everyone around him was dead. Smoke filled what was left of the cabin. He had to get out quickly.

Unlatching his belt, he dropped to what had been the ceiling. Climbing over bodies and debris, he found a hole in the fuselage and escaped. He walked away, nearly unharmed, from United 232, one of the most bizarre crashes in history. But he had no idea that his ordeal had only begun.

Almost two years later, after battling severe depression and "survivor's guilt," Jerry's wife led him to accept Jesus Christ as his savior. Only then did his inner healing begin. He began to see God's purpose in allowing him to go through such an experience. He appeared on national television and became a reluctant celebrity. But when he was asked if the crash had become the best thing that ever happened to him, he replied, "Maybe someday. Not yet. The nightmares still come."

Is there some pain in your life that has not been erased? The Apostle Paul had major struggles, too. He was "in danger from rivers . . . bandits . . . [his] own country . . . Gentiles . . . the city . . . the country . . . at sea . . . and in danger from false brothers" (2 Corinthians 11:26). He worked, hungered, thirsted and went naked. I doubt that anyone has ever suffered more than Paul.

Yet Paul said, "Who is weak, and I do not feel weak? . . . I will boast of the things that show my weakness" (verses 29a and 30b). He was saying, in effect, "If I can persevere, you can, too." If Jerry Schemmel and Paul could praise God through the trials of travel, there is hope for you. Jesus said to Paul, "My grace is sufficient for you, for my power is made perfect in weakness" (2 Corinthians 12:9). Your experience may have been painful, and it may take years to get beyond it. But the love of Jesus Christ is the best thing that ever happened to you.

## December 14
### COMMON DENOMINATOR

"... we should go to the Gentiles, and they to the Jews."
(Galatians 2:9)

Travelers: *Paul and Barnabas*
**Read: Galatians 2:1–10**

Common denominators are used in solving fractions. When you know what the bottom number (denominator) in each fraction has in common, you can perform any mathematical operation, with any fraction. For example, the common denominator in the fractions one-half and one-quarter is "two," because the number two can be divided into both denominators in those two fractions.

Christians are much like a page full of fractions, each looking very different. What are the factors we all have in common?

When Paul became a Christian and was given a major challenge by Christ Himself, to go and preach the Gospel, there was no question in his mind what his mission was. But imagine how all the other Apostles and their closest friends felt. Here's a man who just recently persecuted us and even killed us, and now we're supposed to accept him as one of our own? How do we know he's for real? How do we know he's not just setting us up for a big kill? Will he gather all sorts of information and turn us in?

Galatians 2 tells us what Paul's first encounter with the other Apostles was like: "On the contrary, they saw that I had been entrusted with the task of preaching the gospel to the Gentiles, just as Peter had been to the Jews. For God, who was at work in the ministry of Peter as an apostle to the Jews, was also at work in my ministry as an apostle to the Gentiles. James, Peter and John . . . gave me and Barnabas the right hand of fellowship when they recognized the grace given to me. They agreed that we should go to the Gentiles, and they to the Jews. All they asked was that we should continue to remember the poor, the very thing I was eager to do" (Galatians 2:7–10).

So in this critical encounter, what was the common denominator among those who were serving very different groups of people? Remembering the poor. How much of your ministry, or mine, really does that? Convicting, isn't it?

## December 15
## BLOODY SHINS

> "You were running a good race. Who cut in on you . . . ?"
> (Galatians 5:7)

**Travelers:** *The Galatian Church*
**Read: Galatians 5:1–15**

I'm so old that when I was in high school, we ran track and field meets on a cinder track. And Nike didn't even exist as a shoe company. I ran the half mile and somehow came up with a pair of spikes designed for track. They were a little like golf spikes, except that the spikes were longer, sharper, and they were only on the front half of the shoe, not the heel.

I thought my new spikes were "cool." I felt I was much faster with them on, and that I could beat anyone. But in my first race, I found out that it's not the shoes that make the difference. It's the racing strategy, because all the other guys in the race have the same kind of spikes. In the very first turn of the two-lap race, while all the runners were bunched together, jockeying for position, an opponent cut in front of me. As he did, his spikes treated my shins like a pin cushion, and suddenly I was full of holes and bleeding.

I finished the race. In last place.

And so it is that many will try to tell you how to live your Christian life. If you don't recognize the danger in their spikes, it's trouble: "You who are trying to be justified by law have been alienated from Christ; you have fallen away from grace. But by faith we eagerly await through the Spirit the righteousness for which we hope . . . The only thing that counts is faith expressing itself through love. You were running a good race. Who cut in on you and kept you from obeying the truth?" (Galatians 5:4–7).

What are the basics of your day-to-day living? Going to church, because it's expected of you? Serving on a committee, because you feel you should? Singing in the choir or ushering on Sunday morning, because those are easy and safe activities? Following some ritual because you always have? Falling into patterns is like the law mentioned by Paul.

Only faith, expressing itself through love, counts. What kind of love does that require from you today? What's your strategy for not getting spiked?

## December 16
### MORE ON UNITY

"... tossed back and forth by the waves, and blown here and there ..." (Ephesians 4:14)

Travelers: *You and I*
**Read: Ephesians 4:1–16**

If the Bible doesn't give up on the concept of Christian unity, neither should we. Ephesians 4 is a textbook on unity; what it will look like when we finally achieve it. It's safe to say we have a long way to go.

First, "Be completely humble and gentle; be patient, bearing one another in love" (Ephesians 4:2). When someone stole my seat in church last week, I exhibited none of these qualities, at least not in my heart.

Second, "Make every effort to keep unity of the Spirit through the bond of peace. There is one body and one Spirit—just as you were called to one hope when you were called—one Lord, one faith, one baptism; one God and Father of all, who is over all and through all and in all" (verses 3–6). Aren't these common denominators of the faith?

Third, "It was he who gave some to be apostles, some to be prophets, some to be evangelists, and some to be pastors and teachers, to prepare God's people for works of service, so that the body of Christ may be built up until we all reach unity in the faith and in the knowledge of the Son of God and become mature, attaining to the whole measure of the fullness of Christ" (verses 11–13). What we do does not make us different if we are all fulfilling the same calling, all working to build up the body of Christ.

It's okay to realize that we're not mature yet, that we have a ways to go. But we won't get anywhere unless we set a goal, and that goal must be total unity: "Then we will no longer be infants, tossed back and forth by the waves, and blown here and there by every wind of teaching and by the cunning and craftiness of men in their deceitful scheming" (verse 14).

Isn't it chilling to see how close these verses, written centuries ago, come to describing the current condition of the Christian church as a whole?

## December 17
### PACK THE RIGHT STUFF

"... when the day of evil comes, you may be able to stand your ground..." (Ephesians 6:13)

Travelers: *You and I*
Read: **Ephesians 6:10–20**

Arriving at a hotel late at night is always an interesting experience for me. I open my suitcase slowly, peeking into its depths, before it is fully open, like a child checking for monsters in a dark closet. "What did I forget this time?" I ask myself.

I always forget something. I've forgotten razors, combs, tooth brushes, shaving cream, tooth paste, belts, socks, underwear, shoes, ties, medicine. Each time it's something different. So the adventure is in discovering how to appear presentable just a few hours later. Hotels help out occasionally. They sometimes have a cheery little card on the bathroom sink saying, "Forget something? Call the front desk for a complimentary replacement." Beyond tooth brushes, though, they can't help very much.

I know where most of the 24-hour convenience stores are, and I know what exorbitant prices they charge for things I've forgotten. It's like they know I'm coming and double the price.

There's one thing, though, that is disastrous if forgotten: "Put on the full armor of God so that you can take your stand against the devil's schemes. For our struggle is not against flesh and blood, but against the rulers, against the authorities, against the powers of this dark world and against the spiritual forces of evil in the heavenly realms. Therefore put on the full armor of God, so that when the day of evil comes, you may be able to stand your ground, and after you have done everything, to stand" (Ephesians 6:11–13).

Old fashioned armor in the nineties? You bet! "Stand firm then, with the belt of truth buckled around your waist, with the breastplate of righteousness in place, and with your feet fitted with the readiness that comes from the gospel of peace. In addition to all this, take up the shield of faith, with which you can extinguish all the flaming arrows of the evil one" (verses 14–16). There's your belt, coat, shoes and umbrella. The rest of your wardrobe can be found throughout the Bible. These are items you must pack before you leave. And they are the ones that make you presentable the next morning.

*Faith in Motion*

## *December 18*
### TAKES ONE TO KNOW ONE

"Welcome him in the Lord with great joy . . ."
(Philippians 2:29)

**Traveler:** *Epaphroditus*
**Read: Philippians 2:19–30**

Surely you've witnessed the "tearful reunion syndrome." That's where the first person off the plane is greeted by his girl friend, family and half his high school graduating class, or so it seems. There are signs and balloons and a massive jam, preventing others from getting off the plane.

As a frequent traveler, I often wished I could be greeted at the airport like that, instead of slinking anonymously toward the parking garage for a long drive home. It is a long drive in my case, and it would be ridiculous to ask my wife to meet my flights, especially when there's a good chance of a weather delay or even a change in plans. But like any frequent traveler, I wish sometimes that my return would result in a party right there, where no one else could get by.

Of course, my family greets me wonderfully when I get home, and my Bible study buddies do, too, when I see them. And it makes me wonder how many people never get greeted with gratitude for all they do.

The Philippians sent Epaphroditus to be with Paul when Paul needed help. In the process, Epaphroditus got sick and nearly died. When Paul sent him back home, he wanted to make sure that people recognized what Epaphroditus had done: "Welcome him in the Lord with great joy, and honor men like him, because he almost died for the work of Christ, risking his life to make up for the help you could not give me" (Philippians 2:29–30).

Yes, people who travel for a living risk their lives, and those whose lives are dedicated to Jesus Christ risk their lives for His work. You ought to know: it takes one to know one.

So the question is this: What can you do for people in your local church, to recognize all the sacrifices they make for family and community? Honor those people, with great joy, for what they do. Go ahead, surprise someone!

## December 19
## QUOTA

"... I press on toward the goal to win the prize ..."
(Philippians 3:14)

**Traveler:** *Paul*
**Read: Philippians 3:1–21**

I always thought the corporate budgeting process was absurd, and five-year plans were even more ridiculous. Unless I had a single contract for a fixed amount of money over a long period of time, how could I tell what was going to happen in the coming five years? But that's how sales quotas are born. Management decides to set goals, establish prizes for those who achieve the goals and punishment for those who do not. The goals do not usually reflect reality in the market place.

Usually, luck played a greater role for me than skill. Budgeting was more crystal-ball rubbing than reality. Some years I won, some years I lost. But I always knew that God played a greater role in the outcome, whether I was praised or vilified.

The question is, what is your goal? Is it a one year plan or a five year plan? I think it's the word "plan" that gets to me. In reality, we can't plan anything. So setting financial goals is crazy. It's much easier and less stressful to acknowledge the Source of all things and be grateful for what we get.

There are other kinds of goals that make more sense, like Paul's goal: "But whatever was to my profit I now consider loss for the sake of Christ. What is more, I consider everything a loss compared to the surpassing greatness of knowing Christ Jesus my Lord, for whose sake I have lost all things. I consider them rubbish, that I may gain Christ" (Philippians 3:7–8). Now that's a goal.

And Paul gives a status report: "Not that I have already obtained all this, or have already been made perfect, but I press on to take hold of that for which Christ Jesus took hold of me. Brothers, I do not consider myself yet to have taken hold of it. But one thing I do: Forgetting what is behind and straining toward what is ahead, I press on toward the goal to win the prize for which God has called me ..." (verses 12–14).

Do your goals have that kind of perspective? Do you know with absolute certainty where you stand toward achieving the goal?

## December 20
### BEARABLE BURDEN

> "You know . . . that our visit to you was not a failure."
> (1 Thessalonians 2:1)

Traveler: *Paul*
**Read: 1 Thessalonians 2:1–16**

During his ministry in Thessalonica, Paul said, "Surely you remember, brothers, . . . we worked night and day not to be a burden to anyone while we preached the gospel of God to you" (1 Thessalonians 2:9). So then, what does it mean to not be a burden as guests in a hotel?

When I leave my hotel room, the housecleaning staff can see what I am like as a person. My Bible is there, along with the books I'm reading. So are drafts of these devotions, written as I travel. But they also see newspaper, left over pizza boxes, milk cartons, soda bottles, room service dishes and used towels spread around.

Hotel housekeepers are among the most humble people on earth. I have spent weeks in the same hotel and, particularly on weekends when I'm not away from the room as much, they come and clean while I'm there.

Frankly, they're not usually the kind of people I'd choose as friends. Often barely existing with a low-paying job, often speaking little English, they are accustomed to all sorts of abuse in life and to horrible messes each day. And I contribute to that. Yes, my hotel cost includes their work, but they get paid a tiny fraction of that. And if you stick around to see how many rooms they clean each day, you know that they work as hard as a migrant worker in the fields.

What image do they have of me if I leave a Bible and some other Christian books in a trashy room? They see me the same as everyone else. But what if they enter my room and find it clean, no trash lying around, the towels all on the racks, and the bed covers laid back in place? And what if I left a dollar on the table with a note thanking them for all they do? I'll bet they'd see me as a different kind of Christian, one they'd like to know more about.

I think that's what it means to not be a burden in modern travel. Will you try it?

## December 21
### ONE LAST TRIP

> "And so we will be with the Lord forever."
> (1 Thessalonians 4:17)

Travelers: *You and I and Jesus*
**Read: 1 Thessalonians 4:13–18**

Most modern business travelers would not be caught dead without their task organizer notebooks close at hand, in which their schedules are planned down to the minute. There are so many airplanes to catch, appointments to meet, confirmation numbers to remember and "to do" lists to do; no one can remember it all. As a result we become detail freaks, planning everything as best we can.

But it could very well be in our lifetimes that the Christians among us will all go on one last trip that we cannot plan at all. Those not taken suddenly on this trip will be left behind to face terrible consequences. So when this trip happens, you'll be delighted that it conflicts with your organizer for that day:

> For the Lord himself will come down from heaven, with a loud command, with the voice of the archangel and with the trumpet call of God, and the dead in Christ will rise first. After that, we who are still alive and are left will be caught up together with them in the clouds to meet the Lord in the air. And so we will be with the Lord forever. (1 Thessalonians 4:16–17)

Now that's some itinerary! Imagine what it will be like. All our loved ones who died before us will awaken, as from a nap, feeling as if no time has passed since they left us. And we will join them with Christ in a completely different place. Gone. Vanished. Deliriously happy.

Before being reborn in Jesus, I used to read these verses with hesitation. And the church I attended didn't spend much time talking about them. I thought life here on earth was pretty good, and I wasn't too anxious to leave. Now I know that nothing can compare with the excitement of that day, joy I have never even imagined.

Are you going on that last trip? Are you glad about it? If you're a little hesitant, just ask Jesus right now to speak to your heart. You'll find a peace waiting for you that you didn't realize was there. Better days are coming for the children of God!

## December 22
### THE ROOT OF EVIL

"... flee from all this ..."
(1 Timothy 6:11)

Traveler: *Timothy*
**Read" 1 Timothy 6:3–16**

Most people have heard the saying, "Money is the root of all evil." What many do not realize is that the saying comes from the Bible, 1 Timothy 6:10. But what is the context of that saying? Are we going against the word of God when we travel on business, making money?

First of all, what kind of person are you? Do you have an "... interest in controversies and quarrels about words that result in envy, strife, malicious talk, evil suspicions and constant friction ..." (1 Timothy 6:4–5)? Do you "... think that godliness is a means to financial gain ..." (verse 5)? If not, then you are on the right track, although you probably work with people who fit this description.

Here's the standard that tells whether we have the right attitude about money: "But godliness with contentment is great gain. For we brought nothing into the world, and we can take nothing out of it. But if we have food and clothing, we will be content with that. People who want to get rich fall into temptation and a trap and into many foolish and harmful desires that plunge men into ruin and destruction. For the love of money is a root of all kinds of evil. Some people, eager for money, have wandered from the faith and pierced themselves with many griefs" (verses 6–10).

As I watch countless bus loads of people heading for the gambling towns in Colorado, and as I watch people plunk down their cash for lottery tickets, I see their desire to get rich, rather than be content with what they have. How sad.

If you are not content, if you desire to get rich, you are falling into a trap which can ruin you with temptation and cause you to wander from God. "But you, man of God, flee from all this, and pursue righteousness, godliness, faith, love, endurance and gentleness" (verse 11).

So it's not the money we earn to feed and clothe our families that is evil. It's the desire to get rich, which results in wandering away from God. Big difference.

## December 23
### VISIT A PASTOR

"... he searched hard for me until he found me."
( 2 Timothy 1:17)

**Traveler:** *Onesiphorus*
**Read: 2 Timothy 1:13–18**

A while ago, I was working on a big project in the town of Countryside, Illinois. I was spending a great deal of time there, so I began to take long walks for exercise. I found a three-mile route that winds its way through residential neighborhoods as well as the commercial sector where my hotel was. Along the route is a quaint little Baptist Church.

I walked by that church more than a dozen times. But I never stopped in to say hello. I felt just a little awkward. What would I say? What would the purpose of my visit be? Yet I felt a strange tug on my heart. I just never obeyed it.

Paul gives us a valuable perspective about such tugs: "May the Lord show mercy to the household of Onesiphorus, because he often refreshed me and was not ashamed of my chains. On the contrary, when he was in Rome, he searched hard for me until he found me. May the Lord grant that he will find mercy from the Lord on that day! You know very well in how many ways he helped me in Ephesus" (2 Timothy 1:16–18).

Now, I doubt that the pastor of that little church in Countryside feels like he is in chains, but then how do I know that? Many pastors feel exactly that way, lacking in encouragement and refreshment. And I didn't need to search hard until I found him. He was right there, just a few feet away. How might God have wanted to use me to refresh him? In the future, I can anticipate calling on a local pastor without awkwardness or shyness. This passage from 2 Timothy says it all.

If you're thinking that you don't have time to look up a local pastor when you're traveling, I challenge you to think about it again. Do you have time to eat? Invite him to join you. Do you make time to work out? Walk over to his place for a visit. It doesn't take very long for an encouraging word and a quick prayer for that servant of God.

## December 24
### GIDDY-YUP

"... consider how we may spur one another on toward love and good deeds ..." (Hebrews 10:24)

Travelers: *You and I*
**Read: Hebrews 10:19–39**

As travel words go, "spur" may be one of the most descriptive. It is not a smooth, easy-going kind of word, like "come" or "go." It implies instant action, jerking response.

I've never spurred a horse, because I've not *ridden* a horse. Yes, I live in Colorado, but despite my desire for you to know me as a red-blooded cowboy sort of a guy, the facts are that there were few horses in inner city Cleveland where I grew up, so I'm an urban cowboy in Denver, who relies on *horsepower*, not horses.

Yesterday, I was test driving new cars, because the time has come for me to part with "Old Paint," my trusty Taurus. Not surprisingly, the car I spurred the hardest has the price tag farthest from my reach. But just for a moment, I stuck the pedal to the metal, and its response was anything but lethargic. For a second, I thought I'd boarded the Space Shuttle.

So when the author of Hebrews is encouraging the Hebrews to persevere, he doesn't give them soft, reassuring words like, "Hang in there, folks, better days are ahead." And he places responsibility for consistent behavior on fellow brothers and sisters in the faith: "... let us draw near to God with a sincere heart in full assurance of faith, having our hearts sprinkled to cleanse us from guilty conscience and having our bodies washed with pure water. Let us hold unswervingly to the hope we profess, for he who promised is faithful. And let us consider how we may spur one another on toward love and good deeds. Let us not give up meeting together, as some are in the habit of doing, but let us encourage one another—and all the more as you see the Day approaching" (Hebrews 10:22–25).

We must spur each other as we go. That means being humble enough to meet regularly with others—when we travel, we're alone so often—and let a brother or sister in the faith challenge our behavior.

Are you ready to be spurred forward?

## December 25
### CUTTER CLASS

"... like a wave of the sea, blown and tossed by the wind."
(James 1:6)

Travelers: *You and I*
Read: James 1:1–18

I had never been on a big ship before, only small boats, notably ones caught in big storms in Hawaii and in Colorado. So I had never associated boating with the concept of stability.

That changed when I boarded the giant ferry that crosses Puget Sound from Port Angeles, Washington, to Vancouver Island, British Columbia. Loaded down with hundreds of passengers, cars, trucks, busses and other cargo, the ferry never even noticed the rain squall that moved across the area. It cut the waves and plowed ahead, its engines pulsing confidently. The storm became a pretty sight, rather than a threat.

The book of James speaks well to people who are strong believers in Jesus Christ, but who need to be spurred ahead to better things. All Christians learn how to pray, to put their trust in the Lord, to pray continuously, to become involved in the Christian community and to help the poor. But when we start out, we are like the small Zodiac raft that almost dumped me in high seas off the Napali Coast. No ballast. Hang on for dear life. Wear your life jacket.

But as we begin to learn, to trust God with everything, and most of all not to doubt, we become more like the Vancouver ferry—solid and imperturbable. The storms will always come, but our ability to handle them is tied to the ballast of our faith: "Consider it pure joy, my brothers, whenever you face trials of many kinds, because you know that the testing of your faith develops perseverance. Perseverance must finish its work so that you may be mature and complete, not lacking anything. If any of you lacks wisdom, he should ask God, who gives generously to all without finding fault, and it will be given to him. But when he asks, he must believe and not doubt, because he who doubts is like a wave of the sea, blown and tossed by the wind. That man should not think he will receive anything from the Lord; he is a double-minded man, unstable in all he does" (James 1:2–8).

Don't be a Zodiac. Believe and don't doubt. Cut through storms with Power.

## December 26
### SWAMP COOLER

"Resist the devil, and he will flee from you."
(James 4:7)

**Traveler:** *The Devil*
**Read: James 4:1–12**

A "swamp-cooler" isn't as effective as an air conditioner, but it provides natural goose pimples much cheaper than a high-tech chiller. The swamp-cooler effect (also known as "wind-chill factor") explains why you should always have water-resistant rain gear in the Rocky Mountains, no matter how hot the day.

In other parts of the country, a nice summer rain feels like a warm shower, and it's actually fun to get wet. But where I live, getting caught in a thundershower is the equivalent of jumping into an ice bath, sometimes literally.

That happened to me recently, while conducting a baseball practice. When I left home, there was not a cloud in the sky. But an hour later, nasty, black clouds came racing in, and we got swamped before we knew what had happened. With the wind howling and the temperature dropping thirty degrees in seconds, we all became swamp coolers, feeling the body heat being sucked out of us.

By the time I got home, I was shivering from the chill. But I knew right where to go. My kitchen faces south and west, and it retains solar heat for a very long time. The instant I walked into the kitchen, the chill fled. The warmth of the kitchen was too much for the swamp cooler effect.

James makes the devil look like a sudden mountain thunderstorm, destined to pass on. But my kitchen is like God, who retains all the warmth you need to persevere. But you can't take advantage of the warmth if you don't make a decision to go into the kitchen. You are perfectly free to freeze to death if you choose: "Submit yourselves, then, to God. Resist the devil, and he will flee from you. Come near to God and he will come near to you. Wash your hands, you sinners, and purify your hearts, you double-minded. Grieve, mourn and wail. Change your laughter to mourning and your joy to gloom. Humble yourselves before the Lord, and he will lift you up" (James 4:7–10).

The key to the kitchen is deciding to change your life. Don't get left out in the cold.

## December 27
### GRAPPLING WITH GOD

"... we consider blessed those who have persevered ..."
(James 5:11)

**Travelers:** *You and I*
**Read: James 5:7–12**

Emerging from the blue haze of a smoke-filled construction trailer into glaring sunshine, I was unnerved by the construction manager's threat to sue me personally. Deep in thought as I slogged along a muddy road back to my office trailer, I didn't notice a black limo approaching slowly from behind, until it pulled up next to me. A tinted window, responding to fingertip command, slid down to reveal the dour expression of a well-heeled lawyer. I was informed for the second time in ten minutes that I would be sued.

But this was my client's lawyer! He was supposed to be on my side of the dispute! How could I be accused by both sides in the same dispute? I thought things like this happened only in the movies.

In truth, things like that happen to real people every day. You have probably been caught in a difficult place, too. You're not alone. Jacob spent an entire night wrestling with a man who turned out to be God (Genesis 32:22–30). Hagar was sent by Abraham into the wilderness, with a baby, some food and a little water (Genesis 21:14–21). And the early church suffered endlessly, hoping for the Lord's speedy return (James 5:7–11). But each persevered and was blessed by God.

My trial seemed hopeless, too. In my log book for that day in 1988, I wrote, "If I stay out of court, that is, not get sued, my only armor has been my faith. Without it I am nothing. With it, there must be a way. If this all works out, it will be an eloquent proof of the existence of God." No human cleverness was going to fix this one.

The result? God exists! Not only did I stay out of court, but the dispute was settled and the project went on to become very successful.

Sometimes, like He did for Jacob, God asks us to grapple with some very hard things. Sometimes, like Hagar and her son Ishmael, we cry out in anguish to Him and He hears us: "...we consider blessed those who have persevered...The Lord is full of compassion and mercy" (James 5:11).

## December 28
### C'MON OVER ANY TIME!

"Offer hospitality to one another without grumbling."
(1 Peter 4:9)

Travelers: *You and I*
**Read: 1 Peter 4:7–11**

A friend called to tell me that a missionary he supports was passing through town for one day, just before he was scheduled to return to Eastern Europe. I was asked if I could host him for the evening. Sure, I thought, now that's Christian hospitality at its best. I called the young missionary and invited him to have dinner with us and to stay the night. We were delighted that God chose to use our home in this way.

That day, my wife prepared a nice meal, in anticipation of his arrival. When he didn't arrive on time, we shrugged it off and put dinner on the back burner. By midnight, with dinner long since charred and no call from our guest, we assumed that something had gone wrong. We headed for bed. Just about the time I got my "jammies" on, the doorbell rang. "What?" I grumbled.

I was a terrible host, and his failure to acknowledge the lateness of the hour only aggravated me. I was dead tired after a hard day's work, and I knew I had to get up early the next morning. I tried to talk with him for awhile, but my biological clock goes catatonic at that hour (I'm old, he's young), and I'm sure I insulted him.

I violated the word of God enough times that night that grace is my only hope for forgiveness. Peter said, "Above all, love each other deeply, because love covers a multitude of sins. Offer hospitality to one another without grumbling" (1 Peter 4:8–9). Well, I flunked that one. I showed no love; I covered no sins; I grumbled much.

Hospitality ain't easy. But it's biblical. It's more than a superficial invitation over to the house. It's a commitment and sometimes a sacrifice to love brothers and sisters in the faith. If you know someone who is hosting a visitor, especially for more than a day, call and encourage them. That might make the difference between a grumble and a humble.

## December 29
### STRONG WORDS

> "Many deceivers ... have gone out into the world."
> (2 John 7)

Travelers: *Deceivers*
**Read: 2 John 1–13**

In America, it is almost impossible to imagine what it was like to be a Christian in the first century, after Jesus Christ lived and died. Even in our darkest hours, we have never known religious persecution at its worst (although African Americans and others have suffered personal and political persecution in our history). We are aware of others who suffer terribly, but somehow it all feels so far away. Couldn't ever happen here.

But it could, and in fact it probably will. Right now we live in an age of "diversity," pluralism and inclusiveness. But when God finally decides that America, like Israel of long ago, has abandoned God's special blessing, things will change in a hurry. But for now it's hard to feel unsafe when we interact with the world. Yes, we're treated a little strangely as Christians, but most of us don't feel real threats.

John talks about a time when things were extremely dangerous for Christians, and he gives us warning for what to avoid in our day:

> "Many deceivers, who do not acknowledge Jesus Christ as coming in the flesh, have gone out into the world. Any such person is the deceiver and the antichrist.... Anyone who ... does not continue in the teaching of Christ does not have God; whoever continues in the teaching has both the Father and the Son. If anyone comes to you and does not bring this teaching, do not take him into your house or welcome him. Anyone who welcomes him shares in his wicked work" (2 John 7–11).

Strong words! Harsh words! Divisive words! Politically incorrect words!

I know many, many people who do not believe in Jesus Christ as the Son of God. I work with them, live near them, encounter them every day, tolerate their views in the interests of free speech. Hate the sin, not the sinner. But John is saying something different, something we'd understand better if we knew what real danger is. John is saying that there is a difference between encountering non-believers in daily life and opening your home to them.

Hard to swallow, but true. Be careful.

*Faith in Motion*

# December 30
## TEPID

"... I will come in and eat with him, and he with me."
(Revelation 3:20)

Traveler: *Jesus*
Read: **Revelation 3:14–22**

There's someone even worse than the deceiver and the antichrist mentioned yesterday: "I know your deeds, that you are neither cold nor hot. I wish you were either one or the other! So, because you are lukewarm—neither hot nor cold—I am about to spit you out of my mouth" (Revelation 3:15–16). Even the bad guys, the non-believers, are cold and the Lord holds out hope that somehow they will repent. So what does it mean to be lukewarm, and why is that so abominable to Jesus?

When I think of lukewarm, I think of milk. Hot milk is good for hot chocolate. And cold milk is great any time. But tepid milk comes in a bottle that I left out of the refrigerator too long. It's curdled, spoiled, and as soon as I realize it by the horrible taste, I spit it out, and fast!

What tastes like curdled milk to God? When someone says, "I am rich; I have acquired wealth and do not need a thing" (verse 17). God doesn't just feel sorry for people like that; He gets royally ticked: "But you do not realize that you are wretched, pitiful, poor, blind and naked" (verse 17). A person who uses financial well-being to cruise undisturbed and lukewarm above the storms of life is in fact worse than the worst. I pray that doesn't describe you. If you are rich, I hope you know there is much more you need, and that your spiritual needs are what make you hot for Christ.

There's hope, great hope: "Those whom I love I rebuke and discipline. So be earnest, and repent" (verse 19). Jesus still loves you, even if you're tepid and curdled, and only He has the power to restore your spoiled condition to freshness. If you can do that, if you can humble yourself and admit that your pride and contentment have spoiled you, you can receive the richest blessing ever stated: "Here I am! I stand at the door and knock. If anyone hears my voice and opens the door, I will come in and eat with him, and he with me" (verse 20).

By the way, compared to the world's standards, all business travelers are rich, so don't think this does not apply to you. Do you hear Him? Will you open the door?

December

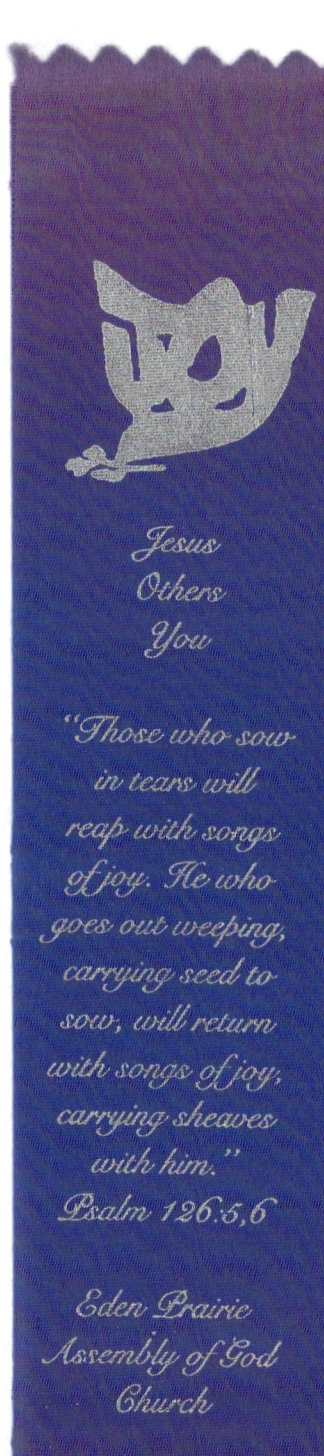

**December 31**
THE BEGINNING

"Amen. Come, Lord Jesus."
(Revelation 22:20)

...e piloted by a man making his last flight, ...was retiring, and there was a great celebra-...turned over the controls long enough to ...enger with a handshake. When we landed ...est landing I had ever known. If I hadn't ..., I'd never have known we landed. As pi-...t."

...o. And we will have an escort even nicer ...t: "Behold, I am coming soon! My reward ... everyone according to what he has done . ...h their robes, that they may have the right ...through the gates into the city" (Revelation ...l take us on this trip!

...Then I saw a new heaven and a new earth, ...rst earth had passed away, and there was no ...ly City, the new Jerusalem, coming down ...pared as a bride beautifully dressed for her ...d voice from the throne saying, 'Now the ..., and he will live with them. They will be ...will be with them and be their God. He will ...yes. There will be no more death or mourn-...old order of things has passed away'" (Chap-

...end of our journey through the Bible to-...God hovering over the deep and ends with ...t books, this one ends with the beginning—...about you, but I can't wait for the Guide to ...l my biggest blessing will be meeting you at

...s. (Revelation 22:20)

381

# NOTES

1. *It Doesn't Take a Hero*. Bantam, New York, 1993. Pg 220.
2. *The Divine Conquest*. Christian Publications, Camp Hill, PA 1978. Pg. 68.
3. *Favorite Poems Old and New,* by Helen Ferris, Doubleday, Garden City, NY, 1957.
4. *Daily Thoughts for Disciples*, Discovery House, 1994.
5. By M.. Powers
6. *The Hospitality Commands*, Alexander Strauch, Lewis & Roth, Littleton, Co., 19██.
7. Contact the Bread of Life Foundation, Denver, CO 80202

To Order Additional Copies of:

## *Faith In Motion*

Send $12.95 plus $3.95 shipping and handling to:

E. Larry Beaumont
12650 W. Belmont Ave.
Littleton, CO  80127
(303) 972-3003

1-800-270-7464